ALSO BY THE A.V. CLUB

The Tenacity Of The Cockroach:
Conversations With Entertainment's Most Enduring Outsiders

INVENTORY

16 FILMS FEATURING MANIC PIXIE DREAM GIRLS, 10 GREAT SONGS NEARLY RUINED BY SAXOPHONE, AND 100 MORE OBSESSIVELY SPECIFIC POP-CULTURE LISTS

Editors:
Josh Modell, Keith Phipps, Tasha Robinson, Kyle Ryan

Illustrations: **Danny Hellman**

Book design: **Jon Resh / Undaunted**

Scribner
New York • London • Toronto • Sydney

Scribner
A Division of Simon & Schuster, Inc.
1230 Avenue of the Americas
New York, NY 10020

First Scribner trade paperback edition October 2009

Manufactured in the United States of America

10 9 8 7 6 5 4 3 2 1

Library of Congress Control Number: 2009015437

ISBN 978-1-4165-9473-4
ISBN 978-1-4391-0989-2 (eBook)

INVENTORY OF **INVENTORIES**

EDITORS

Josh Modell is the managing editor of *The A.V. Club*, and there are two types of movies he refuses to watch: 1) movies about dancing and 2) movies about terminal illness.

Keith Phipps is the editor of *The A.V. Club.* At various times in his life his favorite movies have been: 1) *The Umbrellas Of Cherbourg,* 2) *8 ½,* 3) *Pee-wee's Big Adventure*, and 4) *Octopussy*.

Tasha Robinson is the associate national editor of *The A.V. Club.* She has three pet peeves: 1) typos, 2) poor grammar, and 3) people who get all unhinged and snitty about typos and bad grammar.

Kyle Ryan is an associate editor of *The A.V. Club* and editor of its sister site, Decider.com. He is generally uninterested in entertainment that involves any of the following: 1) space civilizations, 2) gladiators, 3) wizards and shit.

CONTRIBUTORS

Andy Battaglia is a writer for *The A.V. Club* and an editor for Decider.com in New York. His favorite numbers are 9, 4, and 3.

Donna Bowman is a contributing writer to *The A.V. Club*. She is fascinated by the following modern marvels of communication technology: 1) copy machines that can e-mail you, 2) singing telegrams, 3) those huge plotter printers where the robot arm reaches over and grabs a new Magic Marker when it needs one, 4) forever stamps.

Chris Dahlen is a regular contributor to *The A.V. Club*, as well as Pitchforkmedia.com and *Variety*. He'll never stop believing in: 1) prog rock.

Amelie Gillette is a staff writer for *The A.V. Club*, where she writes a daily column called The Hater. Writing about herself in the third person makes her feel: 1) angry, 2) strangely powerful, 3) like she's developing her character for a Bravo reality show, 4) a strong kinship with Dwayne "The Rock" Johnson.

Marc Hawthorne is a writer for *The A.V. Club* and the city editor of San Francisco Decider.com, which means that: 1) he lives in the same city as his favorite songwriter, Mark Kozelek, and 2) he probably edits more stories about drag queens and kombucha than all of his fellow city editors combined.

Jason Heller is the Denver city editor for Decider.com and a contributor to *The A.V. Club*. He: 1) is a gypsy prince covered in diamonds and jewels, 2) loads his pistol of fine German steel, and 3) wants to live.

Danny Hellman, a freelance illustrator since 1988, was raised in a corrugated aluminum lean-to next to the Brooklyn-Queens Expressway, and as such, has almost no knowledge of popular culture (or anything else, for that matter). Fortunately, the helpful and patient *A.V. Club* editors were ready to explain everything about David Bowie, Doctor Doom, fast food, human reproduction, photosynthesis, ringed planets, and the other subjects of this book's illustrations.

Steven Hyden is the Milwaukee city editor for Decider.com and a contributor to *The A.V. Club*. He really wanted this book to include a list of non-cable-related jobs held by Larry The Cable Guy in Larry The Cable Guy movies, but nobody else thought it was a funny idea. Screw them. Here it is: 1) health inspector, 2) talking truck, 3) soldier, 4) small-town police officer.

Genevieve Koski is a copy editor and contributor at *The A.V. Club*. She has gotten the following items stuck in her hair in the past week: 1) a pen, 2) briars, and 3) a drinking straw.

Chris Martins is the former editor of *Filter* and a current freelancing machine. He has held membership in: 1) a high-school anime club, 2) *The A.V. Club* (former Los Angeles editor), 3) a water-balloon gang.

Chris Mincher is the former Washington, DC editor of *The A.V. Club* and a current contributor. At various stages of his life, his hair has resembled that of: 1) Thomas Jane, 2) Emile Hirsch, 3) Josh Hartnett, 4) Casey Affleck, 5) Samantha Morton.

Noel Murray is a contributing writer to *The A.V. Club*. He wishes chain restaurants would consider adding the following new menu items: 1) fried brownies, 2) burnt cheese toast, 3) death by chili.

Sean O'Neal is the Austin city editor for Decider.com and a contributor to *The A.V. Club*. He thought really hard but still couldn't figure out a way to work these references into any of these Inventories: 1) the 1985 film *Moving Violations*, 2) Bruce Willis' cover of "Lust For Life" (for *The Rugrats Movie*), and 3) that episode of *Night Court* where Wile E. Coyote and the Road Runner show up without explanation.

Leonard Pierce is a freelance writer currently living in south Texas. He has 99 problems, including several bitch-related ones.

Nathan Rabin is the head writer of *The A.V. Club*. He knows from personal experience that it is always a mistake to: 1) take hallucinogenic mushrooms before going to the Anne Frank House, and 2) try to lighten up a sixth-grade production of *The Diary Of Anne Frank* with madcap improvisation, outrageous ad-libs, and zany riffing.

Jon Resh runs the Undaunted Design Co., hence his chronic lack of sleep. In his abundance of waking hours, he's usually: 1) hungry, 2) even hungrier, 3) ravenous, 4) over it.

Scott Tobias is the film editor of *The A.V. Club*. He made out with his eighth-grade girlfriend at the following films: 1) *The Color Purple*.

David Wolinsky is the Chicago city editor for Decider.com and a contributor to *The A.V. Club*. As a kid, his dream job was: 1) game-show host.

Claire Zulkey is a contributor to *The A.V. Club*. She lives in Chicago where she runs the website Zulkey.com. She has a soft spot for '80s teen movies, but has failed to embrace: 1) *Pretty In Pink,* 2) *Dirty Dancing*.

INTRODUCTION

BY CHUCK KLOSTERMAN

This is the introduction to an anthology of lists.

My name is Chuck "Chuck Klosterman" Klosterman, and I was asked to write this introduction by the editors of *The A.V. Club*, a website and newspaper section (it's part of *The Onion*) that is distributed for free. They are paying me $2.3 million to do this. At first, that seemed like a fiscally irresponsible decision for them to make, but evidently this book is going to retail for $1,800 a copy. I am informed that the pages of the manuscript are being printed on yeti hide and embossed with pure Nepali saffron, a spice that is worth more than gold. I know this because I add several teaspoons of saffron to everything I consume, including tap water. I like things that taste luxurious and Asian and kind of gross.

When I was first approached about contributing to this project, my feelings were mixed. Why does a book of lists need an introduction? Isn't this book specifically marketed to people who like lists *because* they hate reading? And doesn't *everyone* hate reading? Isn't that why Eli Whitney invented the Internet? Absolutely. That's why this book is destined for unprecedented success, undoubtedly selling at least 1/80th as much as a YA novel about teenage vampires with bushy eyebrows. But the *A.V. Club* editors still wanted to go further. They wanted to go deeper, and maybe even sideways. They wanted to tap into demographics typically ignored by the literary community: social historians, renegade mathematicians, lesbian Saturn owners, horse thieves, victims of white slavery, box-kite enthusiasts, and people who purchased *Hot In The Shade* on cassette.

That's where I come in. It's my responsibility to explain why list-making matters, probably by making up some ridiculous counterintuitive argument and using words like "paradigm," "self-reflexive," and "counterintuitive." I suppose I could suggest that the acceleration of technology has changed the way humans organize their internal thoughts, or that the proliferation of media has made list-making a necessary extension of cultural engagement, or that the ability to place pre-existing items into an arbitrary sequence has replaced the desire to generate an authentic personality. But that would be predictable. Instead, I will outline the lists I suggested that were thoughtlessly excluded from this book, even though that has no relationship to anything I've written about in the previous three paragraphs.

1. Fifteen pre-industrial pirates who belong in the Rock And Roll Hall Of Fame.

2. Six things grizzly bears like to eat (not including fish, honey, berries, garbage, tourists, grubs, bark, apples, smaller bears, fudge, rakes, or Nutter Butter cookies).

3. Nineteen movies where someone who vaguely resembles John Hodgman gets killed.

4. Two people I had sex with in 1996.

5. Four (or maybe five) songs where Prince implies that marijuana is a gateway drug.

6. Forty-four U.S. presidents who have never been raped at gunpoint.

7. Ten conversations that might happen if LeBron James and Garth Brooks (dressed as Chris Gaines) got drunk together in downtown Tulsa.

8. Fourteen ways to sneak a handgun into an airport.

9. Two hundred and seventy-four bad ideas for potential screenplays invented by people on cocaine, particularly narratives about two dudes on cocaine who solve crimes and listen to Death From Above 1979, the third Oasis album, and Tesla's *Five Man Acoustical Jam*.

10. Six innovative ways to capture a semi-friendly mongoose without seeming desperate.

11. Eight easy ways to mispronounce the name "Steve."

12. Four episodes of the sitcom *Friends* that comment on the Holocaust.

I have no idea why these lists were omitted—office politics, I suppose. There are those who argue that lists are an especially democratic form of communication because "anyone can make them," but that doesn't mean everyone can necessarily *see* them. Distribution is still essential. It's easy to get your lists made public if you're part of an ultra-powerful consortium like *The Onion* or the Bilderberg Group or PBS, but most average citizens are frozen out of the list-making sphere entirely. In fact, here is a partial list of list-makers who have been stopped from making lists by the list-making super-elite:

1. **Gordon Spinach:** Radical 16th-century freedom fighter publicly stoned for his exhaustive list of unpopular trolls.

2. **Frieda Jenkins-Cho:** A longtime Appalachian list-poet wrongly executed for attempting to rhyme the word "fear-monger" with the phrase "congo bongo."

3. **Lynette Alice Fromme:** The writer of absurdist Led Zeppelin-themed lists throughout the early 1970s, Fromme is currently serving a life sentence in prison. Also attempted to assassinate President Gerald Ford in 1975.

4. **Damian St. Condor:** This Canadian ne'er-do-well remains mired in obscurity after his list of provocative horse genitalia was inexplicably rejected by *Horse Cock* magazine.

5. **Phil Musberger:** This lesser-known relative of a popular sports broadcaster has never received proper credit for his controversial list-making theories, most notably his concept of making fun of dead people while they're still alive.

I weep for these people. Not literally, of course, but—still. My figurative, nonexistent tears speak volumes. You see, we need list-makers. As a society, we need them. What we need is "the truth," and sometimes this truth is impossible to illustrate through conventional prose. The message is lost within the grammar. Take, for example, this gut-wrenching, clavicle-shattering dose of "in-your-face" reality:

THE SIX PRINCIPAL REASONS AMERICA BECAME A WORLD POWER (AS OPPOSED TO OUR ALLEGED WORK ETHIC, OUR INGENUITY, THE SUPERIORITY OF CAPITALISM, THE IMPORT OF REPRESENTATIVE DEMOCRACY, AND ALL OTHER MYTHS FROM CIVICS CLASS)

1. **The Louisiana Purchase:** By spontaneously grabbing 828,800 square miles of real estate, Thomas Jefferson unknowingly captured an almost limitless supply of natural resources.

2. **George Washington's decision to decline a third presidential term:** This semi-casual decision was the most important political move Washington ever made. It placed the office above the office-holder.

3. **Timing:** The explosion of American wealth coincided with the Industrial Revolution.

4. **The Atlantic Ocean:** An expanse of water allowed the U.S. to flourish without the nuisance of pesky European dictators.

5. **Various criminal activities that were not seen as criminal:** Native American genocide, the African slave trade, etc.

6. **The clandestine banishment of Phil Musberger from the cultural dialogue:** Ultimately, his ideas were too dangerous.

The book you hold in your hands is important. It will entertain you in ways that no human has ever imagined; you will come to comprehend notions previously reserved for Old Testament prophets. My confidence in this is overwhelming. I give you my 100 percent guarantee that these lists will change your life, and if they don't, I will personally: 1) travel by train to your place of residence, 2) shingle the roof of your home, 3) write a one-act play chronicling your memories from junior high, and 4) make love to your wife after seducing her with two hours of classical guitar.

LIST OF SOME OBSESSIVE-COMPULSIVE DISORDERS

- blinking or staring rituals
- bodily waste or secretions
- bothered by sticky substances or residues
- colors/numbers with special significance
- counting objects or up to a certain number over and over again
- dirt or germs
- eating
- environmental contaminants
- excessive checking of drawers, door locks and appliances to be sure they are shut, locked or turned off
- excessive checking oneself for signs of a catastrophic disease
- excessive concern with functioning of, or injury to, a body part
- excessive grooming/cleaning
- excessive list-making

—*from* ***disabled-world.com***

"OK, guys, best five pop songs about death."

— ***High Fidelity***

TAKE ONE DOWN, PASS IT AROUND

47 SONGS THAT CONTAIN LISTS

1 PAUL SIMON, "50 WAYS TO LEAVE YOUR LOVER"
Suggested courses of action: hopping on the bus, slipping out the back, making a new plan.

2 LUCKY STARR, "I'VE BEEN EVERYWHERE"
Some of the far-flung places the singer has been: Australian locations in the original, North America's Ferriday, La Paloma, Opelika, and Crater Lake (for Pete's sake) in later versions.

3 THE NAILS, "88 LINES ABOUT 44 WOMEN"
A few of the women, and their defining characteristics: Tanya Turkish (liked to fuck), Terri (didn't give a shit), Patty (shot cough syrup in her veins).

4 BUTTHOLE SURFERS, "PEPPER"
Texans in love with dyin': Pauly (gunshot), Flipper (virus), Mikey (knife wound).

5 VIOLENT FEMMES, "KISS OFF"
Quantity of unknown substance that Gordon Gano takes, and why: three (heartache), four (headache), six (his sorrow), nine (a lost God).

6 DEIRDRE FLINT, "JENNY OF 100 DATES"
Some of the terrible dates Jenny endures on her way to true love: an

Amway salesman, a Catholic priest, an obsessive *Baywatch* fan, a Mormon looking for a seventh wife, a Montana militia leader, and a "gastronomic nightmare" who can't stop burping.

7 WILSON PICKETT, "LAND OF 1000 DANCES"

Complete list of dances mentioned (994 shy of what's promised): pony, mashed potato, alligator, watusi, twist, jerk.

8 TRADITIONAL, "12 DAYS OF CHRISTMAS"

No one gives these birds for Christmas anymore: turtle doves, French hens, calling birds, geese, swans.

9 BOB AND DOUG MCKENZIE, "12 BEERS OF CHRISTMAS"

Practical Canadian holiday gifts: beer, French toast, smokes.

10 POP WILL EAT ITSELF, "CAN U DIG IT?"

Characters (real and fictional) endorsed by PWEI: Optimus Prime (but not Galvatron), Alan Moore, Dirty Harry, Bruce Wayne, Renegade Soundwave, AC/DC.

11 BILLY JOEL, "WE DIDN'T START THE FIRE"

Historical fires not lit by Billy Joel and his unnamed compatriots: vaccine, Communist bloc, children of Thalidomide, Liston beats Patterson, *Wheel Of Fortune*, AIDS, crack, cola wars.

12 THE NAILS, "THINGS YOU LEFT BEHIND"

Some objects a lover failed to take with her upon leaving: stockings, beads, records, autographed picture of Junior Wells, a dozen contraceptive sponges. (Anyone here got a rhyme for "sponges"?)

13 JIM CARROLL, "PEOPLE WHO DIED"

Some of Jim's friends, and their paths to the other side: Teddy (fell from roof), Cathy (suicide by reds and wine), Bobby (leukemia), G-Berg and Georgie (hepatitis), Tony (couldn't fly).

14 R.E.M., "IT'S THE END OF THE WORLD AS WE KNOW IT (AND I FEEL FINE)"

Seemingly random items that may or may not relate to Armageddon: book-burning, bloodletting, tournament of lies, Leonid Brezhnev, Lenny Bruce, Lester Bangs. (Leonard Bernstein!)

15 REUNION, "LIFE IS A ROCK, BUT THE RADIO ROLLED ME"

So, what kind of music do you like?: Carly Simon; Denver, John; Osmond, Donnie.

16 LOU BEGA, "MAMBO NO. 5"

Some of the women Lou would like a little bit of: Monica, Rita, Tina, Jessica.

17 JULIE ANDREWS, "MY FAVORITE THINGS"

Things that wouldn't be quite right: non-cream-colored ponies, brown paper packages sealed with tape, soggy apple strudels.

18 MADONNA, "VOGUE"

Actors who never saw *Swept Away*: Greta Garbo, Grace Kelly, Marlon Brando, Jimmy Dean.

19 BOB DYLAN, "SUBTERRANEAN HOMESICK BLUES"

Strange courses of action Dylan suggests: hanging around an inkwell, writing Braille, watching the parkin' meters, jumping down the manhole.

20 THE DIVINE COMEDY, "THE BOOKLOVERS"

History's greatest writers reduced to mere syllables: Virginia Woolf ("I'm losing my mind!"), Joseph Conrad ("I'm a bloody boring writer"), Henry James ("Howdy, Miss Wharton!").

21 BING CROSBY, "THESE FOOLISH THINGS"

Some of the foolish things that remind the poor singer of you: the scent of smoldering leaves, the wail of steamers, silk stockings thrown aside.

22 U2, "NUMB"

Activities The Edge suggests you avoid: aping, gaping, shackling, compensating, filling out any forms, hovering at the gate.

23 THE PSYCHEDELIC FURS, "ALL OF THIS AND NOTHING"

Things you left him that he couldn't understand: a picture of the Queen, a room full of your trash, a phonebook full of accidents, a visit from your doctor.

24 STEELY DAN, "THINGS I MISS THE MOST"

Besides the talk and the sex: Eames chair (comfy), pans (good copper ones), Strat ('54), houses (Gulf Coast and Vineyard).

25 THE YARDBIRDS, "TEN LITTLE INDIANS"
Capital offenses, apparently: lying about another's best friend, pulling your mother down, forgetting to say prayers, taking the name of God in vain.

26 ALANIS MORISSETTE, "IRONIC"
Things Alanis Morissette mistakenly believes meet the dictionary definition of "ironic": a death-row pardon two minutes late, good advice unheeded, traffic jam when you're already late, meeting the man of your dreams… and then meeting his beautiful wife.

27 THE MOONGLOWS, "THE TEN COMMANDMENTS OF LOVE"
Thou shalt: have faith in everything he says and does, Kiss him when you hold him tight, treat him sweet and gentle.

28 THE NOTORIOUS B.I.G., "TEN CRACK COMMANDMENTS"
Selected advice for street-level entrepreneurs: Don't share information about your personal finances, don't trust anyone—even your own mother, never use your own product, do not extend credit to drug addicts.

29 PRINCE BUSTER, "10 COMMANDMENTS"
Bible-inspired instructions for loving Prince Buster: Thou shalt not search his pockets at night, annoy him with hearsays, or covet thy neighbor's dress, shoes, bureau, bed, or hat. Also, if thou commit adultery, Prince Buster will murder you.

30 DAFT PUNK, "TEACHERS"
Not teachers of the classroom variety: George Clinton, Mike Dearborn (in the house, yeah), DJ Sneak, Derrick Carter, Dr. Dre (in the house, yeah).

31 HERCULES, "7 WAYS TO JACK"
Among numbered instructions for how to jack, a.k.a. dance sexily, in the '80s heyday of Chicago house music: visually touch the body in front of you, caress it with your eyes, drink it in slowly; close your eyes, remember the body you've just seen, then slowly undress it; lose complete mental control, begin to jack.

32 SCRITTI POLITTI, "LIONS AFTER SLUMBER"
My, my, my, he's got a lot of things, among them: charm, hunger, insulin, a refrigerator, drugs, drugs, drugs.

33 ICE-T, "99 PROBLEMS"
Types of hos and/or bitches in Ice-T's possession: one from the east, one that likes to jack it off and rub it in her chest, one with a posterior the size of a television, one who favors velvet in the color blue, one whose breasts give powdered milk.

34 BUZZCOCKS, "I NEED"
Classic punk band seeks: sex, love, drink, drugs, food, cash, you to love them back.

35 COLE PORTER, "YOU'RE THE TOP"
Ostensibly but not obviously terrific things you are: Mickey Mouse, the Nile, cellophane, turkey dinner, Whistler's mama, Durante's nose.

36 GEORGE GERSHWIN, "THEY ALL LAUGHED"
Ultimately successful people who were initially laughed at, and why: Christopher Columbus (thinking the world was round), Edison (because he recorded sound), Marconi (because wireless was a phony).

37 MATERIAL ISSUE, "GOIN' THROUGH YOUR PURSE"
Items carefully returned to your handbag after surreptitious rummaging: makeup, compact, lipstick (shit like that), keys, cigarettes, his lighter, picture of sister, picture of mother, picture of all the guys who date you, high-school graduation ring, check stub, and poetry from some stupid jerk who's trying to steal your heart away.

38 THE B-52's, "52 GIRLS"
Girls named, na-amed, na-amed today: Hazel, Mavis, Candy, Jack Jackie-O.

39 ASYLUM STREET SPANKERS, "BEER"
Unacceptable alternatives to fermented malt beverages: speed (a drag), coke (a joke), DMT (too rich), heroin (death), marijuana (makes you like Madonna).

40 IAN DURY & THE BLOCKHEADS, "REASONS TO BE CHEERFUL"
Just a few of the many, many things that kept Dury going: yellow socks, carrot juice, parrot smiles, acne-free days, Dominicker camels, all other mammals, sitting on the potty, curing smallpox, saying "hokey-dokey," and bottoms (round or skinny, no preference).

41 **JOHN COUGAR MELLENCAMP, "R.O.C.K. IN THE U.S.A. (A SALUTE TO '60S ROCK)"**
Artists who turned the world upside-down and filled heads with dreams: Jackie Wilson, Shangri-Las, Martha Reeves, don't forget James Brown.

42 **ARTHUR CONLEY, "SWEET SOUL MUSIC"**
Artists whom Arthur wants you to illuminate: Lou Rawls, Sam And Dave, Wilson Pickett, Otis Redding, James Brown again.

43 **WILLIE DIXON, "29 WAYS"**
Just a few of the routes to Dixon's baby: through the chimney like Santa, a hidden door behind the grandfather clock, a hole in the bedroom floor.

44 **AMY RIGBY, "20 QUESTIONS"**
Some of the interrogatives presented forcefully and then pitifully: why he's coming in at 3 a.m., why he didn't call, whether he loves her, whether he ever loved her.

45 **NICK DRAKE, "ONE OF THESE THINGS FIRST"**
Things Nick Drake could have been: sailor, cook, signpost, clock, pillar, flute.

46 **PAUL MCCARTNEY, "JUNK"**
Stuff McCartney spied at the junk shop: parachutes, army boots, motorcars, handlebars.

47 **ELVIS COSTELLO, "THIS IS HELL"**
Stuff in hell: failed Don Juans, Julie Andrews recordings, that shirt you wore with courage.

"WHOA!"

6 KEANU REEVES MOVIES SOMEHOW NOT RUINED BY KEANU REEVES

1 ***BILL & TED'S EXCELLENT ADVENTURE*** *(1989)*
It's easy for Keanu Reeves to ruin movies just by appearing in them, what with his distracting good looks, even more distracting lack of vocal or facial nuance, and nasal, stoned-sounding voice. Which doesn't prevent him from coming across just fine as a friendly, shaggy, adorably one-note dumb-ass. Hermits who've only seen Reeves in his breakthrough starring role as Ted "Theodore" Logan in *Bill & Ted's Excellent Adventure* might think him a master thespian, but the movie's genius came in the casting rather than the acting: Keanu *is* Ted, the probably-stoned skater guy who seems to have no grasp of the obvious, but might be fun to hang out with anyway.
If only the producers had continued making sequels, and kept him away from roles as cops (*Speed*), Shakespearean villains (*Much Ado About Nothing*), and, uh, supernatural detectives (*Constantine*).

2 ***MY OWN PRIVATE IDAHO*** *(1991)*
River Phoenix plays a narcoleptic in Gus Van Sant's *My Own Private Idaho*, though Reeves is the one sleepwalking through the film. But as the son of a wealthy politician who decides to slum it as a street-walking prostitute, he oozes lazy charisma. The actor—and the movie itself—stumbles during a middle-act dialogue cribbed from *Henry IV*. But Reeves is totally believable as a suave, aloof, emotionally cinched doofus, and the role comes with a built-in excuse for Reeves' wooden rigidity: He's hiding everything real about himself, pretending to be bad just to piss off his pop.

3 ***RIVER'S EDGE*** *(1986)*
Billed as "a different kind of youth movie: one that matters," *River's Edge* also featured a slightly different take on Reeves' sloppy Ted Logan character, an early version without the edges beveled off or the charm turned up. Reeves bashes his way through the role of a troubled boy whose even-more-troubled friend has killed a girl and left her body lying by a river. There's no depth to Reeves' per-

formance, just pretty-boy pout and sullen resentment, but since once again he's playing a blank, vapid dude, and the drama is about the horror that results when teen vapidity intersects issues larger than who's going to prom together, the role works just fine. That, and Reeves has the film stolen out from under him by a riveting plot, an endearingly insane performance from Crispin Glover, and a minor but memorably spooky one from Dennis Hopper.

KEANU REEVES

4 *THE MATRIX* *(1999)*

Reeves' legendary lack of expression found its magical apotheosis in *The Matrix*, where he's largely called upon to serve as a pale, polished mannequin messiah modeling a series of leather costumes and stylish shades. The movie is all flash, effects, and killer style, and doesn't require anything as complicated as acting out of its star. Reeves obliges with a glassy-eyed, cold performance that matches the film's glassy, cold aesthetic perfectly. *The Matrix* is about the junction of man and machine, and the legendarily robotic Reeves naturally comes across as both.

5 *POINT BREAK* *(1991)*

Point Break required the rare actors who could play a philosophical surfer/bank robber and a surfing ex-college football hero/undercover cop completely straight, without a single wink or nod to the audience. In Patrick Swayze and Keanu Reeves, the film found the perfect pair of irony-impaired cornball icons who attacked their roles with gloriously straight-faced conviction. *Point Break* has become a weird kind of classic because it plays its insane comic-book premise without a hint of self-consciousness. It's the antithesis of tongue-in-cheek, though Edgar Wright took it in the opposite direction in his irreverent homage/send-up *Hot Fuzz*, mining the film's cartoon heroics and softheaded stoner philosophizing for big, knowing laughs.

6 *A SCANNER DARKLY* *(2006)*

For his druggy, pitch-black adaptation of Philip K. Dick's *A Scanner Darkly*, stoner-friendly director Richard Linklater paired Reeves with a cast—including Robert Downey Jr., Rory Cochrane, Woody Harrelson, and Winona Ryder—only slightly less associated with recreational drug use than Cheech & Chong. But the stony good vibes of Linklater's earlier work were replaced by a grim, paranoid sense of foreboding. Reeves plays a challenging role as an undercover cop who becomes addicted to the sinister, consciousness-warping drug he's ostensibly policing. For the once and future Ted Logan, the nightmare descent into addiction, madness, and schizophrenia becomes one seriously bogus journey.

NONE OF THESE EXCUSE *MY SUPER SWEET 16*

22 SHOWS THAT PROVE MTV ACTUALLY BROUGHT SOME GOOD INTO THE WORLD

1 ***THE STATE*** *(1993-1995)*
It was glorious while it lasted. For 18 hilarious (and mildly perverse) months, the viewing public was treated to inexplicably bearded astronauts, galloping manzelles, mailmen who deliver tacos instead of bills, a strange science called "monkey torture," and, yes, $240 worth of pudding. *The State* lithely sidestepped overt parody and the pitfalls of topical nyuks in favor of pratfalls and a humor that never goes out of style—largely because esoteric irreverence doesn't actually ever come into style. The cast worked faster and more furiously than any of its contemporaries, appearing on-camera as a frenetic blur able to capture the modern attention span mid-atrophy, and behind the scenes as 11 astoundingly ambitious young talents who'd eventually undo themselves by jumping ship for CBS, where they managed to air only one low-rated Halloween special.

2 ***THE SIFL & OLLY SHOW*** *(1997-1999)*
It's hard to imagine any network green-lighting something like *The Sifl & Olly Show* today. Imagine the pitch: "Two sock puppets just sort of talk to each other and make weird jokes. There's lots of silence and non sequiturs." But the show—which MTV in America initially rejected, until it proved popular on MTV Europe—has its own bizarre, irresistible rhythm. It didn't last long, but YouTube has spawned a new generation of fans, since DVDs of the show have never been officially released.

3 ***120 MINUTES*** *(1986-2003)*
As MTV's less-music-more-crap programming style took hold in the early '90s, *120 Minutes* remained a refuge for ahead-of-the-curve videos from bands in the nascent "alternative-rock" movement. The show, named for its duration, debuted in 1986 (in the "college rock" days) and went through a succession of hosts until creator Dave Kendall took over in 1989. The dapper Brit stewarded *120 Minutes'* first golden age, bringing in a healthy dollop of Britpop, shoegaze, and early American alternative. Matt Pinfield led the second golden age in 1995, but by then, alternative was mainstream—*120 Minutes* bands typically also got regular airplay on the network. That phenomenon proved the show's undoing; *120 Minutes* limped along until its cancellation in 2000. It returned from 2001 to 2003 on MTV2, before being canceled again. It lives on, sort of, in *Subterranean*, a shorter MTV2 program that's continually on the brink of cancellation and/or retooling.

4 ***YO! MTV RAPS*** *(1988-1995)*
Back in the days when hip-hop represented just one small segment of MTV's music videos, devoting two whole hours to it probably seemed like a gamble. But from its first episode, *Yo! MTV Raps* was a ratings smash—and more importantly, it helped turn hip-hop into a commercially viable genre, acting as a court where up-and-coming kings from Tupac Shakur to Naughty By Nature to Snoop Dogg came to be crowned, and introducing them to far-flung audiences in Europe, Asia, and Latin America. Although its popularity dwindled in later years as rap became less specialized (thanks in part to the show itself) and the shtick of hosts Ed Lover and Doctor Dre began to wear thin, *Yo!* had a cultural impact that can't be overstated. The

series finale's epic freestyle, starring a summit of decade-spanning hip-hop all-stars, remains a defining moment in music history.

WONDER SHOWZEN

5 ***ROCKUMENTARY*** *(INTERMITTENTLY THROUGH THE LATE '80S AND '90S)*
It seems inconceivable now that MTV would occasionally devote half an hour of airtime to sober, informative documentaries about contemporary and classic-rock artists. Often narrated by Kurt Loder, MTV's version of Walter Cronkite, *Rockumentary* summarized the career stories of everyone from Metallica to Rod Stewart to The Doors, focusing as much on albums and tours as the scandalous "behind the music" stories that VH1 later recycled. For budding music fans, *Rockumentary* offered a handy Cliffs Notes version of pop-music history that encouraged further exploration at the corner record store, maybe the only time MTV's consumerist ethos was used for good.

6 ***HEADBANGERS BALL*** *(1987-1995, 2003-PRESENT)*
MTV and metal have a long history, going back to the music channel's early championing of Def Leppard and Quiet Riot videos. But metal fans didn't have their own corner of MTV's weekly schedule until *Headbangers Ball*. For two hours every Saturday night, the series showcased the poppy metal bands that dominated MTV's primetime video schedule in the late '80s and early '90s, as well as harder-edged bands pointing the way to metal's future. Just as *Yo! MTV Raps* exposed viewers to revolutionary hip-hop acts, *Headbangers Ball* is responsible for turning millions of kids to the dark side of rock 'n' roll.

7 ***UNPLUGGED*** *(1989-2006)*
Make no mistake, *Unplugged* (and *Unplugged 2.0*) foisted some completely forgettable hours of stripped-down entertainment on the world, but some episodes of the show—which features bands playing acoustic (or nearly acoustic)—were absolutely transcendent. Nirvana revealed a new side of itself in a 1993 performance, which included Leadbelly and Meat Puppets covers. Jay-Z and LL Cool J redefined how hip-hop could be performed with their sessions, and Bob Dylan and Neil Young both brought their songs back to the basest levels. Of course, the show is also responsible for the reunion of the original Kiss lineup; whether that's good or bad is up in the air.

8 ***THE PAPER*** *(2008)*
While MTV's fascination with abhorrent teens of the rich-and-spoiled (*My Super Sweet 16*) and/or rich-and-dull (*Laguna Beach*) varieties shows no signs of abating, *The Paper* proves that somewhere, deep down, the network still loves teenagers. Set in the thoroughly suburban enclave of Weston, Florida, the first season of *The Paper* followed the senior editing staff of Cypress Bay High School's student newspaper, *The Circuit*. In many ways, *The Paper* is the anti-*Laguna Beach*: While the *Laguna* kids seemed to live in a kind of everlasting summer, fully ensconced in a romantic melodrama of their own making, the kids of *The Paper* actually attend classes and fill out college applications. And Amanda Lorber, the loveably dorky, showtune-humming editor-in-chief, is a much-needed realistic counterpoint

to dead-eyed, largely mute reality star Lauren Conrad.

9 *THE TOM GREEN SHOW* *(1999-2000)*
MTV isn't entirely responsible for *The Tom Green Show*—it originally aired in Canada, and the MTV version used a lot of the same prank footage—but the network did let Green expand his repertoire beyond annoying his parents (pre-*Jackass*, it should be noted) with lesbian paintjobs and severed cow heads. He ended up delivering "The Bum Bum Song," as well as an hourlong special with guest Monica Lewinsky. All compelling, weird TV.

10 *HUMAN GIANT* *(2007-2008)*
The guys of *Human Giant*—Rob Huebel, Paul Scheer, and Aziz Ansari—honed their chops doing live shows at the Upright Citizens Brigade theater in New York before they got the MTV gig, and while the three main cast members (along with director Jason Woliner) do the majority of the writing, *Human Giant* has featured script contributions and guest appearances from a veritable who's who of indie comedians. It's no coincidence that *Human Giant* sometimes scans like the *Mr. Show* of the 2000s; the two series shared guest stars and guest writers.

11 *BEAVIS & BUTT-HEAD* *(1993-1997)*
Beavis & Butt-head was criticized for the stupidity and violence of its title characters, which misses the point entirely: These are teenage boys who love metal, boobs, and fire. As such, their whole world was pretty spot-on. They laughed at their own stupid jokes, made everything sexual ("Entertain us." "He said 'anus'."), and shot from the hip about music videos. Watching those two watch MTV—a regular part of the show that's largely unavailable on DVD, for legal reasons—is like sitting with the two funniest, stupidest, smartest people alive. The show rarely got credit for being deeply satirical, either: There's plenty to laugh at beyond "I am Cornholio!" (Though that's damn funny, too.)

12-16 *LIQUID TELEVISION, AEON FLUX, THE MAXX, THE HEAD, DARIA* *(1991-1997)*
From its earliest days, when weird, experimental stop-motion and animated bumpers between shows made even the commercial breaks worth watching, MTV did great things for animation that reached far beyond *Beavis & Butt-head's* crudely drawn vision. The network's shorts-and-segments anthology *Liquid Television* gathered bizarre bits of creativity that at the time were rarely seen outside of theatrical touring animation shows. Some of the most popular segments were chapters in Peter Chung's wildly avant-garde future-fantasy *Aeon Flux*, which MTV later gave its own independent series. *The Maxx* adapted Sam Kieth's twisted comic with a surprising faithfulness to its dramatic, striking visual style. *The Head* pitted a collection of creepy but well-meaning freaks against an alien invasion in an ambitious, coherent single plot arc. And *Daria* spun off from *Beavis & Butt-head* as the dryly smart cousin to *Beavis'* gleefully dumb humor. For much of the '90s, MTV had its own animation production company, which it used to foster and support experimentation that had no other home. Those of us who were watching back then are still grateful—though we'd be a lot more grateful if all this material were available on DVD.

17 *TRUE LIFE* *(1998-PRESENT)*
One of the few remaining outposts of MTV's once-respectable news division, the original documentary series *True Life* has thrived for a decade, even as most of the channel's recent unscripted material has burrowed into the slop pile of so-called "reality" programming. Over the course of 150 or so episodes, the series has explored the width and breadth of youth culture, from the mundane ("I'm Jealous Of My Sibling") to the extreme ("I Live In A Brothel"), from the heartbreaking ("I'm Returning To The Gulf Coast") to the enlightening ("I'm In An Arranged Marriage"). Due to the often-touchy subject matter, *True Life* generally avoids the fame-whoring flotsam and jetsam that washes up on most of the channel's other reality shows; instead, it finds relatable subjects with a story to tell. (Though the series has dredged up its share of "characters" over the years, particularly in the snicker-inducing "I'm Getting Married" and "I'm Obsessed With My Dog.") It's still voyeurism, sure, but at least it's voyeurism with a point.

18 *REMOTE CONTROL* *(1987-1990)*
Because this game show was the first original MTV program that wasn't all about music, it might be tempting to lay the network's whole non-musical devolution at its feet. But *Remote Control* was almost too good for that stuck-in-the-'80s cable channel.

Anticipating the snark and kitsch of the '90s, the series revolved around the premise that host Ken Ober had remade his basement into a game-show set, complete with recliners, a wet bar, and wisecracking friends Colin Quinn, Adam Sandler, and Denis Leary, among others. Some of us are still winning trivia contests with information gleaned from categories like "Dead Or Canadian" and "Inside Tina Yothers."

19 *THE JON STEWART SHOW* (1993-1995)

Long before *The Daily Show* made him America's most trusted fake newsman, Jon Stewart was a stand-up comic whose résumé was limited to hosting fringe basic-cable programs like Comedy Central's *Short Attention Span Theater* and MTV's incredibly short-lived *You Wrote It, You Watch It.* Although Stewart lost the chance to be plucked from semi-obscurity to replace David Letterman—that honor fell to Conan O'Brien—MTV demonstrated its uncanny ability to be ahead of the curve when it gave him his very own show in 1993. Stewart's chatfest was sometimes painfully "alternative" (particularly in its host's penchant for wearing leather jackets and baggy jeans), but Stewart's rapport with his guests was loose and funny, the interwoven sketches were surprisingly sharp, and the musical acts included just-under-the-radar artists like Sunny Day Real Estate and Guided By Voices. Put together, *The Jon Stewart Show* made network talk shows look old and out of touch.

20 *WONDER SHOWZEN* (2005-2006)

Perhaps the most beautifully evil show ever funded by MTV (though it was originally broadcast on MTV2), *Wonder Showzen* was the brainchild of John Lee and Vernon Chatman, guys whose idea of funny is dressing a cute kid up as Hitler and having him ask random people, "What do you think is wrong with the youth of today?" Add to that twisted cartoons, wicked puppets, and harsh social commentary, and it's like *Sesame Street* perpetrated by depraved, hilarious animals. The show only lasted two short seasons, but that was long enough to run half an episode backward and devote an entire half-hour to a *Hee-Haw* parody called *Horse Apples*.

> A.V. CLUB
> You Wrote It, You Watch It *also spawned* The State.

21 *JACKASS* (2000-2002)

The *Jackass* disclaimer claimed that its stunts were performed—or at least supervised—by professionals, a sorta-fib so laughable that it became part of the show's humor. *Jackass'* appeal was that its stars *weren't* professionals, just a bunch of silly man-children acting on the simplest of male impulses. To guys, *Jackass* spoke to a reckless pursuit of cheap thrills that no amount of common sense can suppress: It simply looks *fun* to ride a shopping cart down a hill. Borrowing elements of *Candid Camera* (fat guy in a diaper chases a midget in public!) to *MythBusters* (If a dude drinks a gallon of eggnog in an hour, will he puke?), *Jackass* pioneered the novel concept of watching funny people do whatever they think is funny. Yes, Bam Margera went on to hawk deodorant, and Johnny Knoxville embarrassed himself in Hollywood, but in *Jackass'* prime, what guy didn't secretly want to be next to ride a toy horse on the half-pipe?

22 *ACTUAL MUSIC VIDEOS* (1981-1992)

Pointing out that MTV no longer plays videos is such a tired cliché that even pointing out the cliché is itself a cliché. But those old enough to remember long summer afternoons watching cheesy Van Halen and Madonna videos at a friend's house probably still get nostalgic for MTV's kinder, gentler, more musically inclined past. In MTV's early days, when the music channel was so desperate for content that it played any video it could get its hands on, low production values and awkward concepts were *de rigueur*, and absolutely charming. Back then, MTV seemed barely professional, almost like it didn't deserve to be on television. Which made it all the more mesmerizing.

Guest List:
ROBERT BEN GARANT

9 MOMENTS IN MOVIES I HAD TO TURN AWAY FROM

1. When "the Fly" barfed acid barf onto Geena Davis' boss' ankle.
2. When the girl in *Audition* cut off the dude's feet.
3. When Kathy Bates "hobbled" James Caan in *Misery*.
4. When the medic had to find the marine's vein in his leg in *Black Hawk Down*.
5. When he shaves his head in *Clean, Shaven*.
6. When the baby in *Eraserhead* gets "sick." And when the girl in the radiator steps on the... things she steps on. Actually, most of *Eraserhead*.
7. When he eats the boar testicles in *Apocalypto*.
8. *Freaks*.
9. When Gage cuts Fred Gwynne's ankle tendons in *Pet Sematary*.

Robert Ben Garant was a founding member of The State *and* Reno 911!, *and directed the* Reno 911! *movie and* Balls Of Fury.

Top Chef ◀ pizza, Oreos ◀

DOESN'T ANYBODY FUCKING KNOCK ANYMORE?

16 TRAGIC INSTANCES OF MOVIE MASTURBATION

1 *PARENTHOOD* (JOAQUIN PHOENIX)

In the '80s, nobody in mainstream cinema talked about masturbation, except when attributing nasty habits to the creepiest, most maladjusted kids in school. In *Parenthood*, a young Joaquin Phoenix (credited as Leaf) nails the part. He sneaks out of his bedroom with a furtive look, a mysterious grocery bag under his arm, and monosyllabic responses to any questions. His mother (Dianne Wiest) is bewildered by his behavior, until she gets her hands on the bag and pulls out a copy of *Wet, Wild And Ready* (with "XXX" helpfully printed on the label). But leave it to the all-knowing Keanu Reeves to clear everything up: Phoenix has been masturbating, a lot. And that's okay. As Reeves tells Wiest—and the audience—"That's what little dudes do. We've *all* done it."

2 *SPANKING THE MONKEY* (JEREMY DAVIES)

In his breakthrough role, Jeremy Davies bears a strong resemblance to elf/pirate pretty boy Orlando Bloom. But *Spanking The Monkey* shows why some young actors wind up in heartthrob roles opposite Keira Knightley, while others go on to play Charles Manson in a *Helter Skelter* remake. The initially fresh-faced Davies comes home from college and winds up stuck for the summer with his ill, manipulative, sexually frank mother. Davies can't get to his internship, can't escape his parents' demands, and can't even get a little privacy to masturbate. After multiple mid-act interruptions, he can't maintain a normal relationship with anybody, least of all his mother, who—in the film's infamous twist—has drunken intercourse with him.

A.V. CLUB *Rachael Ray's Tasty Travels* ◀ Domino's Oreo Dessert Pizza ◀

3 *THE EXORCIST* (LINDA BLAIR)

As Peter Biskind writes in *Easy Riders, Raging Bulls*, Linda Blair was 12 when director William Friedkin auditioned her for the part of the possessed girl in *The Exorcist*. When Blair explained that she knew what masturbation was ("It's like jerking off, isn't it?"), Friedkin asked if she ever did it herself. She answered, "Yeah, don't you?" Still, home rehearsals couldn't have prepared Blair for her big scene: Deep in the clutches of Satan, she effectively rapes herself with a crucifix, spraying blood all over her nightgown and screaming, "LET JESUS FUCK YOU!" at the top of her voice. Then she jams her mother's face into the mess, screaming "LICK IT!" before casting her aside. "Do you know what your cunting daughter did?" asks Satan/Blair. Yeah, well, it was pretty hard to miss.

4 *THE SQUID AND THE WHALE* (OWEN KLINE)

Owen Kline plays the younger of two sons of stuffy Park Slope, Brooklyn writers Jeff Daniels and Laura Linney. When his parents separate, Kline finds several ways to cope—and the creepiest comes in the school library, when the sight of a girl prompts him to walk over to the stacks with a wrinkled piece of porn and rub himself off against a bookcase; after he ejaculates, he smears his semen along the spine of some books. Later, Kline declares that he's a "philistine" who hates "books and things," by way of rejecting his father's book-based authority and his mother's literary success. Maybe his handling of the library books is another way of acting out against them. Or maybe that's just how writers breed in Park Slope.

5 *JUNEBUG* (AMY ADAMS)

Amy Adams loves Ben McKenzie. They're married; she's carrying his child. But McKenzie is withdrawn and uncommitted. In one scene in the middle of the film, Adams, lying in bed hugely pregnant, comforts herself with a photo of the two of them together, though in the photo, McKenzie looks just as distant as in life. Meanwhile, her husband is in the other room loudly complaining about their marriage. "I woulda gone to Washington D.C. in 12th grade, except for her!" is the last thing she hears before she finishes.

6 *SHORTBUS* (PAUL DAWSON)

In *Shortbus*, the graphic sex serves the plot and the character development. But no matter how mature viewers feel coming into the movie, there's no getting around the curiosity factor in the opening sequence, as a buck-naked Paul Dawson gets on his back, flips his feet over his head, and tries to fellate himself. He gets excruciatingly close and manages a slight insertion before he ejaculates—and then bursts into tears. Minutes later, his lover comes home, and Dawson quickly gets dressed and runs away, while everyone in the theater silently ticks his acrobatic act off their "things to see before I die" lists.

7 *YOUR FRIENDS & NEIGHBORS* (AARON ECKHART)

The arch metropolitan elites of *Your Friends & Neighbors* can't satisfy each other, sexually or otherwise. Aaron Eckhart plays the schlubbiest of the bunch, the closest the film has to a likable character. Discussing his best sexual experience, Eckhart brags, "The best lay I've ever had? That's easy, it's me!" Nothing satisfies him like himself, and he enjoys a post-coital spank better than the real act with his wife (played by Amy Brenneman). But even though he's the one character not dependent on other losers for his own satisfaction, Eckhart gets dumped anyway: While his wife beds down unhappily with the menacing Jason Patric, Eckhart tries but fails to reach orgasm on a sex-chat line. In narcissistic despair, he shouts, "What is the matter! Is it *me*?"

8 *HAPPINESS* (RUFUS READ)

In another grim late-'90s indie flick, *Happiness*, writer-director Todd Solondz suggests that the only true happiness comes at orgasm. Young Rufus Read, whose family has had a really, really rough year, wants to masturbate, but his efforts fail until the end of the film, when the sight of a blonde in a bikini finally brings him to finish. He ejaculates on the balcony railing, and in one of the film's only bursts of comic relief, the family dog licks it up, then runs back inside to lick Read's mother (Cynthia Stevenson) square on the kisser. Read follows him in and announces to his whole family, "I came!" Finally, he's fleetingly happy, and the family has a great story to tell at Thanksgiving.

9 *MULHOLLAND DR.* (NAOMI WATTS)

David Lynch's thriller *Mulholland Dr.* can be broken into two halves—the "fantasy" section, followed by the shorter "reality" section, which kicks off when Naomi Watts' fresh-faced naïveté collapses into a haggard expression, haunted eyes, and a hint of a snaggletooth. But nothing in that section looks as real as Watts masturbating on the couch, sweating and struggling and coming to tears at her inability to climax. The blurred shots of the wall across the room have been interpreted as her attempt to disappear into fantasy, only to crash right back into real life. Watts has described her character as "full of self-loathing," and said that "I kept on weeping and falling to pieces, because I just felt so embarrassed and humiliated."

10 *AMERICAN BEAUTY* (KEVIN SPACEY)

Kevin Spacey opens *American Beauty* in the shower, explaining that his few moments alone will be "the high point of the day." Masturbation sums up the death-like routine of his suburban life, but later in the film, it's the turning point: Smitten with his daughter's high-school friend, he starts to pleasure himself in bed while thinking about her. When the rapid thumping wakes his wife (Annette Bening), they fight, and Spacey finally declares his independence, even throwing her threat of a divorce back in her face. Says Spacey, "It's a great thing when you realize you still have the ability to

surprise yourself"—especially when it comes from something you've been doing since you were 13.

11 *BABEL* (BOUBKER AIT EL CAID)

At the beginning of *Babel*, a young Moroccan boy—after looking at his sister, naked, through a hole in the wall of her hut—takes a break from herding goats to drop trou and masturbate. But his brother interrupts him by taking potshots at coyotes with their brand-new rifle, which leads to a shooting contest between the brothers, which only stops after they wound American tourist Cate Blanchett. Had the boy not been interrupted, Blanchett might never have done a bedpan scene, Gael García Bernal couldn't have shown us the best way to twist the head off a rooster, and Rinko Kikuchi would've gotten a lot less naked. In other words, had the kid gotten off, the whole movie could have been avoided.

12-13 *LITTLE CHILDREN* (GREGG EDELMAN, JACKIE EARLE HALEY)

As a bored, overeducated suburban housewife, Kate Winslet is an easy mark for an adulterous affair. But to keep viewers sympathetic to her needs, *Little Children* writes off her husband, Gregg Edelman, as a total drip. The pale, cave-bug-like Edelman can't stop surfing an amateur sex site run by "Slutty Kay." His obsession grows until Winslet walks in on him at his computer, masturbating to Kay with her mail-order panties stretched like a mask across his face, making him look like a polka-dotted gynecologist. After that, Winslet feels a lot less guilty about messing around behind his back.

A more horrifying scene comes later in the film, when Jackie Earle Haley—playing a sex offender who served time for indecent exposure—takes unlucky date Jane Adams to dinner. When she drives him home, he asks her to pull over by a children's playground and kill the lights. As she tells him how bad her last date was, she notices a strange sound and looks over to see him masturbating and staring at her like a snake, hissing, "You better not tell on me… or I'll fucking get you." The swing-set in the background completes one of the film's most disturbing moments.

> A.V. CLUB
>
> *Six Feet Under uses the same gesture in the third season, when Peter Krause, stalling for time on his way home to a loveless marriage, pulls over and masturbates in his car. Just as in American Beauty, the writers couldn't fix the marriage without offing one of the spouses.*

14 *BAD LIEUTENANT* (HARVEY KEITEL)

Of course, Harvey Keitel perfected the "jerking off in front of girls trapped in a car" scene in *Bad Lieutenant*, when he catches two Jersey teens on the town without their licenses, and threatens to tell their father unless they do what he says. Keitel's abuse of his authority, crossed with the pathetic sight of him playing with himself as the girls humiliate themselves in sexual poses, gruesomely proves the depth of his corruption.

15 *FAST TIMES AT RIDGEMONT HIGH* (JUDGE REINHOLD)

There's no worse nightmare than coming back from your fast-food job, still wearing your sweaty pirate uniform, and getting caught in the bathroom by the girl you're fantasizing about. Still, Reinhold plays this legendary caught-in-the-act scene for laughs, and 30 years' worth of guys have staged their own run-throughs thanks to the vivid shots of Phoebe Cates striding across a misty swimming pool and unsnapping her bikini top. After she finds him, Cates cringes away—but Reinhold wins the round with an exasperated, "Doesn't anybody fucking *knock* anymore?" Nice save, dude!

16 *BEING THERE* (SHIRLEY MACLAINE)

In Hal Ashby's acerbic 1979 satire, Washington D.C. insiders fall over themselves to misinterpret the words of Peter Sellers, a vapid, TV-obsessed, mentally challenged gardener who's accidentally hailed as a profound thinker when his literal statements about his garden are taken for political metaphor. Among the misinterpreters: society wife Shirley MacLaine, who presses herself on Sellers' character as he watches TV in his room. Mistaking his straightforward announcement "I like to watch" for a description of his sexual tastes rather than a summary of his television-focused existence, she struggles with shyness, rolls around grunting on a bear rug, and finally fingers herself to cackling, squealing orgasm, all while Sellers indifferently channel-surfs. So which is more tragic during masturbation, being caught by a potential partner, or ignored by an actual partner?

STICK AROUND FOR THE GHOST MONKEY

22 MOVIES WITH POST-CREDITS SURPRISES

1-3 PIRATES OF THE CARIBBEAN 1-3 (2003, 2006, 2007)

As credit sequences get longer, more filmmakers are rewarding dogged viewers by adding bonus scenes after the last name has scrolled by. *The Pirates Of The Caribbean* trilogy is particularly playful with its post-credits action—each movie has a "stinger" (or "tag," or "button") that sets a completely different tone from the film's actual ending. The first film concludes on a triumphant note, with the cursed doubloons returned to their source, all the ghost pirates returned to mortality, and protagonists Will Turner and Elizabeth Swann together at last, in what seems like a suitable epilogue. But after the credits, the pirates' monkey swims back to the cursed gold and steals a piece, turning back into a hideous shrieking ghost-monkey, as if to suggest that the story isn't over. The second film ends on a grim note, with Captain Jack Sparrow apparently dead, and his friends off to the end of the world to find him—but the post-credits tag offers up a little joke, as the series' dog mascot, last seen being chased by a horde of cannibal natives, is shown sitting on a throne as their king. Finally, one of the third movie's many plotlines sees Will and Elizabeth separated yet again, but a bittersweet post-credits epilogue reunites them 10 years later, as Elizabeth and their son wait by the shore for Will's wandering ship, *The Flying Dutchman*, to return at its appointed hour.

4 THE TRIPLETS OF BELLVILLE (2003)

By comparison, the stinger at the end of the wild French animated feature *The Triplets Of Bellville* is a mere fillip of a sight gag. When an old lady's cyclist grandson is kidnapped and spirited away in a vast transoceanic tanker, she pursues in a rusty pedal-boat, rented from a dismal vendor who charges one franc for a 20-minute outing. She winds up in a lengthy, grand adventure, with gangsters, shootouts, car chases, musical numbers, and a disgusting meal of boiled frogs, but once all the big noisy action is over, the film cuts back to a quiet shot of the vendor still standing by the shore, checking his watch, seemingly baffled about how 20 minutes could seem so long.

5 AIRPLANE! (1980)

A similar gag occurs at the end of the Zucker-Abrahams-Zucker disaster-movie parody *Airplane!* In the opening sequence, former military pilot Robert Hays, now a cab driver, pulls his taxi up to the curb at an airport. Passenger Howard Jarvis jumps in, but Hays says he'll be right back, and runs into the airport to confront his girlfriend, stewardess Julie Hagerty, who's just left him a "Dear John" letter at home. She insists their relationship is over, so he boards her plane to Chicago to continue their conversation. The crew passes out, Hays confronts his traumatic past and takes the controls, and a great deal of classic silliness ensues, but after the film ends, the camera returns to Jarvis, still sitting in that taxi at the curb, checking his watch and muttering "Well, I'll give him another 20 minutes, but that's it."

6 IRON MAN (2008)

Possibly the decade's most-publicized post-credits scene followed *Iron Man*, in a calculated attempt both to keep audiences in their seats through the credits, and to build anticipation for an eventual planned Avengers movie. While the film ends with an abrupt, grin-inducing bang, with Robert Downey Jr. as Tony Stark revealing his secret identity to the press, a stinger finds him coming home later to a mysterious visitor: Samuel L. Jackson as Nick Fury, ready to recruit Stark into the ranks of a super-team slated for its own big-screen outing.

7 *FERRIS BUELLER'S DAY OFF* (1986)

The bonus scene at the very end of *Ferris Bueller's Day Off* likely reached more people than most tags, since the action continues through the credits, with beleaguered, beaten-down principal Jeffrey Jones enduring further ignominies on a school bus. Viewers who watch his suffering all the way through to the end endure a little ignominy of their own when the credits end and Matthew Broderick as Ferris Bueller walks out, gives the fourth wall a patronizing, almost pitying look, and snaps "You're still here? It's over. Go home. GO."

8 *THE PRODUCERS* (2006)

Broderick returned with a similar message nearly 30 years later in a tag at the end of *The Producers*, the film adaptation of the Broadway play adapted from Mel Brooks' 1968 film hit. After the wrap, Broderick and the rest of the primary cast bounce back out for a short, peppy number that shoos stragglers toward the exit with lyrics including "Grab your hat and head for the door / in case you didn't notice, there ain't any more! / if you like our show, tell everyone, but / if you think it stinks, keep your big mouth shut!" Even Brooks himself pops in for a cameo, belting out the final words: "Get out! It's over!"

9 *L.A. CONFIDENTIAL* (1997)

In the tangled web of *L.A. Confidential*, three detectives—Russell Crowe, Guy Pearce, and Kevin Spacey—all investigate a massacre at a diner in different ways. Spacey doesn't survive the process, and a post-credits clip pays homage to his abrupt end. Many of his scenes in the film revolve around his life away from his precinct, serving as consultant on a cop TV series called *Badge Of Honor*. While the film is set in 1950s Los Angeles, it's all in vibrant color with sharp modern cinematography—except for chunks of the opening montage, which uses vintage black-and-white footage and imagery, and the post-credits sequence, in which a stereotyped-to-a-fault whitebread '50s family sits around a TV set, watching an episode of *Badge Of Honor* that's specially dedicated to Spacey's fallen cop.

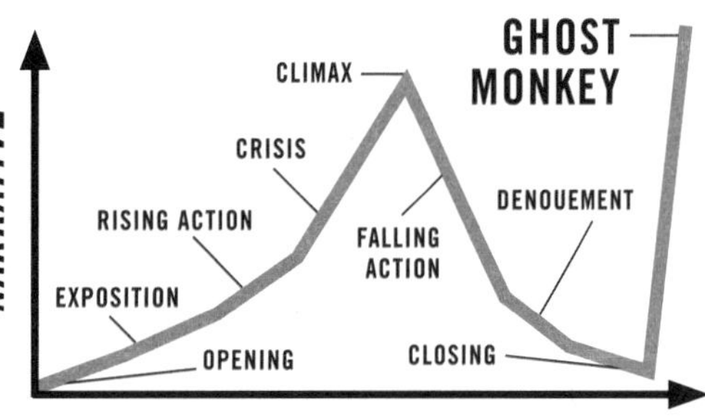

10 *YOUNG SHERLOCK HOLMES* (1985)

Barry Levinson's cheesy but agreeable film about Sherlock Holmes' teen years goes a bit overboard in introducing each of the character's well-known peccadilloes: his relationship with his violin, his first use of "Elementary, my dear Watson," the origin of his deerstalker cap and his pipe, and so forth. For viewers who stick through the credits, it even reveals the origins of Holmes' greatest enemy. It's no huge surprise when one of the good guys turns out to be the film's villain, since that's how so many screen mysteries work. The movie's climax seems to dispose of him permanently, but a post-credits clip shows that he escaped certain death. As he checks into a hotel under the name "Moriarty," he gives the audience a smug little smile, acknowledging the reference and seemingly saying, "You haven't seen the last of me."

11 *HARRY POTTER AND THE CHAMBER OF SECRETS* (2002)

Given the rabid fandom backing the Harry Potter books—and the amount of material that the film adaptations have had to discard to keep the run times reasonable—it's actually surprising that the movies don't throw fans more of a bone with post-credit tags. The only one of the series so far to offer more than a sound clip was the second one, *Harry Potter And The Chamber Of Secrets*, which introduced insufferable egotist and minor villain Gilderoy Lockhart (played by Kenneth Branagh), author of a great many self-aggrandizing books. At the climax of the film, he accidentally erases his own memory; after the credits, he's seen in a straitjacket, making goofy, baffled faces while apparently pimping his latest authorial effort, *Who Am I?*

12 *GHOST WORLD* (2001)

Late in the comic-book-based teen-angst film *Ghost World*, a frustrated Steve Buscemi storms into the convenience store where Brad Renfro works, and attempts to wreck the place as vengeance for perceived mockery. Instead, he finds he's too spindly to overturn a shelf; then a spazzy, mulleted Dave Sheridan attacks him with nunchucks and puts him in the hospital. The jokey post-credits take of the scene shows another story, as Buscemi punches out Renfro (complete with exaggerated ker-pow foley effects), floors and kicks Sheridan, then lunges for the door, screaming profanely. It doesn't fit his nebbishy character, but it's pretty funny.

13 *THE SIMPSONS MOVIE* (2007)

The Simpsons' strangely late-to-the-big-screen outing is framed with scenes of Homer, Marge, and the family at the theater, watching the movie they're appearing in; Homer starts the film by calling everyone a sucker for paying to see something they could get for free at home on TV, and the film ends with them alone in the theater, commenting on the credits scrolling by. But finally, they walk out. The credits continue, with the anonymous pimply teenaged kid who seems to have every menial job in Springfield coming in and scrubbing the gum off the theater floor, muttering "Assistant manager isn't all it's cracked up to be." Even once the credits end, he's still alone, sweeping and grumbling, "Four years of film school for this?"

14 *PLANES, TRAINS AND AUTOMOBILES* (1987)

John Hughes' first "adult" comedy after a series of hit teen comedies tracks Steve Martin and John Candy on a series of torturous attempts to travel from New York to Chicago in time for a family Thanksgiving celebration. The pain starts with the first shot, as Martin and his fellow execs squirm miserably in a meeting, watching the clock and praying for relief as their doddering boss silently examines three layouts of a lipstick ad. Finally—after several comedically excruciating false starts—he puts off choosing one until after the holiday break. And apparently until after the film, as well. The final post-credits shot finds him still in the boardroom, sitting down to a private Thanksgiving dinner—complete with a whole turkey to himself—and continuing to muse painfully over the same three boring ads.

15 *THE ADVENTURES OF PRISCILLA, QUEEN OF THE DESERT* (1994)

Off on a road trip across the Australian outback, two flamboyant drag queens and a transsexual generally make lemonade out of any lemons the trip hands them. When some small-town bigots scrawl "AIDS fuckers go home!" across their tour bus, they repaint the bus pink. When it breaks down in the middle of nowhere, they stage an impromptu drag show with the local aborigines. And when a mechanic takes forever to arrive, they amuse themselves by attaching a grotesque blow-up sex doll to an unwanted dress and making a hilariously camp kite, which they set free when rescue arrives. They go on to further titular adventures, and the renegade kite does too—a post-credits gag shows it touching down in a garden full of Chinese pagodas, somewhere very far from home.

16 *X-MEN: THE LAST STAND* (2006)

The third installment in the X-Men film franchise saw schlock auteur Brett Ratner taking over from series helmer Bryan Singer, and taking the series to staggeringly expensive, overblown new levels. The film made big bucks, but with a $210 million production budget, it was hard to earn back costs—which may explain why a sequel wasn't immediately forthcoming. Nonetheless, *The Last Stand* hedged its bets for future installments. Patrick Stewart said he wasn't interested in reprising his role as X-Men leader Professor X in the event of a fourth movie, so movie number three dutifully killed him off, but a postscript makes it clear that his consciousness survives in a new body, just in case they need to bring back the character, but not the actor, somewhere down the road.

17 *THE FAST AND THE FURIOUS* (2001)

Rob Cohen's surprise 2001 hit is an odd film: It sets out to glorify the racing lifestyle of co-star Vin Diesel, even though he barely races during the film, and it portrays him as such a nice guy that undercover cop Paul Walker lets him walk away from his considerable crimes, even though they aren't remotely justified. By the film's end, Diesel is a complete failure and an outcast on the run, yet a tonally off post-credits coda tries to recapture his poorly established cool by showing him speeding alongside a Mexican beach, reprising an earlier line about how he lives his life "a quarter-mile at a time" and nothing else matters. Way to go, independent rebel who totally blew it. As a secondary bonus, on the DVD release, the Vin Diesel button immediately segues into a laughably awful five-minute music-video-style montage where Walker, now a fugitive, roams the country like Bill Bixby in *The Incredible Hulk*, mournfully winning street races, impressing stray hotties, and generally trying to hook viewers into the upcoming *2 Fast 2 Furious*.

18 *WET HOT AMERICAN SUMMER* (2001)

In a typically straight-faced gag from the '80s-summer-camp-movie parody *Wet Hot American Summer*, a group of counselors stand around having the old "Let's reunite 10 years from now and see what we've become" talk. Except it winds up stretched out into a ludicrous negotiation over exactly what time to meet up in 10 years, and whether to schedule for 9 a.m. "so that way we can be here by 9:30," or just schedule for 9:30 "and then make it your beeswax to be here by 9:30." The scene is dryly funny on its own; the tag at the end, with someone arriving late to that 10-years-later meeting and bringing up the scheduling argument again, doesn't actually add that much.

19 *CONSTANTINE* (2005)

The badly botched 2005 film adaptation of the *Hellblazer* comic-book series messed up the casting, the tone, and the execution, but it at least managed a fairly eerie look, especially for its legion of angels, devils, and half-breeds. That holds true for the tag at the end, where John Constantine (a typically wooden Keanu Reeves) visits the grave of his "apprentice," Chas (Shia LaBeouf), and sees a winged Chas flying up into darkness. Trouble is, like so much of the movie, the scene is baffling. Has Chas earned his wings for fighting the good fight during his lifetime, as a throwaway line early in the film implied was possible? Or—far more interesting—was he an angel all along, sent from heaven to keep an eye on Constantine's hellbound renegade exorcist? The oblique, imagistic scene raises far more questions than it answers.

The Muppet Movie ***is often cited as having one of the earliest post-credit scenes, but it actually just has action all the way through the end of the credits.***

20 *IDIOCRACY* (2006)

"Extremely average" Army drone Luke Wilson is placed into an experimental "human hibernation pod" for what's supposed to be one year, but he wakes up 500 years in the future. His only companion from the past is Rita, a hooker loaned to the Army hibernation experiment by her pimp, Upgrayedd ("with two Ds for a double dose of his pimping"). While Wilson spends the film fretting over his escape back to the past, Rita repeatedly worries that Upgrayedd will think she ran off on him, and that he's coming to get her, not letting a mere 500 years get in the way of the money she owes him. The running joke pays off after the credits, when he turns up as predicted, freshly out of hibernation and still doggedly looking for his ho.

21 *LETHAL WEAPON 3* (1992)

The third outing for Mel Gibson and Danny Glover's mismatched buddy-cop team begins with their showing up at the site of a bomb threat, where Gibson insists on charging in, and Glover, pointing out that he's eight days away from retirement and doesn't want to make any stupid mistakes, begs him to wait for the bomb squad. By the end of the scene, Gibson has accidentally set off the bomb, and they're running for their lives. A ridiculous parallel sequence bookends the film, with the two men yammering manically in voiceover as their car pulls up to another building containing a bomb. The place explodes before they can even enter it, and they hurriedly drive away, yelping, "I hope nobody saw us!" and sharing the series' running-gag line: "I'm too old for this shit!"

22 *NAPOLEON DYNAMITE* (2004)

After *Napoleon Dynamite* became a sleeper hit, distributor Fox Searchlight paid to have an additional sequence shot and added after the credits, reportedly in hopes of getting the movie's cultish devotees to return to theaters to see it yet again. In the button, Napoleon's brother Kip gets married, and Napoleon shows up with an unconventional present. The scene is exactly five minutes long, though it feels like it's at least 50 percent uncomfortable, draggy pause. Not all stingers are worth the wait.

YOU GOT YOUR MOOG IN MY KEYTAR!

10 HIGHLY PRETENTIOUS MUSICAL INSTRUMENTS

1 THE EATON-MOOG MULTIPLE-TOUCH-SENSITIVE KEYBOARD

For years, prog rockers tainted Bob Moog's name by playing his keyboards while wearing shiny silver capes, or standing in the orchestra pit at Rick Wakeman's *King Arthur On Ice* tour. But the late, legendary synth-maker wasn't immune to delusions of grandeur: In 1992, Moog and University Of Chicago music prof John Eaton debuted the Eaton-Moog Multiple-Touch-Sensitive Keyboard, sometimes called "The World's Most Sensitive Musical Instrument." Its 49 keys respond to five kinds of movement—from touch pressure to the way players roll their fingertips and slide them up and down the keys—to adjust the volume, vibrato, and pitch. Reportedly, the prototype sits in Eaton's attic, but the instrument never made it into production. Has anyone pitched it to Keith Emerson?

2 THE CHAPMAN STICK

Art rock—especially '80s-'00s King Crimson—wouldn't be complete without the Chapman Stick, a combination guitar/bass that looks like a 2-by-4 and is played by tapping the strings with both hands. It's forever connected to serious, ponytailed men like Trey Gunn, who look like they treat "picking" and "strumming" with a sniff of contempt. The Chapman Stick is also worn across the chest with the top resting on the player's shoulder, giving the impression that it's so precious, it needs to be cradled.

3 CHILDREN'S CHOIR

A classic example of unearned beauty, the children's choir is a crutch on many "powerful" pop songs. Sure, there are exceptions: The boys on The Rolling Stones' "You Can't Always Get What You Want" sound like they were just caught smoking and dragged to the church by their ears, and the choir's entrance on Talk Talk's "I Believe In You" really is so catch-your-breath beautiful that they earn some slack. But the rest of the time, it's treacly kitsch, not to mention high-maintenance. You have to keep restocking the choirs every few years, and thanks to Pope Leo XIII's 1902 decree, you can't just castrate your star sopranos anymore.

A.V. CLUB

Robert Moog's last name is pronounced with a long "o." It rhymes with "rogue."

4 THE PIKASSO GUITAR

Pat Metheny challenged guitar-maker Linda Manzer to build him a guitar with "as many strings as possible." The cubist three-necked monster she spawned sports 42 strings crisscrossing the body, producing everything from regular guitar tones to harp-like effects. It even featured a pickup for his guitar synth. Manzer's design is a work of art—just ask Boston's Museum Of Fine Arts, which once put it on display. But when Metheny takes it on tour and drags it out for only one or two songs, it's just spectacle, the equivalent of smashing a watermelon with a sledgehammer.

5 BAGPIPE

Who hasn't had a bad experience with a bagpipe? It's the loudest, most boorish acoustic instrument there is, whether it's outside, ruining a perfectly fine public park, or on a concert stage, where—as one example—the Battlefield Band wheels out its bagpiper with almost circus-like fanfare, like the audience is about to watch someone take a cannonball

to the chest. The only safe place to use them is at funerals: That's the only time they don't think they're the guests of honor.

6 KEYTAR

The portable keyboard you strap on like a guitar has graced an embarrassing list of people who should have known better, like Donald Fagen, Herbie Hancock, and "Weird Al" Yankovic. But it still looks like a plastic toy that should have bubbles coming out of the handle. When Steve Masakowski invented it and Moog Music rolled out the first models, keyboardists everywhere who'd been stuck in the back at concerts got the chance to strut across the front, just like the real stars. It didn't take long to figure out that they'd been put back there for a reason.

7 FLUTE

An inflexible, twittery instrument, the flute has barely crossed into popular music: With a few major exceptions, jazz never had a use for it, and neither did rock, until Jethro Tull. Ian Anderson took the flute as his signature instrument, thanks to his groundbreaking "standing-on-one-leg" style of playing, and the sewing-machine-like solo in "My God"—a strikingly pompous performance from a guy who started out aping Rahsaan Roland Kirk. But Anderson is far from the most self-important player in the business. Hats off to James Newton for valuing his work so highly that he sued the Beastie Boys over a three-note sample on *Check Your Head*.

8 VIBES

The syrup on top of the doughy pancake that is most post-rock, the warm, predictable timbre of the vibes is the default stopgap for groups that don't think two drummers and eight retro keyboards is enough to make a groove. It's mostly used for texture, and while a few bands—like the first lineup of Aloha—actually solo on the thing, that doesn't make up for all their griping about hauling it up the stairs to a gig. And while the vibraphone has spawned jazz legends like Milt Jackson and Gary Burton, most listeners secretly love it because it reminds them of the comforting childhood sounds of the xylophone.

9 GRAND PIANO

Tortured pianists clawing their way to a resolution on an imposing, handcrafted instrument... That image has left a legacy that any hack can tap at the drop of a sustain pedal. The drama of the concert hall excuses plenty of weak, meandering music: Grand-piano impresarios can sound like they're moving mountains, even when their ideas don't run deeper than "Sunrise is pretty," or "I wear silk boxers." Keith Jarrett's roughly 20 records of marathon improvisations bring enough rigor and fire to justify the pedestal he puts them on, but the New Agers who followed have bled off the rest of the instrument's credibility.

10 ELECTRIC GUITAR

"Pretentious" means different things to different fans, but the breaking point usually comes when you can smell the artist thinking, "I am fucking *wicked*." And in the 20th century, nothing was more pretentious than the electric guitar. It may be the greatest instrument of our time, but it also lures impressionable young players into losing themselves in musical masturbation: furiously, unproductively stroking the neck of their instrument for hours as they slump into the league of longhaired, overbearing gearheads studying Joe Satriani and Allan Holdsworth instructional tapes in a basement.

...AND WITH HIS KEYTAR, HE IS THE MASTER OF THE UNIVERSE.

TELL ME A TUNE

26 SONGS THAT WORK AS SHORT STORIES

1 JOHNNY CASH, "A BOY NAMED SUE"

Johnny Cash's wise-country-storyteller persona lent itself naturally to story-songs, from traditionally inspired ballads like "Legend Of John Henry's Hammer" to funny goofs like "One Piece At A Time." But one of his best was the epic saga "A Boy Named Sue." Shel Silverstein's dense, witty lyrics follow the titular character on a hunt for the deadbeat dad who gave him his awful name and abandoned him in childhood. Turns out there was method to daddy's madness, which "Sue" accepts in the end, though not to such a degree that he's willing to repeat the process with his own theoretical future kids.

2 KENNY ROGERS, "COWARD OF THE COUNTY"

In his heyday, Kenny Rogers also intermittently donned a wise-country-storyteller persona, though his story-songs tend to be less wryly funny than Cash's, and more tragic. For instance, "The Gambler," "Lucille," and the frankly horrifying "Coward Of The County." Like "A Boy Named Sue," "Coward" follows a young man dealing with a bad paternal legacy—in this case, his father's prison-deathbed command to back away from conflict, 'cause "You don't have to fight to be a man." Eventually, the boy learns that poppa was wrong, and he proves to everyone in his judgmental little county that he ain't yellow after all. Too bad it takes the love of his life getting gang-raped to get him off his butt.

3 JAWBREAKER, "CHESTERFIELD KING"

Viewed through the lens of all the lame emo that's followed it, Jawbreaker's "Chesterfield King" seems kind of quaint. But the song—a lone, bright gem amid all the sludge and glumness of the band's 1992 album *Bivouac*—is the prime example of the emerging literary bent that singer-guitarist Black Schwarzenbach would perfect on Jawbreaker's next two discs. With plainspoken yet vivid lucidity, Schwarzenbach opens the story *in medias res*, with himself and a female friend on the brink of romantic revelation. Fear chases him out of her house, but after sharing a smoke and a beer with a homeless woman outside a 7-Eleven, he races back to his girl's house to seal the deal, poetically and inconclusively, of course. Lines like "I took my car and drove it down the hill by your house / I drove so fast" might sound a little too much like an, um, dashboard confessional, but "Chesterfield King" remains a perfect, roughhewn chunk of prose sunk into one of the catchiest punk tunes of all time.

"Coward Of The County" served as the source of a 1981 TV movie co-starring Rogers.

4 THE TEMPTATIONS, "PAPA WAS A ROLLIN' STONE"

After the high-profile 1968 departure of Temptations singer David Ruffin, Motown songwriter-producer Norman Whitfield helped reinvent the group in his own image, with a trippy, socially conscious brand of psychedelic soul that radically departed from the songs that had made the group famous. The new sound created some tensions, and by 1972, the group had experienced even more turnover and was beginning to resent Whitfield's auteurist approach. But that tension isn't audible in "Papa Was A Rollin' Stone," an expansive track—the full version runs for 12 minutes—in which the singers take turns asking about the father they never knew, only to receive the same answer, "Papa was a rollin' stone." Even as grown-ups, they don't understand:

JOHNNY CASH

They know the details about a "jack of all trades" life of "storefront preaching" and other endeavors, but the sad truth is in the spacious instrumental passages, blanks that the absence uniting them has left them to fill.

5 LOUDON WAINWRIGHT III, "THE MAN WHO COULDN'T CRY"

Loudon Wainwright III pulls off a tough trick with his country-music parody "The Man Who Couldn't Cry"—he pokes fun at tear-in-your-beer story ballads while making his stoic protagonist genuinely sympathetic. The unnamed titular man loses the ability to cry after his tear ducts run dry during childhood. A series of bad things happen to him—his dog is run over, his wife leaves him, he loses his job, a whore laughs at him—but there's "still not a sniffle or a sob." (He even winds up in jail—"you guessed it, no bail," Wainwright adds.) Finally, after landing in a mental hospital, he cries when it rains, and ends up crying for 40 days and 40 nights. On the 41st day, he dies from dehydration. But the story has a happy ending: The man goes to heaven, and everything bad that happened to him in life is corrected. His ex-wife, for instance, dies of stretch marks.

6 TODD SNIDER, "TILLAMOOK COUNTY JAIL"

Singer-songwriter Todd Snider crafts a slyly humorous, Raymond Carver-esque snapshot of a slowly disintegrating loser in "Tillamook County Jail." The details he offers are as important as those only suggested: The first-person narrative begins with the protagonist wondering whether his woman will bail him out of jail, hinting that this isn't the first time he's been in trouble. There's a lump on his head and a boot print on his chest from "the Tillamook County lie-detector test," a "tough test not to fail." He tries to explain what got him here—it started with a fight with a guy on the highway, who said the protagonist "did some things that I didn't do." The cops chased him down the road and hauled him in. His story sounds fishy, but he remains unrepentant. If he ever gets out of jail, he's never coming back to Tillamook County. He'll just raise hell someplace else.

7 DRIVE-BY TRUCKERS, "THE DEEPER IN"

"By the time you were born there were four other siblings," Patterson Hood explains at the start of the funereal-paced "The Deeper In." He goes on to tell the subject of the song her own story: how she met her wayward older brother for the first time when she was 19, how his motorcycle and "jawline" swept her off her feet and into a cross-country run from the law. Positioned as the first song on Drive-By Truckers' most satisfying and arguably most Southern album, *Decoration Day*,

"The Deeper In" either shamelessly exploits the plight of two impoverished hicks, or movingly explains how one damn thing can lead to another. Their brother-sister common-law marriage might've lasted, if only the sister hadn't brought four more inbred kids into the world. But she did, which sets up Hood's devastating finale: "You awoke in a jail cell, alone and so lonely / seven years in Michigan."

8 NEW ORDER, "LOVE VIGILANTES"

Though not generally known for story-songs, New Order kicked off the classic 1985 dance-pop album *Low Life* with this fantastical tale of a soldier who gets his discharge orders and heads home, only to find his wife crumpled over in grief on their floor because—get this—*he's actually dead*! The lyrics are as awkwardly phrased as a junior-high poetry assignment—"You just can't believe the joy I did receive" is a particularly egregious line—but the ending remains a sucker-punch. Maybe the song's impact has something to do with its ironically jaunty melodica solo and bouncy beat. Or maybe it's the simple yearning of the repeated chorus, "I want to see my family."

9 BRIGHT EYES, "LIGHT POLLUTION"

Conor Oberst takes his time setting the scene for this simultaneously sad and triumphant character sketch, starting by remembering a friend who "loaned him books and mic stands" and taught him all about the human wreckage left behind by the free-market system. Then, out of nowhere, Oberst starts piling up the imagery from one particular night. There was a baseball game, and billboards shading the road, and a mall-front highway spitting neon. "And maybe he lost control fucking with the radio," Oberst wails, "But I bet the stars seemed so close at the end." The busy electronic track drops to a hush, and Oberst repeats "at the end" softly over a wisp of electric piano, remembering a man killed by the unchecked corporate sprawl he railed against in life.

10 THE KINKS, "COME DANCING"

This late-period Kinks comeback hit doesn't rock as hard as the band's '60s and '70s classics, and at the time, it seemed like kind of a novelty number, with its retro music-hall melody and brassy arrangement. But "Come Dancing" is of a piece with Ray Davies' formidable body of songs about a vanishing England. The song's narrator remembers "the local palais," where his sister went on chaste dates with boys, while the narrator and their mother stayed up waiting for her to come home. By the end of "Come Dancing," the dancehall has been replaced by a bowling alley and a car-park, and the narrator's sister has become an anxious mother herself. But he urges her to remember the innocent romance of the old days, and to dance again, if only to show a new generation how to do it proper.

> *Ray Davies finds the past similarly bittersweet in the classic story-song "Do You Remember Walter?", in which he recalls an old classmate who he assumes is now "fat and married," and decides he's best left in the past. "People often change," goes the wise, crushing conclusion, "but memories of people can remain."*

11 PULP, "DAVID'S LAST SUMMER"

Another songwriter with a skeptical attitude about the future and a keen eye for detail, Pulp's Jarvis Cocker packs the seven minutes of "David's Last Summer" with details of a summer filled with cider, late-night parties, and a sharply remembered "small pale-skin bikini," the last before the responsibilities of adulthood kick in. By the time summer begins "packing its bags as it prepare[s] to leave town," it's clear that no other season will live so vividly in the imagination.

12 JONI MITCHELL, "THE LAST TIME I SAW RICHARD"

In her heyday, Mitchell preferred to offer impressionistic explorations of moments rather than full narratives, but because the moment she describes in "The Last Time I Saw Richard" has a history, she has to tell a little story in order to bring it to its conclusion. After an extended, somber piano intro, the narrator spends two verses remembering a collegial argument she had in a bar back in 1968—only three years before this song was recorded. Her friend Richard warned her not to be such a naïve romantic, falling over and over for "pretty lies," and she replied that studied cynicism can be a kind of romanticism too. Besides, every song Richard punched up on the jukebox that night was about "love so sweet." In the third verse, Mitchell sums up what happened next: Richard got married and "drinks at home now most nights with the TV on," while she still haunts the bars, though she'd rather be left alone. At the time, this song seemed to bring the curtain down on the '60s, but it still rings true to anyone who ever lived, loved, and fought with more passion than they do right now.

13 JEANNIE C. RILEY, "HARPER VALLEY PTA"

This country standard is so much a start-to-finish narrative that it actually starts off "I want to tell you all a story…", and it inspired a film and a spin-off TV series. The saga begins when a child comes home with a note suggesting that the Parent-Teachers' Association of her provincial school district finds her mother's short skirts and carousing ways inappropriate. The mother promptly shows up at the PTA's next meeting to call out every member by name and publicly reveal their screwin', drinkin', sneakin'-around ways, winding up with the line "this is just a little Peyton Place, and you're all Harper Valley hypocrites." Riley then reveals, in the big finish, that this "really… happened just this way / the day my mama socked it to the Harper Valley PTA." Strangely enough, after the song became a hit, such country luminaries as Dolly Parton, Loretta Lynn, and Billie Jo Spears all recorded cover versions, indicating that the exact same thing "really" happened to their mamas, too.

14 RICHARD THOMPSON, "1952 VINCENT BLACK LIGHTNING"

Having covered English folk ballads like "Matty Groves" from his early days as guitarist for Fairport Convention, Richard Thompson is no stranger to the form. He updated the traditional highwayman ballad with this song from 1991's *Rumor And Sigh*, spinning the tale of a dashingly dangerous robber who bonds with a red-haired beauty over their shared love for the classic motorcycle of the title. It's become his most popular song, and it shows up in nearly every concert he plays, with good reason: It's a masterpiece, a great showcase for Thompson's amazingly fluid fretwork and a powerfully resonant, simple tale of doomed romance that doesn't have a single wasted word.

15 BOB DYLAN, "LILY, ROSEMARY, AND THE JACK OF HEARTS"

Dylan has so many story-songs under his belt, from the surrealist goof of "Bob Dylan's 115th Dream" to the ripped-from-the-headlines "Lonesome Death Of Hattie Carroll," that it's hard to single out just one. But one of his finest yarns turns up on 1975's *Blood On The Tracks*—this Western about a charming rogue who blows into town and gets the better of villainous mine owner Big Jim, with the help of Jim's showgirl mistress Lily and put-upon wife Rosemary. The song's cinematic sweep makes it feel like it might have been a great film in the hands of a director like Howard Hawks or Dylan's friend Sam Peckinpah. And in fact, Dylan tried at least once to get a screenplay based on "Lily" off the ground.

16 SIMON AND GARFUNKEL, "SAVE THE LIFE OF MY CHILD"

Paul Simon also has his share of ballads and story-songs, but few of them are as satisfying or as pointedly conclusive as 1968's "Save The Life Of My Child," which is as much metaphor as story: As a boy sits perched on the ledge of a tall building, a crowd forms, waiting for him to jump. As his mother panics, the bystanders and the cops take the opportunity to dismiss today's youth as disrespectful, irresponsible druggies. The mass conclusion: The current crop of kids is pretty worthless. Naturally, the boy surprises them all by flying away and leaving them in his dust, scoring a point for '60s counterculture.

17 THE HANDSOME FAMILY, "AFTER WE SHOT THE GRIZZLY"

As a lyricist, Rennie Sparks has a lot in common with writers like Flannery

O'Connor and Patricia Highsmith, both for her narrative sensibility and her darkly comic, macabre attitude. "After We Shot The Grizzly," from *Last Days Of Wonder*, follows the grim misadventures of a group of plane-crash survivors who struggle in vain against their inevitable descent into savagery and death—sort of *Lost* as portrayed by the Donner party. Brett Sparks' understated performance and Rennie's deadpan sense of humor make the song something of an anti-epic, with an increasing sense of twilit mystery as the survivors disappear one by one into the darkness and the silent waves, never to be seen again.

18 ELVIS PRESLEY, "IN THE GHETTO"

"In The Ghetto" might be a more soulful song if Elvis Presley didn't sound entirely aware of how very, very soulful he sounds, but the material is still mighty sad—and general enough to be an iconic illustration rather than the story of any one specific person. In an unspecified Chicago ghetto, "a poor little baby child is born" to a mother who can't deal with another mouth to feed. Growing up impoverished and hungry, he becomes mad and desperate, leading to a tragedy that Mac Davis' lyrics present as inevitable. Davis' much-covered (even on *American Idol*) song could stand to be subtler—the bridge where Presley demands "People, don't you understand / the child needs a helping hand / or he'll grow to be an angry young man some day"—is particularly overwrought. Then again, it's also true.

19 HARRY CHAPIN, "CAT'S IN THE CRADLE"

Another weepy classic that's overwrought and true at the same time, Harry Chapin's "Cat's In The Cradle" is a morality tale for absentee parents who have priorities other than their kids. When the narrator's son is a child, he idolizes his dad, "But there were planes to catch and bills to pay… He learned to walk while I was away." Before long, that idolizing kid has become a busy teen, then a grown man who blows off dad the way dad used to blow him off back in the day. The problem, of course, is that the kid spent his childhood saying "I'm going to be just like dad when I grow up," and of course, he's right.

20 ARLO GUTHRIE, "ALICE'S RESTAURANT"

Not so much a story-song as a story sandwich breaded with slices of song, Arlo Guthrie's ironic anti-war saga is almost hypnotic in its meandering, shaggy-dog exigencies. Guthrie starts off "This song is called 'Alice's Restaurant,' and it's about Alice, and the restaurant, but Alice's Restaurant is not the name of the restaurant, that's just the name of the song, and that's why I called the song 'Alice's Restaurant.'" This kind of folky, circular, stoned-sounding double-talk explains why the song takes upward of 20 minutes to perform. Also, the song isn't really about Alice or the restaurant, it's about (to cut to the punchline) how Guthrie supposedly was rejected as a draftee because he was a litterbug. Love it or hate it, it pretty well sums up the '60s.

21 T-BONE BURNETT, "THE STRANGE CASE OF FRANK CASH AND THE MORNING PAPER"

Before he was the Grammy-winning music producer, arranger, and composer for films like *O Brother, Where Art Thou?* and *Cold Mountain*, T-Bone Burnett was a performer in his own right, churning out terrific, quirky songs like "The Strange Case Of Frank Cash And The Morning Paper," in which a down-on-his-luck hustler living on "lonely street" discovers that his daily newspaper lists the scores for next week's football games. He makes so much money on sports betting that he moves out of his crummy apartment and into a sprawling estate on the lake ("And by that, I don't mean *by* the lake, I mean ON. THE. LAKE."). But lo and behold, when football season starts up again, "the damned paper had ceased to prognosticate." Panicked, he rushes back to his old apartment and demands the paper from the new resident, leading to a situation so dire that Burnett himself has to step in to straighten things out. It's tremendously funny in spite of its straight-faced delivery, though the best moment comes when Frank Cash, having realized he's just a character in a song, ineffectually

proclaims that he doesn't believe in Burnett, and that "This song is over!"

22 BARRY MANILOW, "COPACABANA"

Barry Manilow's irrepressibly catchy, annoyingly enduring hit had a strong enough storyline that it eventually became a musical, though ask any 10 people on the street, and they'll probably be able to sing the first line ("Her name was Lola, she was a showgirl") and the chorus, and not much else. Somewhere in between, Lola and her bartender boyfriend Tony work at the Copacabana nightclub until a rich rival for Lola's affections takes Tony down. Cut to 30 years later, when Lola sits alone in her old showgirl outfit "and drinks herself half-blind" at the Copa, now a disco that presumably plays songs like this one.

23 NEIL YOUNG, "CORTEZ THE KILLER"

The soaring mini-epic anchor to Neil Young's 1975 album *Zuma* opens with an extended Crazy Horse jam session before segueing into a delicate, occasionally cryptic mix of the historical and personal. In broad strokes, Young tells the story of conquistador Hernán Cortés, who conquered Mexico for Spain in the early 1500s. At the same time, he gives reverential treatment to the Aztec figure Montezuma, "with his cocoa leaves and pearls," presiding over a world where "the women all were beautiful and the men stood straight and tall." There's no reference to the conflict itself; it's more a reverie for a lost world and a lost people, connected ever so delicately to a stanza about lost love. Then the song finally circles back to Cortés: "What a killer."

24 THE COUP, "NOWALATERS"

On "Nowalaters," Coup frontman Boots Riley lends his gift for novelistic detail and messy humanism to a first-person coming-of-age story about a teen player whose backseat bumping and grinding leads to an unwanted premature pregnancy. The protagonist prepares himself for the solemn responsibility of fatherhood, but then discovers he isn't the baby's father after all. In most rap songs, this final twist would lead to a regressive moral about the innate duplicity of women, but Riley ends the song on a heartbreakingly gracious, tender note by sincerely telling the double-timing temptress, "Thank you for letting me go."

25 EMINEM, "STAN"

Somewhere between funny and tragic, Eminem's saga "Stan" mostly comes in the form of a series of letters from a young super-fan who doesn't understand why his idol won't call him or answer his letters, even though "I left my cell, my pager, and my home phone at the bottom." Stan's clueless desperation veers between laughable and miserable; his life as he describes it is truly awful, and it's sad to think that he's pouring all his energy into reaching out to a celebrity, yet easy to laugh as he goes over the top in his assumptions and demands. The chuckling ends when a despairing Stan crams his pregnant girlfriend into his trunk and deliberately drunk-drives off a bridge, too late for him to be reached by Eminem's warm, detailed, surprisingly caring response letter. It's almost as though Eminem is suggesting that celebrities occasionally don't know whether to be flattered or horrified by their most ardent fans.

Actor Devon Sawa plays Stan in the song's video.

26 JULIE BROWN, "THE HOMECOMING QUEEN'S GOT A GUN"

Part parody of the endless '60s-era ballads about teen romances ending in tragic death ("Teen Angel," "Ebony Eyes," "Patches," etc.), part a standard entry in Julie Brown's Valley Girl character lexicon, and part just an enthusiastic novelty song, Brown's biggest radio hit told the story of a massacre at the big homecoming parade. Peppered with "like" and "totally," and sung in a cheerfully shallow bubblegum style that belies the song's horrible events, the lyrics explain how Julie's best friend Debbie goes from bouquet-carrying, float-riding, pink-chiffon-wearing homecoming queen to cold-blooded mass murderer, "picking off cheerleaders one by one." Ignoring police warnings, Debbie keeps shooting until the cops gun her down; with her last breath, she confesses that she "did it for Johnny." But, like, nobody actually knows who Johnny is. Bummer.

PIE FIGHTS AND THE SUICIDAL FETUS

6 HAPPILY DISCARDED ALTERNATE ENDINGS

1 *TERMINATOR 2: JUDGMENT DAY*

Viewers who found the end of James Cameron's generally terrific *Terminator* sequel kind of weak, with its abrupt conclusion and corny voiceover about the beauty of a machine learning the value of human life, didn't know they'd dodged a bullet until the original ending turned up on DVD. Even then, fans had to enter a coded sequence to access it. For their trouble, they got Linda Hamilton in unconvincing old-lady makeup sitting in a comically neon version of America's future. In front of the U.S. Capitol, happy, happy Americans play with their kids while we learn that John Connor now fights the good fight as a U.S. senator. "His weapons," Hamilton reads into a portable tape recorder, "are common sense… and hope." Kick-ass!

2 *LITTLE SHOP OF HORRORS*

Frank Oz actually shot a much longer, darker ending to his campy musical comedy *Little Shop Of Horrors*, based on the Broadway musical based on Roger Corman's cheapie 1960 horror movie. In the original take, the film's killer-alien-plant antagonist, Audrey II, devours gawky lovers Rick Moranis and Ellen Greene, then spreads and smashes its way across America's cities. While the original ending includes some terrific shots of Audrey II's podlike, toothy heads crashing through buildings, leering and laughing atop the Statue Of Liberty, and devouring an entire train, the whole thing drags on so long, and includes so many pointlessly repetitive shots of buildings collapsing and people fleeing in terror, that even wholesale monster-movie destruction becomes tiresome. Test audiences bitched not about the pacing, but about the leads missing out on a happy ending, and Oz reluctantly subbed in a quicker, brighter wrap-up in which Moranis and Greene defeat Audrey II and run off to their comedically cliché "somewhere that's green" paradise together. Sure, it's sappy, but it's far more in keeping with the film's perky camp tone and loveable leads, who surely deserve better than being turned into plant food.

In a 2007 interview with The A.V. Club, *Frank Oz explained that he believed reshooting the end of* Little Shop *was "the right thing to do," and that he was only unhappy because he lost "a million dollars' worth of great B-movie shots and footage" in the process of cutting the film down.*

3 *ALIEN*

On the laserdisc box-set release of *Alien*, Ridley Scott discussed his original plan for the end of the film, which had already been heavily retooled from Dan O'Bannon's original script. At one point, Scott wanted the final confrontation between Sigourney Weaver and the alien to end with it killing her, then sitting down at a console and recording a distress call in her voice, summoning other ships to come provide it with fresh victims. This time it was the producers rather than test-audience members who vetoed the downer ending. That might have been a mixed blessing. Con: No Sigourney Weaver for *Aliens*. Pro: Without Weaver, much less chance of *Alien 3* and *Alien: Resurrection*. Tiebreaker: *Alien* and its sequels relied heavily on the creepiness of an antagonist that was, well, *alien*—essentially unknowable as well as powerful, dangerous, and not to be reasoned with. Turning the series' aliens into super-smart, English-talking mimics would have leeched most of the

dread out of them, and turned them into something only a little less ridiculous than the singing, dancing *Alien*-creature parody from *Spaceballs*.

WEAK ENDING. CUT HERE.

GETTING HORRIBLY BAD. PLEASE: CUT HERE.

OKAY, SERIOUSLY NOW, C'MON: CUT HERE.

FOR THE LOVE OF ALL THAT IS HOLY — CUT HERE!

4 *THE BUTTERFLY EFFECT*

The basic concept behind 2004's *The Butterfly Effect* was reasonably solid: Boy makes bad decisions and suffers the consequences, boy learns he can travel through time, boy tries to alter his past and just makes things worse. But comically overwrought execution and a clumsy lead performance from overreaching producer Ashton Kutcher made the film a cheesy, critically derided mess. Still, it could have been far worse: In the theatrical cut of the movie, Kutcher's character sacrifices his own happiness by traveling back in time to cut ties with the object of his affections early on, to let her have a better life without him. But in the most radically divergent of the proposed alternate endings on the DVD, he takes that idea a long step further by traveling back to his fetus days, and throttling himself in the womb. Worse yet, a creepy, fatalistic coda implies that all his mother's previous pregnancies ended with similar prenatal suicides. Unsurprisingly, directors Eric Bress and J. Mackye Gruber admit in a commentary that this particular ending got no love from the fine folks at New Line.

5 *CLERKS*

You know how not to end a bawdy, goodhearted comedy? By having its hero die a meaningless death, shot down during an attempted robbery. But that's how Kevin Smith's debut *Clerks* originally wrapped. The final sequence offered a painfully literal take on the notion that the film's hero was living a dead-end existence behind a convenience-store counter. Fortunately, cooler heads—if that term can ever be applied to the Weinstein brothers—prevailed. And with just a few seconds shaved off the end, *Clerks* went from tragedy back to comedy.

6 *WINGS OF DESIRE*

Two words that almost ruined Wim Wenders' delicate meditation on mortality and humanity: pie fight. He actually shot extensive footage of his leads smearing each other with whipped-cream pies, with some thought toward a lighter, more playful ending of the film; he even included that raw footage on the 2003 special-edition DVD, complete with a commentary track encouraging enthusiastic viewers to edit together their own pie-fight ending and send it to him. To top it all off, he said he'd send the best editor a cake as a reward, though he notably omitted any contact information that would make such submissions possible. Maybe even he secretly didn't want to see his most beautiful film desecrated with pie.

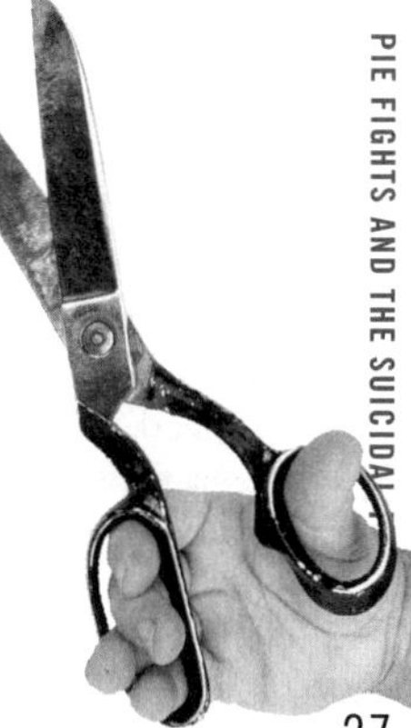

ASH TO THE FUTURE

5 UNFORTUNATELY DISCARDED ALTERNATE ENDINGS

1 ***FATAL ATTRACTION** (1987)*

Arguably, any ending is better than the one *Fatal Attraction* ended up with. Seeking revenge against yuppie adulterer Michael Douglas, Glenn Close turns up at his house and starts going kill-crazy, morphing from a scheming psycho into a high-heeled, impossible-to-put-down Freddy Krueger. The original ending, now included on the film's DVD release, benefits from the addition of poetic justice and the subtraction of nonsense: Close commits suicide, framing Douglas for her death. Though the film gives him an out, this at least keeps with Adrian Lyne's vision of a nightmare world in which Douglas' punishment for straying gets more intense the deeper he regrets his transgression.

2 ***ARMY OF DARKNESS** (1992)*

In the original ending to Sam Raimi's third *Evil Dead* film, hero Ash (the immortal Bruce Campbell) receives a potion designed to let him sleep his way from the Middle Ages back to his 20th-century home. Unfortunately, he accidentally overdoses and wakes up in a post-apocalyptic future. After poor test screenings, Raimi created a new ending in which Ash battles the undead in a K-Mart-esque store, then makes out with Angela Featherstone. It's fun, but not as fun as a sequel combining the best parts of *Evil Dead* and *Mad Max* might have been.

3 ***I AM LEGEND** (2007)*

The alternate ending to the Will Smith version of *I Am Legend* is radically different, and works better in a number of ways, though it has its own problems. In the final cut, Smith sacrifices himself in ridiculous fashion to save new acquaintances Alice Braga and Charlie Tahan, who escape with a precious vial of his blood in hopes of synthesizing a cure for artificial vampirism. Never mind that they're fleeing to a place with no apparent fancy technology, with a small amount of unrefrigerated blood that will doubtless have curdled long before they arrive; we're meant to shut up and enjoy the artificial uplift of Braga's swoony voiceover salute to Smith's sacrifice.

The original ending, available on the DVD, is smarter and even more of a downer, as Smith realizes the artificial vampires he's been testing and tormenting are at least moderately sentient, and negotiates his way into escape. That ending doesn't hold out any more hope for the future of the human race, but it's less overwrought and ridiculous, and it does at least nod to the original ending of Richard Matheson's classic novel *I Am Legend*, which previous adaptations had thrown straight out the window.

4 ***RISKY BUSINESS** (1983)*

Writer-director Paul Brickman only altered his ending to *Risky Business* by a few moments, but they make a crucial difference. Where the theatrical version has Tom Cruise's freshly corrupted high-school student lightly bantering with prostitute Rebecca

De Mornay as they stroll along Lake Michigan, Brickman wanted a more downbeat ending that had the characters sharing a sad embrace over what will almost certainly be their farewell dinner. They've used each other and they're about to head off in opposite directions for good, he to use his new ruthlessness at Princeton, she to resume conning suckers using her body as bait. It's a final chance to enjoy the unexpected warmth between them before it flickers and dies.

5 ***TITANIC*** *(1997)*
The theatrical ending to James Cameron's blockbuster *Titanic* was pared down from the much longer original ending, available as a bonus feature on the 10th-anniversary special-edition DVD set. Theater-goers saw Gloria Stuart sneak out of her bed in the middle of the night and secretly toss her supposedly lost multi-million-dollar diamond necklace back into the ocean. But in the full alternate cut of the ending, her granddaughter and their host Bill Paxton catch her climbing the railing to drop the necklace, and rush to stop her. Cameron gets some visual parallelism to her character's suicide attempt earlier in the film, Stuart gets to explain her seemingly insane actions, Paxton gets closure and the chance to hold the necklace he's been obsessively seeking for three years, and when Stuart throws it overboard, shaggy tech-nerd Lewis Abernathy gets to verbalize what a lot of viewers felt: "Jesus, no! That really *sucks*, lady!" It doesn't tie into the twee "A woman's heart is an ocean of secrets" theme as well as the theatrical ending, but it's richer and more satisfying in every possible way.

OH, THE PLACES YOU SHOULDN'T GO

15 DR. SEUSS CHARACTERS THAT SOUND LIKE SEX TOYS

1 ***FOO-FOO THE SNOO*** *(I CAN READ WITH MY EYES SHUT)*

2 ***THE FOUR-WAY HUNCH*** *(HUNCHES IN BUNCHES)*

3 ***JAKE THE PILLOW SNAKE*** *(I CAN READ WITH MY EYES SHUT)*

4 ***PAM THE CLAM*** *(THE TOOTH BOOK)*

5 ***PEEPING DICK*** *(THE SEVEN LADY GODIVAS)*

6 ***SNEETCH*** *(THE SNEETCHES AND OTHER STORIES)*

7 ***SOUTH-GOING ZAX*** *(THE SNEETCHES AND OTHER STORIES)*

8 ***THING ONE AND THING TWO*** *(THE CAT IN THE HAT)*

9 ***THE ONCE-LER*** *(THE LORAX)*

10 ***THE ROYAL COACHMAN*** *(THE 500 HATS OF BARTHOLOMEW CUBBINS)*

11 ***RUSSIAN PALOOSKI*** *(IF I RAN THE ZOO)*

12 ***VON CRANDALL*** *(YOU'RE ONLY OLD ONCE)*

13 ***WILY WALLOO*** *(IF I RAN THE CIRCUS)*

14 ***SEVEN-HUMP WUMP*** *(ONE FISH TWO FISH RED FISH BLUE FISH)*

15 ***YERTLE THE TURTLE*** *(YERTLE THE TURTLE AND OTHER STORIES)*

DANCING ABOUT ARCHITECTURE

5 ESSENTIAL BOOKS ABOUT POPULAR MUSIC

1 GREIL MARCUS, *MYSTERY TRAIN: IMAGES OF AMERICA IN ROCK 'N' ROLL MUSIC*

Marcus is one of those rare critics whose sheer scholarly diligence can weave familiar cultural strands into a bright, new tapestry. In his seminal essay collection *Mystery Train*, Marcus connects Robert Johnson, Elvis Presley, Randy Newman, Sly Stone, and The Band to classic American folk archetypes, explaining why their music matters from a historical perspective. Marcus isn't as skilled at describing the actual sounds that give people comfort and pleasure through a dark night, but he's a master of the morning-after postmortem.

2 LESTER BANGS, *PSYCHOTIC REACTIONS AND CARBURETOR DUNG: ROCK 'N' ROLL AS LITERATURE AND LITERATURE AS ROCK 'N' ROLL*

Like Hunter S. Thompson and Tom Wolfe, Lester Bangs has inspired more bad writing than a million middle-school breakups—but don't blame him for what his disciples do. Determined to forge a prose style as exhilarating as the trashiest rock song, Bangs shredded critical convention, taking readers deep inside his head as he grappled with why he cared so much about, say, Lou Reed—and why Reed was doomed to let him down. Bangs was one of the few writers who could pen a pan with such enthusiasm that readers felt compelled to buy the record anyway, just to compare notes. This scattershot collection offers Bangs at his purest—which means it's impenetrable as often as it's brilliant.

3 DAVE MARSH, *FORTUNATE SON: THE BEST OF DAVE MARSH*

Marsh's best pieces combine essay and biography, with the frequently cranky critic breaking down albums and artists to find their moral center. The anthology *Fortunate Son* gathers Marsh's musings on rock's power to unite the races and classes, and explains why he gets so pissed when musicians like Bob Seger or Elvis Costello disap-

point him: It's because he counts on them so much.

4 **DAVID CANTWELL & BILL FRISKICS-WARREN, *HEARTACHES BY THE NUMBER: COUNTRY MUSIC'S 500 GREATEST SINGLES***

In playing a country-and-western version of the what-makes-a-great-single guessing game established by Dave Marsh's *The Heart Of Rock & Soul*, David Cantwell and Bill Friskics-Warren forge an alternative history of roots music that explains—and defends—the existence of Faith Hill and Garth Brooks. The two authors analyze 500 great country singles, and set them up against one another in a kind of extended dialectic, looking at what C&W hits have had to say about being poor and powerless in 20th-century America.

5 **CHUCK KLOSTERMAN, *SEX, DRUGS, AND COCOA PUFFS: A LOW CULTURE MANIFESTO***

Because we live in an age of insta-punditry and blog envy, Chuck Klosterman has become an unusually divisive figure, hailed by people who share his cockeyed, inclusive vision of popular culture, and skewered by those who can't see past his championing of hair metal and Billy Joel. In *Sex, Drugs, And Cocoa Puffs*, his most essential essay collection, Klosterman delivers his dissent from the critical hegemony in a voice that's simultaneously witty and honest, full of clever lines and an awareness that mere cleverness won't always cut it when it comes to explaining the schlock that makes our days on Earth tolerable.

FICTIONAL FILM FOLLIES

5 FAILED NARRATIVE MOVIES FROM PROMINENT DOCUMENTARIANS

1 **JOE BERLINGER: *BOOK OF SHADOWS: BLAIR WITCH 2* (2000)**

The surprise 1999 success of *The Blair Witch Project* left Artisan Entertainment unexpectedly flush with cash, and eager to make more of it. When it came time to find a director for a quickie cash-in sequel, Artisan at least made an offbeat choice by bringing in Joe Berlinger, then best known for co-directing the compelling true-crime investigations *Brother's Keeper* and *Paradise Lost: The Child Murders At Robin Hood Hills*. But as the films on this list prove, hiring acclaimed documentarians to helm fiction projects is no guarantee that they'll produce acclaimed films—or even halfway decent ones. *Blair Witch 2* toys with some compelling ideas, commenting on the *Blair Witch* phenomenon in teasingly postmodern ways. Borrowing extensively from the visual vocabulary of '80s horror movies, it follows several tourists as they piece together the murderous events of a night spent in the woods of Burkittsville, Maryland. Watching the first *Blair Witch* movie inspired the trip, but the film's self-reflection ends once it begins limply recycling the horror-movie clichés it ostensibly wants to deconstruct. *Book Of Shadows* killed the *Blair Witch* franchise in its infancy. A humbled Berlinger subsequently eschewed fiction in favor of documentaries with partner Bruce Sinofsky, including the essential metal-legends-in-group-therapy classic *Metallica: Some Kind Of Monster*.

2 **BARBARA KOPPLE: *HAVOC* (2005)**

It must have looked good on paper: Oscar-winning *Traffic* screenwriter Stephen Gaghan rewriting a youth-gone-wild cautionary film originally written by a genuine teenager (Jessica Kaplan, who penned the script at 16 and died in a plane crash at age 24). Throw in rising stars like Anne Hathaway and Joseph Gordon-Levitt, plus multiple-Oscar-winning documentarian Barbara Kopple (*Harlan County U.S.A.*, *American Dream*), and the project looks even more promising. So where did *Havoc* go awry? Probably with the miscasting of fresh-scrubbed Disney princess Hathaway as a trampy teenager drawn to the dark side of Los Angeles. Or the script, which was rife with *Thirteen*-style youthsploitation clichés. Or the unsatisfying, melodramatic ending. Ironically, though semi-predictably, *Havoc* failed as a serious art movie, but succeeded as an Anne Hathaway-getting-naked DVD sleazefest. It even garnered a 2007 sequel-in-name-only follow-up, *Havoc 2: Normal Adolescent Behavior*.

3 ERROL MORRIS: *THE DARK WIND* (1991)

Errol Morris' non-fiction films boast an immediately identifiable visual and stylistic sensibility. But it's hard to discern that authorial stamp on 1991's *The Dark Wind*, the master documentarian's horribly botched adaptation of one of Tony Hillerman's bestselling novels about a Native American detective. In *Fog Of War*, Morris transformed a filmed interview with a senior citizen into riveting drama, yet his storytelling gifts abandoned him in this boring police procedural, which is so glacially paced that rookie cop Lou Diamond Phillips seems to be investigating the grisly murders of Native Americans in real time. Morris gets no help from Phillips' charisma-free performance and gently narcotizing voiceover, or from the dull, convoluted script. (In Morris' defense, he did leave the project at some point due to creative differences with producer Robert Redford.)

4 NICK BROOMFIELD: *DIAMOND SKULLS* (1989)

For his thrill-impaired, terminally unsexy 1989 erotic thriller *Diamond Skulls*, Nick Broomfield brought in some of the seedy tabloid obsessions and class issues that would prove fruitful in later documentaries like *Aileen Wuornos: The Selling Of A Serial Killer* and *Heidi Fleiss: Hollywood Madam*. Unfortunately, he does so via a dark, nudity-laden drama about a wealthy man (Gabriel Byrne) who indulges in a bit of the old hit-and-run following a wild night of debauchery. The muddled drama was a failure with critics and audiences alike, and it flopped on both sides of the Atlantic, in the States under the amusingly generic title *Dark Obsession*. Broomfield had better luck with the respectfully received fact-based docudrama *Battle For Haditha* in 2007.

5 MICHAEL MOORE: *CANADIAN BACON* (1995)

With *Canadian Bacon*, provocateur Michael Moore (*Roger And Me*, *Fahrenheit 9/11*) set out to Trojan Horse his liberal politics into a broad slobs-vs.-snobs comedy for John Candy fans, while simultaneously paying homage to *Dr. Strangelove* through the story of a plot to drive up the popularity of an unpopular president (Alan Alda) by instigating a bogus conflict with our affable neighbors to the north. Moore was more successful than the film's limp reputation suggests; he threw in some wry commentary on Canadian politeness (in an especially droll bit, Mountie Steven Wright writes one of his prisoners a thank-you letter for keeping his cell clean) and the American mania for bloodshed and conflict, alongside funky cameos from Dan Aykroyd and John Cleese. The film was nevertheless a big critical and commercial failure, and Moore unsurprisingly retreated back into the world of populist, bullying comic documentaries.

Guest List: JOHN HODGMAN

6 MYSTERIOUSLY UNHERALDED CHARACTER ACTORS

As you may know, I am sometimes on television and movies. This is largely an accidental career for me, and should it continue, I have no illusions that I will ever be a leading man. For even though I am clearly as pasty as Shia LaBeouf (as science has proven), I am older, paunchier, and far less symmetrical. Despite what you read, my right eye is not lazy; it is merely located somewhat higher in my head than my left. But the result is the same: By movie standards, I am a double-chinned, lopsided monster. Thus, unless there is soon to be a major motion picture on the life of Sartre, I am more than happy to join the long, proud, slightly deformed line of "character actors" who precede me. Certainly you recall:

1. MONTY "BEEFY" MORRIS
Famous for playing the jolly, obese best friend in countless screwball comedies. Catchphrase: "Put some butter on it, brother!" ('30s slang for "calm down," or "I want to eat more.") By 1943, he weighed 719 pounds and was largely immobile. That is why, in 1942's *My Favorite*, he played Cary Grant's irascible younger brother who is always taking a bath, and in 1943's *Two Swells*,

he played a loveable hobo whom Clark Gable had to push around on a special cart. He died at the age of 25.

2. IRMA SCANLON AND HER UNSEPARATED TWIN, IRMITA

Probably the most famous of all the singing unseparated-twin acts of the '40s. Often appeared in army movies singing patriotic songs, and allowing soldiers to rub her third elbow for luck.

3. BUDDY DORP

The tall, double-jointed, rubber-limbed goofball of the '50s comedy ensemble "The Gutter Boys" (a.k.a. "The Ethnic Kids"). Famous for his incredible, gymnastic trombone routines, which might pop up in a Gutter Boys film at any moment, even when they're just hanging around the stoop, playing poker with shards of broken glass. He actually was a very fine trombonist, playing with the Dallas Symphony Orchestra for many years before finally losing control of all his limbs.

4. MACK "COOKIE" McMACK

Most famous as the irrepressible old trail cook on the '50s children's show *Cowboy Tim's Gunfire Hour*. He was probably one of the most legendary "drunk acts" of his time, known for his balletic sway-walk, perfect hiccup timing, and comedic vomiting. He also appeared frequently on TV and film as a drunk hobo, a drunk businessman, a drunk magician, and a drunk drunk. Curiously, he never took a drink in real life, lending truth to the old vaudeville saying "The best drunks are sober men, and also regular morphine users." "Cookie" died of a morphine-addiction-related illness in 1976 while demonstrating his famous chili recipe on *The Dick Cavett Show*.

5. MARIA COTTLE

She was the archetypical successful, well-educated, lesbian black woman on countless '70s sitcoms, from *The Mary Tyler Moore Show*, where she was Mary's third best friend, a wealthy stockbroker, to *Three's Company*, where it was revealed that she was the first person to teach Jack how to cook French food and act gay. However, after Reagan was elected, it was decided that this character no longer existed. Maria Cottle is now a hedge-fund manager, philanthropist, and sculptress who lives on her own private island.

6. JAMBO TUCKER

A famous "heavy" on cop shows throughout the '60s and '70s. A former body-builder, he rarely wore a shirt, even when he played a plainclothes detective in several episodes of *Dragnet*. He was set to play the Jaws character in *The Spy Who Loved Me* until it was discovered that he did not have steel teeth, merely diamond nipples. He later played the sensitive carny who adopts the orphan genius Cosimo in the quickly canceled '80s sitcom *Cosimo*. He still appears regularly on the very small *Cosimo* convention circuit alongside Cosimo himself, Jason Bateman.

John Hodgman is the author of two excellent books, The Areas Of My Expertise *and* More Information Than You Require, *and stars as the PC in a series of Apple commercials.*

NO, SERIOUSLY, I AM SUPERMAN

11 BELOVED SONGS SUNG BY SECONDARY SINGERS

1 THE BEATLES, "YELLOW SUBMARINE"

It wouldn't be ridiculous to assume that Ringo Starr wrote "Yellow Submarine," because "Octopus Garden," one of only a few songs the drummer wrote during his time with The Beatles, also had a lighthearted maritime theme. According to lore, Paul McCartney wrote the tune as a children's song and decided that Ringo should sing it, as the group's most "loveable" member. Though something of a novelty song, it took off, reaching number one on the charts in England and number two in the States, and inspiring an animated movie, thereby establishing Ringo as The Beatles' most talented member and undisputed leader.

2 STYX, "TOO MUCH TIME ON MY HANDS"

Guitarist Tommy Shaw was often at odds with chief Styx singer Dennis DeYoung about the band's direction, but the tracks Shaw sang rarely had the breakthrough power of his curly-haired bandmate. A hit from 1981's *Paradise Theatre*, "Too Much Time On My Hands" ultimately gave Shaw the confidence to leave the band for a solo career in 1984, then take the reins of the reunited Styx when DeYoung departed.

3 THE ROLLING STONES, "HAPPY"

Though guitar-playing is far and away the most important element Keith Richards brought to The Rolling Stones, his backing vocals have always been part of the mix, too—they're rough and ragged compared to Mick Jagger's, but they fit well with the Stones' bluesy ethos. Richards' first solo lead vocal came with the memorable "You Got The Silver" in 1969, and in 1972, he took lead on *Exile On Main Street's* second single, "Happy," a freewheeling rocker that might be a little autobiographical, if the line "I always took candy from strangers" is any clue.

4 R.E.M., "SUPERMAN"

With a frontman as flashy and opinionated as Michael Stipe, it's easy for Mike Mills to fade into the background of R.E.M. (He's also kind of shy and nerdy.) But without Mills' backing vocals, many of the band's songs would be rudderless. And on "Superman," a cover of a 1969 B-side by the Texas band The Clique that served as the second single to R.E.M.'s 1986 album *Lifes Rich Pageant*, Mills steps up to the mic, as Stipe hangs out in the background.

5 THE MINUTEMEN, "TOUR-SPIEL"

The lyrics of this legendary band were always split between the fiercely political work of guitarist D. Boon and the intensely personal songs of bass player Mike Watt, but Boon took on the lion's share of the vocals. When it came time to tell the story of the band itself, though, it came in Watt's rumbling baritone: "Born in the shed with a guitar on," he sings, a slangy punk-rock Proust, "we jammed a shtick to do for gigs."

6 THE VELVET UNDERGROUND, "I'M STICKING WITH YOU"

Moe Tucker did more than provide The Velvet Underground with an unforgettable, primitive drum sound. On a few songs like this utterly charming number from the *VU* album, she also provided a vocal foil to the relentlessly dour Lou Reed. When she opens the song in her light, almost girlish voice, she almost manages to convince listeners that this was a band that could smile occasionally.

7 KISS, "BETH"

A case of the B-side trumping the A-side, "Beth" was first pressed as the flipside to "Detroit Rock City." A string-drenched ballad on which no members of Kiss play, the song gave drummer and "Beth" co-writer Peter Criss a rare moment in the spotlight. Pretty much the source for every icky power ballad of the next decade, the song became a huge hit in 1976, sending out a plea for understanding to a woman left neglected for rock 'n' roll.

8 PIXIES, "GIGANTIC"

It must be ridiculously tough trying to sing in a band with Black Francis, whose insane bark and incredible lyrics put most to shame. But when bassist Kim Deal stepped up to the mic for "Gigantic," she gave the Pixies their first college-radio hit, and big, big love. The Deal-fronted "Silver" appeared on 1989's *Doolittle*, but Francis' reluctance to include Deal's songs contributed to the tensions that ultimately broke up the band.

9 STEELY DAN, "DIRTY WORK"

Donald Fagen's sardonic, heartbroken vocals have become as much an identifier of the Steely Dan sound as endlessly fussed-over solos. But that wasn't always the plan. Though Fagen sings lead vocals on all but three of the 10 songs on the Dan's 1972 debut, *Can't Buy A Thrill*, the earnest-sounding David Palmer was the official lead singer at the time. Palmer took the lead on all the songs in the band's early live shows, and achieved classic-rock immortality on the *Thrill* hit "Dirty Work." Yet by the second album, he'd been relegated to the background, and he soon abandoned the band, leaving room for that much more black humor and regret.

10 THE CARS, "DRIVE"

Casual listeners (and especially video-watchers) could be forgiven for thinking that shades-sporting singer Ric Ocasek was the voice behind every Cars hit. Not so: Many famous Cars songs, including "Just What I Needed" and "Let's Go," spotlighted bassist Benjamin Orr—who died in 2000—on lead vocals. In 1984, the Orr-led "Drive" gave the band one of its biggest smashes.

11 SQUEEZE, "TEMPTED"

By the time Squeeze recorded its fourth album, *East Side Story*, with producer Elvis Costello, the group had become another in a line of British pop darlings that couldn't make any headway in the States. The band's *Billboard*-chart fortunes changed with "Tempted," a soulful mid-tempo ballad that made good use of the band's new keyboardist: former Ace frontman Paul Carrack, who previously had a hit in the U.S. with "How Long." Glenn Tilbrook's sweeter, more nasal vocals take lead on a few "Tempted" lines (and Costello drops down to his foghorn voice for a line or two), but most of the song is delivered in Carrack's smoky, seductive, decidedly un-Squeeze-esque baritone.

RINGO STARR

QUICK, MAN! CLING TENACIOUSLY TO MY BUTTOCKS!

21 CHILDREN'S TV SHOWS THAT FOUND ADULT AUDIENCES

1 *THE MUPPET SHOW* (1976-1981)

From 1969 on, Jim Henson's Muppets were television fixtures, thanks to *Sesame Street*. But while adult viewers could appreciate Henson's puppetcraft, they didn't have as much use for, say, lessons about vowel sounds. Premièring in 1976 and airing in syndication through 1981, *The Muppet Show* operated without any educational burden, so Henson and collaborators like Frank Oz could let their imaginations run wild, and focus on simple entertainment. The show's content was perfectly appropriate for children, but some of the references went way over the heads of kids who probably didn't realize just how weird the show was. A monster/bird-thing obsessed with chickens? An arch-conservative eagle? "Baby Driver" performed by babies? All part of the show's "Why not?" spirit.

2 *INVADER ZIM* (2001-2003)

It's no surprise that Nickelodeon's animated series *Invader Zim* became a hit with older audiences. Its creator, Jhonen Vasquez—best known for his decidedly not-for-kids comic *Johnny The Homicidal Maniac*—always intended for it to be a crossover hit, but the network bosses either didn't get it or didn't want it to happen. It was scheduled at odd times and barely promoted, and what advertising it did get wasn't nearly specific enough about setting it apart from the rest of their young-adult fare. But the older fans who discovered it turned it into a cult hit with a shelf life well beyond its limited series run: The DVD releases, which were clearly aimed at older viewers, played up the satirical jabs at American culture and the dark, absurdist qualities that young viewers never appreciated.

3 *THE ADVENTURES OF PETE & PETE* (1993-1996)

Nickelodeon seemed to have a clearer idea of what it wanted to do with *The Adventures Of Pete & Pete*, which for three too-brief seasons was the strangest thing on TV, as its absurdist plotlines connected with unexpected guest stars. Take, for example, an episode in which Little Pete (as opposed to his brother, Big Pete) has to tunnel out of the house to celebrate Independence Day. He runs into Michelle Trachtenberg—and her father, played by Iggy Pop. In another classic episode, students revolt against algebra, stirring a string of inept teachers, including Janeane Garofalo and Violent Femmes' Gordon Gano. The list (and the weirdness) goes on: Michael Stipe as an ice-cream man, LL Cool J as another teacher, Patty Hearst as an unusual neighbor.

4 *PEE-WEE'S PLAYHOUSE* (1986-1990)

Paul Reubens' Pee-wee Herman alter ego began as a parody of '50s kids shows, aimed at knowing L.A. nightclub audiences who grew up on the stuff. The character came full circle when he got his own Saturday-morning show on CBS. This required Reubens to tone down the act's double entendres and create a show that worked as kids' programming first, and a weird diversion for grown-ups second. *Pee-wee's Playhouse* succeeded brilliantly, providing fast-paced entertainment for sugar-addled kids while making sure adults could pick up on the lascivious nature of neighbor Miss Yvonne and the absurdity of dedicating a full half-hour to the gang's attempt to cure a sick genie by calling in a genie-ologist.

5 *THE REN & STIMPY SHOW* (1991-1996)

Ren and Stimpy were subversive

and scatological in the extreme; it's a wonder they ever appeared on Nickelodeon. Compared to *Doug* and *Rugrats* (which premièred at the same time), *Ren & Stimpy* was a *Fritz The Cat*-like fever dream of nervous energy and Grand Guignol grotesquery, putting its characters through all manner of violence, wink-wink sexual references, and amoral activity with some of the grossest gross-out moments to ever air in a family-friendly slot. (The show was far better suited to its Saturday-night slot in the "SNICK" lineup, which might as well have stood for "Stoners' Nickelodeon.") Creator John Kricfalusi was so often at odds with the network's standards and practices (and, according to the network, he was so often slack with deadlines) that he was fired shortly after the show's first season, and Nickelodeon continued making it without him. In 2003, Kricfalusi unsuccessfully relaunched it on the Spike network as *Ren & Stimpy's Adult Party Cartoon*, which expounded upon the show's more illicit subtexts—including making Ren and Stimpy's gay relationship blatant rather than implied.

6-7 LOONEY TUNES (VARIOUS SERIES) / *TINY TOON ADVENTURES* (1990-1994)

Putting the notion that cartoons are for kids to the test, the Looney Tunes series began living up to its self-proclaimed "lunacy" in the 1930s under Tex Avery, whose gag-a-minute style pushed every boundary on its way to fulfilling his oft-quoted motto, "In a cartoon you can do anything." At the time, that included explosive violence, racy innuendo, racist caricatures, and even the occasional swear word. Though later incarnations were sanitized for audiences' protection, Looney Tunes re-aired endlessly on television, developing a reputation as the wilder, woollier cousin to Walt Disney. That distinction was reinforced in the '90s with the Steven Spielberg-produced spin-off *Tiny Toon Adventures*. That show's frequent satire of politics and pop culture—and the occasional college-kid-friendly detour, like setting an entire episode to They Might Be Giants songs—pegged it as the hip alternative to the saccharine Disney Afternoon, making it an after-school favorite of kids too old for life lessons, but too young to be out ignoring them.

8 *ANIMANIACS* (1993-1998)

A sort-of successor to *Tiny Toons*, *Animaniacs* enjoyed a respectable five-year run on Fox Kids and Kids' WB. But it was always apparent that the after-school cartoon wasn't solely aimed at kids. From the opening song, where the titular characters confess to having "bologna in our slacks" to the show's lack of episode structure, *Animaniacs* had a split personality that kids could appreciate, but only adults could appreciate fully. It's unlikely that children realized that the show routinely parodied *Goodfellas* (with the wise-guy pigeons, "Goodfeathers"), that the super-intelligent lab mouse The Brain sounded like Orson Welles, or that one of the main characters was modeled after Ringo Starr.

9 *THE DEGRASSI SERIES* (1982-PRESENT)

Beginning in 1982 with the series *The Kids From Degrassi Street*—itself derived from a set of after-school specials—Canadian television explored the problems of adolescents and young adults in refreshingly frank, morally complex dramas that play like *Saved By The Bell* as written by David Chase. The *Degrassi* series became a cult hit in the U.S. when PBS began airing *Degrassi Junior High* in 1987; in the early '00s, the cable channel The N found a new set of grown fans for *Degrassi: The Next Generation*, which deals with the children of the earlier series and their more contemporary crises. Goodbye dating; hello date rape.

10 *SPONGEBOB SQUAREPANTS* (1999-PRESENT)

Make no mistake, *SpongeBob* is a kids' show. The premise—a kitchen sponge who lives in a pineapple in an underwater ocean city—sounds like it came from a kindergartner's daydream. But when the show debuted in 1999, creator Stephen Hillenburg seemed to follow the Pixar precedent by finding a sweet spot of humor, heart, and innocence. *SpongeBob* isn't sophisticated, but the show's overwhelming silliness is what makes it so enjoyable. A kung-fu-loving squirrel from Texas who lives in a dome? A snobby tentacled neighbor/co-worker who plays the clarinet? A dim-witted starfish voiced by Dauber from *Coach*? Yeah, sounds about right. And it doesn't hurt that SpongeBob is voiced by *Mr. Show's* Tom Kenny. (His wife and fellow *Mr. Show* castmate, Jill Talley, frequently does guest voicework as well.)

11 *KUKLA, FRAN AND OLLIE* (1947-1957)

Beginning in Chicago in 1947, then going national in 1949, *Kukla, Fran And Ollie* featured 30 minutes of entertainer Fran Allison sweetly interacting with puppets brought to life by show creator Burr Tillstrom. The show had no script, just a series of ad-libbed situations involving a clown-like puppet named Kukla, a dragon named Ollie, and a small supporting cast (also puppets). Kids liked it but adults loved it, including such notables as John Steinbeck, who wrote a fan letter noting "the ease and naturalness delight me." The show ran for almost 10 years, and its characters enjoyed a healthy afterlife of guest appearances for years after that.

12-13 *ROCKY AND HIS FRIENDS* (1959-1961) AND *THE BULLWINKLE SHOW* (1961-1964)

Known collectively as *The Adventures Of Rocky And Bullwinkle And Friends* in syndication and on DVD, the '60s cartoon-miscellany packages *Rocky And His Friends* and *The Bullwinkle Show* have a lasting adult appeal that extends beyond mere nostalgia. The shows' good-natured sensibility and use of anthropomorphized animal characters were just kid-friendly window dressing for gag-a-minute, self-referential humor that's sophisticated in its unabashed corniness. Rapidly deploying puns, innuendo, and fourth-wall-busting asides, Jay Ward's stable of memorable characters make their way through a series of shorts lampooning familiar structures like serials (the adventures of "moose and squirrel," "Dudley Do-Right"), fairy tales ("Fractured Fairy Tales," "Aesop And Son"), and instructional films ("Mr. Know-It-All") via superb writing that transcends the primitive animation and seems as subversively clever today as it did 50 years ago.

14 *THE POWERPUFF GIRLS* (1998-2005)

The fact that *The Powerpuff Girls* was originally conceived as a short film called *The Whoopass Girls*—which ran as part of the Sick And Twisted animation festival—indicates the cartoon's arch underpinnings. Sure, some may find the self-aware cuteness of color-coded super-tykes Blossom, Bubbles, and Buttercup grating in large doses—see the 2002 feature-length film—but the show's hyper-stylized animation and pop sensibilities give it a certain cachet not usually afforded to animated children who grace tiny pink backpacks and little girls' socks. The series' ubiquity—both during its six-season run on Cartoon Network and in the more than $1 billion in merchandising it's racked up over the years—may have dimmed its appeal a bit over time, but it remains one of the turn-of-the-millennium highlights of the kiddie-cartoon genre both for the little'uns who carry Bubbles lunchboxes, and the big'uns who have to shell out for them.

15 *THE TICK* (1994-1996)

It's probably more surprising that *The Tick* gained any traction with kids than that it appealed to adults. The animated version of Ben Edlund's superhero spoof reached levels of stupid-silly absurdity more familiar from current Adult Swim shows than from a Saturday-morning children's programming block. However, the big blue bug of justice and his moth-costumed sidekick Arthur appealed heavily to the big kids who watched it in reruns on Comedy Central and still parrot the show's eminently quotable randomness: "Spoon!"

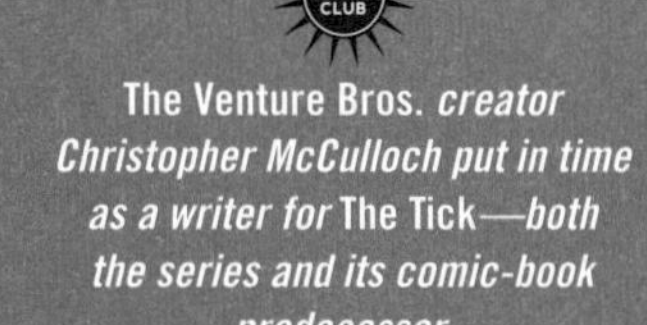

The Venture Bros. *creator Christopher McCulloch put in time as a writer for* **The Tick**—*both the series and its comic-book predecessor.*

16 *THE GUMBY SHOW* (1955-1968)

Part of the potential adult appeal of any kids' cartoon is whether it's fun to watch while stoned. Surely that factored into the cultish embrace of Art Clokey's Gumby. The claymation series debuted in 1953 as a three-minute short titled "Gumbasia"—an homage to *Fantasia*—and that surreal aura clung to most of the *Gumby* cartoons throughout the '50s and '60s. With a dreamlike torpor reminiscent of *Little Nemo*, Clokey's little green golem traveled through books (by melting into them, whoa) and met strange and wonderful friends and creatures along the way.

17 *BATMAN: THE ANIMATED SERIES* (1992-1995)

At a time when most cartoon spin-offs were closer to *Chuck Norris: Karate Kommandos* than *Fantasia*, no one expected much from a new Batman cartoon. But from its first episode in 1992, *Batman: The Animated Series* delivered more than it had to. Combining a dark tone, film noir- and art deco-inspired design, and clever writing, the show quickly picked up teen and adult fans. Many of them stuck around as the creative team—headed by artist Bruce Timm, whose clean, expressive art provided the show with a creative ideal—moved on to other related series like *Superman: The Animated Series*, the futuristic *Batman Beyond*, and *Justice League*. Combined, they created a shared cartoon universe that ran, in one form or another, for 14 years.

18 *MIGHTY MOUSE: THE NEW ADVENTURES* (1987-1988)

Before *The Simpsons*, *The Ren & Stimpy Show*, *Tiny Toon Adventures*, *Animaniacs*, *Batman: The Animated Series*, *The Powerpuff Girls*, and *Futurama*, writers and animators from all these shows cut their teeth working on Ralph Bakshi's controversial, short-lived, mind-blowing *Mighty Mouse: The New Adventures*. Like no network-produced, Saturday-morning cartoon before or since, *MM:TNA* smuggled subversive Dadaism and postmodern weirdness into the minds of impressionable little tykes—and the few savvy adults who quickly seized on the show's embedded headfuckery. The series was cancelled abruptly after an abbreviated second season, partly due to the public uproar when, in the episode "The Littlest Tramp," Mighty Mouse allegedly snorted a drug. It was actually a crushed flower, but the CBS execs who let the man behind *Fritz The Cat* and *Heavy Traffic* near a children's show might have expected controversy would follow.

19 *THE WEIRD AL SHOW* (1997)

With his eponymous Saturday-morning vehicle, beloved song parodist "Weird Al" Yankovic set out to create a gleefully absurdist kiddie version of *Mr. Show*. To that end, he roped in talented collaborators like future *Down With Love* director Peyton Reed, writer Ron Weiner (*Arrested Development*, *30 Rock*), and famed voice artist Billy West. Then, as indelibly chronicled in the darkly funny, unstintingly candid audio commentaries on the show's DVDs, network television sunk its fangs into Yankovic's creation and played havoc with its delicate alchemy. The sinister suits demanded life lessons in every episode, toned down the weirdness, and made the humor broader. But enough of Yankovic's original vision and loveable weirdness came through to posthumously make *The Weird Al Show* a cult hit with adults and kids alike, even though it only lasted a year.

20-21 *BILL NYE THE SCIENCE GUY* (1993-1997)/ *BEAKMAN'S WORLD* (1992-1998)

Maybe it's just a testament to the lackluster quality of science education in our public schools, but ever since the halcyon days of TV's Mr. Wizard, the adult viewing audience has always found a place in its heart for kid-level lessons in physics and chemistry taught on television by colorfully dressed eccentrics. Bill Nye, a former aeronautical and mechanical engineer who began his entertainment career as a stand-up comedian, created his Science Guy persona to teach science to junior-high kids, but his humorous approach and breezy style appealed to older viewers as well; the lesser-known *Beakman's World*, based on a comic strip and featuring puppeteer Paul Zaloom and a rotating cast of assistants, relied more on its kinetic, Pee-wee Herman-ish energy and set design, but still managed to attract adults to its syndicated slot.

PETER PARKER HAD IT EASY

18-PLUS TRULY TOUGH SUPERHERO ADOLESCENCES

1 CLOAK AND DAGGER

The moral to *Cloak And Dagger's* story seems simple: Just say no. But against the backdrop of the '80s war on drugs, writer Bill Mantlo created a genuine tragedy. Tandy Bowen (Dagger) and Tyrone Johnson (Cloak)—a statuesque blonde ballet student and a young black man from the ghetto, respectively—met after they ran away from home and landed in pre-Giuliani New York City. Lured by an offer of food and shelter, they were kidnapped and used as guinea pigs to test synthetic, deadly narcotics. The other subjects died, but the drugs gave Dagger the power of purifying light, while Cloak became the gateway to an endless void. Their beauty-and-the-beast relationship took them through one of Marvel's grittiest urban dramas, as they prowled Hell's Kitchen attacking drug dealers, saving underage girls from peep shows, and rescuing runaways like themselves from a fate far worse than Nancy Reagan ever let on.

WHAT DO YOU EXPECT FROM THE ILLEGITIMATE DAUGHTER OF AN EASTERN EUROPEAN DICTATOR, WHO SUBJECTED HER TO SCIENTIFIC EXPERIMENTS STARTING IN CHILDHOOD?

2 INVINCIBLE

When Mark Grayson discovered his super-strength and invulnerability in *Invincible*, Robert Kirkman's indie take on traditional superheroes, he was the happiest kid in America. He ditched his burger-joint job for a new career of fighting crime and meeting supergirls, and he also formed a new bond with his father, the alien-born superhero Omni-Man. In the series' opening issues, they enjoy touching scenes of father-son bonding, like visiting the tailor to buy Grayson's first superhero costume, or tossing a baseball back and forth—all the way around the globe. But it was too good to last, as Grayson discovered when Omni-Man admitted the truth: He didn't come to Earth to guard it, he came to prepare for the day when his people, the Viltrumites, would conquer and ravage it. With Grayson's powers came the responsibility of stopping his loving father—who paid him back by beating him within an inch of his life, then abandoning him. When they finally reunited, Invincible learned that his father had settled down on a bug-world, married a bug-woman, and sired a half-bug son. His revelation that he never really cared about Invincible's mother—especially not with the passionate love he reserved for Invincible's insectoid stepmom—was just the icing on the crap-cake.

3 RORSCHACH

The signature character of Alan Moore's *Watchmen*—Rorschach, a.k.a. Walter Kovacs—is a multiple-murdering, psychopathic vigilante who makes a point of never backing down, "not even in the face of Armageddon." Even his fellow crime-fighters were uncomfortable around him, and his court-assigned psychiatrist, Malcolm Long, was downright unnerved once he got below Kovacs' emotionless surface. Probing Kovacs' past for defining moments, Dr. Long found a convenient excuse for everything: a thoroughly miserable childhood as the unwanted son of a low-rent hooker who once told Kovacs "I shoulda listened to everybody else! I shoulda had the abortion!" just before beating him for walking in on her and a john. By the time Kovacs was 10, neighborhood kids were mocking him over his "hoo-er" mother; Kovacs retaliated by burning out one boy's eye with a lit cigarette. When he was 16, his mother was murdered; his only response was "Good." As an adult, he described a later event as the true birth of Rorschach, but the foundations for his misanthropic, uncompromising, furiously judgmental superhero identity were dug early and deep.

4 MAGIK

Illyana Rasputin, the little sister of the X-Men's Colossus, was abducted at age 6. Trapped in a hell dimension by the demon-lord Belasco, Illyana saw her friends twisted and murdered as Belasco sealed his control over her, inculcating her in the dark arts. Illyana's relationship with Belasco was a twisted mix of abuse and attraction; she tried to hold onto her innocence, but the lure of his magic and the urge

for vengeance slowly corrupted her. Upon reaching puberty and discovering her mutant powers of teleportation, Illyana fought back and finally defeated Belasco. But even after she returned to Earth and signed up with the New Mutants, she was constantly troubled by her all-too-literal dark side; she became a hero, but she'd lost her innocence in hell.

5 TERRA

Teen Titans readers of a certain age can still remember the sense of outrage when writer Marv Wolfman and artist George Pérez revealed that Terra, the elemental-powered, sweet new addition to the Titans team, was a turncoat working for the team's archenemy, Deathstroke. (What's more, the underage traitor was sleeping with the much-older villain.) But what do you expect from the illegitimate daughter of an Eastern European dictator, who subjected her to scientific experiments starting in childhood? Terra's tough adolescence ended in a bit of poetic justice: Attempting to kill Deathstroke, she buried herself under a pile of rocks.

6 ROGUE

While the *X-Men* movies significantly improved on some characters, others were a letdown; for example, Rogue, a badass white-trash chick and ex-supervillain in the comics, became a largely helpless wimp in the films. But one thing the movies got right about everyone's favorite skunk-streaked mutant was the traumatic moment she realized her powers. The first time she kissed a boy, she instantly absorbed his memories and psyche, leaving him a zapped-out husk. One of the biggest tragedies about her character was the fact that she was an earthy, passionate girl who, because of her absorbing power, could never know what was genteelly referred to as "a man's touch." That's why, at age 18, she already had a bad attitude to rival Wolverine's.

Supervillains don't generally have happy childhoods, either. One nominee for the Toughest Villain Adolescence Award: Victor von Doom. His mother was killed for practicing witchcraft, and as he later learned, she promptly went to a very literal hell. Meanwhile, his father was executed for practicing quack medicine. Von Doom worked hard for his physics scholarship to Empire State University, where he was promptly one-upped by that jackass Reed Richards. No wonder he opted for a career in evil.

7 WARLOCK

Like almost every team of teen superheroes, the New Mutants were a cornucopia of adolescent mope and turmoil. Everyone on the team had problems (in addition to being mutants), but the alien cyborg known as Warlock upped the angst factor considerably. His species, the Technarchy, were sort of a cross between the Borg and vampires: They drained the life force out of living creatures to heighten their own cyber-organic power. That was bad enough when young Warlock had to get used to living on Earth, where this sort of behavior was frowned upon, but then his sire, the Technarchy's brutally violent leader Magus, came gunning for him to fulfill their race's tradition of sons and fathers fighting duels to the death. Some dads make their kids mow the lawn or take out the trash; Warlock had to face down a being who could grow to the size of a star.

8 CLOUD

Sexually confused teenagers are a dime a dozen, but they've got nothing on Cloud, one of the more bizarre characters to emerge from the cosmic glop of Marvel in the 1980s. Originally a sentient nebula, Cloud struck up a conversation with the Cosmic Cube, which told it about Earth's superheroes. (No, really.) So it decided to visit our planet, where it encountered a pair of lovestruck teenagers, but—whoops!—accidentally caused them to die in a car crash. So—since this didn't make any less sense than the rest of the character's ludicrous origin—Cloud decided to assume the form of the dead girl, and become a superheroine who was half super-powerful alien gas cloud, half naked teen. But wait, it gets even stupider: Cloud then fell in love with fellow Defender Moondragon, and assumed the form of the (dead, naked) teenage *boy* to win her heart. Of all the things that can ruin a childhood, growing up reading nonsense like this has to be the worst.

9 SPEEDY

"My ward is a junkie!" So screamed the cover of *Green Lantern* #85, the notorious 1971 comic in which Green Arrow's teenage sidekick Roy "Speedy" Harper goes through the nightmare of heroin addiction. While Speedy eventually made a full recovery from his teen smack habit, the comics (titled "Snowbirds Don't Fly") in which he lived through the ordeal became some of the most celebrated of their time. Denny O'Neil, a skilled comics author and a famous lefty, was one of the first to treat drug addiction as a serious problem, and he was unique at the time in not only portraying users as victims of a sickness rather than villainous criminals, but also showing the unbalanced effect drug abuse had on the African-American community. It reads as hokey today, but it's hard to imagine the impact the story must have had almost 40 years ago.

10 ROBIN

Sure, Batman had it rough—no 8-year-old should have to watch his parents being murdered. But his ward and sidekick, Dick Grayson—the original Robin—suffered the same ordeal as a youngster, when his mother and father were killed in front of him as part of an extortion scheme. One of the most interesting aspects of the Batman/Robin relationship is that while Bruce Wayne's tragedy essentially paralyzed him in time, making him forever a shattered little boy seeking revenge on mom and dad's behalf, Dick Grayson endured the same trauma and managed to grow through it, avoiding grim doom and turning into a relatively well-adjusted adult (albeit one who still dresses up in a silly costume and fights crime).

11 JOHNNY BATES/ KID MIRACLEMAN

In Alan Moore's masterful re-imagining of the Captain Marvel mythos, Miracleman and his young friends were genetic experiments, fed a virtual-reality simulation of heroic deeds until they proved too dangerous to control. When the experiment was terminated, young Kid Miracleman decided to stay in his superhuman adult form instead of returning to the body and personality of weak, frail adolescent Johnny Bates. But the years of isolation and power drove Kid Miracleman mad, and he eventually turned against his mentor, who only survived because KM mistakenly reverted to his Bates alter ego. Terrified at what his other side had done over the intervening decades, Bates lapsed into a catatonic fugue, and while his drooling body rested in a brutal youth home, his psyche suffered nonstop abuse from the KM personality, which tried to goad him into releasing it. Ultimately, he recovered—just enough to meet the other kids in the home, who tormented and eventually raped him, forcing him to defensively become the near-omnipotent Kid Miracleman again. Once more trapped in his own head, Bates watched as KM unleashed a hellish revenge on the world. In a medium filled with traumatic teenhoods, the miserable downward spiral of the once-heroic Johnny Bates may be the worst.

12 SPIDER-WOMAN

It's hard to even remember, since her character has been retconned beyond recognition so many times now, but while Jessica Drew—the original Spider-Woman—didn't necessarily have the most *traumatic* adolescence of any superhero in history, she has to be a candidate for the most *confusing*. In her first few incarnations, she received an almost deadly dose of radiation poisoning, was injected with radioactive spider blood to counteract the poison, got crammed into a genetic acceleration chamber by a deranged scientist-turned-supervillain, had her aging process artificially slowed so she was a 90-year-old woman with the body of a 17-year-old, was raised by a group of super-intelligent animals and nannied by a genetically altered cow, ended her first sexual experience by accidentally electrocuting her partner, was placed in the care of a bunch of ex-Nazi criminal terrorists, was brainwashed into becoming a supervillain, *and* was told that she wasn't really a mutated human, but a mutated spider. Most teenagers just have trouble getting a prom date.

When we say "original" Spider-Woman, we mean the original from the Marvel Comics universe. There were other, far less significant Spider-Women.

13 FIRESTORM

Ronnie Raymond was, by most criteria, a normal, well-adjusted kid, and even though the accident that turned him into Firestorm was no picnic, he did emerge alive and well, and with a bunch of badass superpowers to boot. But getting caught in a nuclear explosion is enough to screw up anybody's year, and worst of all, the accident resulted in Professor Martin Stein's consciousness getting permanently embedded in Ronnie's brain. Constantly hearing voices is bad enough, but when the voice is real—it can hear and see everything you do, say, and think, and it belongs to your *high-school physics teacher*—well, that's going to put a pretty serious crimp in your wonder years.

14 TRIPLICATE GIRL

Unlike most teenage superheroes, the members of Legion Of Superheroes weren't originally seething with sour hormones and unchecked angst, thanks to their origins in more innocent times. They generally maintained the fun-loving, carefree vibe of the early Silver Age. (Later reboots took care of that.) Still, it can't have been easy being Luornu Durgo. Not only did she have a pretty limp power (she could split into three identical versions of herself) and a superhero alias that implied mastery of the secretarial arts, but she also got saddled with the ridiculous Bouncing Boy as a romantic partner, and he was a step down from Matter-Eater Lad. What's more, the evil Computo eventually killed one of her bodies, severely traumatizing the two that remained and sticking her with the even goofier name of Duo Damsel.

15 MISTER MIRACLE

The aptly named Scott Free had one of the worst childhoods imaginable: Born the son of Izaya, ruler of the Utopian paradise planet New Genesis, he was traded for the son of Darkseid, the unimaginably evil lord of Apokolips, in an attempt to quell a war between the two worlds. Raised by one of the most feared supervillains in the universe, he grew up among unthinkable oppression, brutality, and evil, and was sent to a "Terror Orphanage" run by the fearsome Granny Goodness. Still, his yearning for good was unquenchable, and even though he was raised in the worst conditions this side of metro Detroit, he rebelled against his violent upbringing, trained himself to be the world's greatest escape artist, and fled Apokolips with his wife-to-be, Big Barda, another victim of the Terror Orphanages who went against her upbringing. Now that's family values!

16 BATGIRL

The most famous Batgirl had a relatively normal childhood, or as normal as you can get when your dad is Police Commissioner of Gotham. It wasn't until she reached adulthood that she was shot, paralyzed, and sexually abused by the Joker in one of his "down" moods. But Cassandra Cain, the young woman who later picked up the Batgirl mantle, spelled her adolescent trauma with a capital T. The daughter of villainous super-assassins David Cain and Lady Shiva, young Cassie was raised to be the greatest killer of all time. It's nice to have ambitions for your children, but Cain decided not to teach her to talk, and put her through a brutal training regimen that allowed her to read body movements with uncanny skill. While she eventually rejected her father's murderous ways, she grew up with the legacy of his training: She couldn't speak, she could barely read or write, and she naturally had trouble communicating with her fellow human beings. The goth trappings were a natural.

17 PREZ

The star of the bizarre, beloved 1973 DC comic *Prez: First Teen President* was a friendly, resourceful, outgoing all-American teen; his mom even named him "Prez" because she thought he might grow up to be president one day. Problem is, he became president *before* he grew up, once a new law allowed teenagers to serve in high office. (To the irritation of some purists, the book apparently took place within DC Comics' official continuity.) While "America's First Teen President" was generally a cheery kid, it can't have been any fun for a 16-year-old boy to withstand the intense media scrutiny or public anger and judgment stemming from the highest office in the land—especially with the creepy-ass supervillain Boss Smiley always gunning for him, and his mom as the vice president.

18+ ALL THE RUNAWAYS

The entire point of Brian K. Vaughan's ongoing series *Runaways* is its focus on young superheroes enduring miserable adolescences. Vaughan's first story arc introduced a group of kids of various ages who learned that their parents were supervillains, and struck out on their own in rage and disgust. Privation, romantic entanglements, betrayal, insecurity, second thoughts, a great deal of angst and grief, and death all ensued—in short, apart from the big drama and the superpowers, the Runaways are like any kids who leave unhealthy homes and wind up with nowhere else to go. As the series has continued, with arcs written by Joss Whedon and *Stranger In Paradise's* Terry Moore, new kids with similar problems have joined the group, which remains one of the few super-teams that has to focus as much on where the next meal is coming from as what the new villains in town have up their sleeves.

NOT DEAD YET

8 GREAT FILMS MADE BY DIRECTORS AFTER THEY TURNED 70

1 AKIRA KUROSAWA, *RAN* (1985, AGE 75)

In his later career, the great Japanese director Akira Kurosawa struggled to secure funding to make movies, thanks to a reputation as an old-fashioned perfectionist that made him seem like a bad financial risk. He made only four films in the 20 years before *Ran*, and used the unwanted time off to painstakingly craft what would become his last masterpiece—a lavish, deeply personal adaptation of Shakespeare's *King Lear* set during Japan's tumultuous medieval era. Aging warlord Hidetora parallels Lear's descent into madness and obscurity, but also echoes the 75-year-old Kurosawa's own misfortunes, including a 1971 suicide attempt. By the time he made *Ran*, Kurosawa was nearly blind—yet he still achieved stunning, bold cinematography with help from assistants and his own carefully painted storyboards. His signature work is woven through with his lifelong themes of pacifism and deep concern that humanity's dark side might overwhelm us.

> A.V. CLUB
>
> *Kurosawa continued making films for quite a while; his final project, 1993's* Madadayo, *is a touching portrait of an aging teacher whose students gather every year to throw him a party and ritualistically ask whether he's ready to say goodbye. The title comes from his cheery, enthused response, Japanese for "No, not yet!"*

2 ROBERT ALTMAN, *GOSFORD PARK* (2001, AGE 76)

Robert Altman had a couple more great movies in him after he hit 75: His gently naturalist dance-company portrait *The Company* (2003) hearkened back to his observational classics like *Nashville*, and his final film, *A Prairie Home Companion* (2006), seemed designed to marry that style with a regretful but philosophical personal epitaph. But neither film holds a candle to *Gosford Park*, which stands among the best works of Altman's career. Part class portrait, part murder mystery, part comedy, it presents an *Upstairs, Downstairs*-like story about upper-class guests and their community of personal servants at a British country house in 1932. Practically everyone in the fantastic ensemble cast is a hero of British film or television, but they couldn't carry the film without Altman's crisp, precise style; he keeps the camera constantly on the move, separating and uniting the characters, and keeping the many plot threads clear. What could have been a dry procedural becomes viciously witty and surprisingly deep, as Altman spends just enough time with each character to establish how many ugly currents are running through what's meant to be a simple social gathering.

3 SIDNEY LUMET, *BEFORE THE DEVIL KNOWS YOU'RE DEAD* (2007, AGE 83)

Sidney Lumet is a case study in how one classic movie can make up for three terrible ones. As the man who directed *Network, Dog Day Afternoon, Serpico*, and *The Pawnbroker*, Lumet is forgiven for also making *The Wiz, Gloria, Find Me Guilty, A Stranger Among Us*, and many other unmentionables. That's because Lumet has kept working, reliably turning out movies well into his eighth decade. In 2007, 50 years after the auspicious directorial debut, *12 Angry Men*, Lumet made a triumphant return to form with the bleak, cynical thriller *Before The Devil Knows You're Dead*. Loaded with unlikeable, unapologetically tawdry characters, *Before The Devil Knows You're Dead* is an old-school noir from a man who was around to see the genuine article, and a sign that Lumet may still have a masterpiece or two left in him.

4 CLINT EASTWOOD, *MILLION DOLLAR BABY* (2004, AGE 74)

Beginning with *Unforgiven*, which he helmed when he was a wily 62-year-old whippersnapper, Clint Eastwood has remade himself as one of the foremost directors in the world as he's advanced into retirement age. One of the most accomplished films of his career, 2004's *Million Dollar Baby*, is an old-fashioned, emotionally devastating melodrama about the relationship between hard-luck female boxer Hilary Swank and her trainer, played by Eastwood. Displaying a classic command of storytelling and a surprising knack for sentiment, *Million Dollar Baby* is the work of a master craftsman drawing on a wealth of film and life experience.

5 LUIS BUÑUEL, *THE DISCREET CHARM OF THE BOURGEOISIE* (1972, AGE 72)

The Spanish surrealist filmmaker Luis Buñuel would have already been a legend had he done nothing more than his 1929 collaborative short with Salvador Dalí, "Un Chien Andalou." But in the 1970s, Buñuel—who was born in 1900—not only didn't slow down, he entered one of the most productive phases of his career. Invigorated by the political films of Jean-Luc Godard, Buñuel unleashed a trilogy of dreamlike surrealist masterworks, of which *The Discreet Charm Of The Bourgeoisie* is the first and best. Built around a middle-class group of friends and their constantly frustrated attempts to have a dinner party, *Discreet Charm* may be the most subversive film to ever win an Oscar.

ROBERT ALTMAN

6 MANOEL DE OLIVEIRA, *I'M GOING HOME* (2001, AGE 92)

Films after 70? How about films after 90? Portuguese director Manoel de Oliveira was 92 when he made *I'm Going Home*, a melancholy, poetic film about how getting old is all about the repetition of a performance. De Oliveira underscores the point by making his lead character a septuagenarian actor (Michel Piccoli) who gets through his day the way he gets through a play: by doing the same things over and over. In *I'm Going Home*, disruption comes in the form of an accident that leaves Piccoli in charge of his grandson, but while a youngster's perspective helps open the actor up in some ways, he can't completely change the creature of habit he's become.

7 ERIC ROHMER, *AN AUTUMN TALE* (1998, AGE 78)

The final entry in Eric Rohmer's "Tales Of The Four Seasons" film cycle, *An Autumn Tale* found the then-78-year-old director thinking about starting over. Beatrice Romand, one of the endless parade of effortlessly beautiful women who figure prominently in Rohmer's films, plays a widowed winemaker who secretly becomes the object of her best friend's matchmaking scheme. Rohmer provides the film with the kind of warm glow only enhanced by the threat of a chill. He also took to heart the idea that new opportunities can come late in life, taking up newfangled digital filmmaking with his 2001 film *The Lady And The Duke*.

8 CHARLES CRICHTON, *A FISH CALLED WANDA* (1988, AGE 77)

At age 77—and after 20 years away from directing feature films—Charles Crichton collaborated with John Cleese on a throwback farce full of the kind of criminal capers and broad characters that populated Crichton classics like *The Lavender Hill Mob*. On the film's DVD commentary track, Cleese deftly explains how Crichton lets scenes play out with a minimum of cutting and only a few economical camera moves, so the actors can build a comic rhythm. That's one of the virtues of senior-citizen directors: They're never in much of a hurry.

TALKING AT THE MOVIES

15 COMMON TYPES YOU MEET ON DVD AUDIO COMMENTARIES

1 THE IRRITATING ACADEMIC

A longtime staple of Criterion Collection DVDs, Irritating Academics typically introduce themselves, then read whole passages from their books on the semiotics of slapstick (or whatever), while only occasionally

AH BLAH BLAH BLAH BLAH BLAH BLAH BLA

noting what's happening onscreen. And even when they do sync up with the action, their observations tend to overscrutinize every element of the scene, as in this tidbit from *The Lady Eve* commentator Marian Keane: "A silent, random person cuts through the frame, carrying a large object. These quick moments of near-surrealism are Preston Sturges' acknowledgements that just outside this frame, there's a movie set." Um… they are?

2 THE NOSTALGIST

Ah, wasn't the golden age golden? Don't agree? Well, pay attention to The Nostalgist, who will explain why the classic you're watching could never be made today, or in extreme cases, how the film represents an example of a lost art that contemporary filmmakers could never hope to match. In this category, nobody quite rivals Peter Bogdanovich, who uses the term "the classic directors" as an indirect jab against the no-talents of today. From his commentary for *The Searchers*:

"Interesting that [director John Ford] doesn't go to [John] Wayne in a close-up. He does it in the dark. Again, the classic directors were judicious. They knew what an audience needed and what it didn't want."

3 THE NARRATOR

The Narrator somehow imagines that the job of an audio commentator is to painstakingly explain what's happening onscreen for viewers too stupid to follow the action. Though Narrators seemingly derive great satisfaction out of merely explaining a film's storyline in jaw-droppingly literal terms, they're also generally keen on explicating how this relates to resonant themes and character motivation. The ulti-

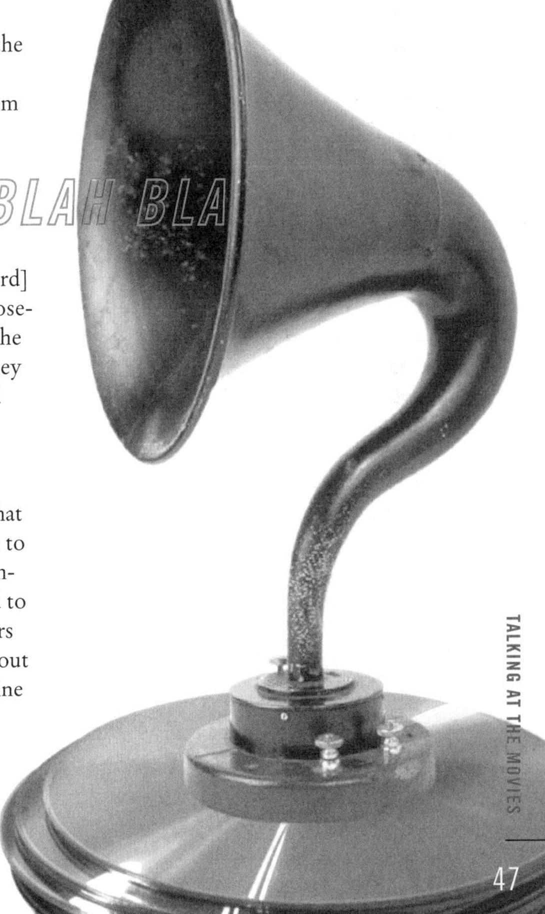

mate Narrator: R. Kelly, who interrupts his breathless narration-commentary of *Trapped In The Closet* just long enough to marvel at his own genius.

4 THE NITPICKER

The Nitpicker is categorically incapable of seeing the forest for the trees, obsessing relentlessly on irksome details most viewers would never notice, while cavalierly ignoring a film's elephantine faults. On the *Glitter* DVD, director Vondie Curtis-Hall behaves as if he'd gladly trade an internal organ for an opportunity to redo tiny technical aspects of the film, while remaining curiously silent on slightly more glaring faults, like Mariah Carey's atrocious lead performance.

5 THE BLOODLESS TECHNICIAN

Bloodless Technicians inexplicably assume that anyone accessing their commentaries has a bottomless need for technical information about every aspect of a film, including where scenes were shot and at what time of day, what lenses were used, and countless other bits of ephemera of interest exclusively to the commentator. (In his commentary for *Confessions Of A Dangerous Mind*, George Clooney also thoughtfully mentions which films he stole each shot from.) The Bloodless Technician stops just short of FedExing call sheets and itemized budgets to everyone listening.

6 THE STRONG SILENT TYPE

Shhhhh! We're trying to watch the movie here! Some commentators like to go light on the commentary. Witness Dennis Hopper's *Easy Rider* track, which contains as many arid stretches as the American southwest seen onscreen. Or listen to virtually any Robert Altman track: They're cheerful and informative enough, but no one seems to be prodding Altman to talk any more than he wants.

REMEMBER THAT OBNOXIOUS PROFESSOR WHO ASSIGNED HIS OWN BOOKS IN ALL HIS CLASSES? THE COMMENTARY-TRACK PROFESSOR IS THAT INSUFFERABLE BLOWHARD TAKEN TO THE Nth POWER.

7 THE FAKE UNDERDOG

According to Fake Underdogs, the odds were so ridiculously stacked against them that it's a staggering miracle they ever got the chance to begin production on the movie they're discussing, let alone see it through to completion. Fake Underdogs invariably portray themselves as plucky Davids taking on formidable Goliaths, no matter how big their budgets or how dependable their source material.

8 THE LECHER

Generally appearing on commentary tracks for vintage drive-in trash, The Lecher relives past glories by lusting anew after the same naked women he cast in his movies decades ago. The quintessential Lecher is nudie-flick kingpin Russ Meyer, who used to drop commentary-track *bons mots* along the lines of, "When gals lay down in the brambles, they get their ass scratched, and I like that," and, "I always liked wrought-iron beds, because they're reminiscent of whorehouses." But Meyer is challenged for Lecher supremacy by softcore smut producer Harry Novak, who opens his commentary for *The Godson* with the line, "I just like watching those big tits there."

9 THE INDIFFERENT CAST MEMBER

There's a law of diminishing returns to group commentary tracks, because while two or three people in a room can make for a lively conversation, four or more often prompts awkward silences, as everyone waits for their colleagues to say something. The worst participants are those actors who probably shouldn't have agreed to appear on the track in the first place. Distracted, reticent, even pissy, these contract-fulfillers are usually the first to poop the party by grumbling, "Who listens to these things, anyway?"

10 THE SMOKER

Listen to the clinking of lighters. Hear the satisfied exhalation of the first drag. Notice the slight mumbling caused by clenched lips. The Smoker can't get through a track without indulging, and doesn't care whether you notice. This type is especially common among the great horror directors. George Romero tends to cough his way through tracks, while it's almost a pleasure to hear how much John Carpenter enjoys his smokes. Almost. (See also Kevin Smith.)

11 THE PROFESSOR

The Professor turns every commentary track into a Xerox of the most insufferable Film Studies lecture you ever suffered through. Take the *Twisted* track, in which director Philip Kaufman tweedily discourses on the resonant themes, enduring archetypes, and timeless brilliance of his nearly universally reviled flop. Remember that obnoxious professor who assigned his own books in all his classes? The commentary-track Professor is that insufferable blowhard taken to the nth power.

12 OWN-FAN-CLUB PRESIDENT

The "I'm President Of My Own Fan Club" types don't see the need for false modesty—or modesty of any kind. They view audio commentaries as wonderful opportunities to bask in their creative brilliance and pay reverent homage to themselves all over again. Prominent Own-Fan-Club Presidents include Michael Bay on *The Island's* commentary track, the especially shameless Damon Dash on *State Property 2*, and Uwe Boll, who's all too willing to spend, say, *Postal's* entire commentary track explaining why he's a genius, and everyone else is a worthless idiot.

13 THE EXPLAINER

Did a movie not go over well at the box office? Audiences didn't engage with it, or critics didn't approve? Maybe they just didn't *understaaand* it. Which is why The Explainer—usually a writer-director, often a first-timer—is there to lay out in detail what's going on in the characters' heads, or just under the symbolic surface. Explainers tend to be hyperbolically sincere as they justify their plots and their characters' actions in minute detail, letting listeners know what they're really seeing onscreen. See: David Duchovny's detailed analysis of his own imagery in *House Of D*, or Rebecca Miller's attempts to take all the ambiguity out of her gorgeous film *Angela* by putting her characters on the psychiatric couch.

14 THE PARTY CREW

Man, it was fun making that film. And man, it's cool to be back together again, watching that film and hanging out with some of the people involved. And man, it's really fun to drink a little, smoke up a little, or just get a contact high from hangin' out with the buds and our movie. Oh, is this all being recorded? And we're getting paid for it too? Dude, cool. There have been plenty of notable Party Crew commentaries, where the commentators seem far more focused on the fun of getting together than on the film or any potential listeners, but Trey Parker and Matt Stone (*Cannibal: The Musical; South Park: Bigger, Longer & Uncut; Team America: World Police*) invariably party the heartiest, with Kevin Smith and friends as a close second.

15 THE DODDERING OLDSTER

It's nice that so many Hollywood veterans are still around to share their memories of working on the classics, but not everyone can be like Stanley Donen, brightening up Criterion's *Charade* DVD with charming anecdotes. Some are more like the late Robert Wise, who couldn't remember much of interest about the likes of *The Set-Up, The Day The Earth Stood Still*, or *Star Trek: The Motion Picture*. And then there's Vincent Sherman, who croaks his way through tracks on Bette Davis and Joan Crawford DVDs, either rambling about his relationships with the actresses, or sharing plainly untrue assertions about the movies. Could these guys not be spared having to deliver a two-hour monologue, and maybe do a short on-camera interview instead? After all, that's why God invented featurettes.

YOU'RE NEXT!

15 MOVIES WHERE THE CRAZIES ARE RIGHT

1 *INVASION OF THE BODY SNATCHERS* (1956)

There's no more famous small-town crazy whom no one's ever going to believe than Kevin McCarthy in *Invasion Of The Body Snatchers*. And there's no more famous unheeded warning than his chilling prediction, delivered straight at the camera, "They're here already! You're next!" This was meant to be *Body Snatchers'* final scene; the alien pod creatures that were slowly replacing our friends and relatives with exact duplicates were supposed to be unstoppable, and as they predicted, McCarthy would be considered a madman for claiming that such an unlikely thing was happening. But the film's producers at Allied Artists found the scene unnerving (damn right, says we) and requested that director Don Siegel add a happy ending where a lucky coincidence pokes a hole in the aliens' cover and (maybe) saves Earth. But it's a testament to the power of the original that McCarthy's hysterical, ignored call to action is the scene everyone remembers.

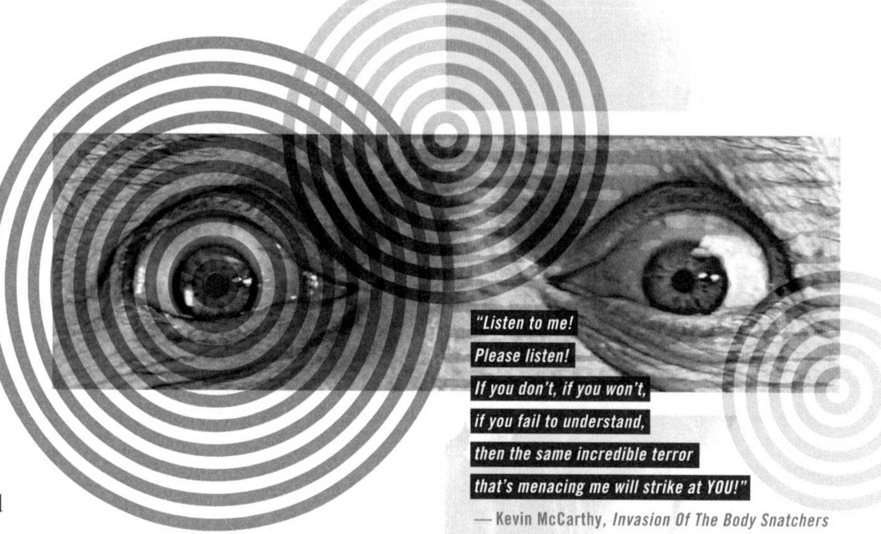

"Listen to me!
Please listen!
If you don't, if you won't,
if you fail to understand,
then the same incredible terror
that's menacing me will strike at YOU!"

— Kevin McCarthy, *Invasion Of The Body Snatchers*

2 *THE NINTH CONFIGURATION* (1980)

In an early scene from William Peter Blatty's criminally underseen *The Ninth Configuration*, two maybe-insane, maybe-not inmates at an experimental military asylum are discussing the arrival of a new psychiatrist (Stacy Keach, who gives a brilliant performance). Jason Miller and Scott Wilson play veterans confined to the facility, where Keach's Col. Kane has been brought in to shake things up. Miller compares Keach to Gregory Peck in *Spellbound*, another big-screen shrink who's nuttier than his patients. Astronaut/ringleader Wilson reacts to this news by requesting that Miller drop from a tree "like an overripe mango," but Miller is right: Keach is damaged in a way none of them could possibly anticipate, as the rest of the hilarious, harrowing film reveals.

3 *TWILIGHT ZONE: THE MOVIE* (1983)

The fourth act of 1983's *Twilight Zone: The Movie* features John Lithgow as a man so afraid of airplane travel that his nervous behavior freaks out the other passengers. And of course it's the mentally unstable guy who witnesses a gremlin tearing up the plane's wing at 20,000 feet. Ultimately, after several increasingly unnerving attempts to sell someone on his crazy story, Lithgow grabs a cop's gun and shoots his window out, depressurizing the cabin and forcing an emergency landing. As Lithgow gets hauled away in a straitjacket, the maintenance crew discovers that the wing actually was damaged somehow. Still, an insane man with a gun is just as scary to have on a plane as a gremlin, so it's just as well that the men in white coats cart Lithgow away.

A.V. CLUB

The Lithgow sequence in the movie is a remake of the old Twilight Zone *episode "Nightmare At 20,000 Feet," written by* I Am Legend *author Richard Matheson and starring William Shatner in the Lithgow role.*

4 *12 MONKEYS (1995)*

Right-leaning politicos have a lot to cheer for in *12 Monkeys*: Anti-capitalist animal-rights advocate Brad Pitt is not only generally considered batshit insane (confirming what most conservatives likely already think about animal-rights advocates and anti-capitalists), he's suspected of all but wiping out the human race as the leader of the Army Of The Twelve Monkeys. (Perhaps because he says things like "Wiping out the human race? That's a great idea.") Pitt, the son of a famous scientist and an expert in viruses, denies any plans to spread apocalyptic disease, but the authorities in his dystopic future world waste their time convinced he's the culprit. Too bad, because Pitt didn't do it, and time-traveling Bruce Willis—who, it should be noted, is also presumed crazy—discovers the actual villain too late to stop him.

5 *DONNIE DARKO (2001)*

In some ways, Donnie Darko is like any other 15-year-old boy: He's socially awkward, he sneaks cigarettes and booze when adults aren't around, and he just wants a girlfriend. But in more clinical terms, he suffers from nightmarish visions and the "daylight hallucinations" usually associated with paranoid schizophrenia; in his visions, he gets visits from Frank, an apparently imaginary friend in a horrifying man-sized rabbit costume. Frank warns Donnie that the world will end in a few short weeks, but he also instructs him to flood his school, bone up on time travel, and burn down the house of a motivational speaker with a "kiddie-porn dungeon." As strange as all this sounds, events play out in a way that suggests time travel is possible, Donnie's actions are justified and sensible, and even a hideous imaginary bunny-man is right some of the time.

6 *THE FORGOTTEN (2004)*

Does any actor portray disturbed individuals with more empathy than Julianne Moore? Too often, she invests those considerable skills into unworthy trash like *The Forgotten*, an otherwise B-level film that builds suspense for 80 minutes, then cops out with a generic "It was aliens!" ending. In *The Forgotten*, Moore is haunted by vivid memories of her son, whom she thinks died a year ago. But no one else remembers him, and doctors link Moore's delusions to a traumatic miscarriage. In spite of evidence, she's tempted to buy into their theories, until she meets another victim of disappeared-child syndrome. The subsequent chases, police action, and half-baked climax ultimately lead toward a happy ending. See, it isn't always bad when the crazies are right.

7 *FRAILTY (2001)*

Does God actually talk to Bill Paxton? That's one of the questions swirling at the center of *Frailty*, along with "Do demons actually exist?" and "Is Matthew McConaughey seriously the voice of reason in this movie?" For the majority of the film, the respective answers are "No, Paxton just thinks He does," "Of course not," and "Surprisingly, yes." Speaking to a shifty, skeptical FBI agent looking for a serial murderer known as the God's Hands Killer, McConaughey reveals that he thinks the maniac might be his younger brother. Then he gives the agent a long account of their childhood, including the night their father (Paxton) told them that God points him toward people who are actually demons that need to be killed, dismembered, and buried in the rose garden. McConaughey says he never believed his dad's nutty story, though his younger brother may have taken up the demon-killing project. But McConaughey lied about a few key points of the story, as the audience learns in the big reveal. Turns out God was talking to Paxton, demons *do* exist, and McConaughey was just *pretending* to be the voice of reason all along!

8 *BUNNY LAKE IS MISSING* (1965)

In Otto Preminger's atmospheric thriller *Bunny Lake Is Missing*, saucer-eyed Carol Lynley plays a young American single mother whose daughter goes missing after her first day of school in London. The problem? The school has no record to indicate that said daughter even exists. As an increasingly unhinged Lynley struggles in vain to find a girl nobody other than her and her brother Keir Dullea has ever seen, she encounters a series of ghoulish grotesques and one seriously unnerving doll hospital,

IN MOST MOVIES, A HYSTERICAL WOMAN BABBLING ABOUT HOW SATAN RAPED HER AND CULTISTS ARE OUT TO STEAL HER DEMON-CHILD WOULD BE BACKGROUND COLOR. IN *ROSEMARY'S BABY*, THAT CHARACTER IS THE PROTAGONIST.

and her hysteria mounts. John and Penelope Mortimer's fiendishly clever adaptation of Evelyn Piper's novel creates a free-floating air of paranoia, piles on red herrings, and cultivates reasonable doubt as to the existence of the title moppet before revealing that Dullea—who shares a creepily intense bond with his flighty sister—is ultimately behind the disappearance of the very real little girl. Ah, family.

Two more films featuring people who disappear, leaving an increasingly unsettled witness to argue with all the people who insist that person never existed: the so-so 2005 Jodie Foster movie Flightplan, *and the terrific 1938 Alfred Hitchcock classic* The Lady Vanishes, *which heavily influenced the other two films.*

9 *MIRAGE* (1965)

In a way, Edward Dmytryk's thriller *Mirage* is just another take on the *Bunny Lake* story, except that instead of a daughter, hero Gregory Peck seems to have lost his mind, his memories, and several entire floors in his office building. After a power outage, Peck wanders around with years of his memories erased, which a psychiatrist tells him is flatly impossible. The key to his amnesia has something to do with his descent into a series of office sub-basements that have magically disappeared. The people around him keep contradicting his understanding of reality, and he gets increasingly unhinged, believing that people are out to kill him and a shadowy figure known only as The Major is stalking him. Strangely, he turns out to be correct on all counts, even about the missing basement floors.

10 *CONSPIRACY THEORY* (1997)

The nature of the devious plot that turns cabbie Mel Gibson into a raving nutbar in *Conspiracy Theory* is a ridiculously complicated mishmash involving brainwashed government super-assassins and an evil Patrick Stewart. But eventually, it all adds up. In a way, that's the movie's only real point: It's designed so audiences first see Gibson as a harmless, dismissible psycho, then realize there's something meaningful behind all his paranoid gabble, then wind up sympathizing with him and understanding that when he bursts in on semi-romantic-interest Julia Roberts, waving a gun and screaming "I was in the belly of a whale! No, they were in a wheelchair, I was crippled! There was a goldfish, and there wasn't any gravy!" he's actually describing real events as accurately as his addled state of mind will permit. Unfortunately, the film goes downhill from that hilariously giddy moment onward.

11 *WINTER KILLS* (1979)

Working from a novel by Richard

Condon (*The Manchurian Candidate, Prizzi's Honor*), first-time director William Richert took a slantwise approach to the Kennedy assassination. Here, it's a fictional president killed in Philadelphia rather than Dallas, but the various conspiracy theories swirling around JFK's death come into play. The kicker: The real story is even wilder than anyone suspected. Jeff Bridges heads a star-packed cast caught in a blackly comic world where everyone has a hidden agenda and paranoia is practically the same as common sense. In some respects, it's a world the filmmakers knew well. Funded by a pair of marijuana dealers, one of whom was murdered during production, the film was barely completed—Richert and Bridges made another movie called *The American Success Company* during a shutdown, in part to secure funds to complete *Winter Kills*. Then it was barely released in spite of glowing reviews. Did somebody get too close to the truth?

12 *THE PARALLAX VIEW* (1974)

John F. Kennedy's death haunted other '70s thrillers, too. In Alan J. Pakula's *The Parallax View*, Warren Beatty's reporter attempts to lift the lid on the Seattle Space Needle death of a maverick presidential candidate. All roads lead Beatty to the Parallax Corporation, a mysterious business whose product appears to be untraceable murder. To infiltrate the company, Beatty poses as an eager-to-be-recruited sociopath, only to find that he's done far too good a job constructing a cover story. Sometimes the crazies aren't just right, they're pawns in the game they're trying to upset.

13 *TERMINATOR 2: JUDGMENT DAY* (1991)

Although the first *Terminator* movie ended on a hopeful note, with Linda Hamilton destroying the robot sent back in time to kill her and the unborn son destined to protect humanity from a future machine revolt, it didn't solve the biggest problem—there was still going to be a nuclear war, and billions of deaths. Director James Cameron brilliantly picked up that loose plot thread for the sequel, in which Hamilton discovers that knowing the future is a curse if nobody believes you. Obsessively driven to survive the coming apocalypse, she winds up locked in an asylum, where her shrink treats her outlandish stories of time-traveling murderous skeleton robots with the seriousness they seem to deserve.

14 *GOD TOLD ME TO* (1976)

B-movie auteur Larry Cohen begins his creepiest film with a sniper on a New York City water tower firing randomly and with deadly accuracy at the crowd below. When city cop Tony Lo Bianco corners him, the gunman smiles beatifically and explains, "God told me to." He seems like a lone psycho—until similar murders break out across the city, with no apparent connection beyond "God" causing ordinary citizens to develop a homicidal

A scene in The Dark Knight *pays homage to* God Told Me To, *as the Joker infiltrates a public memorial service while dressed as a policeman, then opens fire on the crowd.*

religious mania and send their loved ones to heaven the hard way. (In *God Told Me To*'s most infamous sequence, a beat cop played by Andy Kaufman begins shooting wildly during the St. Patrick's Day parade—a scene filmed guerrilla-style during the *real* parade.) Lo Bianco is horrified to discover that the prime mover is a sinister Jesus-meets-Jim Jones cult leader whose brainwashing powers come from the UFO that kidnapped and forcibly impregnated his virgin mother. The God story sounds sane by comparison.

15 *ROSEMARY'S BABY* (1968)

In most movies, a hysterical woman babbling about how Satan raped her and cultists are out to steal her demon-child would be background color, the kind of bit character who exists to make things uncomfortable for the misunderstood protagonist temporarily locked up in a halfway house or an insane asylum. In *Rosemary's Baby*, that character is the protagonist, and she has her story entirely straight. Too bad no one believes her—not that it's any surprise. Her explanations aren't any calmer or more rational than her wacky religious-guilt-inspired horror story.

SHE DON'T LIE, SHE DON'T LIE, SHE DON'T LIE

15 SONGS ABOUT THE POSITIVE SIDE OF DRUGS

1 BLACK SABBATH, "SWEET LEAF"

Leave it to Ozzy Osbourne to address marijuana with relative tenderness ("My life is free now / my life is clear / I love you, sweet leaf"), and leave it to the rest of Black Sabbath to make lighting up seem totally badass via crushing minor chords. "Sweet Leaf" makes the mellow act of pot-smoking safe for metalheads.

2 THE SHAMEN, "EBENEEZER GOODE"

This infectious raver was clearly written as an excuse to get club kids shouting "E's are good!" in a celebration of Ecstasy, the happiest drug around. The titular character is "something of a genius" and "gives a grin that goes around." Sounds like a blast!

3 TOM PETTY, "YOU DON'T KNOW HOW IT FEELS"

Though Petty now criticizes his years of doing hard drugs, he remains unapologetic about the simple joys of marijuana. Some might have thought he was saying goodbye to locoweed in the bitter "Mary Jane's Last Dance," but just one year later, he's singing "Let's roll another joint" in a tone that's celebratory at worst, borderline triumphant at best. In context, the line suggests that being Petty is a difficult task requiring THC enhancement. But the song's slow thump and rising chorus are tailor-made for fist-pumping shout-alongs. We don't all have the rock-star life, but we all need to take the edge off.

4 THE LEMONHEADS, "MY DRUG BUDDY"

Never has the quest for a high seemed more casual and sweet than on this duet between Evan Dando and Juliana Hatfield. This isn't just a song about the benefits of drugs—Dando complains that he's "too much with myself" and is ready to get high and "be someone else"—it's also about the pleasant social aspects of sharing a gentle trip. The singers love their drugs, sure, but the chorus says, "I love my drug buddy," not "I love my drug, buddy."

5 ERIC CLAPTON, "COCAINE"

Eric Clapton has always insisted that this classic hit, written by J.J. Cale, is an anti-drug song. But with its simple bluesy riffing and its slow, slick bassline, it sounds like just the thing to accompany a few late-night toots. With a guitar solo like that, it's easy to miss lines like "Don't forget this fact / you can't get it back."

6 PETER TOSH, "LEGALIZE IT"

Peter Tosh doesn't spend a ton of time talking about how good weed feels in this classic, but he does note—over a gently loping beat, of course—that doctors, nurses, judges, and lawyers all smoke it. And that it's good for flu, asthma, tuberculosis, and "umara composis," which is apparently menstrual pain. If that isn't an endorsement, nothing is.

7 QUEENS OF THE STONE AGE, "FEEL GOOD HIT OF THE SUMMER"

A pounding bassline, a tongue-in-cheek title, and grocery-list lyrics checking off seven recreational drugs all help frontman Josh Homme suggest that the mere mention of some narcotics is beyond exhilirating.

8 THREE 6 MAFIA, "SIPPIN' ON SOME SYRUP"

The *ne plus ultra* of songs devoted to the hip-hop practice of drinking cough medicine to get tranquilized, "Sippin' On Some Syrup" floats over woozy patches of tingle-skinned warmth and cold-sweat chills. The song gets plenty of pro-high competition from other druggy anthems on the same Three 6 Mafia album, *When The Smoke Clears*, but this paean to *sizzuurrrrp* is a classic drug song due to its ability to cast its narcotic of choice as simultaneously creepy and compelling. Plus it adds a little something extra to the prospect of taking NyQuil the next time a cold rolls around.

9 LIL WAYNE, "I FEEL LIKE DYING"

The fascinatingly schizophrenic pro/anti-drug song "I Feel Like Dying" has verses and a hook operating at cross purposes. "Only once the drugs are done, I feel like dying," wails the haunting hook, a cry of despair from a suicidal addict. Yet Wayne's lyrics shamelessly advocate a wide variety of mood-altering substances, dreaming spacily about a game of touch football "on marijuana streets," "Jumpin' off of a mountain into a sea of codeine," and swimming "around a bottle of Louis XIII" like a hip-hop "Lucy In The Sky With Diamonds."

10 THE STREETS, "THE IRONY OF IT ALL"

Pitting a loutish beer-drinker named Terry who likes to "exercise my right to get paralytic and fight" against a peaceful, PlayStation-loving pothead named Tim, The Streets' Mike Skinner provides a salient (though clearly biased) point-counterpoint on the hypocrisy of drug criminalization.

THE SUGARY CHEMICAL RUSH OF THE SONG'S SHOUT-ALONG CHORUS IS ENOUGH TO MAKE EVEN THE STAUNCHEST TEETOTALER LONG FOR THE COZY CONFINES OF A CROWDED BATHROOM.

While "upstanding citizens" like Terry are allowed to roam free, downing eight pints and spitting in an officer's face, Tim sits in his "hazy bubble," watching kung-fu movies, thinking about Einstein, and posing no threat on his settee. Compared to alcohol, anyway, "The Irony Of It All" makes responsible marijuana use seem like an exercise in rationality.

11 CYPRESS HILL, "HITS FROM THE BONG"

While shout-outs to the herb abound in nearly every one of Cypress Hill's songs, their casual reverence pales in comparison to "Hits From The Bong," which is delivered with the sort of adoring, Zen-like focus of stoners who drool over *High Times* pullouts. Punctuated by the burble of bong pulls, B-Real and Sen Dog exhort listeners to "Pick it, pack it, fire it up" as they declare their love for Mary Jane, offering step-by-step instructions on how to clean the screens, plug the carb, and properly inhale.

12 THE ROLLING STONES, "SISTER MORPHINE"

Another example of the razor-thin line between anti-drug and pro-drug songs, "Sister Morphine" initially seems to be resolutely against heroin, with its portrait of a desperate, dying man too weak to do anything but await his next fix. But the snaky intertwining of the acoustic and electric guitars sounds like a heavenly trip, and in the end, the message is unmistakable: If death is inevitable, why not feel good until it happens?

13 ELLA FITZGERALD, CHICK WEBB & HIS ORCHESTRA, "WHEN I GET LOW I GET HIGH"

The 1930s and '40s were full of jazz songs flagrantly pimping pot and its myriad virtues, many of which are compiled on the essential *Dope And Glory* compilations. A particular standout is Ella Fitzgerald's "When I Get Low I Get High," which prescribes copious doobage as the ideal way of coping with life's frustrations and disappointments, from getting dumped by a boyfriend to poverty to the freezing winter. Irresponsible? Maybe. Infectious? Hell yeah.

14 THE VELVET UNDERGROUND, "HEROIN"

Heroin addicts know they're flirting with suicide, and Lou Reed openly admits that it'll "be the death of me." Still, "Heroin" muses over how it's hard to resist the seductive thrall of "when the smack begins to flow" and you stop caring about the "evils of this town"—that, and Reed's giddy, head-rush of a laugh in the last verses make nearly dying sound like the closest thing to heaven. We're surrounded by "dead bodies piled up in mounds," Reed says. Who wouldn't want to shut all that out with a simple spike to the vein?

15 WEEN, "BANANAS AND BLOW"

Cocaine is bad. Jimmy Buffett-style beach-bum songs are also bad. But in the good, crazy hands of Ween, combining the two flips the script, making burning nostrils and steel drums sound not only good, but incredibly appealing on "Bananas And Blow." Listen a little closer, and "Bananas And Blow" isn't quite as chipper as the perky melody suggests—"Eating the bananas and the cocaine off the mirror, looking for a ticket to take me away from here"—but the sugary chemical rush of the song's shout-along chorus is enough to make even the staunchest teetotaler long for the cozy confines of a crowded bathroom stall and a bowl of fruit.

I WATCHED THE NEEDLE TAKE ANOTHER MAN

15 SONGS ABOUT THE NEGATIVE SIDE OF DRUGS

1 NEIL YOUNG, "THE NEEDLE AND THE DAMAGE DONE"

In the space of two minutes on 1972's *Harvest*, Neil Young, accompanied by only an acoustic guitar, managed to record one of the most damning songs about heroin addiction ever, a quiet, breathy tune infused with a heartbreaking sense of loss and waste. Amazingly, it isn't even the greatest song he ever wrote on the subject. Only a year later, after losing two more close friends to the needle, he followed it with the blistering, devastating "Tonight's The Night."

2 LOW, "IN THE DRUGS"

One particularly crushing line in Low's vague, strange "In The Drugs" makes drugs sound scarier than any direct facts could: "I closed my eyes like Marvin Gaye." ("The weight was more than you could stand" is a little scary, too.) The vibe approximates a post-dope comedown—a place no one wants to be.

3 NINE INCH NAILS, "HURT"

Drug addiction rarely sounds less glamorous than it does on Trent Reznor's rumination on turning to the needle: It won him a crown of shit and an empire of dirt, and he's still unable to shake the pain or keep it from spreading to the ones he loves. Still, the song surprisingly unsheathes a modicum of hope before deteriorating into a distant, distorted whine: "If I could start again / a million miles away / I would keep myself / I would find a way."

4 GRANDMASTER FLASH, "WHITE LINES"

Written at the peak of the coke frenzy of the '80s, "White Lines" (actually written by Melle Mel, but credited to DJ Flash) became a huge smash thanks to its numerous hooks and unforgettable bass riff. It perfectly balances its warning message (in the nagging sample of "Don't do it!") with a frenzied energy that recreates the impatient, jumpy buzz of a cocaine high.

5 ELLIOTT SMITH, "NEEDLE IN THE HAY"

Elliott Smith wrote lots of songs about drugs, many touching on his powerlessness against them. None cuts as deep as "Needle In The Hay," in which he mournfully walks to see the man who's going to "make it all okay." It's near bottom for a junkie, the time when he doesn't want to use, but knows he's going to.

6 BRIGHT EYES, "DOWN IN A RABBIT HOLE"

Conor Oberst delivers a haunting, worried postcard to a shut-in junkie who has dropped off the face of the earth after falling into the grips of crack-smoking. It's far from a pretty picture: "No one ever takes the garbage out."

7 SPIRITUALIZED, "MEDICATION"

Jason "Spaceman" Pierce is in a bind—first needing his "medication," then spending all day and night waiting for it to wear off. He hopes the day will come when he can kick it, but knows it won't come soon. Until then, he's "fucked up inside"—a line that lent its name to a terrific Spiritualized live album.

8 EMINEM, "MY FAULT"

This ridiculous song is as funny as it is scary, with Eminem voicing all the characters in a drama about a girl who eats a whole bag of mushrooms and goes crazy. ("She's upstairs crying out her eyeballs, drinking Lysol.") Still, it ends on a downer, with Eminem standing over the dead girl saying "Susan, please wake up!"

9 PHUTURE, "YOUR ONLY FRIEND"

One way to address a drug's power is to personify it, as happens in this Chicago house classic featuring spoken narration by none other than cocaine itself. "This is cocaine speaking / I can make you do anything for me," says a demonic voice over a sizzling dance groove. The list that follows isn't nice: Coke can make you cry, fight, steal, or kill without much effort. Not comforting: cocaine's eventual claim that, "In the end, I'll be your only friend."

10 JAMES BROWN, "KING HEROIN"

"Ladies and gentlemen, fellow Americans, *lady* Americans, this is James Brown. I want to talk to you about one of our most deadly killers in the country today." Brown is talking about heroin, in a mournful, declamatory rap partly written by ex-con Manny Rosen. In a series of short couplets, Brown adopts the voice of heroin, telling us exactly how strung out and desperate the drug will make its users. Brown was so passionate about the topic that one month later, he returned to the studio to record a sequel, "Public Enemy No. 1," this time taking on the persona of a street preacher, testifying about that brown powder that will "take all your money and poison your brain."

11 JOHNNY CASH, "COCAINE BLUES"

Okay, so the Man In Black makes this tale of a drunken cokehead who murders his wife and leads police on a wild chase before being caught sound like a hell of a lot of fun. And the captive audience at Folsom Prison whooped and hollered its approval at every turn when Cash performed it for his famous live album. But the song ends with the protagonist getting a 99-year bid and advising the cons to "let that cocaine be," so it has to be an anti-drug song. Really.

12 JOHN PRINE, "SAM STONE"

There's no ambiguity here: John Prine's tale of a wounded Vietnam vet who returns home with nothing to show for his service but an agonizing wound and a heroin habit is as anti-drug as any song ever written. And with its blood-freezing chorus—"there's a hole in daddy's arm where all the money goes / and Jesus Christ died for nothing, I suppose"—it's also a good candidate for the most depressing song of all time.

13 THE MOUNTAIN GOATS, "FALL OF THE STAR HIGH SCHOOL RUNNING BACK"

This song from *All Hail West Texas* is one of John Darnielle's bluntest character studies. In it, a star football player blows out his knee and takes up dealing to stay popular. At first, it's lots of fun buying new gear and quoting Biggie Smalls, but "Selling acid was a bad idea / and selling it to a cop was a worse one." Things go downhill from there.

14 COCOROSIE, "K-HOLE"

Over a simple beatbox rhythm and a delicate melody, Bianca Casady mutters distorted, surreal lyrics about a drug addict who's undergone a religious experience. At the beginning, she breathes out apocalyptic regret: "Tiny spirit in a K-hole, bloated like soggy cereal / God will come and wash away our tattoos and all the cocaine." It's a creepy enough description of a bad ketamine high to scare anyone off the drug.

15 XZIBIT, "SHROOMZ"

Xzibit came up in The Likwit Crew, and he openly advocates the deplorable practices of drinking and smoking marijuana, but on the trippy anti-drug song "Shroomz," he shares a cautionary tale about the dangers of powerful hallucinogens. After being given two grams of shrooms by cartoonish white boys, Xzibit embarks on a very bad trip as people melt before his eyes, he's filled with mindless aggression, and he ends up emptying his entire shotgun into the floor in a drugged-up panic. It seems safe to assume X will be sticking with weed and booze in the future.

ACHTUNG BJ

9 LYRICS FROM U2'S ACHTUNG BABY *THAT MIGHT BE ABOUT ORAL SEX*

1 "Did I disappoint you or leave a bad taste in your mouth?" ("One")

2 "You ask me to enter, but then you make me crawl" ("One")

3 "Surrounding me, going down on me
Spilling over the brim" ("Until The End Of The World")

4 "Who's gonna drown in your blue sea?
Who's gonna taste your saltwater kisses?"
("Who's Gonna Ride Your Wild Horses")

5 "I'm only hanging on to watch you go down, my love" ("So Cruel")

6 "Screams like an angel for your love
Then she makes you watch her from above" ("So Cruel")

7 "If you want to kiss the sky, better learn how to kneel
On your knees, boy!" ("Mysterious Ways")

8 "Squeeze the handle, blow out the candle" ("Love Is Blindness")

9 "And you can swallow or you can spit
You can throw it up or choke on it" ("Acrobat")

CLICK HERE FOR SEVERED FACE

30 DISTURBINGLY SPECIFIC INTERNET MOVIE DATABASE KEYWORDS

1 murder of family (*Gladiator, The Usual Suspects, The Hitcher*)
2 sex with fat woman (*Sideways, Good Luck Chuck, Family Guy*)
3 defecation scene (*Dances With Wolves, Bruce Almighty, The Rugrats Movie*)
4 infant nudity (*The Godfather II, A Beautiful Mind, Ghostbusters II*)
5 bloody body of child (*The Pianist, Henry V, Desperado*)
6 nude woman murdered (*Sin City, Goldfinger, Angel Heart*)
7 actual animal killed (*Apocalypse Now, Pink Flamingos, Babel*)
8 filthy toilet (*Trainspotting, Jarhead, Desperado*)
9 axe in the head (*Kill Bill: Vol. 1, American Psycho, Tenebre*)
10 drill in the head (*Pi, Scanners, Frankenhooker*)
11 hit in head with fire extinguisher (*Get Smart, The Invasion, Pineapple Express*)
12 child uses gun (*Near Dark, There Will Be Blood*)
13 decapitated child (*The Exorcist III, A.I., 1492: Conquest Of Paradise*)
14 child killed by animal (*Jaws, Moby Dick, My Girl*)
15 shot during sex (*Colors, The Missouri Breaks*)
16 sex with minor (*Manhattan, Fast Times At Ridgemont High, Election*)
17 self mutilation (*Firefly, Letters From Iwo Jima, Harry Potter And The Goblet Of Fire*)
18 finger bitten off (*Return Of The King, Speed Racer*)
19 killed by propeller (*Raiders Of The Lost Ark, A View To A Kill*)

IMDB keywords are submitted by users, then applied to films by users. A lot of people volunteered their time to make sure you can find films based on very specific murder weapons and sex acts.

20 severed face (*The Silence Of The Lambs, A Nightmare On Elm Street, Face/Off*)
21 group vomit (*Stand By Me, The Goonies, The Sandlot*)
22 gay man has sex with lesbian (*Queer As Folk, The L Word*)
23 man forced to strip (*Mr. Woodcock, Foxy Brown, M*A*S*H*)
24 piercing ripped out (*The Punisher, Land Of The Dead, Airheads*)
25 futuristic torture (*Star Trek, Flash Gordon, Impostor*)
26 sexy male vampire (*Buffy The Vampire Slayer, Underworld, Lost Boys, Blade*)
27 footsie under the table (*Ugly Betty, Battlestar Galactica, The Virgin Suicides*)
28 coma rape (*Kill Bill, Talk To Her*)
29 demon rape (*Jacob's Ladder, Xena: Warrior Princess, The X-Files*)
30 non statutory female on male rape (*Married With Children, Oz, Six Feet Under*)

THE MOVIES DON'T WANT YOU, TONY DANZA

28-PLUS FILMS THAT FAILED TO MAKE MOVIE STARS OUT OF TV STARS

1-2 TONY DANZA, *GOING APE!* (1981) AND *SHE'S OUT OF CONTROL* (1989)

Taxi star Tony Danza had two shots to make it as a leading man, riding the crests of separate waves of popularity. In *Going Ape!*, he starred as a con artist who inherits a fortune on the condition that he keep three orangutans alive and healthy for three years. The directorial debut of screenwriter Jeremy Joe Kronsberg (writer of *Every Which Way But Loose* and *Any Which Way You Can*), *Going Ape!* failed to find a theatrical audience, but became a staple on '80s cable TV. As the decade ended, Danza's work on the hit sitcom *Who's The Boss?* led to his part as disturbingly protective father Doug Simpson in *She's Out Of Control*, a completely forgettable film directed by faceless '80s comedy vet Stan Dragoti. *She's Out Of Control* tries to mine laughs out of Danza's creepy obsession with his 15-year-old daughter's burgeoning (though mostly innocent) sexuality, when the material really deserves someone with a keen eye for psychopathology.

3 GARY COLEMAN, *ON THE RIGHT TRACK* (1981)

From 1978 to 1981, *Diff'rent Strokes* was one of the most popular shows on television, and its pint-sized star, Gary Coleman, was one of the best-known and best-liked personalities in the United States. Right around the time the American citizenry began to tire of Coleman's tiny, never-aging face, he made his motion-picture debut, playing a homeless shoeshine boy who sleeps in a Union Station locker in *On The Right Track*. By that time, however, the show and Coleman's "Whachoo talkin' 'bout, Willis?" catchphrase had become cloyingly omnipresent, and another cute-kid role for Coleman seemed like overkill.

4 BILL COSBY, *LEONARD PART 6* (1987)

Bill Cosby's fame as a stand-up comic and TV star allowed him to make films before the massive success of *The Cosby Show* in the mid-'80s, but it's fair to say that *Leonard Part 6* was the Cos' biggest and best shot at becoming a full-blown movie star. Surely a film that the incredibly popular comic co-wrote, produced, and starred in would be a guaranteed smash. Released one week before Christmas, *Leonard Part 6* instead put Cosby on Hollywood's permanent naughty list. The movie was such a colossal failure that even Cosby discouraged people from seeing it, though he refused blame for the debacle, and opted to throw director Paul Weiland under the bus. Unfortunately, Weiland couldn't be blamed for the awfulness of Cosby's next feature, 1990's *Ghost Dad*.

5 MARC-PAUL GOSSELAAR, *DEAD MAN ON CAMPUS* (1998)

In 1994, *Saved By The Bell: The College Years* was cancelled after one season, proving that people didn't want to see Zack Morris as a college student. How Marc-Paul Gosselaar spent the next four years is between him and a box of Just For Men hair color, but when he re-emerged in 1998 as the star of *Dead Man On Campus*, his hair was jet-black and he was wearing wire-rimmed glasses. He looked like Morris in a serious-guy disguise, so *Dead Man On Campus* seemed doomed from the get-go. It didn't help matters that Gosselaar was essentially playing a Morris-like character: a slacking, scheming, charismatic college student—which, again, apparently no one wanted to see. Unsurprisingly, *Dead Man On Campus* failed to launch Gosselaar into movie stardom, but once audiences learned to accept him as a cop on *NYPD Blue*, his TV options became essentially endless.

6 MELISSA JOAN HART, *DRIVE ME CRAZY* (1999)

Melissa Joan Hart made her career playing oddball teens on two popular shows: *Clarissa Explains It All*, where her eccentricities included owning a phone covered in buttons and the ability to break the fourth wall with pie charts, and *Sabrina The Teenage Witch*, where her peculiarity was being a witch. But in *Drive Me Crazy*, her first starring feature-film role, Hart played an eccentricity-free, queen-bee high-school student, complete with a jock boyfriend and disdain for her weird, outsider neighbor (a pre-*Entourage* Adrian Grenier). The result? No one turned out to see it. Not even a hit song by Britney Spears, complete with a Hart cameo in the video, could get *Sabrina/Clarissa* fans into theaters. Afterward, Hart seemed to resign herself to films aimed at *Sabrina* fans, like the ABC Family movie *Holiday In Handcuffs* and the Lifetime movie *Whispers And Lies*.

7 FRED SAVAGE, *THE WIZARD* (1989)

As Kevin Arnold in the much-loved late-'80s sitcom *The Wonder Years*, Fred Savage was the youngest actor ever nominated for an Emmy. While still on *The Wonder Years*, Savage played the lead in the critically panned *The Wizard*. Little more than a feature-length commercial for the hotly anticipated *Super Mario Bros. 3*, the film lazily shoehorned in a narrative about a trio of kids (including a young Jenny Lewis) making a daring journey to California to play the videogame at a tournament. Though *The Wizard* remains a cult classic, Savage has struggled to find his footing in movies: His directorial debut, 2007's *Daddy Day Camp*, snagged him a Razzie nomination for Worst Director.

8 SHELLEY LONG, *IRRECONCILABLE DIFFERENCES* (1984)

Shelley Long's decision to leave the highly rated *Cheers* in 1987 to pursue a film career is Hollywood legend, but in 1983, it didn't look like the grave miscalculation it was. Hot off her Emmy and Golden Globe awards for *Cheers*, Long made *Irreconcilable Differences*, a schmaltzy heart-warmer about a 10-year-old girl (Drew Barrymore) who sues for emancipation from her careerist parents (Long and Ryan O'Neal). It earned Long a Golden Globe nomination, and set the wheels in motion for a series of middling films. By the time *Troop Beverly Hills*—also featuring Jenny Lewis, if anyone's looking for patterns—arrived in 1989,

Long was facing her last chance. The film flopped, and Long's next film was the little-seen 1990 Steve Guttenberg vehicle *Don't Tell Her It's Me.*

9 TED DANSON, *A FINE MESS* (1986)

By 1986, Ted Danson had served four seasons behind the *Cheers* bar, and though he never expressed interest in leaving it like a certain fellow cast member, he tried his hand at movie stardom with this slapstick-y Laurel-and-Hardy homage from Blake Edwards. Playing another variation of his slightly smarmy *Cheers* gigolo, Danson replaced Edwards' intended star, Burt Reynolds, opposite Howie Mandel (filling in for Richard Pryor); they play buddies who learn about a Mafia plan to fix a horse race. Edwards gives Danson plenty of soft light in which to work his hairy-chested charm, but studio interference and endless re-editing resulted in a film as sloppy as its self-prophesizing title. Although Danson later found box-office success in ensemble comedies like *Three Men And A Baby* and the romance *Cousins* opposite Isabella Rossellini, he never proved to be a box-office draw on his own.

10 JAMES VAN DER BEEK, *VARSITY BLUES* (1999)

Varsity Blues should have been a big break into movie stardom for James Van Der Beek, better known as Dawson Leery of *Dawson's Creek* fame. The high-school-football melodrama was No. 1 for two weeks, no thanks to Van Der Beek's wooden delivery of the film's memorable line, "I don't want your life." But following the movie's success, Van Der Beek just went back to playing Dawson—on the TV series until 2003, in 2000's *Scary Movie*, and yet again in 2001's *Jay And Silent Bob Strike Back*. By the time Van Der Beek played Sean Bateman in *The Rules Of Attraction* (2002), audiences were understandably Dawsoned out, even though his role in that film was the complete opposite of his signature character. Could a turn as a secretly gay football star in a segment filmed and dropped from Todd Solondz's 2001 film *Storytelling* have made a difference? The world will have to wonder.

11 ELIZABETH BERKLEY, *SHOWGIRLS* (1995)

Perhaps eager to shed her image as the geeky, wooden Jessie Spano from NBC's *Saved By The Bell*, Elizabeth Berkley took a turn as the somehow violent *and* wooden Nomi Malone in *Showgirls*, a movie hailed upon its release as one of the worst ever made. Cult status has since blessed the film, partially due to Berkley's performance: It takes a special kind of actress to make a nude swimming-pool sex scene so unappealing. Berkley's film career never took off, in spite of serviceable small roles in films like *Roger Dodger*. Lately, she's back where she started, on television, hosting Bravo's *Step It Up And Dance* and fronting an MTV reality self-help program. Of course, everybody involved with *Showgirls* had the last laugh, as the film has been re-released on DVD twice and repeats constantly on television, proving that if you're going to flop, you might as well flop big (and naked).

12 TOM GREEN, *FREDDY GOT FINGERED* (2001)

Anti-comedian Tom Green could always be counted on for outrageousness on *The Tom Green Show*, whether via harmless pranks like aggressively dancing next to ATM users or more squirm-inducing endeavors like humping a dead moose. So when he got a $15 million budget and free rein on his big-screen debut, it was hardly surprising that the minimal plot (about an unemployed cartoonist forced to move back to his parents' house) was just a platform for even grander cringes: elephant ejaculate, newborn babies as projectiles, and child-molestation institutes all factor highly into the absurd story arc. Also unsurprising was the deluge of horrified reviews. Green subsequently acted in a succession of forgettable and more conventional films, but is now more likely to be seen popping up in questionable TV stints, such as 2009's *Celebrity Apprentice 2*.

13 DAVE FOLEY, *THE WRONG GUY* (1997)

Fresh off the conclusion of the beloved sketch show *The Kids In The Hall*, and two years into the rise of his sitcom *NewsRadio*, Dave Foley took a shot at full-fledged movie stardom. Too bad that his aim was askew with *The Wrong Guy*, a little-seen, dull Hitchcock spoof. Foley tried to anchor the predictable tale of mistaken identities, but his prime comic acting couldn't salvage the script he co-wrote, which trucks in cameos from Joe Flaherty, *KITH's* Kevin McDonald, and, uh, The Barenaked Ladies as singing policemen. Aside from a voice-acting turn as Flik in the following year's animated movie *A Bug's Life*, Foley has stayed out of the leading-man spotlight since.

14 ELLEN DEGENERES, *MR. WRONG* (1996)

At the first peak of her career, Ellen DeGeneres was following the standard '80s/'90s comedy path, parlaying a successful stand-up career into minor film roles and eventually a sitcom. But the final leap to feature films took a nasty tumble with *Mr. Wrong*, a gloriously misconceived romantic comedy about a single woman being harassed by an obsessive man with a Jekyll/Hyde complex. DeGeneres' ambiguous sexuality at the time—she came out of the closet a year later—didn't do much for the film's chemistry, and she hasn't approached anything even vaguely resembling a romantic lead since. Not that she likely cares: She rebounded admirably in the '00s, with a top-rated daytime talk show, a hosting gig at the Oscars, and a much more auspicious return to film with her voice performance as Dory in *Finding Nemo*.

15 FRENCH STEWART, *LOVE STINKS* (1999)

It's hard to believe that anyone who watched *3rd Rock From The Sun* ever thought, "That guy with the scrunched-up face and nasal voice—he's leading-man material!" Nevertheless, French Stewart got his own big star vehicle in 1999 with *Love Stinks*, in which he played a sitcom writer whose girlfriend tortures him when he refuses to propose to her. For some reason, audiences didn't turn out in droves to watch a one-note comic actor whose lone asset as a performer is his impeccable pronunciation. Stewart has gone on to a steady career in voiceover work, where no one can see his one facial expression.

16 PAMELA ANDERSON, *BARB WIRE* (1996)

As the chestiest of the chesty lifeguards on *Baywatch*, Anderson bewitched millions of teenage boys who didn't seem to mind that her boobs were so stuffed with silicone that they didn't actually jiggle. But while audiences could buy her as a beach-going bimbette, they weren't ready to accept her as a post-apocalyptic bounty hunter in the campy 1996 shoot-'em-up *Barb Wire*. Injections of synthetic substances can lift a lot, but they can't suspend disbelief.

17 KELSEY GRAMMER, *DOWN PERISCOPE* (1996)

Kelsey Grammer's sonorous voice, mellifluous delivery, and patrician air made him an inspired choice to play psychiatrist Frasier Crane and evil genius Sideshow Bob for roughly eight bazillion years on *Cheers*, *Frasier*, and *The Simpsons*. Those same qualities made him a spectacularly perverse anchor for a slobs-vs.-snobs comedy like 1996's *Down Periscope*, which cast Grammer as a Navy man infamous for having "Welcome Aboard" tattooed on his penis during a drunken bender. *Down Periscope* stacked the deck by casting a slew of ringers opposite its unproven leading man, but not even the heavyweight likes of Rip Torn, Bruce Dern, William H. Macy, and Harry Dean Stanton could transform *Periscope* into a hit, or Grammer into a movie star.

18 MICHAEL RICHARDS, *TRIAL & ERROR* (1997)

With his flyaway hair, spastic energy, and unconventional looks, Michael Richards is nobody's idea of a leading man. But after he lurched into America's collective heart as irascible ne'er-do-well Cosmo Kramer on *Seinfeld*, New Line was willing to take a chance on him. Richards played a zany actor who impersonates lawyer buddy Jeff Daniels in *Trial & Error*, but *Seinfeld*-addicted audiences found it easy to ignore his bid for big-screen immortality. After the well-publicized unpleasantness at the Laugh Factory in 2006, Richards' chances of resurrecting his film career, especially in leading roles, went from slim to nonexistent.

19 AL FRANKEN, *STUART SAVES HIS FAMILY* (1995)

"I'm good enough, I'm smart enough, and doggone it, people like me..." Apparently that was true only for a few minutes at a time. With 1995's

Stuart Saves His Family, Al Franken found that Stuart Smalley, the TV therapist he played on *Saturday Night Live*, wasn't a feature-length prospect for most viewers. The film attempted to give the sweater-bound softie a backstory: He used to be a fat kid, and his family sucks, especially go-to movie codger Harris Yulin as his dad, and Vincent D'Onofrio as his brother Donnie. Smalley's needy, misguided attempts at helping his guests on *Daily Affirmations With Stuart Smalley* made for smartly uncomfortable TV sketches. His attempt to save his family in the movie, while not bad as *SNL* adaptations go, might've looked to some like an unwanted exercise in empathy.

20 JUSTINE BATEMAN, *SATISFACTION* (1988)

As Alex P. Keaton's sexy younger sister on *Family Ties*, Justine Bateman had every right to think that she could follow Michael J. Fox's footsteps to movie stardom. For her first big-screen project, she chose *Satisfaction*, a coming-of-age story about an all-girl rock band that takes the country by storm during a summer coast-to-coast tour. Even by the lax standards of '80s sitcom-star vehicles, *Satisfaction* was pretty cheesy, but since Fox got away with the likes of *Teen Wolf* and *The Secret Of My Success*, audiences should have been able to buy the loveable Bateman as a rocker chick. Alas, the movie bombed, and Bateman's chances at stardom went up in the resulting smoke.

> *One of Bateman's* Satisfaction *bandmates, Julia Roberts, emerged from the wreckage unscathed, as did love interest Liam Neeson. The two would later reteam for the 1996 film* Michael Collins.

21 KIRK CAMERON, *LIKE FATHER LIKE SON* (1987)

Kirk Cameron has been the leading man in crackpot Christian entertainment for so long that today's youth might not know he was one of his era's hottest teen idols. Bolstered by the popular *Family Ties* knock-off *Growing Pains*, Cameron even flirted with movie fame, secular style, with 1987's *Like Father Like Son*, where he played a Mike Seaver-esque slacker who ends up switching bodies with workaholic father Dudley Moore. *Like Father Like Son* was soon overshadowed by *Big*, which came out the following year, and even *Vice Versa*, yet another body-switch movie, this time starring Judge Reinhold and Fred Savage. For his next film, 1989's *Listen To Me*, Cameron played a college debater who argues against abortion rights. The rest, as they say, is history.

22 ED O'NEILL, *DUTCH* (1991)

The critically reviled but popular series *Married With Children* made a cult hero out of irascible character actor Ed O'Neill, and for his first foray into film stardom, the odds on *Dutch* definitely could have been worse. John Hughes' script called for a loveably gruff working-class stiff (O'Neill's specialty), and it combined concepts from Hughes' *Uncle Buck* and *Planes, Trains And Automobiles*, two proven hits. But the film's tough-love story about a guy who smacks and abuses his way into the heart of his girlfriend's spoiled brat was mostly just tough to love, and although O'Neill showed previously unknown depth in the title role, most reviewers found the movie shrill and formulaic. Judging by its tepid box-office returns, audiences agreed. O'Neill later put his talents for bullying to better use in the modest hit *Little Giants* opposite Rick Moranis, but he's never been asked to carry a movie since.

23 JOHN RITTER, *SKIN DEEP* (1989)

By 1989, John Ritter was a household name courtesy of *Three's Company*, but he hadn't yet parlayed that into a film career. Although his pairing with Jim Belushi on 1987's offbeat *Real Men* failed to drum up much interest, Ritter had every reason to believe that starring in one of Blake Edwards' "male midlife crisis" comedies might turn it around. In *Skin Deep*, Ritter plays another of Edwards' romanticized alter egos—an alcoholic, womanizing writer who beds dozens of beautiful girls, including *American Gladiators'* Zap. Unfortunately, viewers found Ritter hard to swallow as an irresistible ladykiller, and the hints of *Days Of Wine And Roses* melodrama were tonally confusing. The press murdered *Skin Deep*, and Ritter later returned to broad comedy in family movies like *Problem Child* and *Stay Tuned*, even earning raves for his nuanced performance in *Sling Blade*. But he ended his career where it began: in sitcoms.

24 JOHN LARROQUETTE AND BRONSON PINCHOT, *SECOND SIGHT* (1989)

John Larroquette was sitcom royalty in the '80s, racking up four Emmys in a row for his performance on *Night Court*. After years of memorable cameos in comedies like *Risky Business* and *Beverly Hills Cop*, Bronson Pinchot found his niche on *Perfect Strangers*, garnering an Emmy nomination of his own. With two well-liked TV stars and a script from Tom Schulman (*Dead Poets Society, What About Bob?*), 1989's *Second Sight* definitely could have been worse. It also could have been much, much better: As a comedy duo, Larroquette's cynical detective and Pinchot's space-case psychic had *Ishtar* levels of chemistry, but without the star wattage to generate even bad publicity. Audiences and critics dismissed it, the film tanked, and Larroquette's next leading role, opposite Kirstie Alley in 1990's *Madhouse*, was his last. Meanwhile, Pinchot went back to a career of making scene-stealing cameos before finally ending up on *The Young And The Restless* in early 2008.

25 GARRY SHANDLING, *WHAT PLANET ARE YOU FROM?* (2000)

Garry Shandling put himself front

Ritter might have made a bigger splash in Skin Deep *if he hadn't been upstaged by the ad campaign, which claimed the film's true star was a glow-in-the-dark condom.*

and center with the innovative sitcoms *It's Garry Shandling's Show* and *The Larry Sanders Show*, but after decades in show business, he hadn't found a cinematic showcase for his talents, past small roles in films like *Love Affair* and *Hurlyburly*. So he wrote one for himself with 2000's *What Planet Are You From?* Directed by Mike Nichols and featuring a solid supporting cast that included Annette Bening and John Goodman, *WPAYF?* was an offbeat sexual satire reminiscent of early Woody Allen. Perhaps, had it succeeded, Shandling could have similarly slipped into a second act of his career, starring in slightly neurotic romantic comedies. (His role in 2001's dreadful *Town & Country* suggested he was at least interested in the idea.) But Shandling's flat performance and the film's reliance on cheap laughs failed to charm critics or audiences, and Shandling has apparently entered semi-retirement.

26 SCOTT BAIO, *ZAPPED!* (1982)

Happy Days was on top of the ratings world in 1977, when Scott Baio was introduced in the show's fifth season as Fonzie's cousin "Chachi" Arcola. Baio was just 15 at the time, but his good looks turned him into a heartthrob as the seasons passed. When Ron Howard left the show before season eight in 1980, Chachi's relationship with Joanie Cunningham (Erin Moran) became a central plot point. Unsurprisingly, around this time, Baio began appearing in films, after-school specials, and made-for-TV fare like 1980's *The Boy Who Drank Too Much*. He debuted on the big screen with a supporting role in 1980's *Foxes*, then moved to top billing with 1981's *Senior Trip*. But the vehicle most people remember is 1982's *Zapped!*, starring Baio as a nerd who develops telekinetic powers, which he uses for typical adolescent pursuits: removing girls' clothes and beating up bullies. Despite the inevitable critical drubbing, *Zapped!* made a respectable-for-the-time $15 million or so, but Baio disappeared from film for five years. Back on TV, the *Happy Days* gravy train continued with the short-lived *Joanie Loves Chachi* spin-off. Baio finally put *Happy Days* behind him in 1984, reuniting with his *Zapped!* co-star Willie Aames for the sitcom *Charles In Charge*.

27 ROSEANNE BARR, *SHE-DEVIL* (1989)

Roseanne debuted in 1988 to immediate high ratings, and by the time *She-Devil* hit the box office in December 1989, Roseanne Barr's signature show was overtaking perennial frontrunner *The Cosby Show* at the top of the Nielsen ratings. Her debut stayed close to *Roseanne's* winning blue-collar formula: In *She-Devil*, Barr stars as the frumpy housewife of Ed Begley Jr., who dumps her after meeting famous novelist Meryl Streep. Revenge follows. *She-Devil* debuted respectably at No. 4 in the box-office rankings, but sunk quickly, disappearing from screens before the month was out, and making Barr look much more bankable on TV than in film.

She-Devil dropped from sight so fast because of tough competition in the theaters, especially from Look Who's Talking, which dominated the top 10 for months in 1989. If you can't beat 'em, join 'em: Barr's next screen outing was as the voice of a baby in 1990's Look Who's Talking Too.

28+ ALMOST EVERYTHING FEATURING CAST MEMBERS FROM *FRIENDS* *(VARIOUS, 1996-PRESENT)*

Friends was a hit out of the gate when it debuted in September 1994. By its second season, it was third in the ratings, and it never dropped below fifth until it went off the air in 2004. As the show became a pop-culture phenomenon, it was inevitable that its young, attractive cast would make movies, but while Jennifer Aniston (and to a much smaller degree, Lisa Kudrow) became movie stars, the show's other principals—Courteney Cox, Matthew Perry, David Schwimmer, and Matt LeBlanc—haven't fared as well. To wit: kiddie-monkey flick *Ed* (LeBlanc), *Almost Heroes* (Perry), *Kissing A Fool* (Schwimmer), *The Runner* (Cox).

WEEBLE FALLS DOWN

34 ACTUAL TOPIC NAMES FROM HASBRO.COM'S "INSTANT ANSWERS"

1. Baby Alive Hispanic Switching Languages
2. Zipper On Butterscotch
3. Baby Alive Won't Chew
4. Pooh Poppin' Piano Recall
5. Secret Strike Pocket Blaster Won't Shoot
6. Blue Play-Doh Too Moist
7. Bulls-Eye Ball Ball Composition
8. Butterscotch Or S'Mores My FurReal Pony Where To Buy
9. Cootie Replacement Parts
10. Selling Mortgaged Properties
11. Smoke Fluid Packs
12. Won't Lie Flat
13. Don't Go To Jail
14. Dream Life Permission
15. Females And Minorities
16. French-Speaking Squawkers
17. FurReal Friend Grinding
18. Getting Out Of Jail
19. Heads Won't Work
20. Kosher
21. Making An Egg
22. Feeding The Lamb
23. Where To Buy Nerf Vulcan
24. No Available Houses
25. Cat Hissing
26. Win Dance Lessons With A Celebrity Coach
27. Real Meal Oven Smoking
28. Eggs Pasteurized
29. Padme Amidala Unleashed
30. Multiple-Birth Program
31. Cuddle Chimp Batteries
32. Cuddle Chimp Fur
33. Cuddle Chimp Cleaning Instructions
34. Cuddle Chimp Will Not Respond

Guest List:

ANDREW W.K.

MY 5 FAVORITE PIANO CHORDS

1. A MINOR 7

I guess this is what some people might call the standard blues chord—it works in any key, but I really like A. The wild part about these Minor 7 chords is that when played as a triad with the 7 on top (or bottom), they're the same notes as the relative major, so an A Minor 7 chord is exactly the same notes as a C Major Triad with the root note octave. Minor 7 chords instantly resonate a certain emotional head-space. Maybe it's the feeling of the blues, but the sound seems more optimistic and powerful than simply sad or down in the dumps. This chord has a unique beauty and sound—the sound of pure human emotion in all its richness.

2. B MAJOR WITH SUSPENDED 4TH

Suspended 4ths have always tickled me in a certain special way. You can hear a great example of a suspended 4th guitar chord in The Who's "Pinball Wizard"—the main strumming riff is working with a suspended 4th chord resolving to a Major triad. There's something so beautiful and emotional about these chords—a suspended 4th truly has a feeling of hanging in the air, unresolved, open to anything, free to jam out with whatever music comes next. But for now, it's suspended, and that feeling of weightlessness is heavy as hell.

3. D MINOR TRIAD

Supposedly this is the saddest key, and therefore the saddest chord. I've enjoyed it frequently, especially since it has only one black key, so the keyboard fingering is a breeze. I've heard so much about how D Minor is the saddest-sounding chord, but I don't remember what people have said is the happiest-sounding chord. I wonder if it would be the relative Major of D Minor (which would be F Major)? I've always thought C Major sounded happy.

4. C MAJOR TRIAD OVER D BASS (OR "4 CHORD OVER 5 BASS")

This chord has a sound familiar to many, as it's been heavily used in popular music. It seems to usually set up a big chorus or appear at the end of a phrase, right before a resolve. "Tiny Dancer" by Elton John uses this move to great effect!

5. G MAJOR TRIAD OVER B BASS (OR "1 CHORD OVER 3 BASS")

When I first played this chord by accident, it was a revelation. In my early years of music-making, there were certain sounds and chords and feelings I had heard in life, yet hadn't figured out how to recreate on the piano. Most of the time, just messing around on the keyboard would eventually lead to some new discovery or breakthrough. The first time I heard this chord, I probably played it by accident, while going through inversions in my right hand. Once I started following the inversions with my left hand, I struck this chord, and *wow*... it was like the sound of my own internal world. There's something about the feeling of these notes that defines human existence. It's the full spectrum of feeling and passion—somehow, it's simultaneously sadder than a chord like D minor, and happier than a regular major chord. I've heard it said that music is the human spirit in full bloom; I think this chord, and its sound, are tapping into the elemental aspect of what it is to be alive. Music, with all its chords and endless variations of melody and rhythm, is our spirit at its richest and most revealed. Music is everything.

Andrew W.K. is a musician, an occasional television personality, and a positive inspiration to everyone he meets.

SHOOT THE WHOLE DAY DOWN

22 GREAT SONGS INSPIRED BY HEINOUS TRUE CRIMES

1 THE SMITHS, "SUFFER LITTLE CHILDREN"

One of Morrissey's most lyrically haunting songs, "Suffer Little Children" laments the sadistic "moors murders" near his Manchester hometown in the early '60s. Ian Brady and Myra Hindley tortured and killed five children and teenagers before being caught—even photographing and audio recording one of them. The song, from The Smiths' first album, refers to the victims and attackers by name, which some critics found morbid and exploitative. Morrissey, though, claimed he was simply empathetic, having been a child in the city at the time. He eventually even spoke with the mother of one victim, convincing her of his good intentions.

2 SUFJAN STEVENS, "JOHN WAYNE GACY, JR."

In a strange bit of soul-searching, gentle Christian singer Sufjan Stevens tried to get inside the psyche of notorious child-killer John Wayne Gacy Jr. Not content with a simple biography, Stevens paints an eerie picture ("In a dark room on the bed, he kissed them all"), then turns the focus on himself: "I am really just like him." That's a harsh self-judgment, but Stevens sticks by it. In an interview with Gapersblock.com, he said, "I believe we all have the capacity for murder. We are ruthless creatures."

3-4 BOB DYLAN, "THE LONESOME DEATH OF HATTIE CARROLL" AND "HURRICANE"

Bob Dylan once accused Phil Ochs of being a journalist rather than a folk-singer. But Dylan himself brilliantly merges art with breathless reporting on his two greatest "issue" songs, "The Lonesome Death Of Hattie Carroll" and "Hurricane." Both songs deal with real-life people who suffered at the hands of a racist legal system—51-year-old murdered barmaid Hattie Carroll in the former, and imprisoned boxer Rubin Carter in the latter—and Dylan states all the pertinent details of their cases without pedantry. Best of all, by reporting the facts succinctly and the emotional truth poetically, he ensured that their stories wouldn't be forgotten once they moved off the front page.

5-6 BRUCE SPRINGSTEEN, "NEBRASKA"; J CHURCH, "HATE SO REAL"

In 1958, 19-year-old Charles Starkweather and his 14-year-old girlfriend, Caril Ann Fugate, embarked on a killing spree that left 10 people dead in Nebraska and Wyoming. The brutality of the crimes and the duo's ability to evade capture held Nebraska hostage for a week. After their arrest in Wyoming, they turned on each other; Fugate claimed she'd been kidnapped, though Starkweather blamed her for some of the deaths. In the end, only he was executed; Fugate was imprisoned until 1976. Decades later, the duo's crimes still awed Bruce Springsteen so much that he opened his 1982 album, *Nebraska*, with a song about the killings. With haunting sparseness, "Nebraska" tells the story from Starkweather's perspective, ending with "They wanted to know why I did what I did / well sir, I guess there's just a meanness in this world." Lance Hahn of the prolific punk outfit J Church took the same perspective in "Hate So Real," packing in more description of the couple's final days together, and nodding to Springsteen in the chorus: "I can't say that I'm sorry for the things I know I've done / for the first time, me and Caril had a lot of fun."

7 ELVIS COSTELLO, "LET HIM DANGLE"

Elvis Costello opens his dark, bitter "Let Him Dangle" with a sticking point in the legal case of Chris Craig

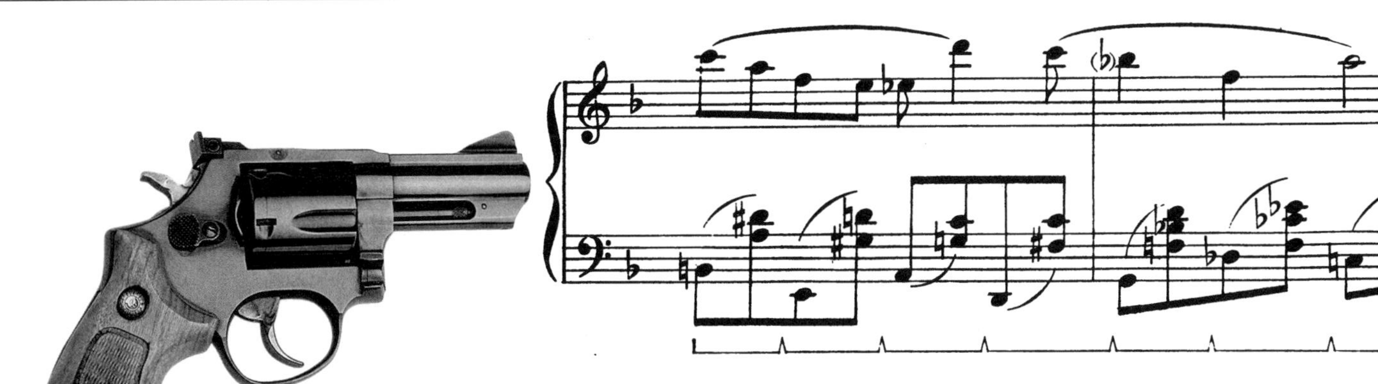

and Derek Bentley, accused of killing a policeman in 1952 England. Craig pulled the trigger, but he was underage at the time, so his friend Bentley was charged with and executed for the killing, largely on witnesses' claim that he said "Let him have it, Chris" before Craig fired the fatal shot. One key question in court was whether Bentley meant "Shoot him" or "Give him your gun and surrender"; another was whether Bentley could be considered guilty of murder when he was already under arrest. Costello's song tells their story without justifying their actions, but he acidly points to the "bloodthirsty chorus" determined to punish murder with more murder, even with the wrong guy at the gallows. With the chilly chorus lyric, "Let him dangle, let him dangle," Costello expresses his contempt for the motives of people who favor capital punishment, even though "it won't make you even, it won't bring him back."

8 NEKO CASE, "DEEP RED BELLS"

For more than a decade, a man known only as the Green River Killer haunted the roads of Seattle and Tacoma, strangling women and leaving their bodies on the banks. Neko Case grew up in the area, and thoughts of the voiceless victims—almost all prostitutes or young, impoverished drifters—plagued her teenage years. She gave them a voice in this song off her *Blacklisted* album. "A handprint on the driver's side" of the truck the killer drove, she sings, "tastes like being poor and small." The song was recorded late in 2001, right around the time a hateful nothing named Gary Ridgway was arrested for the crimes. He was eventually convicted of 48 murders and sentenced to life without parole.

9 THE BOOMTOWN RATS, "I DON'T LIKE MONDAYS"

Given the increasing number of calamitous school shootings, it seems likely that Brenda Spencer's decision to open fire on an elementary school in 1979 would be largely forgotten if Bob Geldof hadn't written a song about it. Geldof read the reports of the San Diego spree—the teenage Spencer wounded eight children and killed two school employees—and was struck by her blunt, remorseless, almost whimsical answer when asked why she did it: "I don't like Mondays—this livens up the day," Spencer told a judge. Using her chilling words as his chorus, Geldof penned a tune driven by arch, hyperdramatic piano swells, and a true-crime classic was born.

10 CAMPER VAN BEETHOVEN, "JACK RUBY"

By the time Camper Van Beethoven recorded *Key Lime Pie*, things had gone sour for the band; creative differences, financial difficulties, personal conflicts, and emotional stress made it their darkest record, lyrically and musically. That's clearest on the mournful, searing "Jack Ruby," an impressionist portrait of the man who killed Lee Harvey Oswald. It begins with creepy little details familiar to anyone who's seen the photographs ("I remember his hat tilted forward / his glasses were folded in his vest") and ends in a world rendered terrifyingly unlivable by the enormity of the crime. Singer David Lowery advises listeners to avert their eyes in shame and pretend that the day of the assassination has no meaning, but suggests that it's impossible, no matter how much we all need "the luxury" of denial.

11 BIG BLACK, "JORDAN, MINNESOTA"

Unlike the rest of the songs on this list, Big Black's savage "Jordan, Minnesota" was based on a crime that wasn't. Steve Albini wrote the song, with its unforgettable refrain of "And this is Jordan, we do what we like," after reading about a child-molestation ring in the Southern Minnesota town. Allegedly, the parents swapped their children like swingers swap partners, and Albini claimed in an interview that no one except the one man who ratted out the rest did any jail time. The dregs of human behavior have long been the fodder for Albini's material, but he got this one wrong: The reason the Jordan case only led to one conviction is because only one person was guilty. The defendant cooked up the whole ritual-child-abuse story at the prodding of an overzealous prosecutor, and the tall tale completely fell apart under questioning.

12 SLAYER, "DEAD SKIN MASK"

"Dead Skin Mask" isn't the most unsettling Slayer tune inspired by real-world horrors: That honor goes to the Josef Mengele bio "Angel Of Death." But the song, from 1990's *Seasons In The Abyss*, still sets a heavy mood. Inspired, like *Psycho* and *The Texas Chainsaw Massacre* before it, by trophy-collecting, cannibalistic serial killer Ed Gein, "Dead Skin Mask" gets its title from one of Gein's craft projects. Still, the song's creepiest element is the female voice crying out beneath bassist-singer Tom Araya in the mix. A cheap trick, maybe, but in the context of lyrics like, "Dance with the dead in my dreams / listen to their hallowed screams," it works.

13 MISFITS, "BULLET"

Given what a repugnant band name "Dead Kennedys" seemed in its time, imagine the reaction to this 1978 single, which graphically detailed JFK's assassination and supported conspiracy theories surrounding the murder. Lyrics such as "Kennedy's shattered head hits concrete" aren't so much offensive as coldly factual, and even though the song seemingly devolves into a forced-sex fantasy involving Jackie O, it's more likely that the rape is a metaphorical reference to the conspirators behind the killing. Much as in the Misfits classic "Who Killed Marilyn?" singer Glenn Danzig implies he knows more about what's going on than he's actually revealing.

14 JANE'S ADDICTION, "TED, JUST ADMIT IT..."

This song, from 1988's classic *Nothing's Shocking*, has a jerky narrative flow, but it makes perfect sense to those in the know about its subject—serial killer Ted Bundy—and his infamous outbursts during the trials that led to his 1989 execution. Using lines from Bundy's own public statements, "Ted, Just Admit It..." is a powerful commentary on the mingling of pornography and violence at the root of Bundy's pathology. No wonder, then, that bits of "Ted, Just Admit It..." ended up on the soundtrack to Oliver Stone's like-minded film commentary *Natural Born Killers*.

15 CHAIN GANG, "SON OF SAM"

Recorded while its subject, confessed serial killer David Berkowitz, was still an anonymous ghoul terrorizing New York City, this 1977 single (later covered by Jon Spencer Blues Explosion) was as much a slice of citizen journalism as a squealing blast of early noise-punk. "People would walk by with the *NY Post* under their arm, selling papers for the seventh day with pictures of the dead bodies," singer Ricky Luanda told *Forced Exposure* magazine in 1998. "Then we'd try to sell our record to these same people passing on 5th Avenue, and they'd say, 'Hey, you people are sick, capitalizing on this.'... Right away we realized we had to compete."

16 THE ROLLING STONES, "MIDNIGHT RAMBLER"

"Midnight Rambler" has become such an essential part of the Stones' live repertoire that it's easy to take the song's inspiration for granted. No, not the vacation in the Italian countryside during which Mick Jagger and Keith Richards first sketched out the lurid, bluesy boogie, but rather the two-year rampage in which a sexual sadist murdered 13 women throughout the Boston area. Albert DeSalvo confessed to the crimes in 1967, earning the handle "Boston Strangler" for his efforts, but the multiple perspectives in the Stones' lyrics express the chilling possibility—echoed by most experts on the case—that DeSalvo wasn't acting alone.

17 THE ADVERTS, "GARY GILMORE'S EYES"

Convicted spree killer Gary Gilmore technically only gunned down two people in 1976. However, following a long media and legal circus around his demand to be executed for the crimes, Gilmore became one of the most notorious (and oddly sympathetic) criminals in U.S. history. By the time Gilmore got his wish in January 1977, The Adverts had written this song about a fictional eye-donor recipient who was indeed "looking through Gary Gilmore's eyes." The band hit the Top 20 in England with the single, their only national charting hit.

18 VIOLENT FEMMES, "DAHMER IS DEAD"

Violent Femmes frontman Gordon Gano knocked out this 38-second throwaway tune after hearing that cannibal serial killer Jeffrey Dahmer—who, like the Femmes, did his major work in Milwaukee—had been bludgeoned to death in prison. But while "Dahmer Is Dead" is easy to dismiss, its catchy melody and bone-simple lyrics—"Dahmer is dead, Dahmer is dead / a broomstick bashed him upside his head"—make it one of the more enjoyable and immediate additions to the Femmes' latter-day catalog.

19 SONIC YOUTH, "DEATH VALLEY '69"

Charles Manson's notorious Family killed more than their nine literal victims in the 1969 Tate-LaBianca murders: Like that same year's Altamont festival, they figuratively stuck a knife in the peace-and-love generation, bleeding a movement of its innocence and optimism. The Family—and Manson in particular—provided the inspiration for countless dark rock songs, but from Alkaline Trio's "Sadie" to System Of A Down's "ATWA," none of those eclipses this 1985 collaboration between Sonic Youth and no-wave banshee poet Lydia Lunch. "Death Valley '69" is a fitting closing track to the Sonics' ultra-pessimistic album *Bad Moon Rising*, with Lunch and Thurston Moore playing out a frenetic dialogue between Family members as the song's propulsive beat and tornado-force guitars convey the confusion, nihilism, and desperation that followed the Family's acts.

20 MOTÖRHEAD, "JACK THE RIPPER"

Screaming Lord Sutch and Judas Priest (to name but two) had already recorded major singles based on Jack The Ripper's unsolved string of prostitute murders and mutilations in 19th-century England, so Motörhead arrived late to the party with this 1992 track. Still, the song is one of the strongest, rawest tunes on Motörhead's commercial-leaning *March Or Die*, and while others have told the Ripper's tale, there's something uniquely creepy about hearing 'Head master Lemmy Kilmister growl the cold truth of Saucy Jacky's legacy: "And so the mystery continues to beguile / the ones who know can never tell you of his smile."

21 WESLEY WILLIS, "RICHARD SPECK"

This song—which follows the same pattern as every other song late, great schizophrenic teddy bear Wesley Willis ever recorded—becomes a sort of alternate-universe TV voiceover, literally relaying the details of Speck's 1966 mass murder of eight student nurses in a Chicago dormitory: "The ninth nurse hid under the bed / she told on him in court about the murders in 1966 / Richard Speck was convicted and sentenced to 1,200 years in prison." Yes, that's all true, but the real magic of "Richard Speck" comes from Willis' inability to keep his own feelings out of the story: "This man is a criminal / he is a dangerous human being / he is an asshole / he'll kill you and put you in the graveyard."

22 NIRVANA, "POLLY"

Nirvana's harrowing "Polly" is based on the 1987 kidnapping and rape of a Tacoma, Washington teenager. Though the song intimates that Polly escaped after pretending to empathize with her attacker, the real Polly actually found freedom when the abuser—Gerald Friend, who was later convicted and is still in jail—took her for a ride and stopped at a gas station. Some Nirvana fans apparently misunderstood Kurt Cobain's intentions; in the liner notes to *Incesticide*, he wrote, "Last year, a girl was raped by two wastes of sperm and eggs while they sang the lyrics to our song 'Polly.' I have a hard time carrying on knowing there are plankton like that in our audience. Sorry to be so anally PC, but that's the way I feel."

VISIONARY OR MADMAN?

16 CAREER-JEOPARDIZING LABORS OF LOVE

1 THE PASSION OF THE CHRIST *(2004)*

Braveheart grossed nearly $76 million in 1995, putting Mel Gibson in a position to dictate terms to the studios for his next directorial effort. But Hollywood balked at the crazy talk coming out of Mad Mel's mouth, as he planned a portrayal of the sufferings of Jesus from Judas' kiss to Golgotha, with Aramaic and Latin dialogue, and no subtitles. He eventually relented on the subtitles, but still, the rest of his personal act of Catholic devotion made it to the screen thanks to independent financing and eventual distribution by Newmarket. Through dumb luck or perhaps divine intervention, the war-torn America of 2004 couldn't have been more primed to wallow in religious violence; audiences took the lashings and the crown of thorns and begged for more, to the tune of $370 million that summer alone. Largely based on the mystical writings of a 19th-century German nun, and reported to have been blessed by John Paul II with the words, "It is as it was," Gibson's nutter gamble practically defines the term "visionary," for better or worse.

2 FITZCARRALDO *(1982)*

Method actors are known for getting into character by researching a role heavily and "living" the part for the duration of the shoot. In that sense, Werner Herzog could be called a method director. In his many films about man vs. nature, he's always been inclined to recreate the arduous physical challenges that other, more practical productions would studiously avoid. His cursed biopic *Fitzcarraldo* concerns a 20th-century rubber baron who aspires to open an opera house in the remote Peruvian city of Iquitos and invite his beloved Enrico Caruso to perform there. But in order to help finance his dream, he first has to pull a giant steamboat over a steep hill to gain access to the rich rubber-mining territory on the other side. Herzog initially cast Jason Robards and Mick Jagger in the lead roles, but that fell through when Robards fell deathly ill during shooting. Herzog started over with the erratic Klaus Kinski in the lead, but that was the least of his problems. Rather than follow the example of the real Fitzcarraldo, who dismantled the steamboat before carrying it up the hill, Herzog employed a team of indigenous people and a primitive pulley system to drag the whole thing uphill. The disasters that followed are captured in Les Blank's great making-of documentary *Burden Of Dreams*.

3 "CHRIS GAINES" *(1999)*

Garth Brooks was so big in the '90s that a blank CD with his name on it would have debuted at No. 1 on the *Billboard* chart. But a Garth Brooks CD with somebody else's name on it? Not so popular. Brooks learned the value of his own moniker in 1999 when he pulled the Bowie-esque move of adopting a musical alter ego called Chris Gaines, a brooding, soul-patch-stroking alt-rocker whose dark persona couldn't be farther removed from Garth's usual populist image. It was a risky idea that appealed to a superstar looking to break out of a highly profitable but stifling pigeonhole, and Brooks sold it aggressively, doing a fake *Behind The Music* episode and hosting *Saturday Night Live* as himself, while playing Chris Gaines as the musical guest. He also made an album, *Garth Brooks In... The Life Of Chris Gaines*, as a "pre-soundtrack" for a planned Chris Gaines film called *The Lamb*. Perhaps Brooks shouldn't have been so pushy; he was so committed to the Chris Gaines character that it turned off even his most devoted fans, who wanted the guy in the big hat and multicolored shirt back.

4 *APOCALYPSE NOW* (1979)

Francis Ford Coppola's Vietnam epic was career-jeopardizing in that it was considered a questionable project to begin with—an adaptation of Joseph Conrad's supposedly unadaptable *Heart Of Darkness*—and in that Coppola wanted to film it in Vietnam, which was considered insanely dangerous. But it put more than his career in danger. He funded it with his own money, and a string of now-legendary production problems (a typhoon that destroyed sets, two ailing and hard-to-work-with stars, various problems related to shooting in the Philippines under Ferdinand Marcos) nearly bankrupted him over the years it took to shoot and edit. And yet unlike so many labor-of-love stories, this one had a happy ending; *Apocalypse Now* became an Oscar winner, a box-office hit, and an enduring classic, albeit not enough of one to justify the follow-up labor of love Coppola suggested: a theater dedicated solely to showing the movie over and over in perpetuity.

5 *CHRIST THE LORD: OUT OF EGYPT* (2005)

It would have been easy, though painful, for Anne Rice to keep on cranking out her inexplicably popular vampire novels until she was as old as Lestat. Give her credit for not doing the safe thing when, in 2004, she announced that she had embraced her childhood Catholic faith and from that point forward, she would "write only for the Lord." Her risky move didn't exactly pay off, either; her legions of fans were already dropping off after a prolonged slump in her writing career, and fewer were willing to follow her into what promised to be a thinly disguised Christian apologetic. Mainstream critics weren't kind to the first installment in a proposed *Christ The Lord* cycle, since it featured the same sort of overwrought purple prose as her vampire books, but without any juicy sex. A sequel followed in 2008.

6 *SOUTHLAND TALES* (2008)

Though it famously bombed during its theatrical run, 2001's *Donnie Darko* amassed such a massive, devoted cult following that writer-director Richard Kelly could be forgiven for imagining that his loyal fans would follow him down just about any rabbit-hole or weird detour. With that in mind, he concocted an entire Philip K. Dick-style universe around his second film, *Southland Tales*, complete with an elaborate mythology mapped out in a pimped-out website and a series of graphic-novel tie-ins. But when a 160-minute cut of the film was met with jeers at Cannes, Kelly's carefully laid plans began to unravel spectacularly. Turns out moviegoers weren't hungering for a trippy pop-art epic about time-traveling action heroes, synergy-crazed porn stars, lip-syncing teen idols, and neo-Marxist revolutionaries. The film's kitchen-sink comic-strip satire struck all but the most indulgent cult-film fanatics as silly rather than inspired.

7 ***THEY ALL LAUGHED*** *(1981)*
Peter Bogdanovich's 1981 romantic comedy *They All Laughed* is a delicate trifle of a film, a dialogue-light, atmosphere-heavy love letter to New York, film, and the giddiness of finding that perfect someone in a city full of intoxicating possibilities. Even with a rare latter-day performance from Audrey Hepburn, it was a long shot commercially, but when co-star (and Bogdanovich's real-life love) Dorothy Stratten was brutally killed by her jealousy-crazed husband, the film went from risky to DOA. Who could lose themselves in the film's airy wonderland in light of Stratten's high-profile murder? When Bogdanovich was unable to find a studio willing to take a chance on his labor of love, he released it himself, at great personal expense. Unsurprisingly, the film bombed, sending Bogdanovich into a steep personal and professional downward spiral from which he has yet to fully recover.

8 ***IT'S ALL ABOUT LOVE*** *(2003)*
Lars von Trier protégé and Dogme 95 founding father Thomas Vinterberg wowed international film fans with 1998's *The Celebration*. For his follow-up, Vinterberg dreamed big, whipping up *It's All About Love*, a mournful, psychedelic mood piece that takes place in a dystopian, 9/11-haunted future where figure skaters are cloned, Africans mysteriously begin floating for no reason, and people die en masse of broken hearts. Vinterberg's *Celebration* buzz helped line up an A-list cast (Joaquin Phoenix, Claire Danes, and Sean Penn) but the bewildering, intermittently moving film was barely released theatrically, and follow-ups like *Dear Wendy* and *A Man Comes Home* haven't fared much better.

9 ***MY DECEMBER*** *(2007)*
American Idol contestants are supposed to behave. Freshly scrubbed likeability is what wins them broad critical support from tweens and grandmothers alike. Besides, it's in their Draconian contract deal, right next to the clause about Clive Davis having dibs on their firstborn. And yet the sort of success that season-one winner Kelly Clarkson enjoyed on the pop charts does buy a certain amount of leverage, and Clarkson decided to use that leverage for her third album, *My December*, a collection of personal songs she wrote or collaborated on herself. When the 75-year-old Davis reportedly hated the album and wanted it scrapped, Clarkson engaged in a public feud in which she said, among other things, that she couldn't see the wisdom in "100-year-old executives making decisions on what's good for pop radio." Turns out Davis was right: The record, perhaps in part bruised by the feud, sold poorly, and Clarkson wound up firing her manager and canceling her summer tour. Bye-bye, leverage. Hello Swedish hitmaker Max Martin.

10 ***INTOLERANCE*** *(1916)*
Though his incendiary Civil War epic *Birth Of A Nation* established him as the world's preeminent film director, D.W. Griffith also fielded a storm of controversy stemming from the film's racist imagery and its unabashed support of white-supremacist groups like the Ku Klux Klan. Intended as a response to his critics, Griffith's mammoth follow-up *Intolerance* attempted to decry "intolerance" through the ages by telling stories on four different timelines, from ancient Babylon to the Judean Era to the French Renaissance to modern-day America. Griffith had massive sets built for the production—including a Great Wall Of Babylon that stood on Sunset and Hollywood for years after shooting wrapped—and spent upward of $2 million on the film, which was unprecedented and astronomical for the time. There's no understating the film's impact on the history of the medium, particularly Griffith's experiments with crosscutting technique, but it flopped spectacularly and bankrupted Griffith's Triangle Studios.

11 ***HEAVEN'S GATE*** *(1980)*
Michael Cimino is blamed for single-handedly ending the golden age of '70s Hollywood auteurism with his infamous boondoggle *Heaven's Gate*, a four-hour, $44 million monument to creative indulgence and unfulfilled ambition. But imagine an alternate reality where *Heaven's Gate* turned out as grand as Cimino envisioned, a sort-of Western to end all Westerns that successfully married the epic majesty of David Lean with the brooding emotionalism of '60s European cinema. In that world, *Heaven's Gate* is one of the greatest films ever made, lauded for its stunning visuals even though the storytelling meanders to the point of incomprehension. But Cimino's standard for success was so maniacally high that the reality naturally fell short.

12 ***TITANIC*** *(1997)*
Before it won 11 Academy Awards and made more money than any film in history, *Titanic* had all the makings of

another *Heaven's Gate*. Like Michael Cimino, James Cameron was an ego-mad control freak who lorded over his cast and crew with the finesse of a military strongman. A penchant for perfectionism caused production delays that pushed back the release date nearly six months, which—coupled with the astronomical $200 million budget—fueled speculation that *Titanic* was a deeply troubled mess, helmed by an egotist reaching beyond his means. But Cameron, who modestly claimed that his magnum opus "could not have been written better," was vindicated in every conceivable way when *Titanic* went on to dominate pop culture—and the American box office, for 15 straight weeks.

13 HOGG *(1995)*

When groundbreaking novelist Samuel R. Delany began working on *Hogg*, he had just completed *Nova*, a book that led Algis Budrys to call him "the best science-fiction writer in the world." By the time he finished *Hogg*, he had also completed *Dhalgren*, a widely praised masterpiece. *Hogg* was... different. It lacked the genre trappings of his famous works, but more notably, its subject matter was beyond pornographic, even for the swinging '70s. Sexuality has always been a major theme in Delany's work, but *Hogg* went light-years further. The plot features a silent pre-adolescent boy (called only "cocksucker") sold into sexual slavery to a rapist named "Hogg" Hargus, who exposes him to the most extreme acts of deviancy imaginable. The overall sensation is compelling (Norman Mailer had high praise for the book) but hugely off-putting at every turn. No one would touch *Hogg* for more than 25 years, until it finally found a publisher in 1995; even then, it still caused shock ripples among Delany's readers.

14 JOHN FROM CINCINNATI *(2007)*

Producer David Milch had a lot of good will to spend after his brilliant, foul-mouthed Western-noir *Deadwood* wrapped up in 2006. But he didn't spend it so much as squander it on the impenetrable New Age surfer drama *John From Cincinnati*. At first, the show looked promising: Milch set up a great credit sequence, cobbled together a top-notch soundtrack, and brought in a raft of terrific actors, including *Deadwood* alums Garret Dillahunt, Jim Beaver, and Dayton Callie. HBO handed him the plum schedule spot right after *The Sopranos*, and a bigger budget than *The Wire* had during its entire run. But once it actually started running, so did audiences, and critics quickly lost patience with the series' baffling, train-wreck combination of family drama, mysticism, and petty crime. The main character levitated and traveled astrally, surfers smoked dope and schemed, and everyone who watched the show tried in vain to figure out what the hell was going on. After 10 episodes, the answer was "cancellation," and America went back to its *Deadwood* DVDs.

15 PEEPING TOM *(1960)*

Movie lovers can wring their hands all they like over the audience-implicating violence of *Funny Games*, but did director Michael Haneke really say anything that Michael Powell didn't say more artfully in 1960 with *Peeping Tom*? Working with screenwriter (and World War II cryptographer) Leo Marks, Powell dealt unflinchingly with the voyeuristic nature of filmmaking, telling the story of a cinematographer who kills women with a bayonet attached to his camera, then films them as they die. Powell and Marks used the premise to comment on sexual repression, the corrupting power of obsession, and the distancing effect of art, but the critics of the time saw *Peeping Tom* as a nasty little movie about a total perv. They condemned the film *and* Powell, effectively ending his two-decade run as an A-list director.

16 TUSK *(1979)*

The massive success of Fleetwood Mac's 1977 album *Rumours* bought the band time and their record label's indulgence in the quest to make the perfect follow-up. They took both. The resulting album was considered a flop because it failed to match *Rumours'* sales. (Few albums could.) Less a collaborative effort than a collection of solo tracks fussily produced by newly minted studio nerd Lindsey Buckingham, and laced with themes dredged up from the band's massive personal drama, it swaps *Rumours'* tense cohesiveness for a fractured, coked-out melancholy. But the years have taken the tarnish off an album that's now widely considered a classic on par with its more popular predecessor, proving that an act of madness can be revealed as genius with time.

GOTTA HAVE A GIMMICK

16-PLUS BOOKS BASED AROUND ODD LITERARY CONCEITS

1-3 NICK BANTOCK'S *GRIFFIN & SABINE TRILOGY* (1991-1993)

Nick Bantock's *Griffin & Sabine* books (*Griffin & Sabine, Sabine's Notebook, The Golden Mean*) are epistolary novels, which isn't anything new. But unlike *The Color Purple* and other books that unfold via correspondence, the three original *Griffin & Sabine* books are told through a series of letters that readers can physically open and unfold, which enhances the delicious sense of voyeurism. Many of the love letters Griffin Moss exchanges with his mysterious, telepathic pen pal Sabine Strohem are written in longhand and tucked inside actual envelopes pasted into the book, inviting readers to invade their privacy. Their private postcards are even more exposed, written out in Griffin's blocky scrawl or Sabine's flowy cursive hand. Their correspondence is visually as well as voyeuristically appealing; Griffin and Sabine are artists, and their letters and postcards feature beautiful, dark, and even disturbing sketches and paintings.

4 ITALO CALVINO'S *COSMICOMICS* (1965)

Calvino was a fabulist and postmodernist, responsible for novels and short stories that stretched the limits of the fiction form while still respecting the inherent virtues of character and narrative. In *Cosmicomics*, Calvino surveyed the dawn of creation and the varied wonders of the universe via a series of short stories told from the perspective of a single-celled organism, a dinosaur, a mathematical formula, and a land-dweller embarrassed by his ocean-dwelling uncle, among others. The concept takes some getting used to, but because Calvino grounded the stories in basic emotions like love, pride, jealousy, and shame, he made the fantastic relatable and the relatable fantastic.

5 ANDY WARHOL'S *A: A NOVEL* (1968)

Andy Warhol's Factory was dedicated to the idea that art could be reduced to a process, and even automated to some degree. Having applied this concept to painting, sculpture, and cinema, Warhol took a crack at literature, recording 24 hours of conversations between himself and Factory regular Ondine (taped over a two-year period), then submitting four separate transcriptions as the completed work, retaining all typos and inconsistencies. For Warhol, the art was in the errors, and the more he kept his hands off, the better the opportunity for magical mistakes.

6 GEORGES PEREC'S *A VOID* (1969)

The English title of Georges Perec's French novel *La Disparition* is a double pun, with both readings of the title—"a void" or "avoid"—referencing the same thing: The book was written entirely without the use of the letter "E." Like James Thurber's 1957 comic novel *The Wonderful O*, about a tyrant who bans the eponymous letter, *A Void* is self-aware and humorous about its key omission, but it also reads just fine as a novel, even though the syntax sometimes strains as Perec circumlocutes around key E-words. *A Void* is an ambitious metaphorical mystery, in which the letter stands in for a missing man, Anton Vowl, as well as the various friends and family members that people lose in a lifetime. Other authors have tried lipograms—works that consciously avoid one or more letters—but *A Void* is the best-known and the most accomplished.

7 GRAHAM RAWLE'S *WOMAN'S WORLD* (2005)

Graham Rawle probably understands that the trick of his novel is at least as important to readers as the actual story: The British writer outlined a book, then set about "writing" it using only clippings from 1960s women's magazines. *Woman's World* is as much a work of collage art as a novel—it's actually composed of the bits and pieces Rawle clipped out and hand-pasted on paper over the course of five years. It's a remarkable achievement, but also a little hard on the eyes, since it's like a 400-page ransom note. More importantly, there's nothing else quite like it.

8 WILLIAM GADDIS' *J R* (1975)

William Gaddis wrote difficult fiction. (So difficult, in fact, that Jonathan Franzen—a man some have accused of being a bit thorny himself—wrote an infamously cranky poison-pen letter to the recently deceased Gaddis in the pages of *The New Yorker*.) One of his overarching concerns was that modern man had been so poisoned by frivolity that he was incapable of the hard work of appreciating a profound novel; in *The Recognitions*, his first book, he made his point by interrupting the narrative with inane radio commercials. His novel *J R* ups the ante considerably. At more than 700 pages, the book—a savage satire of capitalism starring an 11-year-old boy who becomes a business tycoon by gaming the system—consists almost entirely of unattributed dialogue. It's fiendishly hard to keep track of what's happening, but incredibly rewarding; it won a National Book Award the year after its release, and it remains Gaddis' funniest and arguably best work.

9 STEVEN HALL'S *THE RAW SHARK TEXTS* (2007)

Steven Hall's intensely engaging debut novel proves that sometimes a thousand words can make a picture. In a weird world inhabited by "conceptual creatures" that can eat memories, words take on an incredible power to create and destroy. And the shark—called a Ludovician—that's pursuing the narrator eventually shows up not simply in description, but as a creature made up of text. About 50 pages of the book are given over to a flipbook in which an image of a shark made of words swims right at the reader.

10 ROBERT GRUDIN'S *BOOK: A NOVEL* (1992)

Robert Grudin isn't one of the most stylistically daring writers in modern fiction; in fact, his comic thriller *Book* is largely meant as a satire of literary postmodernism and its attendant stylistic trickery. Too bad for him that the most memorable part of the novel comes from its clever use of such trickery. The book itself isn't brilliant, but its enjoyable story about the attempted murder of a professor ranges between hilarious and reactionary as it parodies various trendy academic theories. About midway through the book, however, the novel's footnotes—which previously ranged between informative and impenetrable—begin making snarky commentaries on the text itself. Then they stage a revolt against the entire book, attempting to reclaim the body of the text for their interpretation of great literature. Sadly, they get brutally squashed, leaving only one footnote to guide readers through the rest of *Book*.

IT'S A REMARKABLE ACHIEVEMENT, BUT ALSO A LITTLE HARD ON THE EYES, SINCE IT'S LIKE A 400-PAGE RANSOM NOTE.

11 VLADIMIR NABOKOV'S *PALE FIRE* (1962)

Similarly, in Vladimir Nabokov's brilliant classic *Pale Fire*, the story is all in the notes, though in a different way. Roughly half the book is devoted to an introspective, melancholy, autobiographical 999-line epic poem by a celebrated American poet named John Shade. The other half is analysis and notes by irritating, intrusive fan Charles Kinbote, who gets his hands on Shade's last work upon Shade's death, and claims that Shade nominated him as editor and publisher. Kinbote's half of the book explains Shade's at great length, bending the poem's meanings to suit his own political agendas, and claiming it's all really about Kinbote himself. A great deal has been written about how *Pale Fire* was meant to be read, since it relies so heavily on an unreliable narrator and many aspects are open to interpretation. But these elaborate critical readings are fairly ironic, since the conflicting viewpoints of Nabokov's half-and-half novel seem to be wryly commenting on—and laughing at—the scholars who take it upon themselves to step in on an author's behalf and explain what he *really* meant.

12 MARK Z. DANIELEWSKI'S *HOUSE OF LEAVES* (2000)

Reading Mark Z. Danielewski's debut

novel is almost exactly like entering a funhouse mirror-maze; it quickly becomes difficult to determine which segments are the "real" book, and which are fictional reflections. In a frame story, a tattoo artist comes across a manuscript analyzing a documentary film about a strange house containing a seemingly infinite expanding space. As the tattooist reads it, he becomes obsessed with it and mirrors some of the behavior of its neurotic, dead author. Soon, it becomes clear that the manuscript he's reading is the book *House Of Leaves* itself. While the frame is fictional, the manuscript presents itself as nonfictional, and frequently references real-world books, events, and personalities. Copious interlocked and stacking footnotes further confuse the issue by adding information, sometimes in the form of lists or stories that go on for pages at a time, carving out shapes in the middle of pages. Then other authorial voices and typographic tricks intrude: Some pages only feature a word or two, to keep readers flipping breathlessly during a chase scene, while other pages crowd all the text to the top or bottom or sides to reflect how characters are feeling. Part hypertext, part picturebook made entirely of words, *House Of Leaves* could just as well be called *House Of Cards*: It's an elaborate construct that demands a lot of focus and effort, but ultimately feels airy and fragile.

13-14 B.S. JOHNSON'S *ALBERT ANGELO* (1964) AND *THE UNFORTUNATES* (1969)

The late English novelist B.S. Johnson took literature seriously, and was endlessly frustrated that the novel failed to progress beyond its traditional boundaries. "Why do so many novelists still write as though the revolution that was *Ulysses* never happened, still rely on the crutch of storytelling?" he asked in his memoirs. Johnson never considered his daring experimental touches to be gimmicks; to him, they were ways to move the art of literature forward to where he thought it should be. In *Albert Angelo*, his autobiographical second novel, a hole was cut through the book, partly to reveal an event later in the story that he wanted readers to know about early on, and partly to encourage nonlinear reading. He didn't stop there; a later novel, *The Unfortunates*, was bound into 27 sections. Apart from the first and last chapter, readers were told to scatter the rest of the sections and read them in any order—they made a coherent narrative regardless of how they were assembled.

15 RAYMOND QUENEAU'S *EXERCISES IN STYLE* (1947)

Many of the books on this list can trace their existence back to the Oulipo movement co-founded by daring French experimentalist Raymond Queneau. He and his collaborators —Georges Perec and Italo Calvino among them—were early masters of formalism, and enjoyed assigning each other writing projects characterized by restrictive, arbitrary rules just to see what they could do with them. The most concise—and possibly greatest—example was Queneau's own *Exercises In Style*, in which he tells a simple story (a bus passenger sees a bizarre-looking man snap at another man on a bus) 99 times. The brilliance of the book is how it tells the story in so many compelling ways: a news story, a blurb for a novel, a mathematical formula, a sonnet, an opera. The book was translated into more than a dozen languages, and could serve as a textbook on writing and rhetoric in any of them.

16+ WILLIAM S. BURROUGHS' CUT-UP NOVELS

William S. Burroughs was no stranger to experimentalism, even in his early days; *Naked Lunch* substantially upped the Beats' surrealist quotient and helped infuse American literature with the kind of daring avant-garde work that had previously strictly been the purview of Europeans. By the early '60s, though, inspired by the poet Brion Gysin, he had moved even further into the abstract, writing what are usually referred to as "cut-up" novels. Using hand-cut bits and pieces of newspapers, magazines, and pulp novels, Burroughs didn't so much write books like *The Soft Machine*, *Nova Express*, and *The Ticket That Exploded* as he assembled them. The books contain original writing by Burroughs folded into the cut-up sections, which are, as is sometimes the case with experimental art, more interesting to hear about than to actually experience. But they perfectly complement the narratives' edgy postmodern feel, and occasionally yield word combinations that are lovely or unsettling.

Law & Order: SVU | cotton candy | *Beverly Hills, 90210* marathons | pre-*Sex And The City* Sarah Jessica Parker

I LIKE SHORT SONGS

100 KILLER SONGS CLOCKING IN AT TWO MINUTES OR LESS

1 **Andrew W.K.,** "It's Time To Party" (1:30)
2 **Austin Lounge Lizards,** "Chester Nimitz Oriental Garden Waltz" (1:53)
3 **Bad Brains,** "Rock For Light" (1:36)
4 **Bad Religion,** "No Control" (1:47)
5 **The Beach Boys,** "Little Honda" (1:48)
6 **The Beatles,** "Do You Want To Know A Secret" (1:59)
7 **Belle & Sebastian,** "Simple Things" (1:46)
8 **Big Star,** "I'm In Love With A Girl" (1:48)
9 **Bikini Kill,** "Statement Of Vindication" (1:11)
10 **Black Flag,** "Police Story" (1:32)
11 **Bob Dylan,** "Oxford Town" (1:50)
12 **The Boo Radleys,** "Lazy Day" (1:38)
13 **Born Against,** "Eulogy" (1:39)
14 **Brakes,** "Heard About Your Band" (1:31)
15 **Brian Eno,** "Another Green World" (1:51)
16 **Buddy Holly,** "Think It Over" (1:48)
17 **Buzzcocks,** "Love You More" (1:49)
18 **Captain Beefheart,** "Frownland" (1:41)
19 **Circle Jerks,** "Red Tape" (0:55)
20 **The Clash,** "White Riot" (1:58)
21 **Crass,** "Do They Owe Us A Living?" (1:22)
22 **The Damned,** "Machine Gun Etiquette" (1:49)
23 **Daniel Johnston,** "True Love Will Find You In The End"(1:47)
24 **Dead Kennedys,** "Nazi Punks Fuck Off" (0:58)
25 **Death Cab For Cutie,** "Steadier Footing" (1:47)
26 **Dicks,** "Hate The Police" (1:59)
27 **Dinosaur Jr.,** "I Live For That Look" (1:56)
28 **Eef Barzelay,** "Little Red Dot" (1:11)
29 **Elastica,** "Annie" (1:13)
30 **Elvis Costello,** "Mystery Dance" (1:37)
31 **Elvis Presley,** "All Shook Up" (1:57)
32 **The Fall,** "Prole Art Threat" (1:58)
33 **The Frogs,** "Who's Sucking On Grampa's Balls Since Grandma Ain't Home Tonight?" (0:11)
34 **Fugazi,** "Back To Base" (1:45)
35 **The Germs,** "Lexicon Devil" (1:44)
36 **Guided By Voices,** "Game Of Pricks" (1:33)

Law & Order: Criminal Intent | cotton-candy-flavored lip gloss | *Dr. 90210* marathons | post-*Sex And The City* Sarah Jessica Parker

37 **The Horrors,** "Sheena Is A Parasite" (1:42)
38 **Hüsker Dü,** "Something I Learned Today" (1:58)
39 **The Jam,** "Boy About Town" (1:59)
40 **Janis Joplin,** "Mercedes Benz" (1:46)
41 **Jawbreaker,** "Boxcar" (1:54)
42 **Jay Reatard,** "It's So Easy" (1:06)
43 **Jay-Z,** "Friend Or Foe" (1:49)
44 **Jenny Lewis,** "Run Devil Run" (1:06)
45 **Jerry Lee Lewis,** "Great Balls Of Fire" (1:54)
46 **Jimi Hendrix,** "Ain't No Telling" (1:50)
47 **Jonathan Coulton,** "Mr. Fancy Pants" (1:19)
48 **The Lemonheads,** "Bit Part" (1:52)
49 **Lifter Puller,** "Candy's Room" (1:54)
50 **Los Campesinos!,** "My Year In Lists" (1:49)
51 **Low,** "Streetlight" (0:33)
52 **Madvillain,** "Curls" (1:36)
53 **The Magnetic Fields,** "Reno Dakota" (1:05)
54 **Maurice Williams & The Zodiacs,** "Stay" (1:34)
55 **Meat Puppets,** "Lake Of Fire" (1:57)
56 **Minor Threat,** "Screaming At A Wall" (1:32)
57 **Minutemen,** "Political Song For Michael Jackson To Sing" (1:31)
58 **Misfits,** "Skulls" (1:56)
59 **Mission Of Burma,** "This Is Not A Photograph" (1:57)
60 **Modest Mouse,** "Space Travel Is Boring" (1:54)
61 **Murs And 9th Wonder,** "Murs Day" (1:54)
62 **Nation Of Ulysses,** "A Kid Who Tells On Another Kid Is A Dead Kid" (1:43)
63 **Neil Young,** "Till The Morning Comes" (1:21)
64 **Neutral Milk Hotel,** "Communist Daughter" (1:57)
65 **Nirvana,** "Been A Son" (1:56)
66 **Operation Ivy,** "Knowledge" (1:42)
67 **Pavement,** "Zurich Is Stained" (1:42)
68 **Pixies,** "Tame" (1:55)

"Stay" by Maurice Williams & The Zodiacs is the shortest No. 1 ever recorded.

69 **Porter Wagoner And Dolly Parton,** "We'll Get Ahead Some Day" (1:59)
70 **Prince,** "Sister" (1:32)
71 **The Promise Ring,** "Between Pacific Coasts" (1:51)
72 **The Raincoats,** "No Side To Fall In" (1:50)
73 **Ramones,** "Judy Is A Punk" (1:30)
74 **Randy Newman,** "Dayton, Ohio 1903" (1:52)
75 **The Rezillos,** "Somebody's Gonna Get Their Head Kicked In Tonight" (1:58)
76 **Rocket From The Crypt,** "Middle" (1:02)
77 **The Rolling Stones,** "She Said Yeah" (1:35)
78 **Scott Walker,** "30 Century Man" (1:30)
79 **The Shins,** "Weird Divide" (1:58)
80 **Simon And Garfunkel,** "April, Come She Will" (1:51)
81 **Slayer,** "Necrophobic" (1:41)
82 **Sloan,** "Will I Belong?" (1:20)
83 **The Smiths,** "Please Please Please Let Me Get What I Want" (1:51)
84 **Sonic Youth,** "Nic Fit" (0:59)
85 **Sparklehorse,** "Heart Of Darkness" (1:51)
86 **Spoon,** "Car Radio" (1:29)
87 **The Suburbs,** "Cows" (1:36)
88 **Terrance & Phillip,** "Uncle Fucka" (1:08)
89 **They Might Be Giants,** "Particle Man" (1:59)
90 **Tokyo Police Club,** "Cheer It On" (1:59)
91 **Tom Waits,** "Frank's Wild Years" (1:53)
92 **Van Halen,** "Eruption" (1:43)
93 **The Vaselines,** "Molly's Lips" (1:44)
94 **Ween,** "I'm Dancing In The Show Tonight" (1:55)
95 **The White Stripes,** "Little Room" (0:50)
96 **Willie Nelson,** "Troublemaker" 1:54
97 **Wire,** "Outdoor Miner" (1:44)
98 **X,** "Back 2 The Base" (1:33)
99 **Yo La Tengo,** "86-Second Blowout" (1:32)
100 **Young Marble Giants,** "Final Day" (1:43)

"I Like Short Songs" is a Dead Kennedys song that simply repeats the title 13 times.

RARE READS

17 BOOKS WE WISH WERE STILL IN PRINT

1 GUSTAV HASFORD, *THE PHANTOM BLOOPER* (1990)

Gustav Hasford emerged from the Vietnam War as an insightful, compelling writer, and a troubled individual. Those qualities were evident in his first book, *The Short-Timers*, a dark, gripping collection of stories from his time overseas; it soon formed the basis of the screenplay to Stanley Kubrick's *Full Metal Jacket*. But the story doesn't end there: Three years after he was nominated for an Oscar for the *Full Metal Jacket* script, he completed the sequel to *The Short-Timers*, an astonishing, deeply felt novel called *The Phantom Blooper*. The book follows the further adventures of the cynical grunt (and Hasford stand-in) Private Joker as he deals with the death of his fellow jarheads, rumors of the Phantom Blooper (a renegade Marine who supposedly fights on the side of the Viet Cong), and his own eventual capture by the enemy, whose ways he can no longer distinguish from his own. A compelling, terrific novel and one of the fiercest condemnations of the Vietnam War ever written, *The Phantom Blooper* is available on Hasford's website (run by his nephew), but it makes for difficult reading due to the site design and the white-on-black typography. The book itself has been out of print for more than a decade.

2 JAMES PARK, *ICONS* (1992)

It's never been clear exactly why the hugely enjoyable reference book *Icons*—originally published in Britain as *Cultural Icons*—disappeared so quickly. However, early editions of the book carried Warhol-esque portraits of a number of the figures profiled within, while later ones featured generic blank cutouts with names pasted over them, suggesting that there may have been issues with the art. Whatever the cause, it's a great book: Film writer James Park gathered a group of British authors to compile brief-but-punchy biographies of major cultural figures from the postwar era. An international cast of "the people who shaped our time," from politicians to fashion designers to philosophers to musicians, are given engaging, sometimes contentious mini-biographies in what reads like a hipper version of Larousse's *Biographical Dictionary*. There's even a fun set of clever visual symbols accompanying each bio, like a set of quote marks for self-publicists, a black triangle for downbeat or depressing figures, and a thumbs-down symbol for those who've fallen out of fashion. *Icons* is a bit dated by now, but an updated version would be hugely welcome.

3 OCTAVIA BUTLER, *SURVIVOR* (1978)

Octavia Butler wrote a couple of clunkers alongside her science-fiction classics *Kindred* and *Bloodchild*, but the one novel she disowned, *Survivor*, is far from her worst. While she reportedly dismissed it as a thinly veiled *Star Trek* novel, it's an absorbing alien-encounter story that highlights her usual themes of forced interdependence, unwilling assimilation, personal-dominance wars, and other emotional offshoots of slavery. On a distant planet, two native sects struggle for control, and one decides that the recently arrived group of human missionaries will make an effective weapon, once they're brought under control via a secret addiction to a local food additive. An outcast from the human group—one of few individuals to survive withdrawal from the additive—proves key in sorting out the situation, but as with all Butler novels, there's a painful, ugly cost for everyone involved. Butler's awareness of the book's Trekkie inspirations may have blinded her to its stronger qualities—

it's unmistakably an early experiment for her, but the characters, her alien society, and the emotional stresses they endure are all vivid and compelling, and *Survivor* is well worth revisiting.

4 RUSSELL H. GREENAN, *THE SECRET LIFE OF ALGERNON PENDLETON* (1973)

Acclaimed but little-known writer Russell H. Greenan has published 10 novels since 1968, but good luck finding most of them. His most famous, *It Happened In Boston?*, is a richly textured tale of a world-class art forger who will do anything to meet God; in 2003, it was reissued at Jonathan Lethem's behest, as part of a "20th Century Rediscoveries" series, but the others have yet to receive a similar second look. Even a film version of Greenan's *The Secret Life Of Algernon Pendleton*, released in 1997 and starring *The Matrix's* Carrie-Anne Moss, didn't lead to a "Now a major motion picture" reprint of the book, though no one needs a cinematic excuse to enjoy *Pendleton*. Sly, clever, abundantly detailed, macabre, and at times funny, *The Secret Life Of Algernon Pendleton* centers around the great-great-grandson of a well-known Egyptologist who may or may not be crazy. It's crime fiction, in that several crimes (including a dog murder) are committed. And it's a thriller, in that Greenan's storytelling never hesitates to ratchet up the suspense. But *The Secret Life Of Algernon Pendleton*, like its endearing, intense, possibly insane narrator, isn't so easily classified.

5 JOHNNY CASH, *MAN IN BLACK: HIS OWN STORY IN HIS OWN WORDS* (1976)

Twenty years before *Cash: The Autobiography*—Johnny Cash's second try at a memoir, and the one that's still in print—the country legend wrote (in longhand!) an account of his life to date. There's no question that *Man In Black* is the product of the man in black himself; written before celebrity ghostwriters became widespread, it features his simple style and straightforward approach to storytelling. It's an intensely spiritual work, but that shouldn't scare readers away: The man once known as "God's superstar" isn't the type to strut around in his Christianity, expecting to be congratulated for his superior moral standing. Cash presents his relationship with God with a true respect for salvation, and his principled stance on issues like labor, poverty, racism, and the Vietnam War are in perfect sync with his religious views. A combined set of *Man In Black* and *Cash* would be most welcome; Johnny Cash had enough stories to fill a dozen books.

6 MARSHALL BLONSKY, *AMERICAN MYTHOLOGIES* (1992)

The most prominent American protégé of brilliant French critic and philosopher Roland Barthes, Marshall Blonsky broke out on his own with a book explicitly patterned after his mentor's groundbreaking work, *Mythologies*. Blonsky was hoping to do for the symbolically charged maze of American popular culture what Barthes did for the French, though *American Mythologies*—released in a fancy glossy hardback edition, with a leering pink portrait of Marilyn Monroe on the cover—wasn't an entirely successful copy of *Mythologies*; Blonsky's essays were much longer, more personal and more wide-ranging than those of Barthes. But they were still highly enjoyable, and in several essays—especially on Italian fashion designers and mobster capitalism—very insightful. Unfortunately, the American public was about as interested in semiotic analysis back then as it is now, which is to say, not at all, and the book bombed. Blonsky went on to write some entertaining essays for the late, lamented *Spy* magazine—including a memorable treatise on the use of Barthesian codes in *Beverly Hills 90210*—that were basically shorter, livelier versions of his *American Mythologies* pieces.

7 PIERRE BOILEAU & THOMAS NARCEJAC, *THE WOMAN WHO WAS NO MORE* (1952)

As "Boileau-Narcejac," the writing team of Pierre Boileau and Pierre Ayraud (a.k.a. Thomas Narcejac) were two of the most successful authors of detective fiction in French history, considered the peers of Americans Frederic Dannay, Manfred Lee, and Cornell Woolrich. Their first major collabora-

tion, *Celle Qui N'Était Plus*, was a huge success in France, and it immediately started a bidding war between movie studios for the right to adapt it. The winner—by a matter of hours—was Henri-Georges Clouzot, who went on to make a tremendously suspenseful adaptation of the book under the name *Diabolique*. While French-language editions are still commonly available, the English translation has long been out of print, and it's extremely hard to find, with copies fetching up to $5,000. The pair later compensated Alfred Hitchcock, who came out on the losing end of the bidding war, by writing the book *D'Entre Les Morts* especially for him; it later became his film *Vertigo*. But seeing *The Woman Who Was No More* back in print in English would be a treat: It's more lurid and brutal than Clouzot's film adaptation, with a very different twist, and a sexually charged pulp atmosphere that the film only hints at.

A.V. CLUB

Frederic Dannay and Manfred Lee were another writing team that collaborated on detective books... under the name Ellery Queen.

8 VICTOR "TRADER VIC" BERGERON, *TRADER VIC'S PACIFIC ISLAND COOKBOOK, WITH SIDE TRIPS TO HONG KONG, SOUTHEAST ASIA, MEXICO, AND TEXAS* (1968)

Victor "Trader Vic" Bergeron was an American original. A legendary bartender, restaurateur, and world traveler, he took the lead in bringing tiki culture to America after World War II. And even more than his chain of restaurants, his numerous cookbooks and drinks guides are a testament to what a unique character he was. Like his other books (all likewise out of print, including *Trader Vic's Kitchen Kibitzer* and *Trader Vic's Helluva Man's Cookbook*), *Pacific Island Cookbook* contains plenty of enjoyable recipes, but the real treats are the little personal anecdotes and reminiscences. A complete Rat Pack-era throwback, Trader Vic writes in a hilarious mélange of he-man tough talk, '50s hipster argot, and swinger-jive, as if Frank Sinatra had become a gourmet chef instead of a pop singer. At times, it almost reads like a parody of a womanizing, freewheeling hepcat, except that Bergeron really was a womanizing, freewheeling hepcat. Though the ebb and flow of public interest in tiki culture led to the closing of many of his restaurants in recent years, tiki is resurgent again. Hopefully the plans to open new branches will renew interest in the late Bergeron's books and bring them back into print.

9-11 DANNY PEARY, *CULT MOVIES I-III* (1981-1988)

Danny Peary's three *Cult Movies* books were a godsend for budding cinephiles eager to swim out beyond the safe waters of Oscar-endorsed fare and into stranger, murkier, often more exhilarating territory. Covering 150 films, Peary showed an impressive lack of snobbery, taking on Hollywood classics like *Rio Bravo* and *It's A Wonderful Life* along with bizarre obscurities such as *El Topo* and *Trash*, on the way to compiling his alternative history of 20th-century cinema. Sadly, the book's striking black-and-white stills and Peary's brilliantly concise yet illuminating summaries were the closest many viewers came to actually seeing some of these hard-to-find movies. Now that lost gems like *The Honeymoon Killers* and *Targets* are within easy reach of anyone with an Internet connection and a few bucks to blow, Peary's books are even more relevant for the dedicated filmhound.

12-14 RICHARD STARK, *SLAYGROUND, PLUNDER SQUAD,* AND *BUTCHER'S MOON* (1971-1974)

Under the pen name of Richard Stark, crime novelist Donald E. Westlake created one of the genre's most hard-boiled anti-heroes in the cold, rational, often brutal master thief known only as Parker. Stark enjoyed a great run with Parker in the 1960s and '70s, writing 16 novels chronicling his violent path through the criminal underground, starting with 1963's *The Hunter* (later re-titled *Point Blank*, then *Payback* to fall in line with its movie adaptations). But Westlake hit a creative wall after 1974's *Butcher's Moon*, and was unable to write in Stark's voice anymore. Parker simply "went away for 23 years," as Westlake described it, and the Stark series largely fell out of print. Things remained that way until Westlake was hired to adapt the script for the 1990 movie *The Grifters* from Jim Thompson's novel, a particularly hard-edged con-artist tale that unlocked Westlake's mental block to Stark. That led to a new Parker novel, 1997's appropriately titled *Comeback*, as well as the otherwise terrible Mel Gibson movie *Payback*, both of which rejuvenated interest in the earlier Stark books. Many of them are now back in print for the first time in years, but the latter part of Parker's first run is still MIA. That's a shame, since it contains some of the series' most ambitious writing, including the loosely connected final trilogy *Slayground*, *Plunder Squad*, and *Butcher's Moon*.

15 CAMERON CROWE, *FAST TIMES AT RIDGEMONT HIGH* (1981)

It's no great wonder that the book that inspired Amy Heckerling's beloved teen-sex romp *Fast Times At Ridgemont High* is out of print; in many ways, it's clumsy and amateurish. And yet it comes out of such a brilliant concept… After a couple of years as a young hotshot writer for the likes of *Rolling Stone* and *Creem*, Cameron Crowe hit upon an idea suited to today's stunt-journalism bestsellers: He went back to school and pretended to be an 18-year-old senior for a year, so he could observe and chronicle modern teen life in all its druggy, sexed-up glory. Like the film adaptation, the book he wrote about the experience is a series of vignettes about senior year. But while the movie accurately brings an assortment of those vignettes to the screen, it skipped a large percentage of them for time's sake. Crowe's book is like a collection of DVD deleted scenes, with many more tales of Spicoli, Rat, Stacy and Brad Hamilton, Charles Jefferson (who got short shrift in the film), and some memorable characters who didn't even make it to celluloid. For people more familiar with the film, the book could almost be re-released as *Fast Times At Ridgemont High: The Expanded Adventures*.

16 J.G. BALLARD, *HIGH RISE* (1975)

In his 1962 science-fiction novel *The Drowned World*, J.G. Ballard first visited the idea of people living in the ruins of apartment high-rises. By 1975, having already redrawn the lines of postmodern fiction with *The Atrocity Exhibition* and *Crash*, Ballard returned to that pulpy motif in *High Rise*. But instead of *The Drowned World's* overt post-apocalypse, *High Rise* internalizes the human race's inexorable struggle toward extinction. In a hazy near future, a divorcée moves into a state-of-the-art 40-story apartment building—practically a *Titanic* frozen in mid-sink—with a population of 2,000 and enough shops and schools to make it a self-contained society. As alienation and petty internecine warfare spirals into catastrophe, the building's veneer of civilization warps and blisters; Ballard has said *High Rise* came from his childhood memories of being detained in a Japanese internment camp in China during World War II, a trauma he later probed in his fictionalized autobiography, *Empire Of The Sun*. Like many of Ballard's great novels, *High Rise* has long been out of print in America, although a beautiful edition was issued in England in 2006.

17 THOMAS DISCH, *THE PRIEST* (1994)

Thomas Disch prefaces *The Priest* with a dedication to Father Bruce Ritter, Reverend Alphonsus L. Penney, and a litany of other clergymen convicted of molesting children—then ends the list with Pope John Paul II, "without whose ministry and conjoint power of example this novel could not have been written." Yes, *The Priest* is a novel about a dirty man of God. But it's far from a snatched-from-the-headlines work of exploitation. Disch, a groundbreaking science-fiction writer (and the creator of *The Brave Little Toaster*) who turned to horror in the '80s, used his loathing of the Catholic faith to fuel his tale of fictitious pedophile Father Patrick Bryce. True to Disch's jaundiced view of religion—no doubt influenced by his experiences in Catholic schools—Father Bryce descends into a hell of his own making that's at least as sadistic and imaginative as anything threatened by the Bible. Disch committed suicide in July 2008 at age 68, and the tragically meager outpouring of tribute that followed his death doesn't bode well for the future of his largely out-of-print catalog.

Sigg | postmillennialism | DRM hysteria | Halloween, the holiday

CHICKEN SALAD BETWEEN THE KNEES

16 FILM AND TV CHARACTERS WHO KNOW EXACTLY WHAT THEY'D LIKE TO EAT

1 LARRY DAVID, *CURB YOUR ENTHUSIASM'S* "TRICK OR TREAT" *(2001)*

In typical Larry David fashion, nothing can be easy—not even ordering a salad. Instead of building his own, David orders a Cobb salad with so many changes—"no bacon, no eggs, blue cheese on the side… add cucumber if you can"—that his friends suggest he doesn't really want a Cobb salad at all. He proudly proclaims that it's a David salad, setting the rest of the episode—about the controversial inventor of the real Cobb salad—in motion.

2 STEVE MARTIN, *L.A. STORY (1991)*

In a movie that sweetly skewers Los Angeles life, one silly scene stands out: A group of La-la-landers orders increasingly silly coffee drinks, capped by Steve Martin's deadpan "I'll have a half double decaffeinated half-caf, with a twist of lemon." Naturally, the rest of the table has to add lemon as well. (Eww.)

3 DANNY DEVITO, *GET SHORTY (1995)*

In another "Isn't L.A. ridiculous?" moment, Danny DeVito's hotshot actor character refuses to order off the menu at a restaurant. "I feel like an omelet," he tells the server—but not just any omelet. "Can you make an egg-white omelet, but with shallots, but with the shallots only slightly browned, very little olive oil, and no salt? Why don't you bring one for the table, and we'll pick on it. Oh, I know, how about having those strawberry frappés, you know, little drinks with little strawberries in them?" In further keeping with his diva attitude, he then takes off before the food arrives, leaving everyone at his lunch meeting stuck with his ultra-specific made-up meal, and the bill for it.

Nutrition Facts

Serving Size: 1 Film or TV Show

Amount Per Serving	
Calories 5,000	Calories from Fat 4,999
	% Daily Value
Utter Pretentiousness 300g	**200%**
Showy Pomposity 40g	**80%**
OCD 122mg	**30%**
Clever Cluelessness 13g	**18%**
Probable Eating Disorder 9g	**12%**
Loveable Quirkiness 1g	**2%**
General Self-Absorption 135g	**77%**
Insufferability 480g	**325%**

4 JACK NICHOLSON, *FIVE EASY PIECES (1970)*

Jack Nicholson ordering breakfast in *Five Easy Pieces* is often taken out of context as silly, but it's really another instance of his character simmering with frustration. When he can't get wheat toast in a diner where it isn't on the menu, he specifies: "I'd like an omelet, plain, and a chicken-salad sandwich on wheat toast. No mayonnaise, no butter, no lettuce. And a cup of coffee… Now all you have to do is hold the chicken." When the scornful waitress who denied him toast looks at him askance, he spells it out further: "I want you to hold it between your knees." (Seriously, though, is there a diner in the world that doesn't sell plain wheat toast?)

5 MEG RYAN, *WHEN HARRY MET SALLY (1989)*

The running gag about Meg Ryan's eating habits as Sally was supposedly

Dasani | premillennialism | Y2K hysteria | *Halloween 3: Season Of The Witch* inspired by screenwriter Nora Ephron, and didn't appear in the original script. When she says she likes her meals exactly how she likes them, she isn't kidding: "I'd like the chef's salad, please, with the oil and vinegar on the side, and the apple pie à la mode. But I'd like the pie heated, and I don't want the ice cream on top, I want it on the side, and I'd like strawberry instead of vanilla if you have it. If not, then no ice cream, just whipped cream, but only if it's real. If it's out of the can, then nothing… just the pie, but then not heated." Gah. How even a useless mope like Harry could find this control-freak routine endearing, only Ephron knows.

6 KYLE MACLACHLAN, *TWIN PEAKS* (1990-1991)

When Kyle MacLachlan's Special Agent Dale Cooper rolls into Twin Peaks, nearly everything about his character not announced by his squeaky-clean appearance and impeccable manners gets spelled out by the lengthy, almost monotonal prepared speech he uses to order his preferred breakfast, which includes two eggs over hard ("I know, don't tell me, it's hard on the arteries, but old habits die hard, just about as hard as I want those eggs"), bacon cooked "super-crispy," and grapefruit juice. It's an all-American breakfast for an all-American man who just happens to be extremely particular and just a little off-center. Over hard? Grapefruit juice? Who is this guy?

7-8 DAN AYKROYD AND JOHN BELUSHI, *THE BLUES BROTHERS* (1980)

When Jake and Elwood Blues enter a Chicago diner looking to reclaim Matt "Guitar" Murphy from his life as a short-order cook, they don't have to announce themselves. The waitress—played by none other than Aretha Franklin—simply has to relay what they look like ("Hasidic diamond merchants") and, more importantly, what they'd like to eat, and Murphy recognizes them, sight unseen. For tall, skinny Dan Aykroyd, it's dry white toast. For John Belushi, it's four whole fried chickens and a Coke.

9 BARBRA STREISAND, *WHAT'S UP, DOC?* (1972)

In Peter Bogdanovich's charming 1972 screwball comedy, Barbra Streisand plays a Manic Pixie Dream Girl-cum-grifter who's down on her luck. Happily, she's developed a hustle that serves her well whenever she's within walking distance of a fine hotel and feeling hungry: She calls room service from a pay phone, orders a meal, and asks for the food to be left outside "her" room so as not to wake her sleeping baby. She then hangs out in the hallway, waiting for the tray to be dropped off, whereupon she snags it and feasts at her leisure. As scams go, it isn't very realistic—someone's gotta sign for all that food, after all—but her order is memorable nonetheless: "I would like a double-thick roast-beef sandwich, medium rare, on rye bread, with mustard on the top, mayonnaise on the bottom, and a coffee hot-fudge sundae with a bottle of Diet Anything. You got that?" Clearly beggars *can* be choosers.

10-11 WARREN BEATTY AND JULIE CHRISTIE, *McCABE & MRS. MILLER* (1971)

As played by Julie Christie, the frontier madam Mrs. Miller conveys a sense of refinement, albeit one limited by life on the American frontier. Seeking sustenance, she checks to see if the eggs are fresh, then demands "four eggs, fried, some stew, and I want some strong tea." As her partner and sometime lover, Warren Beatty's McCabe is less demanding, asking for his usual "double whiskey and a raw egg," which he eats mixed together. Why waste any time?

12 HANK AZARIA, *THE SIMPSONS'* "THE DUMBBELL INDEMNITY" (1998)

Poor pitiful bartender Moe can't get a date to save his life, so when he finally lands one with the girl from the flower stand, he wants to impress her with his fine-dining ordering skills. "Hey, hey Sabu. I need another magnum of your best champagne here. And bring us the finest food you got, stuffed with the second-finest." (The joke's on Moe, of course, as the waiter promises "lobster stuffed with tacos.")

13 JASON ALEXANDER, *SEINFELD'S* "THE OPPOSITE" (1994)

George Costanza is so hopeless, he doesn't even realize that a complete, life-changing turnaround just leads him to the same place. When he snaps and decides he wants the opposite of what hasn't been working, and seals the deal with a streak-breaking food order, he doesn't even realize that it's still pretty close to business as usual: "I *always* have tuna on toast. Nothing's ever worked out for me with tuna on toast. I want the *complete opposite* of tuna on toast.

Chicken salad, on *rye*, *untoasted*, with a side of *potato salad*, and a cup of *tea*! Ha!"

14-16 THE MARX BROTHERS, *A NIGHT AT THE OPERA* (1935)

Steward: "You might have some tomato juice, orange juice, grape juice, pineapple juice..."
Groucho Marx: "Hey, turn off the juice before I get electrocuted. All right, let me have one of each. And two fried eggs, two poached eggs, two scrambled eggs, and two medium-boiled eggs."
Chico Marx: "And two hard-boiled eggs."
Groucho: "And two hard-boiled eggs."
Harpo Marx: [Honks horn.]
Groucho: "Make that three hard-boiled eggs. And some roast beef, rare, medium, well-done, and overdone."
Chico: "And two hard-boiled eggs."
Groucho: "And two hard-boiled eggs."
Harpo: [Honks horn.]
Groucho: "Make that three hard-boiled eggs. And eight pieces of French pastry."
Chico: "With two hard-boiled eggs."
Groucho: "And two hard-boiled eggs."
Harpo: [Honks horn.]
Groucho: "Make that three hard-boiled eggs."
Harpo: [Makes quacking noise with horn.]
Groucho: "And one duck egg. Have you got any stewed prunes?... Well, give 'em some black coffee, that'll sober them up."
Chico: "And two hard-boiled eggs."
Groucho: "And two hard-boiled eggs."
Harpo: [Honks horn repeatedly at length.]
Groucho: "It's either foggy out, or make that 12 more hard-boiled eggs."

ALL'S SWELL THAT ENDS WELL

10 AMERICAN TV SERIES WITH SATISFYING ENDINGS

1 *ARRESTED DEVELOPMENT* *(2003-2006)*

One more reason for Americans to envy Britain: short, planned-out TV series that often form a complete story arc, then definitively end. By contrast, most American shows are designed to stay on the air as long as possible, which puts writers under pressure to keep character dynamics static for years, or string out mysteries endlessly, teasing viewers with revelations that never come. When those viewers finally jump ship, shows are often cut off ignominiously, or left open-ended in hopes of film spin-offs and sequels. All of which means that few American series ever reach a definitive, meaningful end-point. One surprising exception is Mitchell Hurwitz's critically beloved, ratings-blah wacky family comedy *Arrested Development*, which was rescheduled, cancelled, rescued, and put on possibly-permanent-we-don't-know hiatus so many times that it's a wonder the writers recognized the axe when it finally fell. Nonetheless, they managed a hilarious final episode that not only provided closure for many dangling plot threads, but also closely paralleled the first episode, making the whole series seem almost like one carefully planned, coherent piece.

2 *NEWHART* *(1982-1990)*

For most of its eight-year run, Bob Newhart's second great sitcom (following *The Bob Newhart Show*, which ran from 1972 to 1978) sure didn't seem like it was working from any kind of a plan. While clever and funny, and with one of the all-time great TV ensemble casts, it had its ups and downs, cast changes, continuity hiccups, and all the other traits that define American situation comedy. But *Newhart's* series finale, "The Last Newhart," virtually defines "satisfying ending." Fed up with his fellow townsfolk's latest insane whim, Newhart announces that he's leaving for good, only to get pelted in the dome by an errant golf ball and wake up in bed next to Suzanne Pleshette, in a perfect echo of innumerable classic scenes from *The Bob Newhart Show*, where Pleshette played his wife. The brilliant twist of turning one of the cheapest, most despised cop-outs in all of storytelling—the "it was all a dream" ending—into a perfectly realized bit of meta-humor cemented "The Last Newhart" as one of the best series finales of all time.

3 *CHEERS* (1982-1993)

It seemed like every beloved TV show post-*M*A*S*H* was required to have a really long, bloated, "event" finale episode, and *Cheers* was no exception. The last installment not only pushed beyond the 90-minute mark, it was preceded by a retrospective "pre-game" special hosted by Bob Costas. Fortunately, the consummate professionalism that marked *Cheers'* writing during its 11-season run followed through to the end. The funny, poignant final episode brought back original (and best) leading lady Diane (Shelley Long) to once again revive her romance with recovering sex addict Sam (Ted Danson). Ultimately, their love wasn't meant to be—for sure this time, apparently—and Sam ends up dropping his plan to sell Cheers and move to California. Back with his only true love, Sam walks not into the sunset, but into the darkness of his back room at closing time, a surprisingly moving final image for one of the most consistently funny sitcoms ever.

4 *THE WIRE* (2002-2008)

Those left unfulfilled by the actually pretty-fulfilling end to HBO's *The Sopranos* had nothing to complain about at the close of *The Wire*'s five-season run. Each character in this massive story was given some type of closure—not all positive, of course, but no loose threads were left dangling. Creator David Simon even used the series' last five minutes to present a montage that flash-forwarded slightly, letting viewers know not just where things stood, but where they were headed. It felt a little too tidy, but that's a minor, minor complaint when talking about one of the greatest series in TV history. (Yeah, we said it.)

*According to Nielsen Media Research ratings, the sometimes-satisfying, sometimes-frustrating M*A*S*H series ender remains the most-watched network primetime program ever, with a 77 percent share. Given the viewership splintering effect of cable, satellite, and alternative networks, it's pretty unlikely that any one program will ever top that number.*

5 *THE FUGITIVE* (1963-1967)

As one of the first TV series to balance episodic storytelling with an overarching narrative, *The Fugitive* kept viewers in suspense for four seasons about whether Dr. Richard Kimble would ever find the one-armed man who killed his wife, thus getting tenacious police lieutenant Philip Gerard off his back. In the two-part finale—which drew the biggest audience in TV history up to that time, with a 70-percent-plus viewership share—Gerard captures Kimble, who permits him to confront the recently arrested one-armed man. They all meet in an abandoned amusement park, where the one-armed man nearly kills Kimble, until Gerard saves the day. Kimble is exonerated, and ends the series as a free man.

6 *SIX FEET UNDER* (2001-2005)

Revealing the conclusions of characters' lives post-story can be a hackneyed way to end a television series or film, unless it's done ironically, like in *Animal House*. But given that *Six Feet Under* was always about endings, the finale was heart-wrenchingly beautiful and satisfying. As Lauren Ambrose speeds off in her car to her unknown future, the episode wraps with flashes of the final moments of all the show's major players. The use of aging makeup wasn't an across-the-board success, but the speedy, unflinching look at death in its various forms was a natural finish. It didn't just settle the questions of what happened to the characters, it reminded viewers of one of the show's ongoing themes, that death can be sudden, protracted, painful, or peaceful, but it's inevitable, and that's okay.

7 *THE MARY TYLER MOORE SHOW* (1970-1977)

At the end of *The Mary Tyler Moore Show's* seventh season, with the story of career-oriented single woman Mary Richards having more or less run its course—and with the show having fallen out of the Top 20—fans were asked to say farewell to Minneapolis

and WJM with an episode in which the station's new owners fire everyone on the news staff except for the ever-unctuous Ted Baxter. When Mary asks for a group hug, the characters can't bring themselves to let go, so they follow each other around the office in a big, funny, poignant huddle.

8 *AVATAR: THE LAST AIRBENDER* *(2005-2008)*

Michael Dante DiMartino and Bryan Konietzko drew a lot of the style of their Nickelodeon cartoon *Avatar* from anime, and they planned it like a typical anime series too, as a complete story with a fixed, planned arc. Each of the three seasons serves as a complete themed "book" following an important part of the development of the central protagonist, Aang, a 10-year-old boy tasked with restoring balance to a world at war. In the final episode, he fulfills his destiny in an unexpected but perfectly typical way, in a sequence that's glorious even by the show's tremendously high visual standards. It's a fabulous story, one with the richness and depth of a terrific fantasy novel, and it's helped considerably by the sense that from the very beginning, its creators knew exactly where they were going.

9 *HARVEY BIRDMAN, ATTORNEY AT LAW* *(2000-2007)*

The Cartoon Network goof *Harvey Birdman*—one of the network's many signature recontextualizations of characters from old Hanna-Barbera series—didn't come across as nearly so planned-out; it felt more like something the network threw together whenever star Gary Cole was available. Still, the show was always worth waiting for, as the title character—a cheesy superhero re-envisioned as a crappy but upbeat lawyer—babbled his way through hilarious court cases on behalf of the likes of Fred Flintstone, Boo Boo Bear, and Apache Chief from *Superfriends*. The show was surreal, fast-paced, and utterly irreverent, particularly in the daring final episodes, which killed Harvey off. (Spoiler warnings be damned: The episode is called "The Death Of Harvey.") Granted, his death is random and accidental, but it comes just as Harvey has achieved a stunning victory that renews his confidence in himself, and he doesn't live to experience disappointment; it's almost like a happy ending. Also, he dies as he lived: randomly, strangely, and without any regard for the rules and conventions governing the old cartoon that spawned him.

10 *BARNEY MILLER* *(1975-1982)*

Much like *The Mary Tyler Moore Show*, *Barney Miller* ended on a bittersweet note, with the men of New York's 12th precinct learning that their rotten old building has been named a historic landmark, forcing all the cops who work there to transfer to scattered posts across the city. Over the course of a three-part episode, some characters were promoted, some contemplated new careers, and all realized how much they were going to miss the leaky, drafty, smelly old office where they spent eight TV seasons processing petty criminals. In the final scene, Barney himself switches off the lights, saying a fitting goodbye.

THOROUGHLY SATISFYING ENDING

PANIC AT THE ARCADE

11 VIDEOGAMES THAT PROMPTED FEAR AND OUTRAGE

1 ***PAC-MAN*** *(1980)*

Videogames are crammed with bizarre images and goals, but far stranger are the scenarios when the world of sprites and polygons comes into conflict with the real world. The first such goofy controversy came in the late '70s, when Taito's groundbreaking *Space Invaders* game proved so popular that it began to seriously cut into the nation's supply of 100-yen coins (at the time, the Japanese equivalent of the quarter). A few years later, what started out as a mere economic hiccup turned into a full-blown tempest in a teapot: 100-yen coins were in such short supply thanks to the widespread outbreak of "*Pac-Man* fever" that politicians in Japan began decrying the game, with doomsayers predicting that *Pac-Man* would ruin the economy, as if the coins were simply being wiped out of existence, rather than simply being funneled into Namco's bank accounts. Eventually, the bogus moral panic died down—but it was only the first of many.

2 ***POLYBIUS*** *(1981)*

By 1981, videogames were a big enough presence in popular culture to spawn their own urban legends. The first—and one of the most persistent and mysterious—involves a game called *Polybius* that was test-marketed in the Portland area, and was so bizarre and addictive that it caused headaches, disorientation, memory loss, and even insanity. Supposedly, *Polybius* was a vector-graphic game (à la *Tempest* or *Battlezone*) that involved outer-space action, but its presentation was so real and its graphics so unprecedented that it sucked players in, then made them lose touch with reality. Like all good urban legends, this story contained the very slightest grain of truth: Supposedly, a few players really did have epileptic reactions to early versions of *Tempest*. And like all good urban legends, it quickly got out of control, with rumors of CIA involvement and the appearance of men in black. Although a few people claim to have been involved with the design of the original game, there's still no hard proof that it ever existed.

3 ***CUSTER'S REVENGE*** *(1982)*

Usually, the appearance of adult themes and ideas in a medium previously associated with children leads to interesting art. That decidedly wasn't the case with the vile *Custer's Revenge*, a game developed for the Atari 2600 by a small-time outfit called Mystique. The company's specialty was ripping off popular platforms and giving them a pornographic theme, and *Custer's Revenge* was its degraded masterpiece. In the game, players take on the role of a crudely pixilated General Custer, naked save for boots and a cavalryman's hat, and sporting an erection. If he successfully evaded a hail of arrows, his reward involved raping a large-breasted, smiling naked Indian woman tied to a post. Gamers have never been and will never be the most politically correct bunch, but even they were grossed out by this display, and the game quickly disappeared, but it's still remembered as one of the most notorious titles ever released.

4 ***E.T.: THE EXTRA-TERRESTRIAL*** *(1982)*

Videogames were serious business by 1982. The young industry thrived, and when Atari announced plans to develop a game based on Steven Spielberg's monster hit movie *E.T.: The Extra-Terrestrial*, they had every expectation that it would be a best-seller. Four million copies of the game were produced, and the company projected massive holiday sales, but a number of factors—oversaturation of the game market, increased competition from personal computers, a software price war, and more demand for good game programmers than there was supply—combined to make 1983 the worst year on record for videogame sales. It didn't help that the *E.T.* game was a mess, alternately confusing and boring; less than half of the cartridges manufactured were sold, and newspapers reported a mass dumping of unsold games in a desert landfill. Atari took a $536 million loss, and the company was sold less than a year later.

5 *NARC* *(1988, 2005)*
The concept for the original 1988 version of *NARC* was by Eugene Jarvis, who had designed *Defender*, *Robotron: 2084*, and *Cruis'n* for Williams Electronics. Two elements made it stand out from the other arcade games of the late '80s: its extreme gore, and the high-resolution monitor that made the gore so easy to see. Because of its simplistic plot—drug-enforcement agents kill dealers and take their money and product—few people complained about the fact that players went around shooting people with rocket launchers so that their burned, bloody limbs were strewn all over the screen. When the game was redesigned for modern console play in 2005, though, it expanded the plot so that the main characters could deal drugs themselves, or even take drugs. This made it a controversy magnet, and Illinois governor Rod Blagojevich, himself no stranger to the wrong side of the law, singled it out as a poisoner of youth; apparently, butchering people with heavy weapons was fine, but taking the occasional puff of weed was worthy of condemnation. Just as in real life, killing is okay, as long as you're killing the right people.

6 *MORTAL KOMBAT* *(1992)*
Only a few years after America shrugged its collective shoulders at the original *NARC's* dismemberments and charred human remains, it got all heated up about another game that it decided simply went too far. From today's perspective, *Mortal Kombat*—developed by Midway to compete with Capcom's successful *Street Fighter* series—seems not exactly tame, but at least cartoonish in its violent content. But parents of the day were so aghast at its beheadings, bloodshed, and gory spine-removals that it became almost a crusade. Likely the only thing that made it a target for censure was its popularity; while *NARC* and *Smash TV* were equally gory, they didn't collect as many quarters, and thus received less attention.

7 *NIGHT TRAP* *(1992)*
It's doubtful one gamer in a hundred would remember it today, but in 1992, *Night Trap* became one of the most infamous games around. A dull full-motion-video action-adventure thriller originally released for the Sega CD system in 1992, *Night Trap* somehow attracted the attention of anti-violence crusaders and then, bizarrely, the Senate. It became Exhibit A in a Judiciary Committee hearing—chaired by none other than Joe Lieberman—on videogame violence, where it became a punching bag for the frustrations of thousands of parents. In what would become a familiar pattern in later years, it became clear that none of the people condemning the game had actually played it; Lieberman claimed that the goal of the game was to "trap and kill women," when in fact players are meant to save them. The hearing, which led eventually to the forming of the ESRB ratings system for videogame content, also marked the very last time anyone expressed any interest in Dana Plato (who played an undercover agent in *Night Trap*) until her overdose death seven years later.

8 ADDICTIVE MMORPGS *(1997-PRESENT)*

Although game addiction wasn't new in the '90s (ask anyone who spent hundreds of dollars in quarters playing *Ms. Pac-Man*, or take a look at South Korea, where it seems to be a leading cause of death), it received a record level of media attention. With the debut of MMORPGs (massively multiplayer online role-playing games) such as *Everquest* and *Ultima Online*, basement-dwelling nerds had a new reason not to emerge from the depths. Every few months like clockwork, a mainstream newspaper features a new article about some goof who lost his or her job, family, and hygienic presentability because of "EverCrack" or the like. The phenomenon continues today, over the likes of *World Of Warcraft*.

9 *GRAND THEFT AUTO III* *(2001)*

Anyone who's scanned the headlines for the words "Rockstar Games" over the last seven years could be forgiven for thinking the company manufactures controversy instead of videogames. Starting with *Grand Theft Auto III*, the first of the "sandbox" versions of the company's popular franchise, bashing Rockstar for enabling the moral corruption of youth has practically been a national obsession. Attorney Jack Thompson has made his name on bashing Rockstar, and every subsequent iteration of *Grand Theft Auto* has attracted more controversy. The absurdity reached its peak in 2005, when the so-called "hot coffee mod" for *Grand Theft Auto: San Andreas* caused a firestorm of controversy and even got Hillary Clinton involved. Apparently, America found the existence of a patch that most gamers didn't know or care about, which allows players to view a mildly sexual cut-scene, far more shocking than the fact that the game involves murdering almost everyone the player encounters.

10 *BULLY* *(2006)*

To Rockstar's credit—or to its detriment, depending on where one stands—the company has always treated the media storm surrounding its products with good humor, often incorporating it into games. (Likely someone there is cognizant that every controversy means an extra million or so in sales.) Rockstar announced its planned release of *Bully* in 2006 while keeping the game's plot close to the vest; naturally, this led the usual suspects to flip out and accuse it of containing all sorts of heinous deeds, before any of them had played or even seen the game. Jack Thompson was again at the forefront of the complaints, accusing *Bully* of being "a Columbine simulator." When the game was finally released, it turned out to be a fun, even charming story, where the main character frequently attempted to *stop* bullies, and any serious misbehavior was instantly punished by the game's authority figures. Thompson would have died from shame, if he had any.

11 *LEFT BEHIND: ETERNAL FORCES* *(2006)*

It was inevitable that the *Left Behind* book series, which sold roughly 80 zillion copies to Bible-believing evangelicals, would spawn its own videogame series. What was a bit surprising is that it attracted widespread criticism, even from Christian groups. In *Left Behind: Eternal Forces*, players control a "Tribulation Force" that, among other duties, is called upon to fight and kill the forces of the antichrist, such as secular humanists, rock musicians, and college-educated nonbelievers. Though the massacre-the-heathens angle was oversold (by, among others, the omnipresent Jack Thompson), and the conversion of enemy forces to Christianity doesn't take place by force, the game is still problematic for its frank depiction of anyone not immersed in evangelical activities as one of the bad guys. Women's groups were also displeased that several key roles in the Tribulation Force could only be filled by men, so the game designers responded by issuing a patch where women could join an elite group of "Prayer Warriors." Panderiffic!

SCREENREADING

5 ESSENTIAL BOOKS ABOUT FILM

1 PAULINE KAEL,
FOR KEEPS: 30 YEARS AT THE MOVIES

Cultural critics like Manny Farber, Susan Sontag, and Robert Warshow all pioneered fruitful ways to look at film from an academic perspective, but no one has had as profound an influence on the actual *writing* of film criticism as Pauline Kael. *For Keeps* spans her whole career, compiling page after page of slangy prose and unpopular opinions, delivered by a woman always unfailingly honest about what she was looking for in movies—namely sensual pleasure, not moralizing—and unafraid to eviscerate filmmakers who didn't toe the line.

2 PETER BISKIND,
EASY RIDERS, RAGING BULLS: HOW THE SEX-DRUGS-AND-ROCK 'N' ROLL GENERATION SAVED HOLLYWOOD

There are few more pitiful spectacles than baby boomers applauding themselves, but Peter Biskind's look back at the culture that nurtured the likes of Martin Scorsese, Steven Spielberg, and Robert Altman is clear-eyed and pointed, showing how a group of bona fide geniuses seized a rare opportunity to make masterpieces within the mainstream… and how they eventually screwed it up. His *Easy Riders, Raging Bulls* is frequently funny and somewhat scary, as much cautionary tale as celebration.

3 HELEN G. SCOTT AND **FRANÇOIS TRUFFAUT,**
TRUFFAUT/HITCHCOCK

Like a lot of directors of his generation, Alfred Hitchcock cagily deflected critical and scholarly attempts to ascribe deeper meanings to his taut psychological thrillers. But when interviewed by critic-turned-filmmaker François Truffaut, Hitchcock opened up, going over the technical and creative details of each of his films, and providing some rare personal insight along with the trade talk. It's the ultimate in Hitchcock analysis, provided by the master himself.

4 JOE BOB BRIGGS,
PROFOUNDLY DISTURBING: SHOCKING MOVIES THAT CHANGED HISTORY!

Joe Bob Briggs started out as the wild-man alter ego of respectable Dallas film critic John Bloom, but this survey of controversial cinema—from *The Cabinet Of Dr. Caligari* to *Ilsa, She-Wolf Of The SS*—is as well-researched and opinionated as anything from a "real" writer. Briggs not only explains why these movies shook people up in their time, he also digs up lively behind-the-scenes anecdotes about how and why they were made, shedding light on genre filmmaking's dim back rooms.

5 DANNY PEARY,
GUIDE FOR THE FILM FANATIC

There are enough film guides on the market to wallpaper every multiplex in Los Angeles, but Danny Peary—best-known for his *Cult Movies* series—whips up something a little different with his gift to film fanatics everywhere. His *Guide For The Film Fanatic* offers snappy opinions and appreciations of more than 1,500 films, divided into categories. It all amounts to an alternative canon, taking into account underground films and disreputable Hollywood fare, adding up to a perfect next step for movie buffs who've already seen the acknowledged classics.

Guest List:
AMY SEDARIS

50 THINGS THAT MAKE ME LAUGH

1. ticks
2. toupee tape
3. grab bars and rails
4. *America's Funniest Home Videos*
5. the Wise potato-chip owl
6. owls wearing graduation caps
7. willow trees
8. mushrooms and toadstools
9. skin tags
10. last-minute shoppers
11. crystal-meth teeth
12. burnt food
13. stains
14. coconut hair
15. snake traps in the home
16. slapping
17. missing teeth
18. verbal fights
19. abandoned cars with doors left open
20. misplaced items in the store
21. messy dressing rooms
22. thin thin thin hair
23. tassels
24. googly eyes
25. skin-disorder books
26. designer shoes involving a lot of hair or fur
27. fur coats
28. mean people laughing
29. customers being mean to service people
30. the word "snoop"
31. spider bites
32. barrister wigs
33. Cockney accents
34. yelling
35. melted candles
36. litterbugs
37. monkeys
38. flat tires
39. cowardliness
40. swelling
41. toe rings
42. crying and driving at the same time
43. bad ideas
44. buck teeth
45. Buddy Hackett
46. uncomfortable moments
47. people falling down
48. sound-effects tapes
49. pain
50. peanut shells on the floor

Amy Sedaris has made people laugh as Jeri Blank on the television series Strangers With Candy *and in plenty of movies. She also penned a book about entertaining called* I Like You: Hospitality Under The Influence.

NOT AGAIN

24 GREAT FILMS TOO PAINFUL TO WATCH TWICE

1 *REQUIEM FOR A DREAM* (2000)

Darren Aronofsky's brutal adaptation of Hubert Selby's novel depicts the horrors of many kinds of substance abuse—heroin, pot, caffeine, prescription pills, hope—with visceral, breathtaking force, and the result is one of the only genuinely effective, non-hysterical anti-drug movies ever made. *Dream* flirts extensively with delirious camp during its fever-dream climax, but retains a pummeling power thanks to Aronofsky's unblinking willingness to trawl deep into the bowels of hell alongside his heartbreakingly fragile characters.

2 *DANCER IN THE DARK* (2000)

Starting with 1996's *Breaking The Waves*, writer-director Lars von Trier commandeered the genre of fantastic but torturous films. *Waves, Dogville, Dancer In The Dark*, and even the less successful *Manderlay* all center on women whose well-meaning but disastrous choices wind up abetting their own financial, emotional, and sexual exploitation. And when presented with such humble, cooperative victims, the people around them tend to abandon any semblance of morality in order to take full advantage of the sacrifices they've been offered. Of the four, *Dancer In The Dark* is particularly painful, thanks to Björk's sweet, nakedly vulnerable performance as a cringing immigrant factory worker trying to conceal her worsening vision until she can make enough money for the operation that will save her son from the same fate. Von Trier calculates his plotlines with exacting, inspired sadism, ensuring that her attempts to reach out to others backfire, her kindness is repaid with betrayal, and every seeming spark of hope exists only to better illuminate the miserable darkness.

3 *THE PASSION OF JOAN OF ARC* (1928)

Von Trier owes his entire painful career to his Danish countryman Carl Dreyer, particularly his silent classic *The Passion Of Joan Of Arc*, which deals with the ultimate case of a woman suffering for her faith. What makes the film difficult to watch isn't so much Joan's persecution at the hands of her ecclesiastical tormentors, or even Maria Falconetti's famously expressive performance, which registers anguish in every crevice of her face. Its disturbing intensity comes mainly from Dreyer's refusal to play by the rules: Defying the most basic tenets of cinematic grammar, which require filmmakers to establish spatial relationship on a 180-degree plane, Dreyer instead constructs the film as a series of extreme close-ups, with little sense of where the characters are in relation to one another. That disorientation, combined with the feverish emotions whipped up by the trial, places viewers in a grim psychic space.

4 *BENNY'S VIDEO* (1992)

Just about every film by Michael Haneke—the fiendishly precise Austrian director of *Funny Games*, *The Seventh Continent*, and *Caché*—could have made this list. An unsparing moralist with a peerless talent for getting under viewers' skins, Haneke backs up his schoolmarm-ish theses on violence with a punishing aesthetic. In *Benny's Video*—a prequel of sorts to *Funny Games*—he shows the title character coldly, dispassionately murder a schoolgirl. Then he shows it again. Then comes the truly bone-chilling stuff: the emotional reaction—or lack thereof—from Benny and his parents.

5 *WINTER LIGHT* (1962)

Perhaps the grimmest entry in Ingmar Bergman's "Trilogy Of Faith" (also

THE PASSION OF JOAN OF ARC

known as the "God's Silence" trilogy, which should be a good indicator of the bleakness at play), *Winter Light* follows a small group of parishioners who have no celestial answers for their anguish. The opening scenes alone constitute one of the sparest expressions of Bergman's dour spirituality: As a rural pastor performs his noon service, a handful of the faithless faithful go through the requisite motions, but with a palpable disconnection from their meaning. Though he offers himself as counselor, the pastor can't comfort them, because he too is in spiritual crisis; after serving in Spain during the civil war, he witnessed so many bloody atrocities that he struggled to reconcile the idea of a just, loving God with the reality of human cruelty. In the end, apostasy is the only answer.

6 BAD LIEUTENANT (1992)

The blunt title turns out to be an understatement: The hard-living detective in Abel Ferrara's *Bad Lieutenant*, played with fearless brio by Harvey Keitel, surely counts as one of film history's most corrupt cops. He's a gambler and an addict, given to pocketing drug seizures for recreational use, participating in sleazy sex-and-drug-fueled bacchanals, and flagrantly abusing the public trust. Ferrara coughs up some repulsive images: a nun getting gang-raped on the altar; a virtual how-to clinic on preparing and shooting up a ball of heroin; a profanity-laced confrontation with Jesus; and most memorably, a scene in which Keitel pulls over two underage girls and agrees to let them go in exchange for sexual favors. The clincher is Keitel's performance—a display of raw, unvarnished emotion from a character whose slumbering conscience and faith are suddenly reawakened.

7 STRAW DOGS (1971)

A forceful, unrelenting statement on masculinity and violence, Sam Peckinpah's *Straw Dogs* sounds like a perfectly watchable home-invasion thriller, concluding as it does with the hero standing his ground and beating back his formidable attackers. But like many of the films on this list, it's a case where the moviemaking is skillful enough to make even its simple revenge scenario seem dangerously potent. Critic Pauline Kael described it as a "fascist classic" for casting Dustin Hoffman as a wimpy, pacifist academic whose questionable manhood is proved via a bloody rite of passage. Hoffman's gruesome showdown with a group of locals is shocking, but the infamous scene prefacing it is even more disturbing: Left alone in their home in a seemingly quaint Cornish village, Hoffman's wife (Susan George) is raped by her former lover and his crony. Initially horrified, she eventually responds with something close to ecstasy, underlining her husband's weakness in the context of an indefensible rape fantasy.

8 ***AUDITION*** *(1999)*
"Kiri-kiri-kiri-kiri-kiri!" ("Deeper, deeper, deeper…") J-horror maestro Takashi Miike has plenty of disturbing images to his credit—a man suspended horizontally by hooks and doused with hot oil in *Ichi The Killer*, the infamous lactation sex scene in *Visitor Q*—but *Audition*, his best film in a walk, unsettles because its shocks are character-oriented, in addition to merely being gross. The first half of the film could be mistaken for austere melodrama, as Miike follows a widowed producer who "auditions" a new wife under false pretenses, and finds a quiet, petite young woman who fits the bill. But she turns out to have a dark agenda, and she answers his deceptions in a horrifically extended torture sequence involving a very long needle. Her retribution is Miike's sick idea of social critique, addressing the problem of female objectification with unspeakable, yet weirdly erotic, acts of cruelty.

9 ***SICK: THE LIFE AND DEATH OF BOB FLANAGAN, SUPERMASOCHIST*** *(1997)*
Simply describing the sadomasochistic stunts pulled by Bob Flanagan, a performance artist who died from cystic fibrosis at age 43, is enough to get half the population wincing as if they were sucking on a lemon wedge. But seeing Flanagan's work in Kirby Dick's surprisingly moving documentary *Sick* is another matter. As a way of combating a body that constantly betrayed him, Flanagan tested his astounding pain threshold in shocking ways, most notoriously by nailing his penis to a board (in close-up). It may sound like something no one would want to watch the first time, let alone twice, but *Sick* is redeemed by Flanagan's wicked sense of humor and courageous defiance in fighting a disease that normally strikes down the afflicted during childhood.

10 ***COME AND SEE*** *(1985)*
Many films use a child's perspective to tell a war story—it's an easy way to chronicle loss of innocence and portray the consequences of violence. Nothing on film drives this point home as effectively as Elem Klimov's *Come And See*, the chronicle of one boy's struggle to defend his Belarusian village from the Nazis in 1943. Aleksei Kravchenko spends the early part of the film eager to join his comrades, finding a damaged rifle of his own and dressing in oversized military clothing, camouflaging his youth before the war actually takes it from him. Repeated close-ups document his transformation—by the film's end, it's hard to tell whether dried dirt or actual wrinkles are violating his once-youthful visage.

11 ***IN A YEAR OF 13 MOONS*** *(1978)*
There's torment enough in Rainer Werner Fassbinder's deeply personal *In A Year Of 13 Moons* long before it reaches the sequence that made it semi-notorious. Fassbinder's hero, a transvestite martyr played by Volker Spengler, is a pitiable Frankfurt drifter who had a sex-change operation years earlier, prompted by an offhand comment ("too bad you're not a girl") from an unattainable object of desire. Spengler convinces neither as a man nor as a woman, and he winds up subjecting himself to his old crush, now a cruel businessman whose towering office space is accessed by the password "Bergen-Belsen." And on top of it all, the film was shot mere weeks after Fassbinder's lover committed suicide. But *13 Moons* saves its most disturbing setpiece for its final act, which contains a monologue on self-mutilation set against footage of the killing floor in a slaughterhouse.

12 ***SAFE*** *(1995)*
A sort-of horror movie in which the monster is the entire world, Todd Haynes' *Safe* follows a rich, empty housewife (played masterfully by Julianne Moore) into the depths of "environmental illness"—a malady that real-world doctors still can't agree on. Is it all in her head, which is half-vacant and in need of something to worry about when all basic needs are met? Or is she just sensitive to low levels of toxic chemicals that most people simply don't notice? The film doesn't offer any clear answer—instead, it follows Moore through excruciating anxieties and unpeggable illnesses. She ends up at a wellness retreat, which at first seems to offer some hope, but she's soon sucked even deeper into the discomfort of her own mind. It's pure bleakness.

13 ***IRREVERSIBLE*** *(2002)*
Gaspar Noé's *Irreversible* picked up some well-deserved notoriety for its centerpiece, a nine-minute single-take sequence in which Jo Prestia anally violates Monica Bellucci at knifepoint in a grimy (and highly symbolic) red underground tunnel, then beats her to an unrecognizable pulp. There's nothing cinematic or subversively sexy about the rape scene; it's a

ghastly, raw experience that seems to go on for hours, with Bellucci's muffled cries and wide, blank eyes becoming increasingly inhuman as the process drags on. But Noé doesn't make the rest of the film any easier to take. Laying out the story in reverse chronological order, he begins with a stomach-churning act of revenge for the rape, then sets his camera spinning slowly end-over-end, preventing viewers from gathering their bearings and turning the film into a ghastly carnival ride.

14 *BOYS DON'T CRY* (1999)

Similarly, the brutal rapes in *Boys Don't Cry* make repeat viewings of the film an act of psychic self-abuse. Based on the real-life tragedy of transgender 21-year-old Brandon Teena—played with haunting depth by Hilary Swank—*Boys* is relentless in its portrayal of barbaric bigotry in small-town Nebraska. After Swank starts a romantic relationship with Chloë Sevigny's Lana Tisdel, Lana's redneck friends forcibly expose Teena as a biological female, then savagely rape her before the hatred escalates to an inevitably horrific end. Just as sickening as the violence, though, is the complicity of Lana's mother—who calls Teena "it" and ultimately gives the boys sanction to "clean up" the situation—and the outright antagonism (bordering on titillation) of the hick sheriff who grills Teena after the rape. The fact that the film's events are based on truth—and the lingering attachment *Boys Don't Cry* has to the hate-fueled murder of Matthew Shepard around the time of its release—only magnifies its gut-crawling impact.

15 *GRAVE OF THE FIREFLIES* (1988)

From the opening scene showing 14-year-old protagonist Seita dying on a train-station floor as harried travelers look on bemusedly, it's clear that *Grave Of The Fireflies* isn't going to be easy to watch. An animated Japanese film as visually beautiful as it is emotionally draining, *Grave* finds tragedy in the horrors of war and the dangers of human pride. *Grave* draws out the story of two Japanese siblings orphaned during World War II, following Seita and his younger sister Setsuko over 88 quietly horrifying minutes as they struggle, and eventually fail, to survive in a bleak, war-torn landscape. In spite of its dark subject matter, *Grave* is brightly colored and peppered with sweetly innocent moments, making the children's eventual fates all the more disturbing.

16 *WHEN THE WIND BLOWS* (1986)

This deceptively sweet little British animated feature emphasizes the cost of war on a very personal level, by observing a quiet rural couple preparing for impending nuclear conflict, then slowly dying of radiation poisoning afterward. Naïvely accepting everything their government pamphlets tell them (though they don't understand much of what they're told, and remain sure that since they can't see or feel radiation, it can't possibly hurt them), they fumble through their gentle days without comprehending either the scope or the causes of the fight that's killing them from afar. Perhaps the saddest part is their conviction that nuclear war will be no different from World War II, which they lived through, and that if they just tough it out and tighten their belts, they can get through lethal radiation poisoning the way they got through wartime shortages. Much like *Grave Of The Fireflies*, *When The Wind Blows* is adorable in its personal, knowing details, and excruciating in its big picture.

17 *LEAVING LAS VEGAS* (1996)

Following a decade of Nicolas Cage films like *Next*, *Ghost Rider*, and *The Wicker Man*, it's hard to remember what a revelation he was in his Oscar-winning role in *Leaving Las Vegas*, as a failed screenwriter pointedly setting out to drink himself to death. The film, written and directed by *Stormy Monday*'s Mike Figgis, is more consciously polished and Hollywood-y than most of the films on this list, but like them, it unstintingly, aggressively delves into just how miserable human beings can get. It isn't enough, for instance, that co-star Elisabeth Shue is trapped in a degrading life as a Vegas prostitute, or that her best friend is an abusive, suicidal drunk who seems content to drag her down with him. It isn't enough when she gets gang-raped, then evicted from her home by landlords clearly uncomfortable with her bruised, limping, disreputable post-rape appearance. No, she actually has to get mocked and abused on her way home after the rape, as her taxi driver, noticing how gingerly she's moving, asks if she got "a back-door delivery you weren't expecting," then tells her she was asking for it by dressing the way she does. Only Figgis' glittery, somber direction and the leads' stellar performances make this miserablist wallow sadly poetic.

18 *JONESTOWN: THE LIFE AND DEATH OF PEOPLES TEMPLE* (2006)

19 *S-21: THE KHMER ROUGE KILLING MACHINE* (2003)

Though they take drastically different approaches, the Jim Jones documentary *Jonestown* and *S-21* are both far too intense and draining for repeat viewing. *S-21* coldly but powerfully appraises the devastating aftereffects of totalitarianism through the firsthand stories of survivors of Khmer Rouge terror. *Jonestown*, meanwhile, traces the tragic rise and fall of Jim Jones, a fiery idealist and social activist corrupted by power. *Jonestown* attains an almost unbearable intensity in a heart-stopping climax that draws extensively on audio footage documenting Jones' endgame strategy of poisoned Flavor-Aid and mass suicide. It's as close to being there as humanly possible.

20 *THE LAST HOUSE ON THE LEFT* (1972)

Taxi Driver is considered the definitive rebuke of '70s vigilante movies, but it's a laugh-a-minute joyride next to the vengeful depravity depicted in *The Last House On The Left*. Drawing from Ingmar Bergman's *The Virgin Spring*, Wes Craven's brilliantly unwatchable first feature is a no-holds-barred depiction of the rape and murder of two teenage girls by a pack of hippie lunatics, and the graphic revenge the girls' parents enact on the murderers. *Last House* looks cheap and amateurish, which adds to its snuff-film-style realism. Never has the gulf between "great film" and "enjoyable" been so wide.

21 *MILLION DOLLAR BABY* (2004)

The first three-quarters of *Million Dollar Baby* play like an old-fashioned sports movie, focusing on the heartwarming father-daughter dynamic between coach Clint Eastwood and boxer Hilary Swank. Then Swank suffers a horrible accident in the ring, and the film heads into ripped-from-the-headlines relevance, as Eastwood wrestles with Swank's demands to be euthanized. The decision is appropriately gut-wrenching, and Eastwood's direction is always tasteful, but who wants to ponder the difficulty of putting a loved one out of their misery?

22 *UNITED 93* (2006)

Writer-director Paul Greengrass dramatizes the events of September 11 on the ground and in the air with a "you are there" veracity that's gut-wrenching and surprisingly probative. From the initial confusion to the panicked response, *United 93* explains what the following years have been like, from shock to violence to exhaustion. But Greengrass' refusal to insert any kind of distancing effects means that viewers get to relive every second of sick horror from one of the worst days any of us will ever experience. A lot of Americans didn't want to see *United 93* even *once*, and it's hard to blame them.

23 *LILYA 4-EVER* (2002)

Just prior to *Lilya 4-Ever*, Swedish writer-director Lukas Moodysson made *Together*, a movie so generous in spirit that a lot of its fans found this follow-up, a comparatively bleak story of a teenage Russian sex slave, too tough to take. Actually, *Lilya* follows logically from *Together* as another profound illustration of how people need people. (A little familial support would've prevented most of the movie's string of tragedies.) But in spite of a spectacular lead performance by Oksana Akinshina—and a lyrical final scene that tries to put a happy spin on human misery—*Lilya 4-Ever* essentially asks its audience to watch the hopes of a bright, pretty girl get crushed one by one. It's powerful stuff that lingers in the memory so strongly that a second viewing may not even be necessary.

24 *NIL BY MOUTH* (1997)

Gary Oldman has openly said that he appears in dreck like *Air Force One* because Hollywood paychecks let him fund his own indie films. So far, though, his only writing-directing project is *Nil By Mouth*, a gritty, grueling drama in Mike Leigh mode. Like *Irreversible*, it centers on a protracted, nauseating act of violence against a woman, framed within a nervy, talky plot. But *Nil By Mouth* is less story-driven; it mostly captures, intimately and unsparingly, the details of working-class life in South London, among addicts and alcoholics. It's an impressively immediate, immersive film, but a hard one to sit through, thanks to its direct look at physical and emotional abuse. Then again, the accents are so dense, and the dialogue flies so fast and furious, that it may be necessary to rewatch just to follow what's going on. Sometimes even the most exhausting films *have* to be watched more than once.

FROM GUMMI TO GUTTENBERG

35 THINGS WE'LL FOREVER ASSOCIATE WITH THE SIMPSONS

1 ***A STREETCAR NAMED DESIRE***
Marge: "I just don't see why Blanche should shove a broken bottle in Stanley's face. Couldn't she just take his abuse with gentle good humor?"

2 **COMIC-BOOK STORE OWNERS**
Comic Book Guy: "This is an arm, drawn by nobody. It is worth nothing."
Bart: "Can't you give me anything for it?"
Comic Book Guy: "I can give you this telephone. It is shaped like Mary Worth."

3 **BEER, DOUGHNUTS, AND TV**
Homer: "Mmm, doughnuts." "Mmm, beer." "Television! Teacher, mother, secret lover!"

4 **DRINKING**
Homer: "To alcohol! The cause of—and solution to—all of life's problems."

5 **MONORAILS**
Miss Hoover: "I hear those things are awfully loud."
Lyle Lanley: "It glides as softly as a cloud."
Apu: "Is there a chance the track could bend?"
Lyle Lanley: "Not on your life, my Hindu friend."

6 **JIMMY CARTER**
Random person in crowd: "History's greatest monster!"

7 **ANYTHING GUMMI**
German man: "That is the rarest gummi of them all, the gummi Venus de Milo, carved by gummi artisans who work exclusively in the medium of gummi."
Marge: "Will you two stop saying 'gummi' so much?"

8 **THE DENVER BRONCOS**
Marge: "I think owning the Denver Broncos is pretty good!"

9 **"IN-A-GADDA-DA-VIDA"**
Homer: "Hey, Marge, remember when we used to make out to this hymn?"

10 ***PLANET OF THE APES,* PARTICULARLY DR. ZAIUS**
Troy McLure: "I hate every ape I see / from chimpan-A to chimpanzee / no, you'll never make a monkey out of me!"

11 **PABLO NERUDA**
Lisa: "Pablo Neruda said, 'Laughter is the language of the soul.'"
Bart: "I am familiar with the works of Pablo Neruda."

12 **POGS**
Milhouse: "Alf pogs! Remember Alf? He's back… in pog form!"

13 **THEME RESTAURANTS**
Marge: "An alligator wearing sunglasses? Now I've seen everything!… Street signs? Indoors? Ha ha! Whatever!"

14 **STEVEN SPIELBERG**
Mr. Burns: "Get me Steven Spielberg!"
Smithers: "He's unavailable."
Burns: "Then get me his non-union Mexican equivalent!… Listen, Señor Spielbergo, I want you to do for me what Spielberg did for Oskar Schindler."
Spielbergo: "Er, Schindler es bueno, Señor Burns es el diablo."

15 **EUDORA WELTY**
Krusty: "Let's get going. I've got a date with Eudora Welty. [Loud offscreen belch.] Coming, Eudora!"

16 ***GLENGARRY GLEN ROSS***
Gil: "Now, let's talk rust-proofing. These Colecos'll rust up on you like that… er… Shut up, Gil. Close the deal. Close the deal!"

17 FROZEN YOGURT
Shop owner: "Take this object, but beware… it carries a terrible curse!"
Homer: "Oooh, that's bad."
Shop owner: "But it comes with a free Frogurt!"
Homer: "That's good!"
Shop owner: "The Frogurt is also cursed."
Homer: "That's bad."
Shop owner: "But you get your choice of topping!"
Homer: "That's good!"
Shop owner: "The toppings contain potassium benzoate. [Pause.] That's bad."
Homer: "Can I go now?"

18 RELIGION
Homer: "I'm no missionary! I don't even believe in Jebus!" [Seconds later, when in danger…] "Oh, save me, Jebus!"

19 JEERING/BOOING
Hans Moleman: "I was saying 'boo-urns'."

20 STEVE GUTTENBERG
Stonecutters: "Who holds back the electric car? Who makes Steve Guttenberg a star? We do!"

21 ARNOLD SCHWARZENEGGER
Rainier Wolfcastle: "My new movie is me, standing in front of a brick wall for 90 minutes. It cost $80 million to make."

22 RACE RELATIONS
Comedian: "Yo, check this out: Black guys drive a car like this. [Leans back, elbow on an imaginary windowsill, and scats.] Yeah, but white guys, see, they drive a car like this. [Hunches forward, scats nasally.]
Homer: "It's true, it's true! We're so lame!"

23 *THE NUTTY PROFESSOR*
The Jerry Lewis-inspired Professor Frink: "Elementary chaos theory tells us that all robots will eventually turn against their masters and run amok in an orgy of blood and the kicking and the biting with the metal teeth and the hurting and shoving."

24 MEANINGLESS AWARDS SHOWS
Joe Frazier: "Webster's Dictionary defines excellence as 'the state or condition of being excellent.' And now, the winner of the First Annual Montgomery Burns Award For Outstanding Achievement In The Field Of Excellence…"

25 SECRET SOCIETIES LIKE THE MASONS
Lenny: "You put that sticker on your car so you won't get any tickets. And this other one keeps paramedics from stealing your wallet while they're working on you."
Carl: "Oh, and don't bother calling 911 any more… Here's the real number."

26 ARBY'S
Homer: "If I can keep down Arby's, I can keep down you!"
or
Terri: "I'm so hungry, I could eat at Arby's!"

27 RORY CALHOUN
Burns: "I've never seen anything so adorable! Do you know who it reminds me of?… The person who's always standing and walking."
Smithers: "Rory Calhoun?"
Burns: "That's it!"

28 MOUNTAIN DEW
Homer: "Now what do you have to wash that awful taste out of my mouth?"
Vendor: "Mountain Dew or crab juice."
Homer: "Blecch! Eeew! Sheesh! I'll take a crab juice!"

29 AL GORE
Al Gore doll: "You are hearing me talk."

30 "BABY ON BOARD" SIGNS
Marge: "Look what I got! Now people will stop intentionally ramming our car!"

31 TITO PUENTE
Tito Puente: "Why wound his body with bullets when I could set his soul afire with a slanderous mambo?"

32 TOM & JERRY
Theme song: "They fight! And bite! They fight and bite and fight! Fight fight fight! Bite bite bite! The Itchy And Scratchy Show!"

33 LUKE PERRY
Luke Perry: "My face! My face! My valuable face!"

34 SPIN-OFFS/ VARIETY SHOWS
Announcer: "And now, the family that doesn't know the meaning of the word 'canceled,' the Simpsons!"

35 PRETTY MUCH EVERYTHING ELSE

Peter Gabriel | Kevin Smith talking about movies | the Algonquin round table

I'M AGAINST (OR FOR) IT

10 THINGS THE RAMONES WANNA OR DON'T WANNA DO

1 **Walk around with you** ("I Don't Wanna Walk Around With You")
2 **Go down to the basement** ("I Don't Wanna Go Down To The Basement")
3 **Be your boyfriend** ("I Wanna Be Your Boyfriend")
4 **Be a good boy** ("Now I Wanna Be A Good Boy")
5 **Be sedated** ("I Wanna Be Sedated")
6 **Be well** ("I Wanna Be Well")
7 **Sniff some glue** ("Now I Wanna Sniff Some Glue")
8 **Grow up** ("I Don't Wanna Grow Up")
9 **Have something to do** ("I Just Want To Have Something To Do")
10 **Live** ("I Wanna Live")

Peter Cetera | Kevin Smith's movies | *Fox & Friends*

GOT ME A MOVIE, I WANT YOU TO KNOW!

18 SONGS ABOUT SPECIFIC FILMS

1 DEATH CAB FOR CUTIE, "DEATH OF AN INTERIOR DECORATOR" *(INTERIORS)*

Woody Allen shocked his fans with 1978's *Interiors*, a heavy, depressing slice of life that offered little hope and little music. Death Cab For Cutie's Ben Gibbard has called the film one of his favorites ever, and he brings it to sad life with "Death Of An Interior Decorator," whose lyrics essentially follow the plot. ("Arriving late, you cleaned the debris and walked into the angry sea.") It's a masterful re-telling of the story.

2 PIXIES, "DEBASER" ("UN CHIEN ANDALOU")

Pixies' second LP, *Doolittle*, opens with this offbeat tribute to Luis Buñuel and Salvador Dalí's avant-garde classic "Un Chien Andalou." "Got me a movie!" Black Francis shouts. "Slicin' up eyeballs!" He's referring to "Un Chien Andalou's" infamous signature image: a razor drawn across an actual eyeball. He's also yoking the Pixies' own brand of pop-shock theater to the tradition of surrealist decadence—and letting listeners know that he once took a film class in college.

3 THE WHITE STRIPES, "THE UNION FOREVER" *(CITIZEN KANE)*

Maybe the reason *Citizen Kane*—perennial consensus best film ever—hasn't inspired more songs is that it already contains a pretty great song. When the *New York Inquirer* attains the largest circulation in the city, the staff gathers to celebrate, and owner Charles Foster Kane brings out the dancing girls to perform a number he apparently wrote in praise of himself:

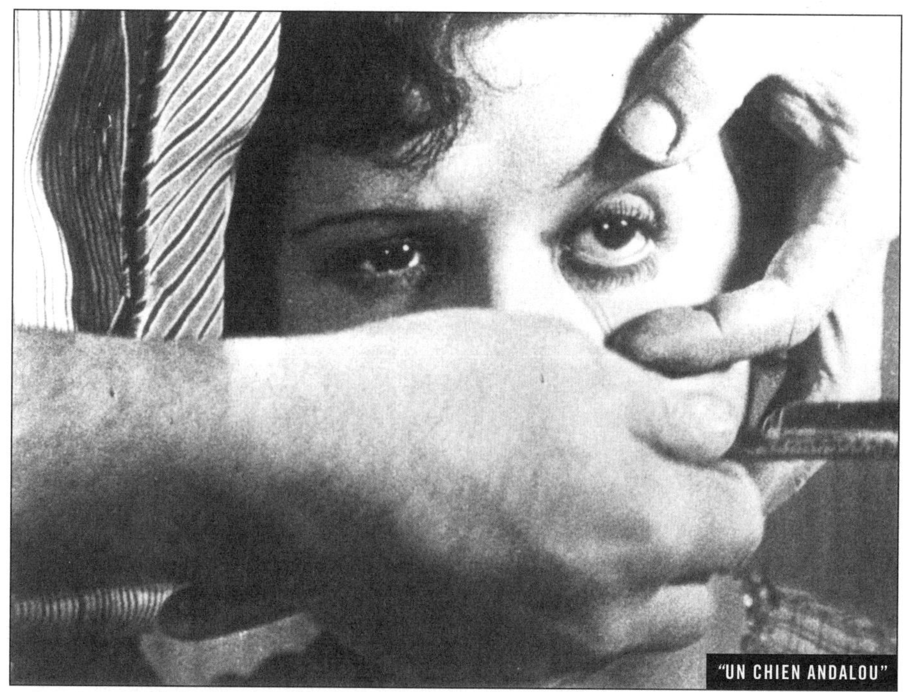

"UN CHIEN ANDALOU"

"Who likes to smoke? Enjoys a joke? And wouldn't get a bit upset if he were really broke?" Jack White solves the problem by talk-singing the first couple of verses of the *Kane* song during the break of "The Union Forever," The Stripes' Cliffs Notes version of the movie. Almost all the lyrics are taken verbatim from the film—including the title, which is the slogan young Charles shouts while playing Yankees-and-Rebs in the snow while his mother arranges to have him sent away.

4 DJ JAZZY JEFF AND THE FRESH PRINCE, "A NIGHTMARE ON MY STREET"

(A NIGHTMARE ON ELM STREET)

This unofficial tribute to *A Nightmare On Elm Street* bogeyman Freddy Krueger was, like all things Will Smith, cheeky bordering on cartoonish: In his intro, Smith refers to Krueger as being "burnt up like a weenie" and calls him out for wearing "the same hat and sweater every single day"—hardly an appropriate attitude toward a man wielding razors on his fingers. That irreverence didn't sit well with Freddy's parent company, New Line, which sued Smith and partner Jazzy Jeff, and successfully scrubbed the song's video from existence. Fortunately, this nightmare had a happy ending, with New Line offering the duo the chance to star in *House Party* (they turned it down) and Smith learning his lesson, resolving to only create limp rap odes to movies starring himself.

New Line was apparently against "Nightmare" largely because it stole attention from 1988's other cheeky, cartoonish Krueger tribute from a non-threatening rap group—The Fat Boys' "Are You Ready For Freddy?" which New Line officially commissioned for A Nightmare On Elm Street 4: The Dream Master.

5 "WEIRD AL" YANKOVIC, "THE SAGA BEGINS"

(THE PHANTOM MENACE)

"Weird Al" writes songs about movies almost as often as he writes songs about food—"Yoda," "Jurassic Park," "Gump," and "Ode To A Superhero" are all explicitly and at length about the plot details of blockbuster films. But he made his definitive statement with "The Saga Begins," a parody set to the tune of Don McLean's "American Pie," containing the entire plot of the *Star Wars* franchise entry *The Phantom Menace*. He describes Lucasfilm as "very supportive, but not to the extent that they would agree to show me a script or let me into an advance screening," so he based his detailed musical spoiler entirely on pre-release plot leaks from sites like TheForce.net and Cinescape. The song is a lot more fun than the film in some ways: It's bouncier, catchier, and contains 100 percent less Jar-Jar Binks.

6 RAMONES, "PINHEAD"

(FREAKS)

Ramones were never known for complicated lyrics, so their adaptation of Tod Browning's classic 1932 horror film *Freaks* is unsurprisingly simple. The band swiped a chant from one of the strange movie's strangest scenes, when the sideshow performers are accepting a "normal" into their ranks with the chant "Gooble gobble, one of us!" (The Ramones' famous version: "Gabba gabba hey!") The lyrics don't tell much of the film's story—just "I don't wanna be a pinhead no more"—but they do capture the spirit.

7 JAY-Z, "NO HOOK"

(AMERICAN GANGSTER)

Jay-Z liked *American Gangster* so much that it inspired him to produce a whole damn album, though the connections between the two are often maddeningly abstract. "Blue Magic" takes its name from the brand of heroin *American Gangster* subject Frank Lucas introduced to Harlem, but the song lacks a more overt connection to the film. On "No Hook," though, Jay-Z lays down samples from the film, then makes the connection between the kingpin of '70s smack and the kingpin of mainstream gangsta rap explicit with, "Compare me to trappers / I'm more Frank Lucas than Ludacris / and Luda's my dude, I ain't trying to dis / like Frank Lucas is cool, but I ain't trying to snitch." In that passage, Jay-Z pointedly associates himself with Lucas' success while distancing himself from Lucas' eventual role as a government informer, the ultimate crime in hip-hop's moral code.

8 HARVEY DANGER, "CARLOTTA VALDEZ" *(VERTIGO)*

Harvey Danger's frenzied, fun look at Alfred Hitchcock's *Vertigo* is also completely unsubtle: It basically re-tells the story ("Kiss Kim Novak where the redwoods grow / I'll bleach her hair and pretend that she didn't die") and even hits its high point with the film's title: "I'll follow anywhere / that is, until you climb too high / 'Cause I get vertigo." Not original, to be sure, but fun nonetheless.

9 NEIL DIAMOND, "HEARTLIGHT" *(E.T.: THE EXTRA-TERRESTRIAL)*

One of the most cloying examples of the movie-to-song phenomenon is this paean to *E.T.*, sung from Elliot's perspective. "Now that he had to go away / I still feel the words that he might say," Neil sings. (Given E.T.'s limited vocabulary, what exactly would those words be?) Many radio listeners in 1982 might not have realized that the song was about Spielberg's alien, unless they remembered that scene where E.T.'s heart lights up when he returns to life inside a scientist's body-bag. Or they could pay attention to the lyrics: "Gonna take a ride across the moon... He's looking for home." It's a catchy (though terminally soggy) song, but something about a grown man celebrating a little kid's relationship with a lost bug-eyed monster—without paid endorser status—puts it a hair on the creepy side.

10 RANDY, "THE EXORCIST" *(THE EXORCIST)*

Plenty of metal bands have turned to William Friedkin's *The Exorcist* for lyrical inspiration, but rather than trotting out hoary old clichés about the devil inside—and in fact, ignoring metaphors altogether—pop-punk band Randy sticks to the facts, offering an honest, *Videohound*-worthy appraisal of all three *Exorcist* films. In short: The first one was scary ("even though... I'm an atheist"), *The Heretic* "wasn't a worthy continuation," and *The Exorcist III* was "not as good as the book, but it was still worth to see." This is what it would sound like if Leonard Maltin was really into Green Day.

> *"Weird Al" managed to see* Phantom Menace *just before his song was mastered, but the plot leaks he'd read were accurate enough that he only needed to tweak a few lines slightly—for instance, changing "he thinks he's gonna marry her someday" to "he's probably gonna marry her someday."*

11 TREY PARKER, "THE END OF AN ACT" *(PEARL HARBOR)*

In a neat bit of cultural recycling, *Team America: World Police* composer Trey Parker finally found a working purpose for Michael Bay's *Pearl Harbor*—as a metaphor for pain. "I miss you more than that movie missed the point," Parker sings, turning intangible yearning into words that everyone can understand. "I need you like Ben Affleck needs acting school." (As a deft bit of meta-critique, the backing swells of power chords and melancholy piano recall a typical, overblown Diane Warren rock ballad—just like the kind Bay films favor.) Though satirical, the song does pose two eternal questions: "How does one mend a broken heart?" and, more directly in the final lines, "Why does Michael Bay get to keep on making movies?"

12 ASS PONYS, "NOT SINCE SUPERMAN DIED" *(HENRY: PORTRAIT OF A SERIAL KILLER)*

Ohio's late, lamented Ass Ponys always loved dark little narratives, so it's no surprise that vocalist Chuck Cleaver was drawn to the chilling indie film *Henry: Portrait Of A Serial Killer*. (*Henry* itself was based on the exploits of Henry Lee Lucas and his partner, Ottis Toole; the song's title is drawn from the answer Toole allegedly gave when asked if he had any heroes.) Over an incongruously jolly, jangling rhythm-guitar riff and a whooping chorus, the song recounts some of the movie's most sinister moments before concluding: "They wrapped her in a plastic bag and threw her over the side / they said 'Ottis, do you ever feel remorse?'" Guess what he answered?

13 THE LEMONHEADS, "6IX" *(SEVEN)*

It was always clear when Evan Dando was simply shitting out lyrics rather than taking time to craft them, which is the case on most of *Car Button Cloth*. (The album still has some fine moments, but they seem more lucky than inspired.) "6ix" repeats the line "here comes Gwyneth's head in a box" over and over (along with some other semi-coherent rambling), and it's easy to picture Dando watching the end of *Seven* (or *Se7en*, as some posters rendered it) with dread, when Gwyneth Paltrow's head is, indeed, delivered to her husband in a box.

14 SONIC YOUTH, "MILDRED PIERCE" *(MILDRED PIERCE)*

Technically, this brief, shattering track from 1990's *Goo* may not be about the classic film noir/weeper starring Joan Crawford. It's a bit hard to tell, because the song's only lyrics, hissed through layers of distortion and compression, are "Mildred Pierce." But honestly, what else could it be about? It isn't like there's a sandwich or a roller coaster called Mildred Pierce. Besides, the song, which starts out with a calm, rustling introduction before exploding into a frenzied chaos, perfectly reflects the character's bourgeoisie pretensions before she descends into madness. If this film had been made in the mid-'90s, this could have been its main title.

15 METALLICA, "ONE" *(JOHNNY GOT HIS GUN)*

Metallica made the inspiration for its searing anti-war song "One" clear when it included clips from Dalton Trumbo's *Johnny Got His Gun* in the song's video, the band's first for MTV. It's a testament to Trumbo's film (adapted from his own 1939 novel) that the tortured black-and-white images of Timothy Bottoms' deformed torso tossing and turning in a hospital bed are easily the most disturbing parts of the video. But anyone paying attention to the song's lyrics will appreciate how faithfully Metallica translated Trumbo's narrative in the context of a totally shredding metal song.

16 BERTIE HIGGINS, "KEY LARGO" *(KEY LARGO)*

Written largely about John Huston's 1948 noir-thriller *Key Largo*, Bertie Higgins' song by the same name benefits from his odd obsession with Humphrey Bogart movies. Unlike his song "Casablanca," though, "Key Largo" is mostly about its corresponding movie, not about watching the film. "We had it all, just like Bogie and Bacall," Higgins sings in a soft-rock, Jimmy Buffett-lite swoon, glossing over the hate-ridden ugliness of the island in the film. He also doesn't sing about gangsters, World War II, or a hurricane, reducing those plot elements to a vague romantic hurdle before "that sweet scene of surrender when you gave me your heart."

17 IRON MAIDEN, "MAN ON THE EDGE" *(FALLING DOWN)*

In "Man On The Edge," a tired, Blaze Bayley-era Iron Maiden wasn't really inspired by the silly Michael Douglas movie *Falling Down*—the song just recounts the plot, then repeats "Falling down, falling down, falling down" as a chorus. The band must've genuinely liked the film, though, because there aren't many commercial reasons for honoring a dumb, not particularly popular movie. Sample lyric: "Once he built missiles, a nation's defense / now he can't even give birthday presents."

18 KEVIN O'DONNELL'S QUALITY SIX, "GIRL FROM NEW YORK CITY" *(THE LAST SEDUCTION)*

After nearly full two minutes of playful jump blues, vocalist Andrew Bird (better known as a solo artist than as a contributor to outfits like Kevin O'Donnell's Quality Six) cuts into "Girl From New York City" to lay out the plot of *The Last Seduction* from the POV of the hapless chump who winds up on the wrong end of Linda Fiorentino's deadly femme fatale. It's an odd song, with a jumble of lyrics piling up in an artfully haphazard way that recalls Lambert, Hendricks and Ross' vocal additions to jazz standards, but it's swinging and catchy. It also manages to give away most of the film's plot twists in a few bare lines, including the big reveal at the movie's end. Spoiler warning, Andrew!

STAY OFF THE HELL BUS

13 SONGS ABOUT THE HORRORS OF BUS TRAVEL

1 THE FATIMA MANSIONS, "ONLY LOSERS TAKE THE BUS"

Not everyone on the bus is crazy, but there's no denying that public transportation offers myriad opportunities to mingle with society's wildest and woolliest. In one of the most enjoyably bewildering songs of the late '80s, Fatima Mansions frontman Cathal Coughlan barks out the kind of nonsense that would inspire a hurried seat change: "Churchill was a shopping bag / can you draw the Chinese flag?" Then he returns over and over to his thesis about how only losers ride the bus. It's far too easy to picture him as that raggedly dressed, booze-scented dude in the back-row, glaring and muttering about everything and nothing.

2 KRIS KROSS, "I MISSED THE BUS"

Teen hip-hop outfit Kris Kross is best remembered for its infectious debut single "Jump," though Chris "Mac Daddy" Kelly and Chris "Daddy Mac" Smith were almost as well known for wearing their clothes backward. Maybe that wasn't a fashion choice; maybe they were just in a hurry trying to get to their ride. "I almost broke my neck tryin' to get out the door," they sing on *Totally Krossed Out's* "I Missed The Bus," which narrates the story of a frustrated, sleepy kid who can't catch a transportation break. He misses one bus by oversleeping, then lies back down for a minute and winds up missing a second one. Bus drivers don't care that missing school is going to get him grounded all weekend; they don't even care that he's chasing them down the block until "I lost my lunch money, book bag busted / scuffed up my sneakers and I'm really disgusted." They've got schedules to keep. At least the narrator finds a lesson in dragging into school late: "I learned to never miss my bus again."

3 MEST, "FUCK GREYHOUND BUS"

The inclusion of this song is by no means an endorsement of Mest, whose one-note pop-punk might charitably be classified as dull. But this song is so hilariously honest that it's tough to dismiss: A blow-by-blow account of a band trip to Green Bay, Wisconsin, it features hairy women, a mean driver, and stinky people. Add to that the fact the fare isn't even that cheap—$99—and you've got a hell ride. "Fuck the Greyhound bus, fuck you!" goes the spirited chorus.

THE INTERMINABLE WAIT, HAVING TO SCROUNGE UP BUS FARE, TRANSFERS THAT DON'T WORK... IT'S ENOUGH TO MAKE HITCHHIKING AND CAR-THIEVERY LOOK DOWNRIGHT APPEALING.

4 BUFFALO TOM, "THE BUS"

The bus ride as metaphor for frustration seems pretty obvious, and Buffalo Tom's trudging, down-and-out rocker "The Bus" packs the discomfort into words and sounds alike. It also raises the question of whether the singer is one of the crazies on the ride, or is struggling not to be: "Had a staring contest with a guy I did not know today / outstared everyone on the bus today." Either way, most people probably don't want to share a seat with him.

5 "WEIRD AL" YANKOVIC, "ANOTHER ONE RIDES THE BUS"

If hell is other people, then a crowded city bus is like a traveling First Circle, where lost, faithless souls are piled on top of each other to stew in their hopelessness. On his journey through this divine comedy, the song's hapless protagonist is forced to stand in the back "with the perverts," where he suffocates under the crush of his fellow man: "There's a suitcase poking me in the ribs / there's an elbow in my ear." Yet even though everyone's "packed in like sardines," the bus keeps stopping "to let a couple more freaks get on." And when there's no more room in hell? The deadbeats shall walk the earth.

6 ZZ TOP, "WAITIN' FOR THE BUS"

In just nine lines—three of which are reprises—ZZ Top sums up the shittiness of everyday life. The singer has been waiting for a bus all day, with nothing but a sack lunch to keep him company, and when the bus finally arrives, it's ridiculously crowded. Yes, the bus gets him home, but he makes a solemn vow that he's only going to ride it "'til I Cadillac." But there's no indication that better days are coming any time soon.

7 VIOLENT FEMMES, "WAITING FOR THE BUS"

Regulars, like ZZ Top, know that the only thing worse than riding the bus is waiting for it, essentially putting your fate in the hands of an unsympathetic bureaucracy that, like God, is all too eager to laugh at your plans. So never mind Gordon Gano's pleas to the bus driver to "don't be slow," because he's got somewhere he's got to go: He and the rest of his motley crew ("the mother and the kids, the guy and his date") are stuck standing on the corner waiting, getting mad and getting late, and there isn't a damn thing they can do about it. Sure, they could follow his rallying cry, "Let's call the mayor, let's complain," but City Hall is generally less than sympathetic to a bunch of lowest common denominators who can't even afford cars.

8 DEL THE FUNKY HOMOSAPIEN, "THE WACKY WORLD OF RAPID TRANSIT"

Del The Funky Homosapien was such a wonderful anomaly in the G Funk-addled West Coast hip-hop scene of the early '90s that he might as well have been a purple-skinned Martian. While his thugged-out competition rapped about making the ass drop on their old-school Chevys and digging the scene with a gangsta lean, Del spends "The Wacky World Of Rapid Transit" kvetching about the hassles of public transportation: the interminable wait, having to scrounge up bus fare, transfers that don't work, missing your stop, having to dodge the leftover grease of nearby Afro Sheen enthusiasts, and thuggish kids ice-grilling you from across the aisle. It's enough to make hitchhiking and car-thievery look downright appealing.

9 WESLEY WILLIS, "STAY OFF THE HELL BUS"

When not singing about his favorite bands, people, or mythological creatures, Chicago artist-musician-schizophrenic Wesley Willis frequently bemoaned—in keyboard-centric songs, using a built-in demo tune—particularly shitty bus rides through the city. Not to be confused with his "Hell City Bus," "Freakout Hell Ride," or "Hell Me On The Bus," "Stay Off The Hell Bus" actually feels like a traveling song. After the soul-sucking sound of a bus kicking into gear, Willis shouts, "This is a bad bus ride / it is no fun at all—it is a *hell* ride!" To be fair, Willis doesn't really give himself a chance to enjoy this public-transportation outing, since as he gets on the bus, he calls the driver a "no-good cocksucker." Unsurprisingly, Willis is subsequently ejected—but he didn't hold a grudge, as he went on to write pro-bus anthems like "Harmony Joy Bus Ride" and "Get On The Jitney Bus" before his death in 2003.

10 MUDDY WATERS, "BUS DRIVER"

Riding the bus can be dangerous in non-obvious ways, too—you can even lose your love to the damn driver, like Muddy Waters does in "Bus Driver." He doesn't offer much explanation of why a city employee with no upward mobility outperformed the one and only Hoochie Coochie Man. Perhaps making love to a woman in five minutes' time isn't something to brag about after all, since it leaves 10 minutes to wait for the next man to come along. All Muddy can do now is complain. "It don't seem right," he sings. "He used to give her rides in the daytime, now she gives him rides at night."

11 SOUL COUGHING, "BUS TO BEELZEBUB"

As if it isn't bad enough being on the highway to hell, in this song from Soul Coughing's brilliantly loopy debut, *Ruby Vroom*, you have to take public transportation to get there. While the music cascades with frenetic energy drawn from a sample of Raymond Scott's classic cartoon theme "Powerhouse," vocalist Mike Doughty offers up a strange, disjointed psychedelic vision of… well, it's hard to be sure what's going on, given lyrics like "I absorb trust like a love rhombus." But a bus to Beelzebub is a pretty clear invitation to sin, probably of the carnal sort: "It's a grind grind, it's a grind… I'll scratch you raw." And the repeated chant of "Yellow No. 5, Yellow No. 5" implies that it's a *school* bus to Beelzebub, and that chemical enhancement is involved. So: stoned high-school kids doing the nasty on their way to class, maybe? Yeah, that's the devil's bus.

12 RAFFI, "THE WHEELS ON THE BUS"

What better way to drive yourself completely insane than by narrating the action of your bus ride in song? "The wheels on the bus go round and round / round and round / round and round." Yes, thank you, irrepressible traditional children's song, they do. Why do you want to make our bus rides worse by putting this repetitive tune in our heads whenever we're traveling?

13 JONATHAN RICHMAN, "YOU'RE CRAZY FOR TAKING THE BUS"

If, like Jonathan Richman, you're a romantic type who appreciates humanity in all its tragicomic beauty, riding the bus can be like tossing yourself into a mutable Tennessee Williams play: "Well, a welfare gal and her drunk galoot… you meet folks this way you just don't see while flyin'." No argument there—and true, you don't have to deal with the baggage claim, and your guitar can ride right next to you—but Jojo sounds less than convincing when he raves about the "Pepsi cans rolling around the bus" creating all that grit and slime. Sure, he says he sleeps fine, but people get used to prison cots after a while, too.

Guest List: TOM LENNON

8 MORE RECENTLY REDISCOVERED TENNESSEE WILLIAMS PLAYS

1. *BIRD OF MARZIPAN*
Delilah, a young widow of Natchitoches, discovers that her late husband, the dashing, well-liked Rox Manhaven, was never employed at Natchitoches Life Insurance, but rather spent his workdays dressed in a latex Nazi uniform at the Natchitoches docks, luring young men into "checkers matches." The text totals 480 pages. A stage production would run approximately 12 hours.

2. *BONAVENTURE CEMETERY*
Glenhour Manrox, a fit young senator's son from Savannah, prepares to visit the grave of his great-uncle Pomfrit. For some reason, young Glenhour spends most of the first and second acts doing crunches. The actual cemetery visit happens offstage. Then he returns and takes a shower in act three.

3. *THE WONDERFUL DILDO SHELF*
A strikingly similar story to *The Glass Menagerie*, with a young invalid and her collection of dildos. Entire passages of *Glass Menagerie* dialogue appear in the text, which has led some experts to believe it is, in fact, a first draft of *Glass Menagerie*, not a knock-off.

4. *DIA DE LOS ABDOMINALES*
This work is unfinished, but it seems to be either a sequel or a prequel to *Bonaventure Cemetery*. It involves an unnamed character (possibly Glenhour Manrox) doing crunches with a shirtless Latin man, who also goes unnamed. Williams experts are currently debating whether this is in fact a play at all. Many argue that it is, in fact, just a series of drawings.

5. *SKYLARK AND THE LADYFINGER*
At just three lines, this stands out as Williams' shortest play. It unfolds as follows:
Skylark: "They've found another corpse down by the levee."
Ladyfinger: "Oh, really?"
Skylark: "I reckon either the birds will get it, or those awful children will use it as a scarecrow."
OUT.
That's it. A stunning example of Williams' economy with language.

6. *TURNS OUT CLYDE MAXWELL WAS GAY*
The title pretty much says it all. Clyde Maxwell, a respected judge in New Orleans, turns out to be gay.

7. *PIGGYFRIEND*
This was Williams' failed attempt at a major commercial project. The storyline is remarkably close to a film made almost 40 years later, the 1997 hit *Air Bud*. In Williams' version, a young invalid befriends a basketball-playing pig, and they go on to win the state championship. Perhaps Williams' *Piggyfriend* was never produced for the screen because in the final moments of the championship, the young invalid dies offscreen. An unnamed character enters and tells the pig the news, but the pig doesn't understand, because he is a pig. The pig also doesn't understand that he's just won the championship, for the same reason. The whole manuscript of *Piggyfriend* leaves the reader with an overwhelming sense of grief and futility.

8. *722 TOULOUSE STREET*
Again, Williams examines the fit young character of Glenhour Manrox. An abbreviated synopsis of the action is as follows: "Glenhour Manrox enters a shared apartment at 722 Toulouse Street in the French Quarter. He pours himself a Pernod, then shaves his balls in the sink." Note: this is an abbreviated version. The actual text devotes far more description to the action that Glenhour performs in the sink, and has specific notes for casting the role of Glenhour.

(The authenticity of all of these works is, of course, suspect. Teams of Tennessee Williams experts are currently meeting to debate their provenance, on a case-by-case basis. This process is time-consuming, as most meetings of Tennessee Williams experts devolve into mojito-drinking-and-skinny-dipping parties.)

Tom Lennon is a co-creator and original member of The State *and* Reno 911!, *a show on which he regularly wears short-shorts.*

SUPERDRUNK!

10 FILM ALCOHOLICS WHO SOBER UP TO SAVE THE DAY

1 TOM HANKS, *A LEAGUE OF THEIR OWN* (1992)

Perhaps the most familiar cinematic archetype of the inveterate drunk is the disgraced hero. In *A League Of Their Own*, Tom Hanks plays a prime example of the type: a former baseball star whom team owner Garry Marshall pressures into coaching for the women's league. Hanks finds the whole gig so humiliating that he shows up loaded for his team's first game, introduces himself by taking a leak in the ladies' locker room, then sleeps through subsequent games. But once he realizes the girls can play—and that he has no other options—he sobers up and becomes the hard-driving-but-loveable coach the team needs.

2 DENNIS HOPPER, *HOOSIERS* (1986)

Hopper plays the disgraced-star-turned-lush archetype in *Hoosiers*, though his fall from grace happens on a much smaller stage: the small town of Hickory, Indiana, where the former basketball star is now the town drunk. A chance at redemption arrives when high school basketball coach Gene Hackman recruits Hopper to help coach the Hickory Huskers, an undeveloped but potentially great team. The usual battle between progress (coaching a game solo after Hackman is ejected) and personal demons (Hackman dunking Hopper's head in a sink to sober him up) follows. When the team finally makes it to the state championships, Hopper relapses and ends up listening to the game on a radio in the hospital. Whether that's failure or redemption rides on the outcome of the game.

3 DEAN MARTIN, *RIO BRAVO* (1959)

In a famously pointed reversal of *High Noon's* premise, Howard Hawks' no-nonsense Western *Rio Bravo* stars John Wayne as a sheriff who doesn't want his neighbors' help, but gets it anyway. The one he trusts most is the town drunk, Dean Martin, whom Wayne forces to kick the habit and assist in the protection of a prisoner who's due to be transferred to the feds. Martin gets the shakes but he holds it together, and even guns down a bad guy waiting to ambush Wayne from the rafters. How did he know the fiend was there? A drop of blood fell in Martin's glass of beer. Booze saves the day!

4 PAUL NEWMAN, *THE VERDICT* (1982)

In the early '80s, Paul Newman briefly specialized in louts needing redemption, in dramas as diverse as *Absence Of Malice* (in which he plays a liquor distributor with mob ties) and *The Color Of Money* (in which he plays a liquor distributor with a knack for billiards). In *The Verdict*, Newman stops distributing liquor long enough to gulp some down himself. His character is a lawyer who specializes in easy settlements with insurance companies, though when a friend brings him a medical-malpractice case involving a young woman in a coma, Newman sees a chance to argue on behalf of all the people like himself who've been screwed over and left for dead. That is, if he can put down his quaking shot glass long enough to make the closing statement of his life...

5 HUMPHREY BOGART, *THE AFRICAN QUEEN* (1951)

Bogey won his only Oscar for his role in John Huston's charming action movie as the bedraggled World War I-era riverboat captain who rescues prissy missionary Katharine Hepburn after Germans attack the African village where she was working. They're on the same side, but they share an instant mutual loathing—of the kind that actually masks a deepening attraction, which is the story's main driving force. Bogart mocks Hepburn's plan to destroy the Germans' lake-patrolling gunboat as a foolhardy suicide mission, and turns his back on the idea by sinking even further into his already-substantial boozing. He's horrified to wake up after a particularly inebriated evening to find her methodically tossing his gin bottles overboard one by one—which is, of course, just the wake-up call he needs to rediscover the hero inside himself.

6 BILLY BOB THORNTON, *BAD SANTA* (2003)

If anything can shake mall Santa Billy Bob Thornton out of his binge drinking and overall sleaziness, it's the love of a snot-nosed, pudgy, self-described "dipshit loser" kid who believes Thornton is the real Santa, in spite of repeated proof to the contrary. At rock bottom, Thornton pisses his pants, tells children that his beard falls off because he "loved a woman who wasn't clean," and has anal sex with an overweight woman in a dressing room. But reluctant affection for the kid who gifts him with a homemade, bloody wooden pickle (and ultimately, the Christmas spirit) inspires Thornton to get off the drink and beat the crap out of the kid's schoolyard bullies. Sure, he'll still rob the mall where he's been working, but this time, he'll steal the kid a present.

7 BOB HOSKINS, *WHO FRAMED ROGER RABBIT* (1988)

What drove *Who Framed Roger Rabbit's* hard-boiled private investigator Bob Hoskins to love the bottle and hate cartoons? His love interest, Dolores, sums it up: "'Toon killed his brother… dropped a piano on his head." Though Hoskins is the son of a clown, which should predispose him for laughter, he spends much of his time downing liquid courage and somberly investigating a series of noir cliché leads with zany cartoons. But once the titular mystery takes him into Toontown, a fictional Los Angeles burb populated by animated characters, he decides he'd better face his cartoon demons without booze. Which is just as well—he needs all his coordination and mental agility to come up with the song-and-dance routine that saves the day.

> *For the opposite take on the superdrunk movie archetype, there's Jackie Chan's 1994 Hong Kong kung-fu classic* Drunken Master II *(a.k.a.* The Legend Of Drunken Master*), in which the hero doesn't sober up to save the day. Quite the opposite—the more he drinks, the better he fights.*

8 KENNETH BRANAGH, *THE GINGERBREAD MAN* (1998)

In Robert Altman's re-imagined version of John Grisham's story, Kenneth Branagh plays a drunken lawyer fuckup who helped imprison the menacing father of one of his one-night stands. Now a hurricane is bearing down on Savannah, the psychotic dad is out of jail, and Branagh needs to escape the bottom of his shot glass long enough to save his children from revenge—and find out what was really going on with that waitress who asked him for the favor. The crazy ex-con dad is the ostensible villain, but Branagh's true nemesis is Altman, who deprives his star of any courtroom scenes, adds in the fury of nature as another enemy, and disparages the honorable legal profession by making just about every lawyer on display soggy and inept.

9 PIERCE BROSNAN, *EVELYN* (2002)

This nauseatingly treacly melodrama about a real-life landmark Irish court case sugarcoats virtually every aspect of its story, yet goes out of its way to portray protagonist Pierce Brosnan as an alcoholic sot. When his wife runs off and the state claims his kids, he responds by drunkenly assaulting a priest, then even-more-drunkenly trying to break them out of the church-run school that's holding them. Roughly a quarter of the movie is devoted to him sucking down whiskey, singing in bars, and bemoaning his lot. But eventually, his obligatory saint-like love interest refuses to smooch him, saying it would be "like kissing a soggy beer-mat." When she orders him to "give up the drink," he whines, "For God's sake, that's the hardest thing to do." But soon, he's choosing lemonade, humbly quoting the Bible in court, saving his sickeningly precious kids from the orphanage, and single-handedly changing the face of Irish law. (He gets some help from bonus superdrunk Alan Bates; a retired barrister and former rugby star who guzzles and weaves his way through the movie, Bates comes out of boozy retirement to offer up the key strategies that win the case. No lemonade for him; he responds to the judges' final decision with a long, relieved pull on his flask.)

10 DUDLEY MOORE, *ARTHUR 2: ON THE ROCKS* (1988)

Arthur 2: On The Rocks practically defines the concept of "unnecessary sequel": Everyone lived happily ever after at the close of 1981's *Arthur*, with true love winning out and Christopher Cross getting caught between the moon and New York City. But seven years later, the principals reunited for some reason. Arthur—played by the inimitable Dudley Moore—loses all his money, thanks to his ex-fiancée's vengeful father. Then he loses wife Liza Minnelli. Soon, he's homeless and in a perpetual drunken stupor, which isn't as charming when he's broke. If only Moore's prim butler/disciplinarian Hobson, played by John Gielgud, hadn't died in the first movie. But that's easily solved with a dream sequence/drunken hallucination, wherein Gielgud returns and orders Moore to get his shit together. Soon Moore is off the sauce and on the road to getting his fortune and wife back. Thanks, ghost of dead best friend!

KEEP 'EM COMING, GLEEP-GLOP

1 AMAZING MID-'90S SKETCH-COMEDY SHOW THAT TOWERS ABOVE ALL OTHERS AND STILL PROVIDES ENDLESSLY QUOTABLE MATERIAL MORE THAN A DECADE LATER

1 *MR. SHOW*

In just 30 episodes, *Mr. Show* cemented its place among devotees of smart, weird, cutting comedy. Part of the reason the show was so brilliant was that it never seemed contrived: Masterminds Bob Odenkirk and David Cross just brought what truly made them laugh to the small screen. That meant that the *Mr. Show* dynamic could turn on a dime from simple absurdist gags—like a convenience-store employee who has to call all the way up the chain to the president of the United States to determine whether he can make change for a customer's dollar—to more direct social commentary. One of the show's most memorable characters was Ronnie Dobbs, a wife-beating idiot who got famous for being arrested multiple times on a *COPS*-style reality show. The Dobbs sketches combined everything great about *Mr. Show:* a reflexive sense of humor, a smidge of commentary about America's ridiculousness, and some plain old fearless jokes. Though it wasn't a hit while it aired, *Mr. Show* lives on via DVD and the later successes of its cast, including Sarah Silverman, Jack Black, Brian Posehn, Patton Oswalt, and Tom Kenny, a.k.a. the voice of SpongeBob SquarePants.

DAVID CROSS, BOB ODENKIRK

STEAL THIS LIST

14 MUST-READ BOOKS FOR ASPIRING YOUNG REBELS

1 ABBIE HOFFMAN,
STEAL THIS BOOK

How do you learn how to rebel in the first place? Try taking some advice from social/political activist Abbie Hoffman, starting with the title of his infamous 1971 tome *Steal This Book*. Many of the book's detailed guides to miscreant acts like starting a pirate radio station, stealing food and clothes, and obtaining a free buffalo from the U.S. Department Of The Interior are long obsolete, but it's still a good starting place for today's forward-thinking rabble-rouser. A word of warning: If you're wondering, "What the hell would I do with my own buffalo?" then you probably aren't a rebel.

2 NOAM CHOMSKY,
THE CHOMSKY READER

Rebels are all about sticking it to The Man, and The Man doesn't hate anything more than an 80-year-old America-bashing anarchist. With his trenchant, often devastating criticism of U.S. foreign policy, media, and capitalism, Noam Chomsky is the go-to source for the college student who wants to be known as the campus badass libertarian socialist with anarcho-syndicalist sympathies. *The Chomsky Reader* is as good a place to start as any, even though buying the book will contribute to a sick, inherently unfair economic system that subjugates the poor and benefits the rich and powerful.

3 HOWARD ZINN,
A PEOPLE'S HISTORY OF THE UNITED STATES

Nothing screams, "Hey, look at me, I'm a budding young leftist!" like toting around a copy of Howard Zinn's *A People's History Of The United States*. The 1980 book introduces the radical, mind-blowing ideas that history is written by the winners and that there's a dark, repressive, warmongering underbelly to the American dream, in case you didn't know that already.

4 WILLIAM POWELL,
THE ANARCHIST COOKBOOK

William Powell wrote *The Anarchist Cookbook* in the late '60s, when the idea of blowing shit up on American soil didn't have the connotation it does post-9/11. The book's recipes for whipping up explosives and other such sedition may seem laughably outdated today, but the word "anarchist" is still enough to raise an eyebrow—even though Powell has long since disowned the book, saying it was a "product of my adolescent anger at the prospect of being drafted and sent to Vietnam… I consider it to be a misguided and potentially dangerous publication which should be taken out of print."

5 FRIEDRICH NIETZSCHE,
HUMAN, ALL TOO HUMAN

Valuing personal excellence over herd mentality, living one's life as though it were a work of art—grand statements like that make excellent excuses for skipping class, screwing over your roommates, and not calling that one-night stand the next day. Hey, as Nietzsche says in *Human, All Too Human*, it's just part and parcel of humanity's inherent "will to power," which is our way of "coming to grips with chaos and emptiness." For those who need a personal philosophy without having to do the homework, Nietzsche offers a slash-and-burn template for chucking the whole damn thing.

6 ARTHUR RIMBAUD,
COMPLETE WORKS

Need a literary companion to *The Doors: Greatest Hits?* Fear not, poetic outsider: Arthur Rimbaud's *Complete Works* is your new blueprint. Jim

Morrison was famously a big fan of the doomed, moody 19th-century French writer, whose most famous work, *A Season In Hell*, was written under the influence of massive doses of opium and absinthe. Hopefully that dime bag and 12-pack of Pabst in your dorm room will have the same effect.

7 SYLVIA PLATH, *THE BELL JAR*

Subtitled—or at least it should be—*The Emo Girl's Bible*, *The Bell Jar* is Sylvia Plath's lone novel, an apocalyptically depressing fictionalized chronicle of the mental illness that culminated in Plath's suicide in 1963, a month after the book was published. Checking out early is the ultimate rebellion.

8 ANTON LAVEY, *THE SATANIC BIBLE*

Satanism was a much scarier word in the '70s: Right after Anton LaVey's *The Satanic Bible* came out in 1969, America was awash in urban legends about ritualistic kidnapping and human sacrifice. LaVey, the founder and head of The Church Of Satan until his death in 1997, embedded a much more sinister mandate in his bible, though. His strident advocacy of selfishness, hierarchy, and the superiority of the strong over the weak reads more like a playbook for today's neocon movement. Spooky.

9 CHARLES BUKOWSKI, *FACTOTUM*

Drunkenness isn't just tolerated in college culture, it's encouraged and even glamorized beyond all reason. The same could be said of the work of poet and author Charles Bukowski, the so-called "poet laureate of Skid Row," who made filthy, hopeless alcoholism and indiscriminate skirt-chasing somehow seem admirable. Bukowski's autobiographical 1975 novel *Factotum* details his attempt to forge a writing career while working a series of menial jobs and slowly drinking and fucking himself to death. Sounds awesome, huh?

10 HUNTER S. THOMPSON, *FEAR AND LOATHING IN LAS VEGAS*

In his most famous work, *Fear And Loathing In Las Vegas*, Hunter S. Thompson painted "the search for the American Dream" as a nonstop bender fueled by marijuana, cocaine, psychedelics, liquor, and "a whole galaxy of multi-colored uppers, downers, screamers, laughers"—in short, exactly the kind of rampant self-abuse that most college kids take on as a secondary night course. Most people who read Thompson's work picture themselves in the Good Doctor's place, making pithy, poetic observations on the human condition and eloquently pointing out the hypocrisy of squares, all while blasted out of their skulls. Of course, the reality of Thompson's grueling work ethic and painstakingly honed gift for prose usually runs a distant second to merely replicating his self-indulgence, which is why there haven't been too many noteworthy works from his besotted disciples.

11 HERMAN HESSE, *SIDDHARTHA*

A tale of restless contemplation and great indulgence, *Siddhartha* is a great way to invest the wanderings of youth with meaning. It at least hits a sympathetic note with those prone to sitting on riverbanks and holding drawn-out intellectual debates. Helpfully, Hesse's book is short—his prose chisels down the tale of an Eastern spiritual searcher during the time of Buddha with searing sparseness. That also means that many paperback editions fit nicely in a pocket, keeping young protégés in easy reach of handy quotes like, "Let me warn you, you who are thirsty for knowledge, against the thicket of opinions and the conflict of words," or, "Your mouth is like a freshly cut fig."

12 KURT VONNEGUT, *SLAUGHTERHOUSE-FIVE*

When a budding scholar gets buried under mounds of Spenser and Milton, it's nice to be reminded that prestigious literature can embrace kaleidoscopic storylines, outrageously bizarre humor, swear words, and crude drawings of boobs. As demeaning as it may seem, Vonnegut's books are an ideal read for those with short attention spans, many of whom must be grateful that *Slaughterhouse-Five* put so much meaning into little nuggets like "So it goes." Vonnegut smears a devastating war story, satire, and science-fiction ramble into the tale of Billy Pilgrim, who becomes "unstuck in time" and experiences the firebombing of Dresden and life in a zoo on the planet Tralfamadore, among other things.

13 WILLIAM S. BURROUGHS, *NAKED LUNCH*
Tie off that vein, shower humanity with your wicked contempt, let all those thoughts flow out in unruly tangles, and a sordid revolution is on. Can you keep track? Who the fuck cares? In fact, it's arguable that nobody's supposed to keep track of this novel, a garishly vivid satire spilling all over itself and sliced into randomly ordered bits. Its ruthless vision of addiction and sex makes for constant disorientation, even when it's blazingly funny. Still, it's probably a bit easier to follow than your average Allen Ginsberg poem, and recent editions include Burroughs' handy guide "Letter From A Master Addict To Dangerous Drugs."

14 TOM ROBBINS, *EVEN COWGIRLS GET THE BLUES*
Here's the deal: If you're a freshman in college, you're probably going to read this book and think it's awesome. Then years later you'll think back and wonder what was so awesome about it. If we could remember, we'd tell you.

I FEEL SPECIAL RIGHT NOW, CARLA

2 ACTORS BORN TO PLAY THE MENTALLY CHALLENGED

1-2 GIOVANNI RIBISI AND **JULIETTE LEWIS**
Giovanni Ribisi and Juliette Lewis already had solid acting careers when they accepted their respective roles as Daniel McMann and Carla Tate in Garry Marshall's pandering, borderline-evil attempt at dramatic depth, 1999's *The Other Sister*. Like a minstrel show with goofy expressions and ridiculous voices substituting for blackface, the film aims for "heartwarming and truthful," but settles for ridiculous. Still, the casting is genius. Never before or again would Ribisi and Lewis fit so well into their roles: Ribisi is ultimately more believable as a developmentally disabled, sex-obsessed marching-band aficionado than he was as a stockbroker in *Boiler Room*, and Lewis makes more sense as Carla, the mentally challenged rich girl, than she does as the singer in a real-life rock band. Too bad such roles only tend to come around once in a career.

(* *ACTUAL DIALOGUE FROM* THE OTHER SISTER)

DON'T JUST SAY URKEL

25 SURE SIGNS THAT A SITCOM IS TERRIBLE

1 There's a talking animal.
2 It's all live-action dinosaurs.
3 Jim Belushi is in it.
4 It's called "Tyler Perry's" anything.
5 It leans heavily on one or more adorable, precocious children for laugh lines and reaction shots…
6 …or uses animals for the same purpose.
7 It's about a single girl trying to navigate the wacky world of dating while also maintaining a career.
8 Robots, aliens, or Bigfoot-type things are involved.
9 There's a fat, obnoxious man married to a beautiful, understanding woman who isn't named "Marge Simpson."
10 It stars an actor who previously appeared in a much more popular sitcom.
11 The star was once a respected rapper.
12 Every episode ends with hugging or learning.
13 It's predicated on the idea that one of the main characters has some quality or property that only one other character knows about or believes in.
14 There are more than two but fewer than three men mentioned in the title.
15 It centers on a ridiculous artificial situation, like a mistaken identity, or people who openly hate each other being forced to live together.
16 There's a "cool" uncle, who may or may not wear leather vests.
17 It stars Bill Cosby but is called anything except *The Cosby Show*.
18 At least once per episode, the studio audience is prompted to lasciviously "Woooooo!"
19 It awkwardly, repeatedly beats viewers over the head about what city it's set in.
20 It's a short-lived spin-off of a long-running success.
21 It's based on a film not called *M*A*S*H* or *The Odd Couple*.
22 It's a vehicle for a former sports star.
23 Week after week, great pains are taken to make sure that nothing about the characters or their circumstances ever changes.
24 The premise is taken from a Geico commercial.
25 Twins.

WHITHER *THE WRATH OF MOM?*

14 FAILED ATTEMPTS TO START FILM FRANCHISES

1 *THE ADVENTURES OF BUCKAROO BANZAI ACROSS THE EIGHTH DIMENSION* (1984)

Buckaroo Banzai came to theaters less as a film than as a prepackaged, planned cult phenomenon, complete with merchandising, a Marvel comic-book adaptation, a computer-game version, and a closing credit commanding viewers to watch out for the upcoming sequel, *Buckaroo Banzai Vs. The World Crime League*. But the movie bombed, its production company went bankrupt, and the sequel rights were blocked in litigation, for reasons that are still a source of lively Internet debate. In theory, the sequel would have followed up on scenes cut from the theatrical version of the film and restored on the DVD version, in which supervillain Hanoi Xan, head of the World Crime League, killed the parents of weird-science hero Buckaroo Banzai (Peter Weller). As it is, that film-end promise of a sequel mostly stands as just another bit of weird texture in an already very weirdly textured cult hit.

> A.V. CLUB
>
> *As a backhand* Buckaroo Banzai *reference,* Free Enterprise *ended with a title card asking viewers to watch for* William Shatner Versus The World Crime League.

2 *DOCTOR DETROIT* (1983)

After the success of *Night Shift* and *Risky Business*, the "ordinary guy who becomes a pimp" genre was flying high. Then came this lackluster comedy starring Dan Aykroyd as a henpecked professor conned into managing a stable of prostitutes. Faced with a hostile takeover by a mob boss known only as "Mom," Aykroyd dons a fright wig, green pants, and a steel glove (the ultimate "pimp hand") and adopts a bizarre, Carol Channing-esque voice to transform himself into "Doctor Detroit," the city's most feared pimp. In spite of a James Brown cameo and a rousing Devo theme song, *Detroit* is essentially a mediocre skit stretched to feature length, and Aykroyd's character is so unbearably forced that 90 minutes with him is already far too many. It's no wonder that the sequel proposed in the credits—*Doctor Detroit II: The Wrath Of Mom*—never happened.

3 *THE ROCKETEER* (1991)

Adapted from Dave Stevens' comic book, this adventure film about a boy and his rocket pack brims with 1930s atmosphere, from its hero's gee-whiz enthusiasm for do-goodery to the art-deco sets to the classic film references to Jennifer Connelly's throwback pin-up looks. Director Joe Johnston (*Honey, I Shrunk The Kids*) gives it a sense of high-spirited adventure that's simultaneously affectionate toward old-time serials and determined to top them. Sound familiar? While it's foolish to compare *The Rocketeer* to the similarly inspired *Indiana Jones* and *Star Wars* films, it's smart and funny enough to make it one of the more unfortunate dead-ends on this list. Johnston proves himself a sure hand with the comic action setpieces, but just as capable at capturing the full corruption of bad guy Timothy Dalton (playing a Nazi-sympathizing variation on Errol Flynn). The final scene sets up a sequel that short-of-expectations box-office prevented.

4 *DAREDEVIL* (2003)

Better minds could have turned Marvel's *Daredevil* comic into a long-running series. The character—a blind lawyer turned nighttime vigilante—has bottomless potential, and over the years, creators like Frank Miller and Brian Michael Bendis have created a considerable archive of classic stories and characters that could be used as source material. And Ben Affleck wasn't a bad choice for the lead, either. (Honestly!) Too bad irritatingly flashy director Mark Steven Johnson tried to squeeze too much into one movie, turning his hero into a mean-spirited, bloodthirsty jerk in the process.

5 *DICK TRACY* (1990)

In retrospect, an ancient comic strip centered on a bland, strait-laced, middle-aged hero—and well before the current comics-to-movies craze—wasn't likely to produce a box-office hit. Still, Disney poured massive resources into Warren Beatty's *Dick Tracy* in the hope that Chester Gould's comic would yield a candy-colored franchise rooted in strong themes of honor, moral turpitude, and law and order. Beatty-as-actor can probably shoulder much of the blame for the film's disappointing performance, though a square-jawed do-gooder like Dick Tracy doesn't leave much room for interpretation. But Beatty-as-director, with peerless assists by production designer Richard Sylbert and cinematographer Vittorio Storaro, succeeded in creating a singularly beautiful gangland in bold primary colors.

6 *GODZILLA* (1998)

When *Godzilla* was released just be-

Godzilla's *Devlin and Emmerich were apparently braced for bad reviews; they preemptively dissed the critics by naming their villainous mayor Ebert, and his assistant, Gene.*

fore Memorial Day in 1998, there was no reason to believe it wouldn't be a record-breaking smash: The producer-director team of Dean Devlin and Roland Emmerich were hot off the runaway hit *Independence Day*, and they were reviving the biggest movie monster this side of King Kong, with built-in sequels that could pit the beast against Mothra, Mechagodzilla, and even the Smog Monster if they wanted to go the environmental route. They paid for their hubris. The film was a classic case where a script that wasn't worth two cents got inflated into a $100 million-plus megaproduction, ensuring that anything but a blockbuster success would be a financial failure. Which is what Devlin and Emmerich got.

7 *MASTER AND COMMANDER: THE FAR SIDE OF THE WORLD* (2003)

The awkward title shoves together two of Patrick O'Brian's addictive seafaring adventure stories of the Napoleonic war, but it also teases viewers with the possibility that there might be more entries in the *Master And Commander* series. Peter Weir's initial glorious escapade concludes with Captain Jack Aubrey (played with pudgy enthusiasm by Russell Crowe) realizing that he's been foiled by a dastardly French trick, and heeling his ship around to chase his evasive target. By ending the story there, Weir seemed to be pledging that Aubrey and his friend Stephen Maturin (Paul Bettany) were still out there climbing the yards and running out the guns, and that he'd eventually rejoin the chase in progress, but so far, the Aubrey-Maturin novels remain untapped cinematic ground.

8 *WING COMMANDER* (1999)

The first entries in film series are often chockfull of clumsy exposition that only pays off in later installments. But what happens when those later installments never arrive? That was the case with 1999's ill-fated *Wing Commander*, an exposition-heavy adaptation of a popular videogame series that feels like both the sequel to a film not worth seeing and a prequel to sequels that never arrived. Then again, considering Freddie Prinze Jr.'s wooden lead performance and the film's hopelessly convoluted screenplay, it's probably best that the *Wing Commander* franchise never limped past its aborted would-be film-series launch.

9 *SAHARA* (2005)

According to the tagline on the *Sahara* poster, "Adventure has a new name." But the movie not only failed to turn Clive Cussler's pulpy explorer-hero Dirk Pitt into the next franchise movie character, it also prompted Cussler to sue the producers, claiming a loss of future income because they botched *Sahara* so badly. Cussler particularly blamed the casting of zonked-out sun-worshipper Matthew McConaughey as his man-of-action. The producers' defense? Cussler's books aren't as popular as he claimed they were, so they were the ones who were defrauded. If *Sahara* ever does get a sequel, maybe it'll be a documentary about this case.

10-11 *THE PHANTOM* (1996) / *THE SHADOW* (1994)

Lee Falk's costumed cartoon hero pre-dates Superman, and still has a home on many daily comics pages, but audiences in 1996 didn't go for the purple-clad "Ghost Who Walks," perhaps because *The Phantom's* '30s setting and bloodless serial-style dust-ups seemed too self-consciously retro. The same fate befell the movie version of *The Shadow* two years earlier. Both movies had strong leads (Billy Zane in the former, Alec Baldwin in the latter) and crisp, clean storytelling, but in an action world, mere adventure rarely sells.

12 *THE AVENGERS* (1998)

Even though the original British TV version of *The Avengers* trafficked in absurdity and pop surrealism, it still maintained a sense of subtlety completely lacking from this 1998 big-screen abomination. Outside of casting Ralph Fiennes and Uma Thurman to play the stylish, droll secret-agent heroes, little apparent effort was made to match the original's natty spirit. Instead, a TV classic of an earlier era was ground up in the American blockbuster machine—residual explosions and all.

THE FILM WAS A CLASSIC CASE WHERE A SCRIPT THAT WASN'T WORTH TWO CENTS GOT INFLATED INTO A $100 MILLION-PLUS MEGA-PRODUCTION, ENSURING THAT ANYTHING BUT A BLOCKBUSTER SUCCESS WOULD BE A FINANCIAL FAILURE.

13 *THE MOD SQUAD* (1999)

This misbegotten, "quick, our option is expiring" 1999 adaptation of the '60s cult TV series takes the updating-for-a-new-generation idea to its ridiculous extreme by allowing Giovanni Ribisi, Claire Danes, and Omar Epps to slack it up as cops too cool to actually do anything. While the cast acts as surly and strange as they want, some villain or another periodically wanders into the frame and explains the plot to them, occasionally even goading them into action. At the end of the film, the three principals gather on a pier to decide whether to continue as undercover cops. They all shrug. "Yeah," Epps says, "I guess so." Predictably, America shrugged right back.

14 *WILD WILD WEST* (1999)

While Will Smith was busy boasting to any showbiz reporter in earshot about how he "owned" the summer, his *Men In Black* collaborator Barry Sonnenfeld was struggling to figure out how to turn a stubbornly oddball science-fiction Western into a tent-pole franchise. *Wild Wild West*'s problem is that its clumsy, cloddish blockbuster side—embodied by the cocky-to-a-fault Smith—gets in the way of its funky, fanciful side. But those flashes of imagination and wit—largely embodied by Kevin Kline, playing a wide-eyed inventor—are enough to make any fan of eccentricity curse the demands of big-budget filmmaking, which often clobber good ideas to a premature death.

RATTLE AND DUMB

8 ROCK MOVIES THAT MAKE THEIR SUBJECTS LOOK LIKE DICKS

1 U2, *RATTLE AND HUM* (1988)

Even before they were rock superstars, the members of U2 flirted with megalomania, particularly Bono, who aspired to be both larger-than-life (with a spectacularly bushy, Mel Gibson-in-*Lethal Weapon*-style mullet, no less) and a John Lennon-esque pop politician. With 1987's *The Joshua Tree*, record sales finally matched the band's hefty ambitions. Having finally been handed enough rope to hang themselves, they made a movie charting their awkward transition from beloved cult band to backlash-ready stadium-rock ego factory. *Rattle And Hum* attempted to recast the Irish group as the next great American rock band, showing U2 covering Bob Dylan, jamming with B.B. King, and recording at Sun Studios. While the music in *Rattle And Hum* is often good, U2's eagerness to place itself in the rock pantheon was at best premature, and at worst, unseemly, annoying, and pompous. Even U2 seemed to agree, and it radically reinvented itself on its next album, the brilliant *Achtung Baby*.

2 ROBBIE ROBERTSON, *THE LAST WALTZ* (1978)

The Band emerged in the late '60s as the embodiment of the era's ideal of communal generosity. In The Band, everybody sang, made crucial creative contributions, and was both leader and follower. But by the middle of the '70s, the "Me Decade" had taken its toll, and songwriter-guitarist Robbie Robertson began elbowing out the rest of the group. Martin Scorsese's film *The Last Waltz* is practically *The Robbie Robertson Show*; he appears in nearly every frame, and frequently talks over his bandmates in interview clips. (Richard Manuel, once described by Eric Clapton as "the true light of The Band," is mostly M.I.A.) As good as *The Last Waltz* is in many ways, Scorsese seems bent on lionizing his good friend Robertson at the expense of his equally worthy partners, which wasn't lost on critics like Dave Marsh, who quipped that Robertson is "one of the few people capable of making Bob Dylan seem humble." Speaking of which…

3 BOB DYLAN, *DON'T LOOK BACK* (1967)

In 1965, Bob Dylan was paradoxically one of the world's most famous pop stars and one of its most sought-after political commentators. This meant the press simultaneously took him way too seriously and aggressively badgered him with condescending questions. In the fly-on-the-wall documentary *Don't Look Back*, Dylan responds to a toxic mix of hero worship and clueless media inquisition with withering contempt

for nearly everyone and everything. It's hard to blame him, as the film's never-ending run of press conferences and monotonous concert performances conveys just how wearying stardom can be. But Dylan often just seems like a jerk for no good reason, coldly ignoring tour-mate Joan Baez—their romantic relationship entered its final stages around this time—and playing silly mind games with even the more thoughtful journalists. At one point, Dylan tells a *Time* writer to "print the truth," which he says would be "a photo of a tramp vomiting in the sewer." Deep.

4 LARS ULRICH, *SOME KIND OF MONSTER* (2004)

Lars Ulrich was a target of media ridicule after becoming the public face of Metallica's lawsuit against its own fans for Napster-aided music piracy. But *Some Kind Of Monster*, a memorable behind-the-scenes film about Metallica's least memorable album, *St. Anger*, suggests that Ulrich was hated just as much in his own band. James Hetfield, for one, appears on the verge of decking his pint-sized, art-collecting, bleached-blond drummer every second they're in the same room. He isn't alone. Whether he's talking in insipid therapy-speak ("Aggressive music can be made using only positive energy") or generally acting like a self-pitying boob, there isn't enough of Lars Ulrich to go around for all the viewers who would want a piece of him after watching *Some Kind Of Monster*.

5 PAUL MCCARTNEY, *LET IT BE* (1970)

How can you hate a guy who worked overtime to prevent The Beatles from breaking up? It's a tall order, but Paul McCartney earns the anger in *Let It Be*, a document of the acrimonious sessions for the aborted *Get Back* album (later released as *Let It Be*). McCartney was the only Beatle fully engaged in the band by 1969, and judging from *Let It Be*, he corralled the other members by being an overbearing bully. The film's most famous scene features George Harrison finally breaking down under McCartney's constant nagging, promising to play whatever Paul wants, or to not play at all. Small wonder McCartney played all the instruments himself on his first solo album.

6 ANTON NEWCOMBE AND COURTNEY TAYLOR-TAYLOR, *DIG!* (2004)

The engaging documentary *Dig!* pits a pair of rock friends against each other, painting one as a true artist who can't play by the rules, and the other as a ponce all too eager to sell out. They each come across as bad in their own way, but Dandy Warhols frontman Courtney Taylor-Taylor gets the worst of it. In contrast to his rival, Anton Newcombe of The Brian Jonestown Massacre, Taylor-Taylor seems pompous beyond his band's ability. ("I sneeze and hits come out," he wrongfully brags.) Newcombe, on the other hand, just seems crazy, but at least he isn't desperate and reeking of sleaze, like his ex-friend.

7 LIL WAYNE, *THE CARTER* (2009)

Dwayne "Lil Wayne" Carter stumbles purposefully through *The Carter* in a codeine and marijuana haze. Ensconced in a bubble of narcissistic self-love, the self-proclaimed "best rapper alive" brags about losing his virginity at an early age, terrorizes a hapless interviewer who asks earnest questions about his place in the history of New Orleans music, tells another reporter that if he ruled the world he'd end all alimony and child support, and spends as little time as possible with his adorable, adoring daughter. The alternately likeable and obnoxious superstar would be wise to heed Public Enemy's prophetic words and stop believing his own hype.

8 EVERYBODY, *THE DECLINE OF WESTERN CIVILIZATION PART II: THE METAL YEARS* (1988)

Rock historians usually trace the commercial decline of '80s hair metal to the release of Nirvana's *Nevermind* in 1991, but the seeds of the scene's destruction were actually sown three years earlier with Penelope Spheeris' invaluable time capsule *The Decline Of Western Civilization Part II: The Metal Years*. Funny and depressing in equal doses, *Decline* features interviews with rock stars and wannabes working on L.A.'s Sunset Strip. Everyone comes off badly, regardless of star status—whether it's Paul Stanley of Kiss lying in bed with half a dozen girls half his age, club owner (and future MTV VJ) Riki Rachtman talking about how girls who dress "sleazy" get in his bar easier, or, most infamously, W.A.S.P.'s Chris Holmes nearly drinking himself to death in his swimming pool while his mom looks on. Surprisingly, metal didn't seem so cool after that.

DON'T BLOW IT

10 GREAT SONGS NEARLY RUINED BY SAXOPHONE

1 DAVID BOWIE, "YOUNG AMERICANS"

In pop and rock music, saxophone should be used like cayenne pepper: Sprinkle a bit on, and you'll get a spicy jolt. Add even a bit too much, and an otherwise-delicious dish will sink into pain. In the carefree '70s, David Bowie got soulful with the album *Young Americans*, but he wasn't proficient enough to realize that pouring sax on the title track would drown it. It'd be easy to argue that the sax actually *makes* "Young Americans," but imagine the greatness it could've achieved without the constant nagging and yipping.

2 THE CURE, "A NIGHT LIKE THIS"

Robert Smith has been known to overstretch, but nearly all of The Cure's 1985 classic *The Head On The Door* is pretty untouchable. Until, that is, the lovely lament "A Night Like This" heads into its final 90 seconds. A sax solo straight out of a rainy movie interrupts the weeping, adding purely fake emotion and an ugly air of professionalism to a song that didn't need it. Only the sax's final bleat—which sounds a bit like an accident—makes sense in this context. In the song's video, the sax player doesn't even show up, and the band looks uncomfortable.

3 BROKEN SOCIAL SCENE, "ALMOST CRIMES"

Broken Social Scene's kitchen-sink approach to songwriting is part of what makes the Canadian band so intriguing, and "Almost Crimes" packs in fuzzy radio sounds, distant voices, and insistent rhythms. During one forceful breakdown, though, BSS gives in to free-jazz madness, interrupting the mood completely. If the bleating were any more prominent, it might derail things completely, but it's thankfully pretty buried.

4 THE HOLD STEADY, "HOSTILE, MASS."

In its quest to be the new-millennial E Street Band (or at least the world's greatest bar band), The Hold Steady injected sax into this defining track from *Almost Killed Me*. It definitely delivers the "Hey, we're not a regular indie band!" message, but it runs so far in the opposite direction—and competes so gruffly in the mix with churning guitars—that it feels like overcompensation. Save it for the places it makes sense, gents—don't use it just because it's there.

5 BRUCE SPRINGSTEEN, "JUNGLELAND"

It wouldn't be a saxophone list without Clarence Clemons, the beating heart of The E Street Band—so much so that Bruce tended to overuse him. The first half of the incredibly lengthy solo in "Jungleland" adds depth to a pretty incredible song, but then everything just devolves into a strutting cheese factory. The song recovers, but maybe The Boss should have let Clemons stop when things were still going well.

6 RADIOHEAD, "THE NATIONAL ANTHEM"

Radiohead in experimental mode is every bit as exciting and compelling as Radiohead in pop-leaning mode, and this *Kid A* track exemplifies the things that go right when the band leaves hooks behind. There's a monster bassline, a semi-nonsensical lyric delivered through echoey effects, and a general sense of dread. Then comes the sax, nearly turning things into a skronky jam-fest. Proof that it's questionable: The song inspired a group called Radiohead Jam Band.

7 MADNESS, "IT MUST BE LOVE"

Here's another case of a band trying

to get its money's worth from a sax player: The honking is tasteful and integrated throughout most of this sweet little piano-driven song, but like so many bands on the radio in the '80s, Madness apparently felt the need for a solo. Blame Duran Duran. At least this one is mercifully short.

8 THE REPLACEMENTS, "I DON'T KNOW"

The tasteful two-note sax bit that repeats throughout this snarler from *Pleased To Meet Me* isn't the problem; it's when The Replacements let the sax-man do his own thing that it gets ugly (and incongruously mainstream). Live, The Replacements didn't bother bringing the sax player. (Or being sober.)

9 GALAXIE 500, "BLUE THUNDER (WITH SAX)"

The warning is right there in the title. "Blue Thunder" is a magnificent example of the evils of saxophone, because both versions—with and without—are readily available. One is a majestic precursor to the slowcore movement, ambling along gently. The other is like a bucket of cold water dumped on an unsuspecting dreamer.

10 SWERVEDRIVER, "NEVER LOSE THAT FEELING/NEVER LEARN"

A sadly forgotten hero of the shoegazer movement that never really fit the mold, Swervedriver added gauze to songs that rocked far more directly than contemporaries like Ride. "Never Lose That Feeling/Never Learn," the final track from 1993's mega *Mezcal Head*, would be one of the band's greatest accomplishments, if only Swervedriver had let it end at the five-minute mark. Instead, it stretches out to nearly 12 minutes, filled with wandering saxophone that gets more annoying as time elapses.

Guest List:

TIM HEIDECKER AND ERIC WAREHEIM

OUR FAVORITE *SHREK* MOVIES, IN ORDER OF PREFERENCE

1. 3
2. 1
3. 2
4. 4-D

Tim Heidecker and Eric Wareheim are the creators and stars of Tom Goes To The Mayor *and* Tim And Eric Awesome Show, Great Job! *In their spare time, they film unsolicited promos for* Shrek *movies.*

WRITTEN WITH LIGHTNING

12 FILMS THAT DEFINED THEIR DECADES

1 "MR. EDISON AT WORK IN HIS CHEMICAL LABORATORY" *(1897)*

This early "actuality" runs 30 seconds, showing Thomas Alva Edison fussing with Bunsen burners and beakers by himself in a lab. Except that it isn't a lab—it's a set, constructed outdoors because no one had yet invented lights powerful enough to illuminate an indoor scene. And Edison likely wouldn't have been tinkering alone like this, since by this point in his career, he was more of a manager, supervising his employees rather than doing much inventing himself. Even the movie cameras capturing this staged event—the patents for which were tightly held by Edison—were conceived and constructed by somebody else. So here, at the dawn of cinema, we have one of the first object lessons in how an image can be carefully and even deceitfully built, as Edison offers an illusion of truth to a public fascinated by this new age of technological wonder.

2 "THE MAN WITH THE RUBBER HEAD" *(1901)*

Primed to captivate a public weary of actualities, Georges Méliès became one of the first filmmakers to treat the camera like a toy, playing with time-lapse photography, multiple exposures, fade-ins, and fade-outs. In "The Man With The Rubber Head," a mad scientist copies his own head, puts it on a table, attaches a bellows to it, expands it like a balloon, and then deflates it. Then his assistant comes in, grabs the bellows, and takes the experiment too far. The whole film is over and done in three minutes, just long enough to baffle viewers, tease them with impending disaster, let them off the hook, then bring the disaster to fruition. And all this during an era of innovation and experimentation where real science was so arcane as to almost seem like magic.

3 *INTOLERANCE* *(1916)*

"It was like writing history with lightning," Woodrow Wilson was famously quoted as saying about *The Birth Of A Nation*, D.W. Griffith's incendiary masterpiece about the Civil War and its aftermath. Though the film changed cinema forever, baring the racial and regional divides that still fractured the country, Griffith's epic follow-up *Intolerance* was even more wide-ranging. Upset by the controversy over *Birth Of A Nation*'s racist content, Griffith embarked on one of the great follies in film history—a three-hour opus that spanned four time periods, stretching back to Babylon in 539 B.C. and jumping ahead to Christ's persecution and crucifixion, the Renaissance period in France, and a modern-day tale of labor unrest and injustice in California. By far the most expensive film ever made in its day, *Intolerance* attempted to show man's inhumanity to man throughout the ages, and love's power to intercede and transcend. In the process, it took the pulse of a nation in transition, one that was still finding itself while bracing for a new conflict overseas.

4 GREED *(1924)*

In Erich von Stroheim's *Greed*, fatalism and opportunity clash at every possible turn. Though adapted from Frank Norris' 1899 novel *McTeague*, it's perfectly suited for the boisterous '20s, a decade that promised to cast off the mistakes of the past, but could never escape the shadow of a recent World War, or the inevitable sense that it wouldn't be the last. The hulking Gibson Gowland plays the slow-witted son of struggling miners; improbably, he falls into the trade of dentistry through less-than-conventional means. He's happy for a while, but soon learns that the American dream has its limits, as he bungles toward an ending that defines hell on earth. Shooting on location in a San Francisco that's more Victorian than modern, von Stroheim captures an era flowering into its own even as it falls prey to the faults that have haunted humanity since Adam.

5 I AM A FUGITIVE FROM A CHAIN GANG *(1932)*

The Great Depression, Marxist critique, and the flat griminess of Warner Brothers' "social-problem films" collide in *I Am A Fugitive From A Chain Gang*, a fleet, tense prison drama in which the metaphorical leg-irons weighing down "forgotten man" Paul Muni exist long before he gets arrested, and long after. Guilty only of being poor, Muni is accused of a murder he didn't commit, and he lands at an inhumane Georgia prison farm. Then he escapes, only to get blackmailed into a lousy job and a crummy marriage. Like a lot of early sound films, *Chain Gang* has a spare look and a crackly soundtrack, but it also burns with intense rage at how people can screw each other over.

6 THE THIRD MAN *(1949)*

The '40s began with *Citizen Kane*, an ahead-of-its-time stylistic wonder contemplating the neuroses of a great man; Orson Welles made the film shortly before America entered World War II and had to confront the soul-staining cost of doing the right thing. And the decade ended with Welles playing a devilishly practical opportunist in Carol Reed's *The Third Man*, a sophisticated thriller about the moral compromises of post-war Europe, shot in a style that owed an equal debt to *Citizen Kane's* cockeyed expressionism and the then-spreading shadows of film noir. In one of the film's most deliciously metaphorical moments, do-gooder American writer Joseph Cotten gets knocked dizzy and grabs a wooden railing for support, only to find that the top of the railing is loose. After 10 years of concentration camps, atomic bombs, and increasingly complicated Hollywood heroes, there were apparently no places for a traditional good guy to find his bearings.

7 WILL SUCCESS SPOIL ROCK HUNTER? *(1957)*

Ace gag-man Frank Tashlin pioneered live-action techniques as a standout animation director for Looney Tunes, but found his greatest fame as a live-action satirist whose personal obsessions—television, advertising, the gaucheness of youth culture, the cult of eternal upward mobility, the Barnum-esque nature of capitalism, sensual curves—adroitly reflected popular preoccupations of the '50s. *Will Success Spoil Rock Hunter?* is Tashlin's simultaneously loving and scathing send-up of advertising, television, pop stardom at its most Warholian, and the all-American mania for success, '50s-style. As a loveable ad-man duped into pretending to be the boyfriend

ORSON WELLES, *THE THIRD MAN*

of movie star Jayne Mansfield, Tony Randall brings an infectious sense of joy and innocence to the part of a fundamentally sane man driven a little batty by the ridiculousness of the dizzy pop world around him.

8 *WEEKEND* (1967)

In the late '60s, a free-floating sense of revolution energized the radical left, especially in France following the tumult and turmoil of 1968. No film reflected the simultaneous horror and hope of revolts to come more powerfully or directly than Jean-Luc Godard's *Weekend*, a scabrous black comedy about a hideous upper-class couple stuck in a bloody Marxist revolution. *Weekend* and Godard's early masterpiece *Breathless* serve as perfect bookends for the decade Godard loomed over as a trickster-god. For all its darkness and nihilism, *Breathless* conveys the excitement and electricity of the early '60s, while *Weekend* captures the mounting despair of a decade whose good vibes and dreamy idealism darkened gradually but dramatically into a state of apocalyptic paranoia.

9 *NASHVILLE* (1975)

The mounting Vietnam- and Watergate-fueled despair that characterized the early '70s finds assured expression in the crazy-quilt Americana of Robert Altman's masterpiece. Veterans, drifters, political wonks, stars, would-be stars, burn-outs, and enigmas all drift through a town in which entertainment has been confused with politics, and vice versa. Altman slides the tone from comedy to tragedy as the film makes its tuneful progress toward an apocalyptic vision of the world at mid-decade. As usual, he leans on his cast members, who, though they're mostly non-singers and non-songwriters, generally supplied their own perfectly suited songs. It's like there was something in the air.

10 *BACK TO THE FUTURE* (1985)

Like David Lynch's *Blue Velvet*, another quintessential '80s film, *Back To The Future* suggests that behind the white picket fences and carefully manicured lawns of Ronald Reagan's "Morning In America" lies all manner of Oedipal weirdness. Lynch turned that thesis into art; Robert Zemeckis transformed it into crackerjack entertainment with a deceptively dark subtext. In *Back To The Future*, underachieving teen Michael J. Fox—who embodied the '80s as yuppie-in-training Alex P. Keaton on *Family Ties*—lives out the fantasies of Reagan and his backward-looking acolytes by literally returning to the Eisenhower era, where he must ward off the sexual advances of disconcertingly hot mom Lea Thompson in order to avoid disintegrating. It doesn't seem at all coincidental that one of the film's sharpest gags finds mad scientist Christopher Lloyd snorting with disbelief upon being told that the hammy B-list actor from *Bedtime For Bonzo* would eventually become president of the United States.

11 *PULP FICTION* (1994)

For better or worse, Quentin Tarantino's postmodern gangland smash dominated the '90s. Like Nirvana's *Nevermind*, *Pulp Fiction* proved the retail clout of an emerging generation, showing how a punk ethos—or its cinematic equivalent, irony—could sell to ex-latchkey-kids raised on TV, Saturday matinees, '70s chic, and hard-rock records spun in dank, wood-paneled basements. Just as the radio was soon filled with Nirvana wannabes, post-Tarantino multiplexes were flooded with twisty, pop-culture-savvy crime capers, almost none of which matched *Pulp Fiction's* wit, style, or informed homage to art and trash. The twentysomethings who watched *Pulp Fiction* dozens of times over weren't just looking for cool movie characters, they were returning repeatedly to a cinematic universe that imbued the detritus of their youth—the theme restaurants, the movie quotes, the meaningless banter about trivia—with meaning.

12 *25TH HOUR* (2002)

Many movies were at various stages of production in New York around 9/11, but while others rushed to digitally airbrush out the Twin Towers and pretend that nothing had happened, Spike Lee seized the moment. Lee's best films have always tried to capture the tenor of the times, and *25th Hour* beautifully incorporates 9/11 into a story about the loss and regret of a condemned man (Edward Norton) who realizes that while he's serving the prison sentence he's heading for, New York as he knows it will evaporate just as surely as it did on that day. The moving opening-credits sequence—an artful framing of the "Tribute In Light," which temporarily filled the two gaps in the skyline—establishes a mournful tone that's sustained throughout, and a montage near the end unexpectedly celebrates the resilience, diversity, and humanity that the tragedy couldn't extinguish. By sheer chance, the right artist was there at the right time to capture the defining event of the young century.

FUCK THIS TOWN

18 KISS-OFF SONGS TO CITIES

1 ROBBIE FULKS, "FUCK THIS TOWN"

Country smart-aleck Robbie Fulks moved to Nashville during the post-Garth Brooks gold rush of the early '90s; there, he worked for a publishing company that shopped songs to country artists. The experience was understandably soul-crushing, so Fulks penned this bile-filled "fuck you" to Music Row—peddlers of "soft-rock feminist crap" to a "moron market"—on his 1997 debut, *South Mouth*. He's since grown more forgiving of Nashville, but "Fuck This Town" is another example of a great musical tradition: Writing off entire cities in song.

Key line: "So fuck this town, fuck this town / fuck it end-to-end, fuck it up and down / can't get noticed—can't get found—can't get a cut, so fuck this town."

2 IKE & TINA TURNER, "NUTBUSH CITY LIMITS"

Any burg that birthed and raised Tina Turner should be pretty amazing. But The Queen Of Rock 'N' Roll was more than happy to escape her hometown of Nutbush, Tennessee, as evidenced by this 1973 hit, Ike & Tina's last as a duo. Over heavy wah-guitar action and unsettling synthesizer, Tina belts out a list of Nutbush's main attractions—"A church house, gin house, schoolhouse, outhouse"—before railing against the constricting effect the village had on a wild soul like herself.

Key line: "A one-horse town / you have to watch what you're puttin' down in old Nutbush."

3 DIXIE CHICKS, "LUBBOCK OR LEAVE IT"

Shaking off the dust of a one-horse town is a common theme in modern country music, though that sentiment is rarely laced with the amounts of vitriol Dixie Chicks' Natalie Maines spits in this kiss-off to her hometown. Obviously still smarting from the thrashing she received from conservative America

following her anti-Bush statements in 2003, Maines scorns the religious pretense and general hypocrisy of the small Texas city, pointing to the painting of fellow Lubbockite Buddy Holly outside the city's airport and wondering if "Maybe when I'm dead and gone I'm gonna get a statue too."
Key line: "Throw stones from the top of your rock thinking no one can see / the secrets you hide behind your Southern hospitality."

4 THE BOTTLE ROCKETS, "INDIANAPOLIS"

A million songs have bemoaned the hard-knock life of a small-time touring musician, but The Bottle Rockets capture it on the most tedious level here: a van breakdown that strands them in Indianapolis. Ten days into a tour, the novelty has worn off, and frontman Brian Henneman openly fantasizes about ditching his bandmates for a ride home. The waiting, and Indiana's favorite son, may drive him over the edge: "Who knows what this repair will cost, scared to spend a dime / I'll puke if that jukebox plays John Cougar one more time."
Key line: "Is this hell or Indianapolis?"

5 JOHN DENVER, "TOLEDO"

Whatever little notoriety Randy Sparks' satirical song "Toledo" ever managed can largely be attributed to John Denver, who sang it in concert with a big, corny smile, the tee-hee-I'm-being-naughty expression of the teacher's pet reading somebody else's mildly dirty words off the bathroom wall. As fuck-this-town sentiments go, "Toledo" is relatively mild, but its barbed mockery was a notable departure from Denver's normal squeaky-clean, country-loving persona, especially in the way it rips on a Midwestern town for being so numbingly boring. "They roll back the sidewalks precisely at 10 / and people who live there are not seen again," Denver cheerfully sings. Funny, he always seemed like the kind of guy who'd be in bed at 9:30 sharp himself.
Key line: "You ask how I know of Toledo, Ohio? Well, I spent a week there one day."

6 THE PRETENDERS, "MY CITY WAS GONE"

It's one thing to feel alienated in a strange town; it's another to come home and find everything you once knew and loved has disappeared. In "My City Was Gone," head Pretender Chrissie Hynde visits her hometown of Akron, Ohio, and finds that the countryside has been "paved down the middle," with shopping malls and parking lots standing in its place. The most poignant moment comes when Hynde visits the house where she grew up: "I stood on the back porch, there was nobody home." Turns out Thomas Wolfe was right all along.
Key line: "The farms of Ohio had been replaced by shopping malls."

7 LOU REED AND JOHN CALE, "SMALLTOWN"

It took the death of their mentor Andy Warhol to bring Lou Reed and John Cale back into the studio together, 22 years after Cale left The Velvet Underground. The result, 1990's *Songs For Drella*, probed Warhol's life with tenderness and brutal honesty—especially on the album's opener, "Smalltown," an account of the young artist's struggle to ditch Pittsburgh in favor of New York. Reed, speaking as Warhol, complains about the bigotry and lack of opportunity in Pittsburgh, singing, "If they stare, let them stare in New York City."
Key line: "Where did Picasso come from? / There's no Michelangelo coming from Pittsburgh."

8 JIM CROCE, "NEW YORK'S NOT MY HOME"

A native Pennsylvanian, Jim Croce spent a short time in New York City at his record label's behest; there, he and his wife recorded and promoted an album together. The album was a flop, and the disillusioned Croce moved back to his home state, where he took odd jobs working construction and driving trucks. During that time, he wrote his breakthrough album, *You Don't Mess Around With Jim*, which included "New York's Not My Home," a ballad mourning the hectic yet empty interactions of his former big-city life. Croce's short career was typified by this low-key workingman vibe, an aesthetic that clearly couldn't bloom in the concrete confines of Manhattan.
Key line: "Been in so many places /

you know I've run so many races / and looked into the empty faces of the people of the night / and something is just not right."

9 FEAR, "NEW YORK'S ALRIGHT IF YOU LIKE SAXOPHONES"

Lee Ving has long been notorious as one of punk's prime assholes, and he certainly proves it with the line "New York's all right if you're a homosexual" on "New York's Alright If You Like Saxophones." In a poor attempt at humor, the song blasts The Big Apple for being cold, dangerous, and full of drunks—but Ving, an L.A. native, sounds particularly enraged about the "art and jazz" that apparently ruined the New York scene. John Lurie was surely shaking in his shoes.
Key line: "New York's all right if you wanna get pushed in front of a subway / New York's all right if you like tuberculosis."

10 SOUL COUGHING, "THE INCUMBENT"

Sometimes when a starry-eyed naïf hits the big city, the big city hits back—and it had a hell of a right hook. On "The Incumbent," Soul Coughing's Mike Doughty chants the embittered mantra of the failed dreamer who now sees New York as nothing but a horrifying "red sucker mouth." Broken ambitions fester like poison, and all he wants now is for the city that never sleeps to stop giving him insomnia. Prophetically, "The Incumbent" was the last song on Soul Coughing's last album; after the band's 2000 breakup, Doughty left New York for an extended sabbatical in Asia.
Key line: "New York, New York, I won't go back."

One of the more hate-filled tracks on Fear's debut, The Record, *"Saxophone" was infamously taped during the band's 1981* Saturday Night Live *appearance; a gang of rowdy young punks—including a teenage Ian MacKaye—were bussed in to cause trouble on the set.*

11 THE CLASH, "LONDON'S BURNING"

Before London called to Joe Strummer and crew, it burned—at least metaphorically—on "London's Burning," one of the strongest tracks from the band's 1977 debut. Still steeped in the punk look and sound, The Clash crafted a raw yet tuneful assault on street-level boredom, that great enemy of angry, disenfranchised youth. At its core, though, there's a sadness and hopeful desperation that points to the maturity and complexity the group would soon grow into—even while it remained wary of the stultifying urban landscape.
Key line: "The wind howls through the empty blocks looking for a home / I run through the empty stone 'cause I'm all alone."

12 THE WEAKERTHANS, "ONE GREAT CITY!"

"I hate Winnipeg." It doesn't get simpler than the refrain that The Weakerthans ascribe to a variety of the Canadian city's weary inhabitants—a dollar-store clerk, a bus driver, even a wrecking ball. Weakerthans frontman John K. Samson sarcastically reappropriates Winnipeg's civic-pride slogan in the song title, then goes on to bash not only the city's favorite sons (The Guess Who) but also its former pro hockey team, the Jets.
Key line: "Let his arcing wrecking ball proclaim, 'I hate Winnipeg.'"

13 HORACE PINKER, "BURN TEMPE TO THE GROUND"

Teen rebellion expresses itself in many ways; what young punk rocker hasn't wanted to torch his boring hometown? But this isn't a disaffected teenager anthem—it's a disaffected early-twentysomething anthem. Horace Pinker's bassist Bill Ramsey and drummer Bryan Jones lament friends treading water, caught in the easy-living rut that ensnares many inhabitants of college towns like Tempe, Arizona.
Key line: "This town, I'd let it burn to the ground / and I hope my friends are the ones who set it."

14 J CHURCH, "THE SATANISTS CONVENE"

San Francisco was a frequent muse to frontman Lance Hahn, in whose songs the city practically became

another character, like New York in a Woody Allen film or, um, *Sex And The City*. In "The Satanists Convene," he quietly catalogs the disappeared/disappearing quirks of San Francisco that helped give the city its personality, from goofy museums to the Church Of Satan. People love to lament about how something "used to be cool, man," but "The Satanists Convene" gives a real sense of the blandness encroaching on San Francisco.
Key line: "Banality now keeps the city wound."

15 CIRCLE JERKS, "BEVERLY HILLS"

When Keith Morris left Black Flag to form Circle Jerks, he brought along a healthy misanthropy. The Jerks' 1980 debut, *Group Sex*, was a chance for Morris to rant about many things, including how much he hates the star-studded Platinum Triangle. Rather than cracking his head against the windshield, though, future Bad Religion guitarist Greg Hetson slows "Beverly Hills" to a snarling crawl as Morris condemns the town and all its snooty inhabitants. He loses a few punk points, though, by being savvy enough to dis Fiorucci by name.
Key line: "All the people look the same / don't they know they're so damn lame?"

16 PUBLIC ENEMY, "BURN HOLLYWOOD BURN"

In Public Enemy's "Burn Hollywood Burn," Chuck D and guest rappers Ice Cube and Big Daddy Kane rail against Hollywood movies that feed America's racism. D wants to take out his frustration on the town where the movies get made: "Burn Hollywood burn, I smell a riot," he says in the song's opening line. "Let's check out a flick that exploits the color," Ice Cube sarcastically suggests, while Big Daddy Kane says they should follow Spike Lee's example and make their own films.
Key line: "For all the years we looked like clowns, the joke is over / smell the smoke from all around."

IT'S ONE THING TO FEEL ALIENATED IN A STRANGE TOWN; IT'S ANOTHER TO COME HOME AND FIND EVERYTHING YOU ONCE KNEW AND LOVED HAS DISAPPEARED.

17 RANDY NEWMAN, "I LOVE L.A."

Randy Newman is beloved by millions for his soft-pedaling soundtrack songs, but he got famous as a sarcastic bastard. "I Love L.A." is just one of many Newman compositions that drip with double meaning. It's actually tough to tell whether the song is entirely against L.A., though, and Newman has never been entirely clear in interviews. (It's easy to interpret the song as completely pro-Los Angeles, which is part of its charm.)
Key line: "Look at that mountain / look at those trees / look at that bum over there, man, he's down on his knees."

18 DEATH CAB FOR CUTIE, "WHY YOU'D WANT TO LIVE HERE"

Death Cab frontman Ben Gibbard has mentioned that this song is less about hating Los Angeles than about trying to convince someone not to move there. But "Why You'd Want To Live Here" makes a convincing case against L.A., touching on everything from inaccurate star maps to traffic to Hollywood egos.
Key line: "It's a lovely summer's day / and I can almost see the skyline through a thickening shroud of egos."

LOST IN TRANSLATION

20 NOT-SO-GOOD MOVIES BASED ON GOOD BOOKS

1 *SLAPSTICK (OF ANOTHER KIND)* (1982)

It's a testament to Kurt Vonnegut's slippery weirdness—and the filmmakers' ultimate stupidity—that his novel could become this movie. The basic plot elements are the same: A freakishly large twin brother and sister seem dumb, but when they're in physical proximity, they're geniuses. The novel—which, it should be noted, Vonnegut considered his worst—explores loneliness and belonging with an incredibly light touch. But the filmmakers, plus leads Jerry Lewis and Madeline Kahn, destroy any vestige of its heart. Not even Marty Feldman can make things right.

2 *THE BONFIRE OF THE VANITIES* (1990)

It isn't that "master of suspense" Brian De Palma is *incapable* of directing social satire of the Tom Wolfe variety. De Palma's early films were wicked comedies, and his fans would argue that a lot of his thrillers work on satiric levels, too. But a volatile cocktail of directorial hubris and studio interference helped retch up the truth that should've been obvious from the start: *The Bonfire Of The Vanities* is an unfilmable book. The novel's analysis of New York City class politics works because of Wolfe's insider's-view descriptions of stockbrokers, social activists, tabloid reporters, and civil servants; even with Bruce Willis providing occasional pieces of sub-Wolfe narration, it was impossible for De Palma to get that tone and meaning right. Oddly, Jason Reitman's adaptation of Christopher Buckley's *Thank You For Smoking* out-Wolfes Wolfe, perfectly mimicking his deadpan sketches of the likeably unsympathetic and the sympathetically unlikeable.

3 *BICENTENNIAL MAN* (1999)

Isaac Asimov's original novella—later expanded into a novel—subtly examines what it means to be human, by telling the story of a robot with a mechanical brain so advanced that he begins to develop emotion and creativity. But big Hollywood movies don't do subtle well, especially not with Chris Columbus directing and Robin Williams starring. Columbus and screenwriter Nicholas Kazan pour on the schmaltz, while Williams bats his eyes innocently and pats little children's heads. Meanwhile, moments that are supposed to involve deep ruminations about man and machine become impassive stare-downs, accompanied by 101 Strings. Here's a tip: If you want to know what it means to be human, don't ask the creators of *Mrs. Doubtfire*.

4 *THE LEAGUE OF EXTRAORDINARY GENTLEMEN* (2003)

Although the narrative gap between comics and movies is narrowing, the gap between Alan Moore's dense comics and Hollywood movies sadly isn't. Moore's wildly inventive *League Of Extraordinary Gentlemen* comics are a gimmicky cross between turn-of-the-century literature and Silver Age superheroes, with fictional folk like Allan Quatermain, The Invisible Man, Captain Nemo, Dracula hunter Mina Murray, and Dr. Jekyll banding together, Avengers-style, to save the British empire. In theory, this sounds like perfect film fodder, but in practice, Stephen Norrington's version is overloaded with thudding plot, clumsy setpieces, and CGI-enhanced slugfests, devoid of any feeling for what makes the combatants unique. The grizzled, somewhat tortured figures that Moore revealed inevitably disap-

pear, replaced by generic punchers and shooters.

5 *THE SCARLET LETTER* (1995)
Striptease is generally considered the movie that short-circuited Demi Moore's career, but as an act of commercial and aesthetic miscalculation, it has nothing on 1995's misbegotten adaptation of Nathaniel Hawthorne's classic story of guilt, sin, and betrayal in colonial New England. Casting a dubiously accented Moore as Hester Prynne in a "free adaptation" of Hawthorne's book was a recipe for disaster, but even by lowered expectations, *The Scarlet Letter* turned out astonishingly poorly. "Freely adapted" apparently means adding a softcore coupling between Prynne and Gary Oldman's Rev. Dimmesdale that wouldn't be out of place on Cinemax After Dark. There's also some politically correct business involving Prynne's long-lost husband going native with the local Algonquin tribe, a voyeuristic interlude featuring a horny slave girl and Prynne furtively pleasuring herself in a bath, and a widely reviled happy ending for a book that pointedly lacks one.

> The League Of Extraordinary Gentlemen *also worsened relations between Moore and Hollywood when screenwriters Larry Cohen and Martin Poll sued 20th Century Fox for plagiarism due to similarities to a script they'd pitched in 1993. After being forced to give a deposition defending himself, Moore told journalist Rich Johnston that he would have been better treated if "he'd molested and murdered a busload of retarded children after giving them heroin."*

6 *ALL THE KING'S MEN* (2006)
When this version of Robert Penn Warren's powerful staple about abuse within the American political system was first conceived, it seemed like the stencil-work on its Oscars could safely be done in advance. Warren's thinly veiled take on Huey Long, the charismatic Louisiana populist whose gubernatorial reign was tainted by demagoguery and corruption, had obvious resonances in 2006's political climate. Add in the sterling pedigree of writer-director Steven Zaillian, who won an Oscar for adapting *Schindler's List*, plus a murderer's row of stars (Sean Penn, Jude Law, Kate Winslet, Mark Ruffalo, James Gandolfini, and Patricia Clarkson, among others), and the project seemed like it was in good hands. Yet it would be hard to imagine a more leaden adaptation. The cast struggles haplessly with their Louisiana accents (Penn and Gandolfini have never been worse), every scene drags on several beats too long, and James Horner's brutal percussion score makes for an oppressive exclamation point.

> *Had Zaillian needed a road map, he could have turned to Robert Rossen's superb 1949 film version of* All The King's Men, *starring Broderick Crawford.*

7 *THE HUMAN STAIN* (2003)
Okay, armchair casting agents: Who's the perfect actor to play a septuagenarian professor who's a half-Jewish, light-skinned African-American? Who's the perfect actress to play his lover, a dowdy, illiterate, dirt-poor janitor half his age? Were you thinking Anthony Hopkins and Nicole Kidman? No? Because those were the leads selected for *The Human Stain*, a perversely miscast adaptation of Philip Roth's fiery novel about identity politics and the absurdities of academia. It's easy enough to buy Hopkins as a college professor, but the character's fluid, ever-shifting sense of self is key, especially once he causes a scandal by using the unfortunate word "spooks" (as in "ghosts") to describe two absent students who turn out to be African-American. As for Kidman, the world's most glamorous actress can only be de-glammed so much. Together, they're a major distraction in a movie already burdened by the difficult work of adapting Roth's jaundiced vision, which continues to stymie filmmakers.

8 *THE HOURS* (2002)
Michael Cunningham's 1999 novel

The Hours weaves together the stories of three women's lives with the care of a fugue. Themes repeat, echo, and get reversed, and the subtlety of his prose only strengthens the book's emotional impact. The inexplicably acclaimed Stephen Daldry adaptation knows nothing of subtlety. It pounds the material into powder with over-the-top visuals and overreaching performances. And in an odd twist, the film's one truly affecting scene—John C. Reilly's quiet monologue about finding a post-war paradise in America—isn't in the book at all. Maybe they should have started with that and thrown out the rest.

9 ***STARDUST*** *(2007)*

Some book-to-screen adaptations are just plain bad. *Stardust*, however, is a mildly entertaining film that only falls apart when held up to its source. Where Neil Gaiman's beloved original is a brisk, crystalline fairy tale, Matthew Vaughn's version is flabby and plodding; alchemically morphing charm into ham, Vaughn squashes characters to a single dimension and turns Robert De Niro and Michelle Pfeiffer loose to swallow scenery whole. Even worse, their gluttonous mugging nulls the spell that Gaiman's story casts, and it overpowers the already anemic chemistry between leads Charlie Cox and Claire Danes.

10 ***DR. SEUSS' HOW THE GRINCH STOLE CHRISTMAS*** *(2000)*

Throughout his life, beloved children's author Theodor "Dr. Seuss" Geisel was notoriously reluctant to license the contents of his books for movies or toys; aside from a handful of animated cartoons, including the wonderful TV special "How The Grinch Stole Christmas!" by his friend Chuck Jones, the Seuss brand didn't extend that far beyond its original sources. That changed when Geisel died in 1991 and his widow green-lit Ron Howard's feature-length, live-action version, starring Jim Carrey in the title role. The concise storytelling and typically delightful rhymes went out the window, and the exaggerated design of Seuss' book was amplified into a garish nightmare of color and noise. Decked out like a green, feral, pot-bellied dog, Carrey overplays Seuss' diabolical Grinch with his aggressive slapstick, which is separated from his usual rubber-faced yahoo routine only in its mean-spiritedness. (Mike Myers' take on *The Cat In The Hat* three years later was even worse, but mainly because it used this film as a template.)

11 ***PORTNOY'S COMPLAINT*** *(1972)*

Though Richard Benjamin proved a perfect Philip Roth surrogate in both *Portnoy's Complaint* and *Goodbye, Columbus*—Woody Allen even cast Benjamin in his own Roth homage, *Deconstructing Harry*—even his inspired casting couldn't save 1972's ill-fated adaptation of *Portnoy's Complaint*. It preserved much of the crudity but little of the wit and deceptive warmth of Roth's groundbreaking exploration of the sexual neuroses of Jewish males. Six-time Oscar nominee Ernest Lehman has an astonishing track record as a screenwriter (*West Side Story, Sweet Smell Of Success, North By Northwest, Who's Afraid Of Virginia Woolf?*) but *Portnoy's Complaint* snuffed out Lehman's directorial career in its infancy: His first directing job was also his last.

12 ***TROPIC OF CANCER*** *(1970)*

According to his amazing autobiography, Robert Evans ended up green-lighting 1970's *Tropic Of Cancer* as part of a bet with good buddy Henry Miller. Yet even by the standards of the freewheeling Hollywood of the late '60s and early '70s, the resulting film was self-indulgent and rambling, and its X rating didn't do much for its box-office. It could be worse: Claude Chabrol's *Quiet Days In Clichy* cast Andrew McCarthy, of all people, as Henry Miller (a big step down from *Cancer's* ever-dependable Rip Torn), though the casting makes a little more sense in light of the film's subplot about Miller falling in love with a beautiful mannequin come to life.

13 ***BEE SEASON*** *(2005)*

There might be a terrific, touching movie to be made of Myla Goldberg's terrific, touching debut novel about a champion speller and her unraveling family, but the 2005 film wasn't it. God bless Richard Gere, but he's simply the wrong choice to play an overbearing, academic Jewish dad. More importantly, dual directors Scott McGehee and David Siegel apparently skipped the part of the text that explores this family's motivations for its various obsessions. It's the perfect example of a film draining the life out of a book without really changing a detail.

14 *STUART LITTLE* (1999)

In 1999, E.B. White's beloved 1945 classic about the child who happens to resemble a 3-inch-tall mouse got the standard computer-animated, celebrity-voiced, trumped-up-antagonist treatment. And while some of the updates are understandable (it was hard to resist the video-game-friendly toy-roadster chase), the movie eviscerates the book's poignant message. Instead of setting out to find his fortune in the manner of heroes from time immemorial, Michael J. Fox's Stuart gets lost and has to find his way back to the embrace of his adoptive parents. Way to encapsulate the fleeting family-values zeitgeist of the '90s, filmmakers: Life's ultimate meaning shrinks from the expanses of adventure and autonomy to the provincial comforts of hearth and home.

15 *EVEN COWGIRLS GET THE BLUES* (1993)

There was no chance Tom Robbins' sprawling, trippy picaresque novel *Even Cowgirls Get The Blues* could make it to the big screen intact; his loopy run-on thoughts, philosophical musings, bizarre extended metaphors, and meta-references are hilarious and dreamlike on the page, where he can burrow into his weird ideas at length and readers can meander back and forth through them, looking for sense. The book is like a crazy, drug-addled conversation between Robbins and the reader, with Robbins helpfully explaining what "the author" is attempting. But the film is more like a drunken, overbearing monologue. Compressed for film and stripped of much of the explorative depth and colorful language, the book's basic events become shallow, ridiculous, and incoherent, and the forced attempts to make them funny are just embarrassing.

COMPRESSED FOR FILM AND STRIPPED OF MUCH OF THE EXPLORATIVE DEPTH AND COLORFUL LANGUAGE, THE BOOK'S BASIC EVENTS BECOME SHALLOW, RIDICULOUS, AND INCOHERENT.

16 *THE HITCHHIKER'S GUIDE TO THE GALAXY* (2005)

Similarly, Douglas Adams doesn't read as a good film source; his *Hitchhiker's* novels are comically dense, and they play with context, rhythm, and extended farcical narrative diversions. The characters' lines are the easiest part to put on film, but they're also the least funny part of his humor. The 1981 BBC miniseries managed the tone fairly well by letting animated interludes follow some of Adams' narrative rabbit trails verbatim, but the low budget just wasn't up to dealing with two-headed, three-armed Zaphod Beeblebrox. The tech caught up to the story by the time of 2005's film adaptation (though it still cheated on Zaphod's second head), but that version was straining far too hard to be wacky. With so much hilarious Adams material available, why discard so much of it in favor of dumb slapstick and lumpy, overstretched comedy? And the tacked-on ending, which attempted to bring a sort of fakey closure to an open-ended story, was irritatingly at odds with the rest of the material.

17 *THE SEEKER: THE DARK IS RISING* (2007)

The idea of a film adaptation of Susan Cooper's Newbery-winning children's classic *The Dark Is Rising* was odd in the first place; it's the second book in a five-book series, it's more about atmosphere than action, and it feels more than a little like Madeleine L'Engle's *A Wrinkle In Time*, in that the story's child protagonist is in the midst of a battle far larger than he can comprehend, and his place in it is more observer and student than hero. In part a primer in Celtic lore and tradition, it's a slow, thoughtful book, full of allusion and description. The badly botched film version changes the protagonist into a teenager and puts him at the center of an action-oriented, videogame-like plot where he has to collect randomly distributed power-ups, one of which turns out to be himself. *The Seeker: The Dark Is Rising* isn't just a mishandling of the book, it's a loud, clumsy, shallow insult to Cooper.

18 *THE BLACK CAULDRON* (1985)

Similarly, Disney's animated take on the second book in Lloyd Alexander's five-book children's epic (also a Newbery winner) attempts to simplify matters for the kids by stripping out all the depth and half the characters, and Disney-fying the rest. Disney films have always had a glancing relationship with their book sources, at best—*Bambi* the film and *Bambi* the book share a title and a character name, while *Mary Poppins* the movie turns a bitter, shrewish, preposterously vain nanny into a big ball of singing, dancing Julie Andrews sweetness. But both those films get away with it by being gorgeous, magical fun; even Disney's *Hunchback Of Notre Dame*, with its tacked-on happy ending, managed some breathtaking scenes. But *The Black Cauldron*—Disney's first PG animated movie, and reportedly nearly its first R film, before some gruesome killings were excised—was a muddled, uninspired, plodding mess, critically panned and a wash at the box office.

19 *BREAKFAST AT TIFFANY'S* (1961)

Sure, there's plenty to recommend Blake Edwards' lively adaptation of *Breakfast At Tiffany's*, the novel that made Truman Capote's name. Audrey Hepburn's sparky performance as Holly Golightly is perfect, and while George Peppard makes for a lumpen, leaden protagonist, he's a reasonable interpretation of the book's all-but-absent narrator, seen more as a camera lens than an onscreen presence. Far less perfect: Mickey Rooney's embarrassing mugging as a buck-toothed, squint-eyed, fake-accented Japanese neighbor. But mostly, Edwards' film version is infuriating for its butchered "happy" ending, surely one of the biggest copouts in film history.

20 *STEPHEN KING'S THE SHINING* (1997)

This entire list could be composed of botched adaptations of Stephen King books, and there are plenty of King films lousier than the ABC miniseries version of his 1977 novel. But for irony alone, *Stephen King's The Shining* can't be beat: Long rankled by Stanley Kubrick's loose adaptation of his book, King wrote the teleplay as a corrective to the great director's creative butchering, but the new version is vastly inferior in every conceivable regard. King never cared for Jack Nicholson's iconic performance in the earlier film, which he felt tipped off the character's descent into madness too plainly, but Steven Weber (a.k.a. that guy from *Wings*) was no one's idea of an upgrade. So too Courtland Mead (a.k.a. that annoying dough-faced kid from the Disneyworld commercials), who stepped into the pivotal role of a boy touched by ESP. But the made-for-TV format wreaks the most havoc: Sustaining tension, much less delivering scares, over a squeaky-clean 273-minute sprawl isn't really possible, and King and director Mick Garris don't help their cause with action-halting flashbacks, reams of expository dialogue, and cheesy effects sequences. *Stephen King's The Shining* is proof that movies aren't marriages, at least in the sense that fidelity isn't always a virtue.

PLAY IT AGAIN, ONLY BETTER

14 COVER SONGS THAT OUTDO THE ORIGINALS

1 STEVIE WONDER, "WE CAN WORK IT OUT"

The Lennon/McCartney-penned single "We Can Work It Out" comes from the middle of The Beatles' most radical creative reinvention, the 1965 shift from the straightforward pop of *Help!* to the multifaceted *Rubber Soul*, which revolutionized their music, and by extension, everybody else's. So it's fitting that when Stevie Wonder covered the song on 1970's *Signed, Sealed & Delivered*, he was in the middle of a similar transition from teen Motown wunderkind to the socially conscious, super-funky artist he became in the mid-'70s. Wonder's performance is so powerful, in fact, that it changes the meaning of the song without changing a word. The Beatles' original is a desperate plea for reconciliation, delivered with passion but little hope. But Wonder's version is all about the hope, and his joyous, sizzling funk makes "We Can Work It Out" a promise, not a plea.

2 BRYAN FERRY, "IT'S MY PARTY"

Few rockers have taken more irreverent glee in radically re-conceptualizing familiar songs than Bryan Ferry, who has made covers one of his specialties. On "It's My Party," a standout track from the early covers collection *These Foolish Things*, Ferry throws himself into the girlish teen emotions of the Lesley Gore hit with hilarious abandon. It's almost possible to see Ferry sobbing softly in a corner, his tuxedo hopelessly rumpled, as he recounts the horrors of betrayal happening at his very own party.

3 THE BLIND BOYS OF ALABAMA, "WAY DOWN IN THE HOLE"

Tom Waits' offbeat gospel song is one of the highlights of his 1987 disc *Frank's Wild Years*, and it's even better on the subsequent live album *Big Time*, where Waits interjects a grizzle-voiced sermon about using hydraulic-powered faith healing to blast the devil out of your soul. But both versions take a mockingly ironic tone toward Waits' perspective character, a tent-revival preacher promising heaven in exchange for your cash, and neither completely shakes a sense of theatrical artificiality. That definitely isn't the case for gospel group The Blind Boys Of Alabama, whose smoking, bluesy rendition of the song on 2001's *Spirit Of The Century* hits with genuine fire and fervor. It also picked up added resonance when the producers of HBO's terrific *The Wire* used it as the theme song for the show's first season, perfectly encapsulating the series' complicated dance with good and evil.

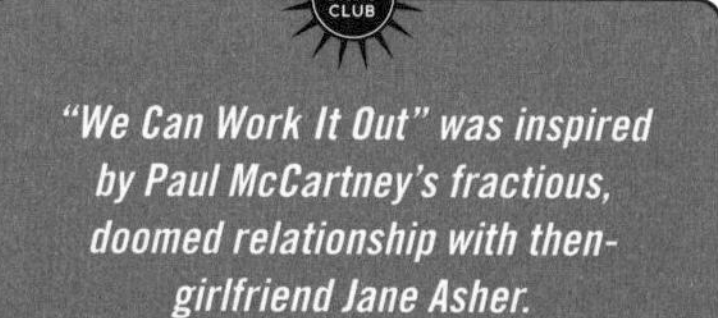

"We Can Work It Out" was inspired by Paul McCartney's fractious, doomed relationship with then-girlfriend Jane Asher.

4 IKE & TINA TURNER, "PROUD MARY"

As the Turners begin their version of "Proud Mary" with a delicate, subdued preface, Tina explains the plan: "We *never, ever* do nothin' nice and easy. We always do it nice and *rough*." Translation: "Thanks, crackers. We'll take it from here." The Turners then tear that quiet intro to shreds by kicking up the tempo, adding horns, and driving it all with a beat that practically demands that people dance. By comparison, Creedence Clearwater Revival's original midtempo rocker sounds positively bland. The amped-up energy of the Turners' version makes the original's easygoing charm sound unnatural.

5 THE WHO, "SUMMERTIME BLUES"

When Eddie Cochran recorded the snappy "Summertime Blues" in the late '50s, he was also writing a near-perfect Who single, at home next to both the kinds of songs that consistently worked for The Who between studio albums. Roger Daltrey sings the part of a trapped teenager with just enough "My Generation"-style conviction, and John Entwistle's deep-voiced interjections as various stodgy grown-ups are reminiscent of oddities like "Boris The Spider." Cochran's lyrics aren't innocuous—they call out his congressman alongside Dad and the boss—but The Who's version makes the original sound a little jokey by comparison, especially alongside the other revamped covers on *Live At Leeds*.

6 ELVIS COSTELLO, "(WHAT'S SO FUNNY 'BOUT) PEACE, LOVE, AND UNDERSTANDING?"

Nick Lowe's original version of "(What's So Funny 'Bout) Peace, Love, And Understanding?", recorded in 1974 with his pub-rock band Brinsley Schwarz, is a minor classic of English pre-punk, and it doesn't sound terribly different from the one recorded by Lowe's buddy Elvis Costello five years later. On the plus side, it actually kicks in with some sweet harmonies after the line "where is the harmony, sweet harmony?" On the debit side, there's Lowe's dated, hippieish talking bit about how we need to save the world for "the children of a new generation." Costello's arrangement is tighter and more assertive, all the better to get right to the point: Why the hell can't people stop being total bastards to each other? The passionate fury in Costello's voice transforms "Peace, Love, And Understanding" into a condemnation of humanity's propensity for cruelty, violence, and war—and elevates it into one of the greatest songs in the rock canon.

7 THE MOUNTAIN GOATS, "THE SIGN"

Though he doesn't play it anymore, Mountain Goats leader John Darnielle turned his interpretation of Ace Of Base's cheesy mid-'90s hit into one of the best covers ever performed onstage. There's a relatively straight version of it—with the programming replaced by an acoustic guitar, of course—on the *Bitter Melon Farm* compilation, but when Darnielle played it live, he peppered it with the Swedish band's backstory. The result was beautifully hilarious, and not just because he could get a club full of hip indie kids to enthusiastically sing along to the chorus. Though Darnielle starts off the recorded version by saying "I never get tired of this song," he eventually eliminated it from his set list because, as he explained, "It sort of seemed like every indie band in the world had some pop staple they played for laughs. I really loved 'The Sign,' thought it was an awesome song, [and] didn't want anything to do with anything that might resemble liking something ironically."

8 SELF, "WHAT A FOOL BELIEVES"

As an exercise in songwriting, Michael McDonald and Kenny Loggins' "What A Fool Believes" is amazing—a pop gem endowed with an expansive melody that flawlessly navigates tons of rhythmic quirks and chords. Unfortunately, The Doobie Brothers' recording hasn't aged very well, mired as it is in late-'70s faux-soul maximalism and airwave overexposure. Rescuing it from the bargain bins just in time for the new millennium, however, Self's *Gizmodgery* version recasts the ultra-complicated song in the coolest possible way—using children's toys. Nailing all the essential elements on instruments such as the Little Tikes Xylophone and the Mattel Star Guitar, Self's Matt Mahaffey brings the ornate elements together in a leaner, funkier version that's a terrific tribute and a memorable piss-take.

9 ELVIS PRESLEY, "HEY JUDE"

Covering The Beatles is often futile. The original versions sound as definitive as if they were issued from on high, which, in a manner of speaking, they were. There's nothing wrong with The Beatles' take on "Hey Jude," but it lends itself to interpretation more than much of the catalog. Maybe it's the unexpected lyrical content—like "She Loves You," it's an impassioned request for someone else to find love. Maybe it's because Paul McCartney's vocals sound like a blueprint for more dramatic readings to come. Wilson Pickett tore into it memorably, but for a truly transcendent version, look no further than Elvis. Presley recorded his version in Memphis during his late-'60s renaissance, but its slow-building gospel fervor remained unheard until the 1972 album *Elvis Now*, when the fires of his artistic revival had begun to flicker. Surrounded by Vegas-ready versions of "Help Me Make It Through The Night" and "Put Your Hand In The Hand," it's remained an overlooked track that captures much of what's great about Elvis and The Beatles in four and a half minutes.

10 NAKED EYES, "(THERE'S) ALWAYS SOMETHING THERE TO REMIND ME"

A beautiful song with slowly descending chords that match the theme of being brought down by constant reminders of an ex-lover, "(There's) Always Something There To Remind Me" has long been a standout in the songwriting catalog of Burt Bacharach and Hal David. The original 1964 recording by American soul singer Lou Johnson was actually pretty good, but its mediocre placement was all but obscured by Sandie Shaw's UK number-one version a few months later. It's awful—going all epileptic-showgirl at just the moment the lyric calls for introspection. But Naked Eyes achieved genuine pathos in its 1983 version, with emotive synths in place of strings. Of course, it didn't hurt that this tale of love leaving a painful reminder exploded internationally at the exact same time as herpes.

11 JIMI HENDRIX, "ALL ALONG THE WATCHTOWER"

Bob Dylan is one of the most-covered musicians in history for a reason: Besides writing some of the best songs of the rock era, he's made lots of recordings that sound unfinished, even skeletal—in other words, perfect frames to flesh out. *John Wesley Harding's* "All Along The Watchtower" is searing and eerie in its own rickety way, but the song didn't become truly epic until Jimi Hendrix unleashed his rendition, a mere nine months after the original. Instead of stiff drums and tubercular harmonica, Hendrix summons a supple, elemental groove that channels pure myth and mystery. Of course, it wouldn't work without Dylan's apocalyptic lyrics and chilling chords, but Hendrix's solos actually *sound* like wind howling and wildcats growling—and his voice is a roar that stalks the song's despair-drenched depths. Prince played a decent version during the 2007 Super Bowl, but when it comes to "Watchtower," no one beats Hendrix.

12 JACKIE WILSON, "LIGHT MY FIRE"

Sometimes it's hard to listen to any Doors song with a straight face, let alone "Light My Fire," a serviceable tune that's been eroded by way too much airplay. Two years after its 1967 chart blitz, Jackie Wilson—surfing on a renewal of popularity thanks to Brunswick's in-house geniuses Eugene Record and Barbara Acklin—decided to have some fun on *Do Your Thing*, an album padded with covers both banal ("Hold On! I'm Comin'") and bizarre ("Eleanor Rigby"). Best, though, is Wilson's vastly superior version of "Light My Fire," which starts with a pseudo-Latin flutter before pumping out some stark, sinewy funk that predicts Al Green's imminent godhood. Punctuated by Wilson's signature squeals and screeches, the song—rendered more sexy than psychedelic—also benefits from an understatement that The Doors never stumbled upon.

13 DEVO, "(CAN'T GET NO) SATISFACTION"

Why is Mick Jagger so sexually frustrated? The Rolling Stones classic is a slow burn with a syncopated grind, a come-on disguised as a lament. Devo turns the song into a real soundtrack for impotence. Over a jittery bass riff, Mark Mothersbaugh stutters the lyric at breakneck speed like he hasn't got no satisfaction in his entire adult life. Before confessing his losing streak, he hollers "baby baby baby baby" for eight full bars without taking a breath, thanks to the magic of looping. This "Satisfaction" is the perfect confessional for lonely, horny geeks.

14 LANGLEY SCHOOLS MUSIC PROJECT, "DESPERADO"

Grade-school recitals are often exercises in well-meant musical torture. But in the late 1970s, a British Columbian schoolteacher named Hans Fenger orchestrated a piece of left-field wonderment almost by accident when he decided to let his children's choir tackle then-current pop songs by the Beach Boys and David Bowie, among others. The songs were forgotten for nearly 25 years until their rediscovery in 2001, when outsider-music archivist Irwin Chusid compiled them on the disc *Innocence And Despair*. The title came from Fenger's description of the album's haunting high point, a winsome, wistful performance of The Eagles' "Desperado" by 9-year-old Sheila Behman. Though Behman mangles the lyrics a bit, creating bizarre new imagery in the line "she'll beat you if she's a bull," the simplicity and seriousness of her sad-angel singing lends the song a surprising poignancy that Don Henley's considerably glossier original doesn't approach.

WE'RE *ALL* AN ATHLETE AND A CRIMINAL AND A PRINCESS

15 RIDICULOUS LIES PERPETUATED BY JOHN HUGHES MOVIES

1 If they just spend a day together, members of radically different social cliques will decide they're all worthy equals. (*The Breakfast Club*)

2 Similarly, the most obnoxious guy on the planet becomes endearing after a long bout of miserable forced togetherness. (*Planes, Trains & Automobiles*)

3 The hottest, most popular jock in school might notice and pursue a nerdy underclassman with "smallish tits." (*Sixteen Candles*)

4 High-school-age dudes are capable of regret and remorse. (*Weird Science, The Breakfast Club*)

5 Upon realizing that her boyfriend wants to have sex, a high-school-age girl would be so appalled that she'd instantly dump him, side with her overprotective, irritating babysitter against him, and later condone his kidnapping and threatened torture at the hands of said babysitter. (*Uncle Buck*)

6 The school's biggest dork can randomly score a beautiful girl by dressing up. (*Pretty in Pink*)

7 All adults are dumb. Not just ignorant of what's really going on in young people's lives, but embarrassingly, mouth-breathingly, uselessly stupid. (*Ferris Bueller's Day Off, Sixteen Candles, Home Alone, The Breakfast Club*…)

8 Violent, sadistic, ADD-afflicted children are cute and funny. (*Home Alone*)

9 Molly Ringwald could act well enough to deserve a film career. (*Sixteen Candles, The Breakfast Club*)

10 Freaky goth girls would be happier if they just put on a little makeup and acted normal. (*The Breakfast Club*)

11 A smartassed, arrogant, smug prick who casually uses and abuses everyone around him will be universally beloved by everyone in his high school who isn't a blood relation. (*Ferris Bueller's Day Off*)

12 Burnouts are the biggest drug users in high school. (*The Breakfast Club*)

13 It's even remotely plausible that an old lady who isn't starring in a porn film would react to her granddaughter's recent physical development by saying "They're so perky!" and grabbing her boobs. (*Sixteen Candles*)

14 Getting married and having a child will eventually fix all relationship problems, commitment problems, emotional-maturity problems, and general dissatisfaction with life. (*She's Having A Baby*)

15 Apart from scattered cheap one-note stereotypes, minorities don't exist. (All Hughes films.)

IT ONLY HURTS WHEN I LAUGH

13 SAD MOVIES ABOUT PEOPLE TRYING TO BE FUNNY

1 *LENNY* (1974)
Ah, the sad clown, laughing on the outside but sobbing internally. It's an archetype with many different faces, real and imaginary, but a depressingly predictable arc. For instance, Bob Fosse's electric 1974 biopic *Lenny* examines the life of Lenny Bruce, the quintessential tortured comic. Dustin Hoffman plays the poster boy for profanity and transgression as a magnetic combination of tenderness and cruelty, rebellion, and disarming sweetness. The first two acts are pure cinematic jazz, a bohemian free-associative ramble that crackles with nervous energy. But the film slows as it reaches its inevitable conclusion. In a harrowing static take late in the film, a trenchcoat-clad, heroin-addled Bruce struggles to convey to a mortified audience the thoughts and emotions racing through his poisoned mind. Years of relentless persecution and heroin abuse have robbed him of his greatest gift: the ability to alchemize pain into comedy and truth.

2 *MICKEY ONE* (1965)
Two years before *Bonnie And Clyde* helped kick off a golden age of experimentation and risk-taking in American film, star Warren Beatty and director Arthur Penn teamed up for 1965's *Mickey One*, a much less commercially successful but still intriguing attempt to bring the live-wire intensity and meta commentary of the French New Wave to American film. The film casts Beatty as an edgy stand-up comedian who incites the wrath of the Detroit mob, then hightails it to Chicago, where he plies his trade under an assumed name, never knowing when the hammer will fall and his past will catch up with him. It's a moody film suffused with paranoia and dark comedy that posits the stand-up comic as the ultimate nowhere man, an existential loner at the mercy of crowds, clubs, and the sinister men who own them.

3 *PUNCHLINE* (1988)
Before he won back-to-back Oscars for *Forrest Gump* and *Philadelphia*, Tom Hanks made an indelible impression in 1988's *Punchline* as an unhappy, self-destructive stand-up who becomes his own worst enemy. To prepare for the role, Hanks developed a brief stand-up routine and hit comedy clubs, giving his bittersweet performance and the film an air of verisimilitude enhanced by the cast-

ing of numerous real-life stand-ups in supporting and bit roles.

4 ***JO JO DANCER, YOUR LIFE IS CALLING*** *(1988)*

Few dramas are as nakedly autobiographical as Richard Pryor's *Jo Jo Dancer, Your Life Is Calling*, which meanders through the life of a suspiciously Richard Pryor-like Midwestern boy made good, then bad, then good again. From a childhood in a Peoria whorehouse to stand-up fame and self-destruction through booze, coke, and wanton bad behavior, Pryor mines his tragicomic life for pathos and comedy. Alas, the film mirrors the arc of Pryor's career. The ample promise and vivid storytelling of its first half gives way to a shambling, elliptical second half that stumbles blearily from one overwrought nadir to another.

5 ***WIRED*** *(1989)*

Similarly, John Belushi indulges in a magical posthumous misery tour courtesy of wisecracking guardian angel Ray Sharkey in the infamous 1989 film adaptation of Bob Woodward's Belushi bio *Wired*. Larry Peerce's *Wired* revels in its subject's sordid indiscretions, but lacks the gravity, depth, and quality to elevate its seamy story to tragic levels. The film offers an ugly burlesque of Belushi's excesses and drug dependency, while completely missing the vulnerability and child-like sweetness that made him an icon. Crude and exploitative, *Wired* is sad for all the wrong reasons.

IT'S A MOODY FILM SUFFUSED WITH PARANOIA AND DARK COMEDY THAT POSITS THE STAND-UP COMIC AS THE ULTIMATE NOWHERE MAN, AN EXISTENTIAL LONER AT THE MERCY OF CROWDS, CLUBS, AND THE SINISTER MEN WHO OWN THEM.

6 ***KING OF COMEDY*** *(1982)*

In Martin Scorsese's viscerally unnerving 1982 film *King Of Comedy*, Robert De Niro plays a kicked-around loser who kidnaps a Johnny Carson-like talk-show host (Jerry Lewis, in a rare dramatic performance) as a backward, criminal way of kick-starting his DOA stand-up career. De Niro's stand-up act is rooted in childhood trauma that belongs in an analyst's office or a mental hospital rather than on the nightclub stage, but he nevertheless desperately clings to his tawdry show-biz dreams. *King Of Comedy* is a harrowing exploration of how the lust for fame at any cost can warp the human psyche.

7 ***MAD DOG AND GLORY*** *(1993)*

Eleven years after *King Of Comedy*, producer Martin Scorsese and star Robert De Niro re-teamed for 1993's *Mad Dog And Glory*, another pitch-black comedy/character study about a terrible stand-up comic with enough issues to occupy an entire psychiatric convention. In a revelatory dramatic performance, Bill Murray plays a full-time mobster and part-time comedian who prowls the stage of a club called Comic-Cazie like he owns the place, because he does. Murray's Cosa Nostra-themed jokes go over like gangbusters with his goons and henchmen, though shy cop De Niro proves tougher to please, even after he pitches Murray some terrible one-liners of his own.

8 ***THE LIFE AND DEATH OF PETER SELLERS*** *(2004)*

Funnyman Peter Sellers was, by most accounts, a singularly gifted comic actor and a deplorable human being. The Emmy-winning TV movie *The Life And Death Of Peter Sellers* flashily, frustratingly dramatizes Sellers' blank, sad offscreen personality and onscreen gifts by having Geoffrey Rush play a version of Sellers who impersonates people from the comedian's troubled personal life in monologues delivered directly to the camera. The results are muddled and ridiculous, but the film boasts juicy supporting turns from John Lithgow and Stanley Tucci as Blake Edwards and Stanley Kubrick, respectively, and an awesomely awkward scene where Rush's Sellers sits down to tell his wife (Emily Watson) and children that he's leaving them to be with Sophia Loren, oblivious that his great romance with the famous sex bomb exists only in his mind.

9 *WHERE THE TRUTH LIES* *(2005)*
Atom Egoyan's *Where The Truth Lies* plunges deep into the seamy subterranean underbelly of a happy-go-lucky comedy duo overtly based on Dean Martin and Jerry Lewis through a mystery concerning the death of hotel employee Rachel Blanchard who doesn't survive an evening of boozy, drugged-up debauchery with two of America's favorite funsters. Colin Firth radiates brittle, sarcastic despair as an amalgam of Dean Martin and Peter Lawford, while Kevin Bacon convincingly captures Lewis' haughty, pretentious side as well as his silliness. Too bad the girlish Alison Lohman is miscast as a reporter who gets way too close to her story.

10 *MR. SATURDAY NIGHT* *(1992)*
In the mid-'80s, Billy Crystal used *Saturday Night Live* to introduce the character of Buddy Young Jr., a Borscht Belt-scented comedian who's part Don Rickles, part Milton Berle, and part self-parody. He loved the character so much, he centered his 1992 directorial debut, *Mr. Saturday Night*, on him. Under layers of unconvincing old-man makeup, Crystal plays the insult comic as a sour misanthrope whose contempt for his audience, his loved ones, and himself keeps him from attaining the rarefied heights of superstardom. Alas, this is a Billy Crystal movie, so the few moments of bracing darkness are buried under oceans of schmaltz and sentimentality. Feh!

11 *THE JIMMY SHOW* *(2001)*
Like Robert De Niro in *King Of Comedy*, Frank Whaley's desperate sad-sack protagonist in *The Jimmy Show* uses stand-up comedy as a form of free therapy, a way of exorcising his demons and discussing his woes without having to pay for a head-shrinker. *The Jimmy Show* is part of that curious subgenre of indie miserablist dramas about characters who start out with almost nothing, then lose even that. In this case, Whaley's fidgety loser loses longsuffering wife Carla Gugino and a shitty job at a supermarket as he spirals further and further into depression. Hilarity fails to ensue.

12 *THE ENTERTAINER* *(1960)*
Laurence Olivier's showboating tendencies found a perfect outlet in the flashy role of an alcoholic, over-the-hill dancehall performer facing a bleak personal and professional crossroads in Tony Richardson's masterful 1960 adaptation of John Osborne's *The Entertainer*. Painted up like a streetwalker and full of superficial bonhomie masking profound sadness, Olivier's desperate clown tries to get funding for one more show from the family of happily deluded sexual conquest Shirley Ann Field, who doesn't realize Olivier can't save himself or his career, let alone help her achieve her show-biz dreams.

13 *WILDE* *(1997)*
Oscar Wilde's tragic life story fails to benefit from the middlebrow trappings of Brian Gilbert's 1997 biopic *Wilde*, which traces the legendary wit's ascent to theatrical superstardom, and his harrowing fall following a disastrous gay fling. But it's almost redeemed by a virtuoso lead performance from Stephen Fry, who captures Wilde's stinging wit and his underlying sadness. Surely a man whose name has become synonymous with droll sophistication deserves better than the standard biopic treatment.

SECOND VERSE, (ALMOST THE) SAME AS THE FIRST

14 RELATIVELY OBSCURE BANDS THAT MORPHED INTO SOME OF OUR FAVORITES

1 FLAKE MUSIC (THE SHINS)
Before they were The Shins, they were Flake Music, a slightly more rocking version of the Sub Poppers who would find extra fame via the use of "New Slang" in the movie *Garden State*. Flake Music left one full-length release behind—*When You Land Here It's Time To Return*, which is clearly nascent Shins, with bits of gritty Pavement thrown in to place it in historical context. It isn't as good as anything the newly minted Shins would record, but it's still a must for fans.

2 ZUMPANO (THE NEW PORNOGRAPHERS)
It's evidence of pure luck that Carl Newman broke through with The New Pornographers after finding only obscurity with his earlier band, Zumpano. The Canadian pop outfit released two albums on Sub Pop in the mid-'90s that are every bit as catchy and enjoyable as the music Newman went on to release with the NPs, but they've gone almost completely unnoticed, even in the wake of his later success. New Porno fans would be wise to track down the 1996 Zumpano release *Goin' Through Changes*.

3 TREEPEOPLE (BUILT TO SPILL)
As the frontman of Built To Spill, Doug Martsch has a signature guitar style built on the kind of intricate fretwork generally missing from indie rock. He developed it in the late '80s and early '90s with his previous band, Treepeople, in the richly complex interplay with the group's other fleet-fingered singer-guitarist, Scott Schmaljohn. The band stayed closer to its punk roots—its members did time in Boise punk band State Of Confusion—but added layers of guitar acrobatics that sounded like nothing else in indie rock at the time. Treepeople released three full-lengths, but the EP compilation *Something Vicious For Tomorrow/Time Whore* remains an enduring classic.

4 RITES OF SPRING (FUGAZI)
One of the biggest names in the cloistered D.C. punk scene of the '80s, Rites Of Spring inadvertently co-spawned emocore, the bastard descendents of which are currently mewling on a radio near you. The group, which featured future Fugazi members Guy Picciotto and Brendan Canty, played a bare dozen or so shows, released only one full-length, and disbanded in less than two years. But the group's intensity—live and on record—made it legendary. Abandoning straightforward hardcore for something more varied and textured, Rites Of Spring helped create the "D.C. sound" that defined post-punk in the late '80s and '90s. Its anthology, *End On End*, is essential listening for fans of the style.

5 THE 101ERS (THE CLASH)
Joe Strummer wasn't always the voice of "The Only Band That Matters." Starting in 1974, Strummer—then going by the even goofier *nom de rock* of Woody Mellor—was in a Brixton-based pub-rock band called The 101ers, named for the house where members of the band squatted. Though it lasted for more than two years and did the festival circuit, the band never really took off, releasing only one full-length, *Elgin Avenue Breakdown*. In 1976, at the Nashville Room, Sex Pistols opened for The 101ers, and as Strummer said later, "I knew we were like yesterday's paper."

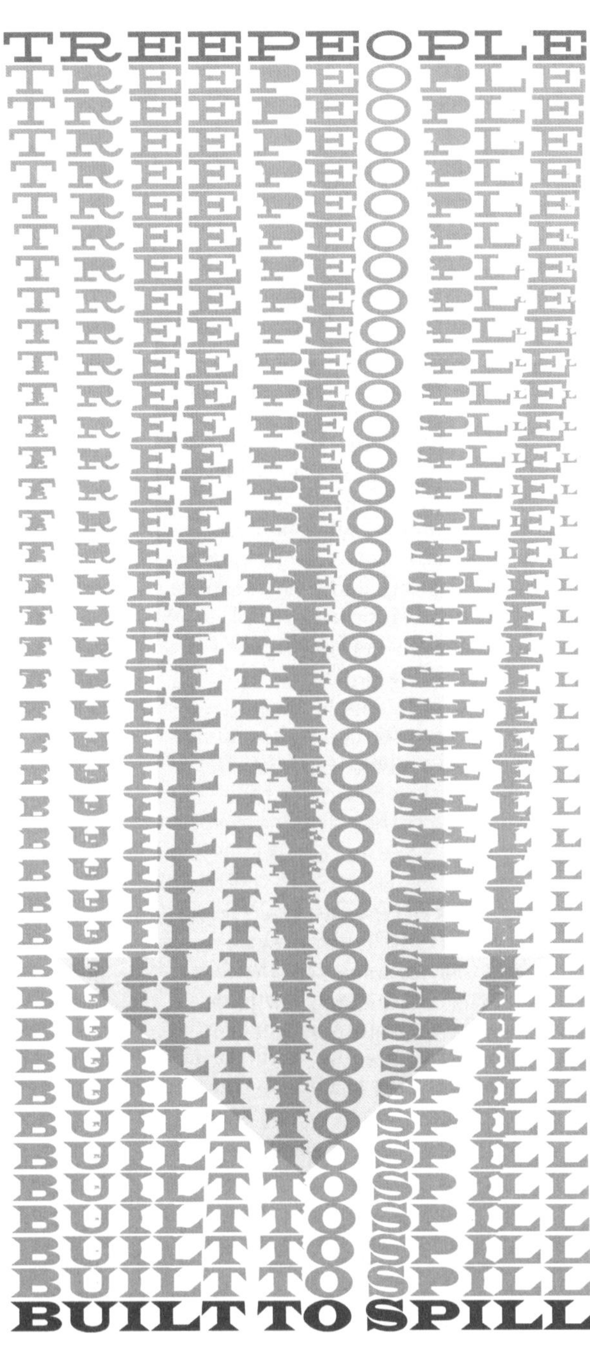

6 HEATMISER (ELLIOTT SMITH)

Before and during his transformation into the saddest, sweetest, quietest indie-rocker around, Elliott Smith was part of the songwriting team behind Heatmiser—a band he would eventually disown, proclaiming that he was playing music he didn't even like. But plenty of the songs he contributed to Heatmiser—especially the band's final album, *Mic City Sons*—were clear indicators of where he was going: "Plainclothes Man" and "See You Later" feel just like louder versions of solo songs. A quiet version of the latter was even released on Smith's posthumous *New Moon* compilation.

7-8 EXCUSE 17/HEAVENS TO BETSY (SLEATER-KINNEY)

Sleater-Kinney sprang from nowhere, according to *Rolling Stone* and some of the other media outlets that appointed them the saviors of rock 'n' roll in the mid-'90s. Actually, the band already had an impressive pedigree. Guitarist Carrie Brownstein had been in the pioneering queercore band Excuse 17 since 1993, while singer Corin Tucker was at the front of the groundbreaking riot-grrrl group Heavens To Betsy. The two bands released material around the same time and toured together often enough to form a friendship, and soon enough, Brownstein and Tucker started dating. Sleater-Kinney was conceived as a side project of the two bands, but didn't stay that way for long.

9 ROCKET FROM THE TOMBS (PERE UBU/ THE DEAD BOYS)

For decades, Cleveland's short-lived Rocket From The Tombs was the great lost band of American punk. Existing for just over a year, and heard only on live recordings, demos, and a sought-after single, they splintered by 1975 into two of the most legendary groups of the era. Singer Crocus Behemoth reverted to his real name, David Thomas, and formed Pere Ubu along with doomed RFTT lead guitarist Peter Laughner and Tim Wright; the band's rhythm guitarist and drummer, Cheetah Chrome and Johnny "Blitz" Madansky, eventually became members of The Dead Boys. What's more, both bands had early hits with songs that were originally RFTT material—Pere Ubu with "Final Solution" and "30 Seconds Over Tokyo," and The Dead Boys with "Sonic Reducer" and "Caught With The Meat In Your Mouth."

10 LIFTER PULLER (THE HOLD STEADY)

If Lifter Puller hadn't split up in 2000, it probably would've morphed into The Hold Steady anyway. The key connective tissue between the two bands is incredibly strong: Craig Finn's voice and elaborate lyrics didn't change at all between bands. The Lifter Puller catalog just sounds like The Hold Steady before it decided to embrace that whole "best bar band in America" thing, which essentially means more keyboards and fewer guitar solos.

11-12 JONATHAN FIRE*EATER/ THE RECOYS (THE WALKMEN)

After running in the same tight-knit, prep-school circles in Washington, D.C., the future members of The Walkmen split into two camps when they hit New York: Jonathan Fire*Eater, whose arresting, theatrical garage-rock was driven by Walter Martin's furious Farfisa and Stewart Lupton's Jagger-esque howl; and its spiky brethren The Recoys, featuring the strangled croon of Martin's cousin Hamilton Leithauser. While JFE imploded under major-label expectations and Lupton's increasingly erratic behavior, and The Recoys dissolved into the ether without ever making a proper album (though Troubleman Unlimited released a posthumous compilation in 2004), the childhood friends reconvened as The Walkmen to find commercial and creative success nearly overnight. That's because the groundwork was laid long beforehand: The Walkmen's warm, vintage textures were kilned in Jonathan Fire*Eater's more subdued moments like "Winston Plum: Undertaker" and "The Shape Of Things That Never Came," while Leithauser was already honing his sozzled, sentimental streak on Recoys tracks like "Song Of The Paper Dolls," "That's The Punchline," and "The Blizzard Of '93"—the latter two of which were reworked for The Walkmen's debut.

13 THE BOYS NEXT DOOR (THE BIRTHDAY PARTY/ NICK CAVE AND THE BAD SEEDS)

Even in its earliest incarnation as The Boys Next Door, the band that would become The Birthday Party (and later, Nick Cave And The Bad Seeds) had a reputation for chaos that made it one of the most talked-about punk acts in Australia. Unfortunately, there's barely any hint of that on its lone album, *Door, Door*, which more or less follows the spiky power-pop formula of groups like The Jam and fellow Australia outfit Radio Birdman. Cave and his bandmates almost immediately disowned the record, dismissing it as too poppy—a fair judgment, considering what was to come—but Cave disciples shouldn't overlook it entirely. Even at its most nascent, Cave's voice is engaging and theatrical, and hearing it boom confidently over the gritty, sax-laden stomp of straightforward glam numbers like "Brave Exhibitions" elevates the otherwise-middling material considerably. Then there are the fascinating hints of all the beautifully strange turns to come, such as the creeping paranoia of "Somebody's Watching" and the melodramatic, kids-aren't-all-right ballad "Shivers," elements of which can be heard throughout Cave's work.

14 SCUD MOUNTAIN BOYS (THE PERNICE BROTHERS)

Retro-pop tunesmith Joe Pernice leaned more toward Buck Owens than Burt Bacharach when he started Scud Mountain Boys in the early '90s. But the band's gentle pop tunes never fit comfortably in an alt-country scene defined by rough-and-tumble rock 'n' roll bands like Uncle Tupelo and Whiskeytown. By the time of its final album, 1996's *Massachusetts*, SMB had moved past the alt-country scene to embrace the richly melodic soft rock—notice the Bee Gees reference in the album title—that brought Pernice wider acclaim two years later with The Pernice Brothers' stand-out debut, *Overcome By Happiness*.

TV GUIDES

5 ESSENTIAL BOOKS ABOUT TELEVISION

1 BILL CARTER, *THE LATE SHIFT: LETTERMAN, LENO, AND THE NETWORK BATTLE FOR THE NIGHT*

While the TV columns were abuzz in the early '90s with speculation about who would replace Johnny Carson when he retired from *The Tonight Show*, Bill Carter of *The New York Times* had rare access to what was really going on, as old friends turned on each other and network executives hatched schemes in private. In real-world terms, the stakes were low, but the way the story played out spoke volumes about the machinations of media empires in the corporate conglomerate age, and about the fragile egos of the men who get paid millions to make us laugh.

2 JAMES MILLER AND TOM SHALES, *LIVE FROM NEW YORK: AN UNCENSORED HISTORY OF SATURDAY NIGHT LIVE AS TOLD BY ITS STARS, WRITERS AND GUESTS*

To help sort out the legends from the facts regarding *Saturday Night Live* drug abuse, infighting, and flashes of era-defining brilliance, James Miller and Tom Shales let all concerned tell the story in their own words, even when one account contradicts another. The resulting oral history shortchanges the '80s and '90s, but it's full of fascinating inside information about the ongoing high-wire act of producing a live weekly television broadcast on Saturday that people will be talking about on Monday.

3 ALEX McNEIL, *TOTAL TELEVISION*

The Internet has largely taken over the print-encyclopedia slot when it comes to looking up the basics on any topic. But nothing can beat the true interactive experience of a book like *Total Television*, which contains entries on every broadcast-network series (plus some cable shows) that aired between 1948 and the present, with appendices that lay out the primetime lineup for each year, and chart out TV movies and specials of note. Looking up one show in *Total Television* inevitably leads to flipping through the book to find out about others in a freeform, impulsive hunt.

4 HARLAN ELLISON, *THE GLASS TEAT*

Harlan Ellison is one of the most prolific writers in the history of pop literature, and also one of the most cantankerous. In this collection of TV criticism—culled from alternative-press columns published in the late '60s and early '70s—Ellison rages righteously against the tide of pap that in the decades since has shown up on Nick At Nite and TV Land, under the label of "classic" television. Faux-subversion, lazy gag-writing, leaden prestige fare... Ellison guns away at all of it, like a boob-tube version of Pauline Kael.

5 RAY RICHMOND, ED., *THE SIMPSONS: A COMPLETE GUIDE TO OUR FAVORITE FAMILY*

Fan-penned TV-episode guides have been cluttering up bookstore shelves since the publication of *The Twilight Zone Companion* and *The Columbo File*, but this ongoing series of *Simpsons* guides has become the industry standard, compiling memorable quotes, subtle sight gags, and detailed plot recaps. It's an apt salute to a show that's been rewarding close TV-watching since 1989.

NOISES OFF

15 MOVIES WITH GREAT DIALOGUE-FREE SCENES

1 *2001: A SPACE ODYSSEY* (1968)

There's a good reason the opening scenes of Stanley Kubrick's *2001* don't have any dialogue: They take place before anyone had any dialogue. Set at the moment when humanity achieved a higher type of intelligence—with, per Arthur C. Clarke's story, a little outside help—the sequence features a tribe of ape-men getting close to a black monolith and figuring out better ways to survive in a cruel world. Their solution: a cleverer kind of cruelty. In *2001*, being human means killing to survive, at least during the millennia between learning how to club an enemy to death and using technology to reach for the stars.

2 *THE RED SHOES* (1948)

Hollywood musicals in the '50s went ballet-happy, often breaking for lengthy expressionistic dances that abstractly restated their stories and themes. None matched the nesting quality of the central ballet in Michael Powell and Emeric Pressburger's 1948 melodrama *The Red Shoes*. Ingénue ballerina Moira Shearer drives herself to the point of exhaustion for taskmaster impresario Anton Walbrook, all to play the part of a girl who can't stop dancing in a ballet adaptation of Hans Christian Andersen's bleak fairy tale. Shearer's actual performance starts on a practical theater stage, but as the dance plays on, that stage subtly dissolves into a massive set, and the players become figures from her own experiences. Life becomes art becomes life.

3 *THERE WILL BE BLOOD* (2007)

The first 15 minutes of Paul Thomas Anderson's masterful oil-and-religion epic isn't entirely dialogue-free, but it's close enough: Daniel Day-Lewis, playing prospector Daniel Plainview, whispers happily at a piece of silver, "There it is." (And this is after he's fallen down a well and shattered his leg!) But the other sounds that introduce the film are the sounds of men working—grunting, striking at rock, coaxing buckets of oil from a deep well—and Jonny Greenwood's buzzing modern score. Those sounds, along with the wide vistas of the American West, do more to set up the film's pacing and central character than hours of historical verbiage could.

4 *MON ONCLE* (1958)

French comedian Jacques Tati spent the bulk of his career playing one character: Monsieur Hulot, a quiet, perpetually confused older gentleman who does his best to stumble unobtrusively through a modernized France. In *Mon Oncle*, M. Hulot visits his family in the suburbs, where they live in a blocky house surrounded by winding paths and shiny steel. Left alone in the kitchen, Hulot fidgets with the automated gadgets, unable to figure out what goes where, or why everything is designed the way it is. He accidentally drops a rounded plastic coffeepot, which bounces back up. He drops it again, delighted. Then he drops a glass tumbler, which, predictably, shatters all over the floor. That's what they call "the shock of the new."

5 *THE LADIES MAN* (1961)

Jacques Tati probably turned *vert* with envy watching Jerry Lewis' 1961 comedy *The Ladies Man*, especially the scene where Lewis explores his nebbishy hero's new lodgings in an all-female boarding house. While rhythmic swing music plays, Lewis moves the camera across his elaborate, multi-level set, watching the women wake up, wash up, get dressed, and head to breakfast in clockwork unison. Lewis shows the house room-by-room, building to the big reveal of the entire set, as his character heads down the grand staircase to the dining room full of females on the ground floor, awaiting him like a nest of vipers.

6 *THE BIRDS* *(1963)*
In a film that studiously avoids all sorts of dramatic convention—no background music, no portentous pacing, no explanation for why swarms of birds attack a sleepy town on a California bay—one scene in Alfred Hitchcock's *The Birds* all but screams in its wordlessness. Before the extent of the birds' savagery is fully known, the story's mysterious mother figure goes to visit a friend on his farm. As she wanders inside, she finds a line of mugs shattered in the kitchen, then a splayed bird smashed in a window, then a pair of bloody legs stretched out on the floor. And then, in a famous series of three silent camera zooms, the face of the farmer with his eyes pecked out. The silence is amplified as the old lady flees, mouth agape. She gasps and tries to grunt something to a nearby farmhand, but she's too terrified to talk.

7 *ONCE UPON A TIME IN THE WEST* *(1968)*
A Western that opens with a gunfight is nothing new. But how about a Western that spends several wordless minutes with the killers before the gunfight, showing them standing around and looking bored before the action starts? It happens in the opening sequence of *Once Upon A Time In The West*, Sergio Leone's elegiac epic about the death of the Western myth, where a wealth of classic Western "guest stars" (including Jack Elam and Woody Strode) wait at a train station for Charles Bronson to arrive. They swat flies, wipe water off their hats, and crack their knuckles, as the tension builds amid the mundane dawdling. A violent payoff appears inevitable, but Leone is in no hurry to get there. Instead, he revels in showing what most Westerns don't, using only the extraneous sounds of the Wild West to tell his story.

8 *WHAT TIME IS IT THERE?* *(2001)*
Director Tsai Ming-liang shoots whole scenes in long static takes, but his best work infuses those drawn-out shots with beauty and an occasional wit that's indebted to the silent classics of Buster Keaton and Harold Lloyd. And sometimes what happens in those shots is miraculous, as in *What Time Is It There?*, his melancholy comedy about a woman and her son grappling with the loss of her husband. The mother, whose grief sends her off into religious fervor, starts to believe that her late husband has been reincarnated, specifically as a cockroach that she finds crawling across the kitchen floor. In one wordless take, her skeptical son drops the cockroach into their fish tank, which is occupied by a giant ghostly whitefish. As the bug trickles down the far end of the tank, the fish hovers apathetically on the other side; just when the roach is about to hit bottom—bam!—the fish swoops over and swallows it whole. It's simultaneously funny, sad, and unexpectedly wondrous.

9 *STROSZEK* *(1977)*
The final eight minutes of Werner Herzog's masterful, depressing *Stroszek* is almost completely dialogue-free—it's broken up by a single line—but it's far from silent. As the title character goes off the deep end, he ends up in a roadside arcade in which caged animals provide amusement: A chicken dances, a duck plays a drum, etc. Meanwhile, when that racket isn't going, a hootin'-and-hollerin' (and terribly disquieting, in this context) Sonny Terry song plays.

10 *RIFIFI* *(1955)*
Jules Dassin's 1955 classic remains the quintessential heist film, largely on the strength of a 30-minute robbery sequence that plays out with no music and not a whisper of dialogue. Aside from the ambient pops of dust on the soundtrack, the only sounds are the muted chisels and drills manned by four thieves as they gingerly chip their way through the ceiling of a jewelry shop. The sequence has been imitated many times—most notably by the bravura Langley break-in in *Mission: Impossible* and by Dassin himself for *Topkapi*—but it's still untouched for its suspense and its respect for the hard-nosed professionals who pull off the operation.

11 *BIG NIGHT* *(1996)*
Stanley Tucci and Campbell Scott's

bittersweet ode to food, art, and brotherhood climaxes on a sour note: Co-starring as the owner of a struggling Italian restaurant, Tucci has just hosted an expensive party in honor of singing great Louis Prima. His chef brother, played by Tony Shalhoub, is an uncompromising perfectionist in the kitchen, and for this one night, he has dazzled the guests with an endless feast of traditional Italian delights. But when Prima fails to show, essentially dooming the restaurant to ruination, the simmering tensions between the brothers finally explode. Then, in the magical morning-after coda, Tucci emerges from his hangover and sets about making frittatas for himself, a waiter, and, finally, his brother, affirming that the fissures between them aren't permanent.

12 ***AKIRA*** *(1988)*

So much of Katsuhiro Ôtomo's animated masterpiece *Akira* is filled with squabbling politicians, shrieking crowds, and the nervy babble of the central gang of biker-kids that every space without chatter becomes unsettling and eerie. Ôtomo uses that contrast to powerful effect, filling his dialogue-free interludes with chilling images, particularly during two nightmare segments. In one, a boy in the process of coming into unimaginable power dreams that he's returned to his childhood playground, but both his city and his body are crumbling to pieces. Later, he confronts gigantic killer monsters out of a toy box, as a children's choir punctuates the moment with an eerie staccato song. Finally, once his power manifests, he flies silently into the outer atmosphere to destroy a satellite that's being repurposed to kill him and end the massive threat he poses to the human race.

13 ***CODE UNKNOWN*** *(2000)*

The full final 10 minutes of Michael Haneke's *Code Unknown* proceed without dialogue, as if in reaction to the talky, nerve-racking scene that precedes them. On the Paris Metro, a successful, independent stage and screen actress (Juliette Binoche) is harassed and humiliated. Afterward, she silently exits and disappears into the sanctum of her home. When her boyfriend arrives, he finds she's changed the security code to her apartment, where he—and possibly the rest of the world—is clearly no longer welcome. Meanwhile, in a parallel scene, unemployed illegal immigrant Luminita Gheorghiu returns to the street corner where she used to beg, but finds another woman has taken her place; she tries to claim a new spot, but is politely sent on her way. Like Binoche's boyfriend, she's abruptly rudderless and displaced. From the moment Binoche leaves the train, no audible words are spoken: The driving beat of a deaf children's drum troupe dominates the soundtrack, and Haneke's camera holds an unusually impersonal medium shot, distancing itself from the action and the emotions on display.

14-15 ***ALIEN*** *(1979)* AND ***JAWS*** *(1975)*

These two blockbuster horror classics both end roughly the same way: With a single frightened survivor facing off against an implacable, inhuman killer. With no one else present, there's no use in words, and with life in the balance, there's no time for them either. In *Jaws*, Roy Scheider has just watched a giant shark make an improbable leap onto his boat, smashing it and eating his shark-hunting partner Robert Shaw alive. As the boat swamps, Scheider frantically, wordlessly deals with repeated incursions from the determined shark, but he's fast running out of ways to stay out of the water. After a long struggle, the silence breaks and the sequence ends when Scheider mutters his famously defiant, make-or-break line "Right. C'mon. Show me the tank. *Smile*, you sonuva—" In *Alien*, Sigourney Weaver ends up in a similar position after she blows up her alien-infested ship. In a long, languorous coming-down sequence, she silently strips for cryogenic sleep, then realizes the alien is in the shuttle with her, and she slowly walks through the prep for her last stand. Eventually, she tries to bolster her nerve by singing "Lucky Star," which comes out in a breathless, choked whisper. No matter: In space, no one can hear you speak *or* sing.

MY BOY SAYS HE CAN EAT 50 EGGS, HE CAN EAT 50 EGGS

12 DISGUSTING MOVIE MEALS

1 MR. CREOSOTE'S LAST SUPPER, *MONTY PYTHON'S THE MEANING OF LIFE* (1983)

"It's only wafer-thin" is one of the most-quoted lines from 1983's *Monty Python's The Meaning Of Life*, but the repulsive Mr. Creosote scene has more yucks than yuks. A mountain of a man ambles into a restaurant, projectile-vomits everywhere, and eats everything on the menu, barfing a bit onto his gigantic shirtfront. Obsequious French waiter John Cleese offers him a tiny mint at the end, then runs off as if he just pulled the pin on a grenade. The joke is that this "wafer-thin" morsel is what literally causes Mr. Creosote to explode. What's grosser than the quarts of bile tossed all over the other diners? The living carcass of Mr. Creosote, exposed ribcage, beating heart and all. It's stomach-turning, but it's meant as humor, not horror.

2 ADVENTURES IN INDIAN CUISINE, *INDIANA JONES AND THE TEMPLE OF DOOM* (1984)

Practically taunting *Raiders Of The Lost Ark* fans with its relentlessly darker tone, *Indiana Jones And The Temple Of Doom* ups the gore and gross-outs at every turn. Even a dinner scene is cause for serious skin-crawling when Indy, Willie, and Short Round are served four courses of disgusting "delicacies" involving giant insects, chilled monkey brains (served straight from the head), and "Snake Surprise." *Doom's* gruesomeness not only led to the creation of the PG-13 rating, it also got the film banned in India, where local Hindus—who are primarily vegetarian—were obviously offended by their portrayal as eel-slurping maniacs. But even to American moviegoers schooled on gore, the dinner sequence is so objectionable that there's a "fan edit" of the film that removes it while leaving in the scene where a man's still-beating heart is pulled from his chest.

3 EGGS BY THE DOZEN, *COOL HAND LUKE* (1967)

Bored in prison? What better way to kill time than to make yourself fantastically sick for your friends' amusement and financial enrichment? As the title character in the '60s rebel classic *Cool Hand Luke*, Paul Newman keeps his reasons under wraps, so it isn't entirely clear why he decides to down 50 hard-boiled eggs in a sitting; it seems like he's just defying those who say it can't be done. Pointless rebellion is sort of a theme for ol' Luke (he gets sent to prison in the first place for decapitating parking meters), but the egg scene, the movie's most famous setpiece, comes off as more nausea-inducing than sexily nonconformist. Just ask Johnny Knoxville, who reenacted it years later on *Jackass* and ended up, unsurprisingly, puking his guts out.

4 BUBBLY, BEANS, AND CHOCOLATE, *TOMMY* (1975)

Hand it to Ann-Margret, she went for the gusto in the 1975 film adaptation of The Who's rock opera *Tommy*. After watching her exploited son on TV from her all-white bedroom palace, Tommy's mother throws a bottle of champagne through the screen. Out pour white, foamy suds, in which she rolls around while wearing a white mesh catsuit, as if to wash away her sins. The catsuit doesn't stay white for long, though. Next, a blast of baked beans shoots through the screen, and she rubs them over herself orgasmically. Then, naturally, there's a flood of liquid chocolate. After flinging the slop around, Ann-Margret humps a now-sullied cylindrical white pillow. It doesn't look like the tastiest recipe around, but it does look pretty fun.

5 MAGGOTS, *RESCUE DAWN* *(2007)*

In the age of *Fear Factor*, eating bugs no longer carries much stigma; in fact, with high-protein cricket snacks on the market, the practice has even gone upscale. But there are culinary distinctions to be made between crickets processed into crispy treats, and the live maggots consumed by Christian Bale's Dieter Dengler and his band of imprisoned comrades in *Rescue Dawn*. Shot down over Laos and thrown into a prison camp in the early days of the Vietnam War, American fighter pilot Dengler had to endure the guards' abuses, but also the famine that was sweeping the country. And when the guards are starving, the prisoners don't get filet mignon. The inspiring thing about Dengler (and Bale, who gamely participated) is that he eats those maggots with the same enthusiasm and lust for life that later leads him to carry out a daring escape plan.

6 "MENSTRUAL TEA," *ANATOMY OF HELL* *(2004)*

When it comes to sex, director Catherine Breillat (*Fat Girl*) has always gone out of her way to provoke, but *Anatomy Of Hell* takes it to another level. The premise concerns a woman who pays a gay misogynist (played by porn legend Rocco Siffredi) to analyze her body, and their clinical relationship leads to many horrifying images that can't be unseen. Between lines about how "the anus never lies" and shots of a garden tool slipped into the slumbering belle, Breillat has her heroine offer up a bloody tampon in a teacup. Bottoms up!

7 EXPIRED PINEAPPLES, *CHUNGKING EXPRESS* *(1994)*

How often is eating disgusting food simultaneously stomach-turning and poignant? That's the tone Wong Kar-Wai strikes in the first part of his magical 1994 diptych *Chungking Express*. After splitting with his long-term girlfriend May, a cop resolves to buy up every can of pineapples he can find with an expiration date of May 1, which also happens to be his birthday. He says, "If May hasn't changed her mind by the time I've bought 30 cans, our love will also expire." When May doesn't change her mind, he's left with a broken heart and a pile of cans, so what can he do in his misery but devour tin after tin of rotten pineapples until he gets sick?

8 SPAGHETTI AND SUDS, *GUMMO* *(1997)*

Harmony Korine's directorial debut *Gummo* doesn't lack for disturbing imagery, but one scene finds a particularly poetic pitch amid some retch-worthy nastiness. After weathering a number of dirty deeds done all around him, the weird-looking kid at the center of the story endeavors to take a bath. The water is dark brown, and for some reason a piece of bacon has been taped to a tile on the wall. After he conscientiously cleans between his toes, his mom walks in with a plate of spaghetti and a glass of milk, which the kid eats in the tub while his mother shampoos his hair. Then comes a candy bar, which gets dropped in the water before meeting its end in a mouth still slathered with marinara.

9 CORNISH GAME HENS SERVED A TOUCH ON THE RARE SIDE, *ERASERHEAD* *(1979)*

The grossness of eating is a running theme in David Lynch's work, all the way back to his first film, *Eraserhead*. When Henry Spencer goes to meet his girlfriend's family, the most grotesque batch of Cornish game hens in history is on the menu: They're still moving, and they bleed when cut. Then Henry learns that his girlfriend is pregnant, all while a slew of puppies nurse maniacally from a mother dog stationed nearby. It's about the least appetizing meal situation imaginable, and enough to make one swear off Cornish game hens (or any kind of chicken product) permanently.

10 LARDASS EATS A PIE, *STAND BY ME* *(1986)*

Even before Davie "Lardass" Hogan takes his revenge with a "complete and total barf-o-rama" in Gordie's campfire story-within-a-story, *Stand By Me's* infamous pie-eating scene has already set stomachs roiling. The smears of pie crust and blueberry hanging from the actors' faces, the guttural grunting as they dig into their tins like pigs at the trough: The lines between man and animal and food and excrement have been crossed even before the burbling begins deep in Lardass' stomach "like a log truck coming at you at a hundred miles an hour," and the entire county-fair crowd sprays each other with vomit. It's rough for viewers, too.

11 AUTO-CANNIBALISM, *A NIGHTMARE ON ELM STREET: THE DREAM CHILD* *(1989)*

Freddy Krueger's murders are among the most chilling in horror filmdom, because they play on our deepest psychological fears, particularly those with vanity at their root. For *Dream Child's* anorexic model-wannabe Erika Anderson, the big bogeyman is food, so being forced to attend one of her mother's dinner parties is already a nightmare even before Freddy shows up in a chef's hat. Locking her into a high chair like a fussing baby, Freddy force-feeds Anderson chunks of her own flesh—giving him opportunity to drop the typical Krueger-ism, "You are what you eat!"—until, her cheeks distended with dripping meat like a Grand Guignol vision of Dizzy Gillespie, Anderson dies choking on the one thing she feared most. Most terrifying of all, her chances of landing a *Vogue* cover are forever ruined.

12 EVERYTHING IN SIGHT, *ANIMAL HOUSE* (1978)

Much like Bill Murray in the similarly ramshackle *Caddyshack* two years later, John Belushi became the symbol and signature of *Animal House*, even though he has little screen time or relevance to the plot compared to the other leads. He's mostly around to show just how depraved and debauched the burnouts of Delta House can get. In particular, there's the wholly improvised scene where he wanders through a cafeteria line, building himself a massive meal that consists of whatever he can reach: an entire bunch of bananas, handfuls of doughnuts, multiple entrée plates, a wobbly green dessert dumped upside-down on top of the whole mess. To supplement that, he smushes food into his pockets. He eats half a hot dog and takes bites out of wrapped sandwiches, then returns them to their respective trays. Then he sucks a square of Jell-O off a plate in one swift gulp. At the point where he crams an entire hamburger into his mouth in a few queasy bites, he's apparently still hungry. The audience isn't.

50 MILLION PEOPLE CAN BE WRONG

7 TERRIBLE MOVIES ON THE TOP 100 ALL-TIME BOX-OFFICE-HITS LIST*

1 *STAR WARS: EPISODE I—THE PHANTOM MENACE*
(#19, 1999)

It's possible to defend George Lucas' *Star Wars* prequels on the grounds that they look fantastic, they're aimed at children, and they do realize Lucas' idiosyncratic personal vision of a universe well-stocked with fast cars and broad ethnic stereotypes. But let's face it: *Star Wars: Episode I* didn't make so much money because millions of people deeply love it. The movie rose to the top of the box office on sheer momentum, buoyed by a combination of nostalgia, hype, and pained disbelief that a cherished franchise could've gone so wrong. ("Maybe we just didn't get it," *Star Wars* fans said en masse. "Better see it again to make sure.")

2 *MEET THE FOCKERS*
(#37, 2004)

Powered by greed, naked calculation, and free-floating contempt for its target audience of easily amused mouth-breathers, the repellent 2004 sequel *Meet The Fockers* ratcheted up *Meet The Parents'* raunch and scatological jokes while recycling pretty much all its jokes. Discriminating audiences punished the filmmakers' hackwork and cynicism by making *Meet The Fockers* the top-grossing live-action comedy of all time, with a worldwide gross of more than half a billion dollars. Seldom has H.L. Mencken seemed more on-the-money about how no one goes broke underestimating the intelligence of the American public.

3 *THE GREATEST SHOW ON EARTH*
(#54, 1952)

1952 Best Picture win aside, Cecil B. DeMille's two-and-a-half-hour salute to spectacle and romance under the big top is a bloated, hammy, overheated string of melodramatic plots spaced out with endless scenes of parades and clowning. In other words, the title ain't exactly truth in advertising.

4 *BRUCE ALMIGHTY*
(#51, 2003)

It's a measure of *Bruce Almighty's*

(* ADJUSTED FOR INFLATION)

surreal paucity of imagination and invention that when benevolent deity Morgan Freeman grants infinite, unimaginable powers to wacky reporter protagonist Jim Carrey (at his rubber-faced, maudlin worst), Carrey seems exclusively concerned with getting a better gig on local news and improving his girlfriend's rack. The Carrey-free sequel, *Evan Almighty*, was just as dumb, but this time around, the audience saw it coming, and it met the fate its predecessor richly merited, becoming one of the biggest box-office bombs of all time.

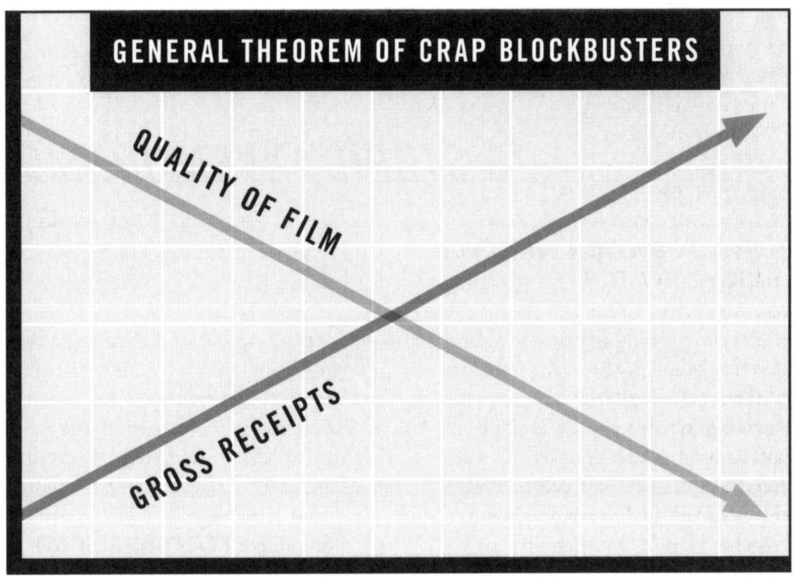

5 ***TWISTER*** *(#75, 1996)*
The mid-'90s were dire times for blockbuster-movie fans, with Steven Spielberg off prepping Oscar-bait while the likes of Stephen Sommers and Simon West dominated the multiplex. No wonder we let ourselves get whipped into a frenzy over this dopey Jan de Bont disaster flick, in which the real villain is our collective reluctance to warn ourselves about tornadoes. Oscar- and Emmy-caliber stars Helen Hunt, Bill Paxton, and Philip Seymour Hoffman do yeoman work in what's essentially an effects-laden two-hour commercial for NOAA Weather Radio.

6 ***MRS. DOUBTFIRE*** *(#84, 1993)*
Robin Williams was at the peak of his popularity when he collaborated with director Chris Columbus on this movie about an out-of-work actor masquerading as his own children's nanny. Maybe it's because Williams went to the "find your inner child" well once too often, or maybe it's because all that '90s "inner child" business now seems arrogant and obnoxious—but *Mrs. Doubtfire* exemplifies the cruddiness of '90s Hollywood comedies the way *Twister* defines clunky '90s action.

7 ***DR. SEUSS' HOW THE GRINCH STOLE CHRISTMAS*** *(#96, 2000)*
Ron Howard has helmed award-winning, critically acclaimed movies, but he also can't seem to say no to a fat paycheck—even if it means dropping a smelly, splattery black mark on his filmography. In expanding Dr. Seuss' classic Christmas story, Howard and company created a shrill, lumbering beast of a movie, in which Jim Carrey's perpetually mugging Grinch is really no worse than the consumerist Whos down in Whoville. Audiences flocked to see this take on *Grinch* during the 2000 Christmas season, but with good reason, it didn't become an annual holiday tradition like the version where the bad guy lacks a cheesy backstory.

TOILETS ARE FOR CHUMPS

24 STUPID INVENTIONS FOR LAZY AMERICANS

1 HANDY SWITCH WIRELESS LIGHT SWITCH

You've come to grips with the idea that you're never going to exercise again. You skip going to the movies because Netflix will bring Hollywood to you. Peapod puts your weekly Twinkie order right on your counter. It's come down to this: The only calories you ever burn are from moving around your own house, and clapping to activate The Clapper. No more! If the light switch across the room is just too far, the Handy Switch—a handheld remote-control light switch—will free you from the tyranny of walking. "Tired of getting out of bed every night just to turn out the lights?" goes the commercial. Now you don't have to. Check and mate.

2 ELECTRIC SCISSORS

On his incredibly funny, incredibly bitter CD *It's Not Funny*, comedian David Cross offers as much exasperation at Americans over the existence of electric scissors (widely available from a variety of companies) as he does for politicians and other assorted assholes. In a way, he has a point: For certain tasks, like difficult-to-cut fabrics, they might make sense. But if you're just using them to clip coupons, you've saved no time or energy at all. Quoth Mr. Cross: "It'll save you over 2.7 seconds. That shit adds up. When you're ready to die, and Death quietly and nurturingly takes you by the hand and says 'It's your time…' 'But I used electric scissors for 40 years!' 'All right, you've got another three and a half minutes.'"

3 FRESCHETTA PRE-SLICED FROZEN PIZZA

Pizza technology made huge leaps in the 20th and early 21st centuries, with the advent of ready-made dough, canned sauce, pre-shredded cheese, and sliced toppings saving hours of laborious kitchen work. Combine those into the ingenious invention of frozen pizza, and you've saved a day in the kitchen—and without too huge a drop in quality. All you had to do was cook the pizza, cut it, and serve. In early 2008, the fine folks of Freschetta finally removed the 30-second middle step, offering pre-sliced frozen pies. Next up from the Freschetta labs: a frozen pizza that carries itself from the freezer to the oven, cooks itself, then hovers in front of your mouth while you eat it.

4 ROBOMOWER

Lazy Americans are often cheap Americans, looking not only to save steps, but to save precious money with which to purchase time- and energy-saving devices. The RoboMower, like its cousin the Roomba, is fairly expensive, which must make it a tough sell for the $9.99-or-less "as seen on TV!" crowd. "Think of the free time you'll have!" trumpets the manufacturer. How much free time will you have after programming this little lawn-mowing robot to your yard specifications, then keeping a nervous eye on it the whole time it's working, to make sure it doesn't choke on a stick, chew up your garden, or swallow a neighbor's pet? Also, it's nearly $2,000. For that price, lazy Americans could hire industrious immigrants to mow their lawns for a decade—if lazy Americans weren't so hell-bent on keeping immigrants out.

5 FLIPFOLD

Humans are born with an inherent love of folding clothes, so thank goodness for the creatively capitalized FlipFOLD, which makes the process longer, more complicated, and more expensive by involving more equipment. Did you ever wish that your pile of T-shirts could be perfectly folded right before you crammed them into the drawer? Dream no longer! Simply pull out the FlipFOLD and place onto an appropriately large space, carefully arrange your shirt on the apparatus, flip, fold, remove, and repeat! It's like fantasy camp for aspiring Gap employees! Comes in various colors for extra fun.

6 BEER HATS

When are lazy people also beasts of burden? When they have two beers fastened to their heads and they're chugging them simultaneously, thanks to a tri-valve plastic hose. Beer hats (which a variety of manufacturers make in styles including trucker caps, football helmets, and cowboy hats) let their users enjoy the miracle of hands-free drinking while also more efficiently downing two beers at once. And thanks to the invention of the Beer Belt—which can hold an entire six-pack "no further than an arm's length"—stumbling trips to the refrigerator are now a thing of the past. All that's missing from the equation is a self-emptying catheter.

7 SLEEVED BLANKET

The sleeved blanket (marketed variously as Snuggie and Slanket) is basically a blanket with sleeves. No, wait, that isn't completely accurate. It's actually a magic sack of lazy: a blanket meant to wrap around its sloth-like owner like a gigantic, nap-inducing fleece hospital gown. The sleeves don't permit much range of motion, but it should suffice for low-impact activities like reaching for another pile of Double Stuf Oreos, or changing the channel. Unsurprisingly, one of the Slanket's slogans is, "Call in sick, it's just one day," though it seems geared more to the slovenly and unemployed.

8 THE SEGWAY

If inventors are going to create devices that aid customers in avoiding exercise, the least they could do is push the price point below $5,000, and the weight limit above 250 pounds. The Segway, a motorized two-wheel stand-up "human transporter," was laughably overhyped before it hit the market in 2001—inventor Dean Kamen predicted in a *Time* interview that the Segway "will be to the car what the car was to the horse and buggy," while the media hyperbolized about how it would change the way cities are built. Instead, it merely surfaced in *Frasier*, *Arrested Development*, and "Weird Al" Yankovic's "White And Nerdy" music video, as Americans continued to grow fatter on their couches, secretly wishing they could ride a Segway just once, if only for a rare, magical low-speed spin around the block.

9 BATTER PRO

The problem with fast food isn't that it's unhealthy, it's that it isn't nearly fast enough. That's where the Batter Pro and its 10-second battering method comes in—simply drop batter, your favorite raw foods, and breadcrumbs into the "revolutionary" (but suspiciously Tupperware-like) tiered bowls, shake 'em, and voilà! You've covered some foods in batter, which clearly couldn't be done in any way not involving special equipment, and you're officially a depressing, pathetic loser gullible enough to buy a highfalutin Shake 'N Bake appliance. (Bonus loser-points if you actually own a deep fryer with which to cook your newly battered food.) Batter Pro also comes with a recipe guide and utensils, but let's face it: Soon after receiving it in the mail, you'll be battering everything from tubes of cookie dough to fried chicken.

10 EZ-CARRY

Consider EZ-Carry a counterpart to *Mr. Show's* Bag Hutch—except that it's a real product, actually available for purchase. It's an "ergonomically designed" soft-grip handle with an attached hook to carry up to 50 pounds of shopping bags. Why is it necessary? Supposedly it saves you trips, since it's impossible to grip the actual handles of more than one plastic bag at a time, but EZ-Carry holds them all together so it's possible to carry more than one bag at once... kind of like an actual human hand. A set of EZ-Carrys runs about $20, and comes with a complimentary "leather" tote, apparently to help you practice the art of latching objects onto hooks without even leaving the house. Too lazy to go shopping? They also double as the most ineffective brass knuckles imaginable.

11 BOOT AND GLOVE DRYER

Take heed, high-maintenance slobs adventurous enough to wander out into the elements: The Boot And Glove Dryer is here to end the plague of wet boots and damp gloves that has gripped the nation since before the invention of the regular dryer. But the Boot And Glove Dryer claims superiority in its field via a base with a built-in fan, baking-soda-filled pans for deodorizing, and pegs with airholes to facilitate circulation. And although it also boasts the ability to dry soggy "accessories of varying lengths," truly lazy people would either toss their soaked garments on the floor after coming inside, or never venture outside to begin with.

12 FLOWBEE

Remember when getting a haircut was as simple as driving to the barber's, hopping in the hydraulic chair, and grunting, "A little off the top"? Well, upon further inspection, that's *entirely* too complicated. Fortunately, San Diego carpenter Rick Hunt invented the Flowbee after noticing an industrial vacuum's ability to suck sawdust from his hair, and realizing the fashionable possibilities. Essentially a vacuum-cleaner attachment with blades, the sucking/cutting Flowbee is an excellent tool for people who want to cut off some hair, and don't really care how they look afterward. If you're too lazy to go to the barber, you're probably also too lazy to go outside and interact with people who might laugh at the haircut you gave yourself with your vacuum cleaner.

13 P.B. SLICES/SPAM SINGLES

Maybe you think you were ahead of the peanut-butter-and-jelly-sandwich-making curve because you were an early adopter of Goober Grape. Maybe you think because you've discovered Uncrustables, you've found the laziest possible way to make the simplest sandwich in the world. But in fact, there you are, still fumbling around with microwaving your Uncrustable, while smarter lazy people have already finished their meal, thanks to P.B. Slices, essentially a sandwich-ready "slice" of peanut butter cling-wrapped like a slice of American cheese. These chemical abominations save you even the minimal prep time it takes to open a bottle of peanut butter and slather some on bread. They also mark select consumers as so incredibly lazy that "unwrapping" is the most complicated culinary procedure they can handle. The venerable meatoid substance known as Spam has also gotten in on the overpriced convenience game: Spam Singles feature a single sad gray specimen of their mysterious product sealed in a foil pouch for people who aren't afraid to announce to grocery-store clerks that cutting up their own Spam is just too exhausting to contemplate. As the website says, "For on the go! For on the couch!" Guess which option is way more likely.

THE WORST THING ABOUT AMERICA'S TENDENCY TO CATER TO THE LOWEST COMMON DENOMINATOR IS THAT IT TENDS TO MAKE THE HIGHER DENOMINATORS CYNICAL.

14 3-IN-1 BREAKFAST MAKER

The marketing geniuses who come up with these stupid inventions in their Unabomber-style thinkin' shacks are faced with the constant challenge of describing their products without saying "You should buy this because you're a fat, indolent bastard." The classic favorite descriptions are "convenient," "easy to use," and "innovative," though the last only appeals to the 5 percent of their clientele who know four-syllable words. With the 3-in-1 Breakfast Maker, the gimmick is "space-saving." The product is a toaster oven with a tiny hot plate on top and a single-cup coffee maker on the side. It's convenient, economical, and really pathetic.

15 HOG WILD TWIRLING SPAGHETTI FORK

There are two schools of thought about the proper way to eat spaghetti: suckers and twirlers. Adherents of both styles disapprove of each other's crudeness, slovenliness, and lack of couth; then there's usually a big food fight. But both sides agree that the Hog Wild Twirling Spaghetti Fork is a total waste of time and cash. Colorful, exciting, and using two AAA batteries where none are needed, the Twirling Spaghetti Fork does exactly what its name implies. It promises less mess, which is only possible if you leave the batteries out, and it delivers a pasta-eating method for people too lazy or enfeebled to rotate their own forks. It also features "100% twirling fun," unlike those other shitty mechanical forks that deliver 90 to 95 percent twirling fun, tops.

16 ELECTRIC TOOTHBRUSHES

Similarly, electric toothbrushes are all about wasting batteries on a simple, minimal physical process. Too lazy to move your own toothbrush up and down or back and forth? Skip a few of those meals you're brushing out of your teeth, and maybe that up-and-down arm motion won't give you chest pains.

17 ELECTRIC FLY SWATTER

Although the name conjures images

of a hydraulic-powered machine for people who lack the muscle power to kill a housefly, the electric fly swatter is not, like Homer Simpson's battery-powered hammer, a crude thing of kinetic energy. It's much more elegant and pointless: a sort of portable mini bug zapper. In fact, it's just the thing for the psychotic insecticidal craftsman who, not content to take out dozens of flies and mosquitoes a minute with a traditional bug zapper, instead chooses to carry around this miniature electrocution griddle and rid the world of pests one grisly execution at a time. The electric fly swatter's bizarre form (it's sort of like having a big hammer with a gun inside it) and delightfully strange claim that it may only stun larger insects—what does one do with a stunned cockroach?—makes it a lazy-stupid classic.

18 INVOCA 3.0 VOICE-ACTIVATED REMOTE CONTROL

The worst thing about America's tendency to cater to the lowest common denominator is that it tends to make the higher denominators cynical. The InVoca voice-activated universal remote, for example, probably wasn't created so much for the lazy and stupid as it was the invalid and paralyzed. But we'd bet the gadget's $50 price tag that the majority of purchasers aren't stroke victims, they're just lazy schmucks who can't be arsed to press a button in order to watch that *King Of Queens* marathon. Even the InVoca's ad copy is a bizarre mixture of creepy and slothful: "Tell your TV what to do," it says—what's with the authoritarian tone?—"without lifting a finger." And since a finger is all that's required to operate any remote, it's pretty clear that the target market for voice-activated remotes is people who consider Stephen Hawking a tireless athletic dynamo.

19 SAKURA AND STAEDTLER BATTERY-OPERATED ERASERS

Although it's sold at art-supply stores, which ostensibly gives it more class than a checkout-rack item at Walmart, the battery-operated eraser is still patently unnecessary. What type of mistake requires 12,000 rpm of torque to erase it? Whatever it is, Sakura is ready: Its 2.8-ounce eraser, powered by two AAA batteries, is "meant to handle any type of mistake." They mean pen or pencil, but there's something strangely comforting in that promise.

Lazy, stupid, and desperate for your own Batter Pro or RoboMower? Or just suspect we made these items up? Many of them are available through AsSeenOnTV.com.

20 STADIUM PAL/ STADIUM GAL

David Sedaris is known to exaggerate details in his writing for comic effect, but he wasn't making up the Stadium Pal when he wrote about it for *Esquire* a few years back. Even his talented mind couldn't fabricate a self-adhesive condom with 18 inches of tubing connected to a 34-ounce "collection bag." Described by its makers as "the ultimate portable urinal," Stadium Pal gives people all the benefits of pissing their pants without the indignities of adult diapers or smelly trousers. Just apply the external catheter—available in five sizes determined by the sizing guide—tie the bag to your calf, and let 'er rip. Ladies can enjoy the same convenience with Stadium Gal.

21-22 SELF-STIRRING MUG/ MOO MIXER SUPREME

Indulging in your morning coffee can be an arduous process, what with all the hefting of heavy mugs and flexing of throat muscles. Thankfully, the Self-Stirring Mug takes some of the burden off the shoulders of the fiending caffeine junkie, via a propeller spinning at 3,000 rpm for mixing in creamer, sugar, and that peskiest of hot-drink additives, honey. (It's also presumably good for splashing scalding-hot coffee or tea on its users' desks, counters, and faces.) For lazy-ass little'uns who haven't graduated to big-kid vices, there's still plenty of propulsive beverage-mixing fun to be had with the Hog Wild Moo Mixer Supreme, which whirls users' chocolate milk into a spinning vortex of lethargy and shame.

23 THE VOICE RECOGNITION GROCERY LIST ORGANIZER

What slothful bastard doesn't like food? And yet the process of coming up with grocery lists is repetitive and taxing enough to kill any hearty appetite. Which is why Hammacher Schlemmer markets a $100 computerized device that listens as you dictate your grocery list, then prints it out. That's great for people without hands, or rich pen fetishists who'd normally be taking grocery-list notes with a $100 pen anyway, but it seems ridiculously pricey and pointless for the rest of the world.

24 JIMMY DEAN PANCAKES & SAUSAGE ON A STICK

Frankly, we could pack five more pages with horrible "convenience" foods for the lazy, from push-up mac-and-cheese in a tube to Hot Pockets. But after a while, it all starts to look the same, like one big greasy, gelatinous, preservative-packed mass. Still, room must be made for one of the most ridiculous "food" products on the mass market: Jimmy Dean's breakfast take on the corn dog, with a pancake (your choice of chocolate chip or blueberry) wrapped around a pork sausage on a stick. The only thing that could make this insanely unhealthy, fundamentally gross product worse would be layers of scrambled egg and cheese between the pancake and the meat. Unfortunately, in some lab somewhere, enterprising convenience-food techs are no doubt working on that right now. If only marketers were as lazy as their customers.

AND I FEEL FINE

17 GREAT SONGS UNAFRAID OF THE APOCALYPSE

1 R.E.M., "IT'S THE END OF THE WORLD AS WE KNOW IT (AND I FEEL FINE)"

Listen closely and use your best abstract-thinking skills, and R.E.M.'s classic is pretty scary ("Locking in, uniforming, book-burning, bloodletting"), but there's no real fear at the end. Mike Mills' backing vocals tell the greatest part of the story: "It's time I had some time alone." Another hint is right there in the title.

2 TOM WAITS, "EARTH DIED SCREAMING"

Tom Waits' best songs sound like he's already gutter-bound and well into a bottle of Jack, so it's no surprise that his take on the apocalypse is as surreal as a Bosch painting and as ragged as a stumbling bum. (And no wonder Terry Gilliam used it in his apocalyptic science-fiction movie *12 Monkeys*.) In his roughest guttural yawp, Waits belts out a woozy report of airplane-sized crows and three-headed lions. Behind him, an orchestra of clanking sticks intended to create the sound of a marching army of skeletons adds an ambience of cartoonish foreboding.

3 THE LOUVIN BROTHERS, "GREAT ATOMIC POWER"

Prophets have foretold the end of the world for thousands of years, updating the details as necessary when God fails to flip us the Big Finger as predicted. In 1952, it seemed obvious to a few Christians that when the rapture came, God's will would be ushered in with a massive nuclear strike. Some gospel musicians began cheerfully praising the atomic bomb as a manifestation of the holy fire that would sweep good people to heaven (including, naturally, the singers and their friends) and leave the rest to wail and gnash. The sweet, uplifting melody of Ira and Charlie Louvin's close-harmony number is a classic of the Eisenhower era, but it's creepy that they're so happy about the prospect of fiery wrath raining down on everything except them.

4 THE HANDSOME FAMILY, "IF THE WORLD SHOULD END IN FIRE" / "IF THE WORLD SHOULD END IN ICE"

Rennie Sparks' cheerfully morbid

outlook could qualify her for membership in the Addams Family. In this pair of songs from her band's 2003 disc, *Singing Bones*, she ruminates on doom, whether it comes as a bang or a whimper. Her decision, delivered with due gravity in a sepulchral baritone by her husband, Brett, is to sit quietly and remember better days—not major moments in her life, necessarily, but smaller grace notes like the transient beauty of clouds or robins hopping across a yard.

5 PRINCE, "1999"

It seems quaint now, but 1999 was once so amazingly far off that it was an easy shorthand reference for a time when we'd all be flying around with jetpacks, or even more drastically, waiting for the end of the world. The children of the '80s lived in terror of nuclear war, and the feeling of impending doom became pervasive in pop culture. Prince took on the topic several times, sometimes with an earnest, stop-the-madness angle on songs like "Ronnie, Talk To Russia." But his 1982 hit "1999" just shrugs its shoulders. Faced with the purple skies of Judgment Day, he figures there's no point in doing anything but dancing: "Life is just a party, and parties weren't meant 2 last."

6 MORRISSEY, "EVERYDAY IS LIKE SUNDAY"

Those who tag Morrissey as a goth are missing the point completely, but the lyrics to "Everyday Is Like Sunday" offer some ammo for doubters: With the lines, "Come Armageddon, come Armageddon, come!" he practically begs for the apocalypse to end his boredom (and he channels John Betjeman's poem "Slough" in the process).

7 JOHNNY CASH, "THE MAN COMES AROUND"

It's easy to imagine Johnny Cash as the voice of the apocalypse, and on the title track of the final album released in his lifetime, *American IV: The Man Comes Around*, that's basically what he becomes. Beginning and ending with quotations from the biblical book of Revelation, the Man In Black solemnly informs us that "there's a man going 'round taking names, and he decides who to free and who to blame." He isn't talking about Santa Claus, either. Cash loads his lyrics with gnomic biblical and pseudo-biblical references ("the virgins are all trimming their wicks"), delivering his warning without anger or joy, just a weary matter-of-factness.

8 TALKING HEADS, "NOTHING BUT FLOWERS"

David Byrne keeps his eye on the important things: The total collapse of human civilization means no more Slurpees. With his usual wry wit, Byrne describes living in a kind of Edenic paradise, with all our malls and factories overgrown by lush vegetation: "This was a Pizza Hut. Now it's all covered with daisies." Sounds beautiful, right? Well, it turns out that the Age Of Plastic had plenty to recommend it. Byrne looks back with nostalgia at the days of asphalt and gas-guzzling, when he could eat cherry pies and candy bars instead of rattlesnake meat. "If this is paradise," he sighs with resigned irritation, "I wish I had a lawnmower."

9 YOUNG MARBLE GIANTS, "FINAL DAY"

Like many Young Marble Giants songs, "Final Day" is sparse and spooky, but also demure and laid-back, as if the apocalypse just isn't worth getting bent out of shape about. In fact, in the course of the 90-second song, judgment day begins to sound

pretty nice. "As the final day falls into the night / there is peace outside in the narrow light," Alison Statton intones in her typically shy, singsong delivery. Sure, she also describes horrible stuff going on as the Earth falls apart—but who cares? It'll all be over soon, and then we can finally get some peace and quiet.

10 THE CLASH, "LONDON CALLING"

There's no denying the suffocating sense of dread that suffuses "London Calling." And yet the song's alarm-ringing tone isn't preachy or blatantly activist; instead, Joe Strummer and company seem equally terrified and electrified by the onset of zombies, underworlds, and nuclear winter. "A nuclear error / but I have no fear," barks Strummer, who sounds almost bestially rapturous imagining a Three Mile Island-style meltdown in the middle of London. And the song's calling card—Strummer's signature, wolf-like howl—serves as a chilling, perverse celebration of societal breakdown and anarchy as much as a lament for the extinction of mankind.

11 BOB DYLAN, "TALKIN' WORLD WAR III BLUES"

Although he's just describing a dream, Bob Dylan's "Talkin' World War III Blues" evokes a familiar vision of post-apocalyptic America, with deserted streets and pockets of paranoid survivors fleeing each other. What's remarkable, though, is how relaxing it all sounds: Dylan lights a cigarette and walks around like nothing happened, tries to pick up a girl so they can "go and play Adam and Eve," then takes a joy ride in an abandoned Cadillac. ("Good car to drive after a war.") Turns out the psychiatrist he's reporting all this to has had the same dream, but with him wandering around on his own instead of Dylan. In fact, everyone's having the same vision, which may imply that it's prophetic, or may just suggest a nation of overcrowded solipsists who, like R.E.M., long for some time alone.

12 OINGO BOINGO, "JUST ANOTHER DAY"

Before becoming Tim Burton's go-to guy for eerie film scores, Danny Elfman established his love for ghoulish music with Oingo Boingo, especially the 1985 album *Dead Man's Party*—which contained the hellish title track as well as the more subtly creepy "Just Another Day." Like some Reagan-era fever dream, Elfman paints a nightmare scenario where "the world was set on fire," followed by a list of holocaust effects. But instead of lamenting all that wholesale destruction, Elfman—as if he were one of Burton's own gleefully morbid creations—sings "But there's a smile on my face for everyone."

13 FISHBONE, "PARTY AT GROUND ZERO"

According to Fishbone, there are two ways to deal with the world's end: Duck and cover, or jump up and dance. In 1985—the same year Sting gazed navel-ward and wondered if the Russians loved their children, too—the frenetic ska-funk band yelled "Fuck it!" and painted the inevitable World War III as "a B-movie starring you" in which the world turns to "flowing pink vapor stew." Then, after throwing in some facetious, flyboy jingoism that presaged *Top Gun*, and celebrating the chance to "sing a new war song," Fishbone issued its most philosophically resonant reason to learn to love the bomb: "Just have a good time, the stop sign is far away."

14 NAPALM DEATH, "DRAGNET"

It's hard to tell where most '80s metal bands stand when it comes to the apocalypse. If their music is any indication, they were simultaneously tickled pink and scared shitless at the prospect of mutually assured destruction. But Napalm Death circa 1987 was no mere metal band; the grindcore pioneer's debut, *Scum*, tore thrash's barbed-wire snarl into a pile of razor-sharp shavings. In just over a minute of garbage-disposal riffs and acidic puke, the disc's closer, "Dragnet," practically drools in anticipation of the oncoming "atomic genocide," and it portrays man's suicidal extinction as merely the inevitable conclusion to its evolutionary cycle.

15 BAD RELIGION, "FUCK ARMAGEDDON... THIS IS HELL"

On its 1982 debut, Bad Religion wasted no time establishing its ethos with all the subtlety its moniker implies. The title, *How Could Hell Be Any Worse?*, came from the lyrics to "Fuck Armageddon... This Is Hell," a song that practically welcomes the apocalypse. Frontman Greg Graffin lambastes the hypocrisy of pious Christians and nationalists who preach God and country while harming their fellow men. "How can hell be any worse when life alone is such a curse?" Graffin asks with inimitable optimism.

16 **BILLY JOEL, "MIAMI 2017"**
In this stormy rocker, some unnamed "they" has destroyed New York, though they were pretty selective about it, saving the Yankees but sinking Manhattan. The song's narrator is tasked to "keep the memory alive" of how he and his neighbors kept on partying in the face of destruction. Now, of course, they all live down in Florida, presumably old and beaten-down, and only able to revive their spirits through bouts of nostalgia. For this, they needed an apocalypse?

17 **CONSTANTINES, "INSECTIVORA"**
A lot of songs by the Canadian indie-rock act Constantines seem to have been written from the perspective of a man barricaded in an attic, scrawling out his panicked final thoughts. "Insectivora" is one of the few that makes the crisis clear. While grunting about "chaos agents" and "hunting dogs" coming to "drag him out," frontman Bryan Webb sounds a warning: "I'm learning to survive on earthworms and houseflies," he gasps. He's in for the long haul.

NOT DEAD YET, TOO

13 GREAT ALBUMS MADE BY MUSICIANS AFTER THEY TURNED 50

1 **JOHNNY CASH, *AMERICAN RECORDINGS*** *(1994, AGE 62)*
It was a simple idea: Give Johnny Cash a guitar and some great songs, then press "record." And yet no album in Cash's storied career was quite like 1994's *American Recordings*, a stark collection of new Cash songs and covers of tunes by Nick Lowe, Glenn Danzig, and Loudon Wainwright III. Looking like something out of the book of Revelation on the striking, black-and-white cover, Cash suddenly became cool to a whole new generation of kids. But it's the music that makes the album a highlight of Cash's career. By stripping down to just his booming voice and chugging guitar, Cash reminded everyone why he mattered once, and why he always would.

2 **LORETTA LYNN, *VAN LEAR ROSE*** *(2004, AGE 70)*
The quintessential comeback album, *Van Lear Rose* was released more than four decades into Loretta Lynn's career. Her career has no shortage of high points, but *Van Lear Rose* solidified her legacy while granting her a new kind of cachet. Thanks in no small part to album collaborator/producer Jack White, who lends a gritty, bluesy bent to the country legend's down-home honky-tonk, Lynn produced a stunning, nearly universally revered crossover hit that reintroduced her to an industry looking for the newest old thing to drool over.

3 **NEIL YOUNG, *SILVER & GOLD*** *(2000, AGE 54)*
Neil Young was well into his 50s when *Silver & Gold* came out. To be fair, he'd been kicking some of its songs around for years—particularly the title track, written in 1982—but this throwback to his gentlest solo material is openly nostalgic in ways Young needed to age into. Here, he reminisces beautifully about old sounds—and about old bands, on "Buffalo Springfield Again."

4 **ROBERT WYATT, *SHLEEP*** *(1997, AGE 52)*
Something of an "old soul" even when he helped conceive the psy-

chedelic prog-rock band Soft Machine in the '60s, Robert Wyatt was 52 when he issued *Shleep*—and he sounded all the younger for it. One of the wondrous paradoxes of Wyatt's work has always been the way he delivers a wizened worldview with the spirited voice of an innocent, and his unique trills and intonations sound all the more guileless within *Shleep*'s charmingly sophisticated jazz-dream arrangements. In certain songs, Wyatt sounds like a distracted child humming to himself at night, but it takes a wealth of life experience to make sense of lyrics like "Given free will but within certain limitations, I cannot will myself to limitless mutations."

5 LINDSEY BUCKINGHAM, *UNDER THE SKIN* (2006, AGE 57)

In the wake of yet another less-than-fulfilling Fleetwood Mac reunion, Lindsey Buckingham dialed down and went it alone on *Under The Skin*, a quiet solo album given a quiet release on his 57th birthday. The lyrics bear all the marks of searching remembrance and wistful contemplation, with an opening song that circles an impassioned question: "What am I doing anyway, telling myself it's not too late?" Buckingham doesn't sound sad so much as curious about what makes him continue to tick, and his alternately fragile and furious guitar (most of it acoustic, to suit the modest mood) does a fine job of invoking his Fleetwood Mac past while slipping outside its shadow.

6 VASHTI BUNYAN, *LOOKAFTERING* (2005, AGE 60)

British folk enchantress Vashti Bunyan made her name in London with one lone album in 1970 before setting off, as the story goes, in a horse-pulled carriage for a life in the country. She took more than three decades to return, and she came back on *Lookaftering* with a special kind of homey knowledge. Over gently picked acoustic guitars and flutes blown by a twilight breeze, she sings of days gone by with a warm, intimate voice untouched by time. In one particularly touching song, "Here Before," Bunyan sings about her own children as if still awed by the little things they did when they were barely as tall as the wheat around them. It's a testament to the special kinds of experience that become all the more meaningful in memory.

7 BOB DYLAN, *TIME OUT OF MIND* (1997, AGE 56)

It was accepted wisdom in the mid-'90s that Bob Dylan was 15, maybe even 25 years past his creative peak. But then a combination of factors crystallized, allowing him to hear his muse again—a snowbound period on his Minnesota farm left him with nothing to do but write songs, and a near-fatal heart ailment gave him something to write about. Working with producer Daniel Lanois to cook up a raw, bluesy sound influenced by the '50s rock that inspired Dylan as a young man, the master songwriter created an album that surprised even his longtime fans, and netted his biggest critical and popular success in years: a slow, rumbling, brooding meditation on mortality, captured in the chilling refrain "it's not dark yet… but it's getting there."

8 ORNETTE COLEMAN, *SOUND GRAMMAR* (2006, AGE 76)

It's generally only in the youth-obsessed world of pop music that no one is expected to produce anything worth listening to after they hit 40; in jazz and concert music, plenty of people have put out fine new works well past retirement age. Even so, free-jazz pioneer Ornette Coleman still sounded astonishing on *Sound Grammar*. Having almost single-handedly invented a new musical vocabulary in 1959, he did it again with this live session almost 50 years later. Featuring some of his best playing and a dynamic new approach (building his free-jazz attack on clever citations of various other works), Coleman put out one of the best records of his legendary career—and won a Pulitzer Prize in the process.

9 SCOTT WALKER, *TILT* (1995, AGE 52)

Groomed for teen stardom, Scott Walker became a bona fide hitmaker with The Walker Brothers in the '60s, then turned inward with a string of solo albums at the end of the decade. But his 1984 disc *Climate Of Hunter* introduced a new Walker: Steeped in esoteric influences like avant-garde minimalism and even Gregorian chants, it was an angelically tragic,

JOE STRUMMER MURAL, NEW YORK CITY

challenging stunner. It took him 11 years to follow it up, but in 1995, he issued his masterpiece, *Tilt*. Offering even less of a guide rope than *Climate*, *Tilt* meanders, clatters, whispers, and moans through songs so cosmically resonant, they might have been made by some eons-old deity instead of a mere fiftysomething.

10 FRANK SINATRA, *STRANGERS IN THE NIGHT* (1966, AGE 50)

Frank Sinatra, a man by no means friendly with the odds throughout his tumultuous career, was up against an unbeatable adversary when he turned 50 at the end of 1965: The Beatles. He responded with *Strangers In The Night*, his first chart-topping full-length since 1960. But it's more than just a commercial triumph. Ditching the concept-album format of many of his preceding LPs, *Strangers* was instead a sterling collection of impeccable standards, show tunes, and the monstrous, canonical singles "Strangers In The Night" and "Summer Wind." In one 28-minute burst of brilliance, Sinatra cemented his second big comeback and proved he still had power, eminence, and oceans of cool—even in the age of Lennon and McCartney.

11 PORTER WAGONER, *WAGONMASTER* (2007, AGE 79)

Country-music legend Porter Wagoner had suffered through a near-fatal illness and decades of critical and commercial neglect when he and protégé Marty Stuart recorded *Wagonmaster*, which would be Wagoner's final album. A lifelong Wagoner fan, Stuart encouraged the man who made Nudie suits fashionable to return to his roots, reviving some of the darker tales of murder, infidelity, and psychological torment that helped make Wagoner a star in the '60s. Like June Carter Cash's lyrical swan song "Wildwood Flower," *Wagonmaster* summed up a great artist's career, letting one excellent album serve as a self-written epitaph.

12 SOLOMON BURKE, *DON'T GIVE UP ON ME* (2002, AGE 62)

The title is the only element that invites pity on this stunning comeback album from the veteran soul man who once did a healthy side business selling fried chicken and something called "Solomon's Magic Popcorn" to musicians on tour with him. An all-star cast of songwriters, from Elvis Costello to Bob Dylan to fellow soul vet Dan Penn, contributed songs that Burke converted into gospel-tinged mixes of hope and regret.

13 JOE STRUMMER, *STREETCORE* (2003, AGE 50)

Joe Strummer turned 50 four months before his death in December 2002, as he worked on what would be his final album, *Streetcore*. The album, his third with backing band The Mescaleros, wasn't done when Strummer died, so producers Martin Slattery and Scott Shields made do with unpolished early vocal takes—or, in the case of "Midnight Jam," excerpts of Strummer's radio show. Regardless, Strummer had already finished *Streetcore*'s music, and it's the rising tide that lifts all boats. The acoustic cover of Bob Marley's "Redemption Song" is stunning, but the album-closing "Silver And Gold"—a cover of Bobby Charles' "Before I Grow Too Old"—strikes the most poignant note with its lines about making the most of the time you have left.

ASK A MOVIE QUESTION, GET A MOVIE ANSWER

30 FILM-TITLE QUERIES, AND THE ANSWERS THE FILMS GIVE

1 ***DUDE, WHERE'S MY CAR?***
Answer: Over there where you left it, behind the mail truck.

2 ***WHERE IN THE WORLD IS OSAMA BIN LADEN?***
A: Dunno, but that isn't the important thing about our relationship with the Middle East.

3 ***WHATEVER HAPPENED TO BABY JANE?***
A: She got old and became Bitchy Jane.

4 ***WHO CAN KILL A CHILD?***
A: Anyone who wants to survive when faced with a sufficiently deranged, evil child.

5 ***WHO'S AFRAID OF VIRGINIA WOOLF?***
A: Nobody in this movie. She should be afraid of them, though.

6 ***WHO'S THAT GIRL?***
A: Madonna.

7 ***O BROTHER, WHERE ART THOU?***
A: All over the South.

8 ***WHY DO FOOLS FALL IN LOVE***
A: Because they're fools, obviously.

9 ***WHAT'S UP, TIGER LILY?***
A: Apparently a great secret recipe for egg salad.

10 ***WHAT ABOUT BOB?***
A: He's a total ass.

11 ***WHAT HAPPENED TO KEROUAC?***
A: He got drunk and fat and moved in with his mom.

12 ***WHO'S HARRY CRUMB?***
A: A complete fuck-up. You should probably just call the police.

13 ***WHAT PLANET ARE YOU FROM?***
A: The kind of mixed-up world where Annette Bening would fall for Garry Shandling.

14 ***MOTHER, MAY I SLEEP WITH DANGER?***
A: No, but it's not like you listen to me anyway.

15 ***THEY SHOOT HORSES, DON'T THEY?***
A: Yes, but you shouldn't be asking questions, you should be dancing.

16 ***WILL SUCCESS SPOIL ROCK HUNTER?***
A: Temporarily.

17 ***JACKIE CHAN'S WHO AM I?***
A: You're Jackie Chan. Dude, your name is *right there in the title*.

18 ***WHERE WERE YOU WHEN THE LIGHTS WENT OUT?***
A: In New York, macking on Doris Day, for all the good that did me.

19 ***WHEN YOU COMIN' BACK, RED RYDER***
A: As soon as this loudmouthed jack-ass quits hollerin' at everybody.

20 ***WHAT BECOMES OF THE BROKEN-HEARTED?***
A: They're forced to star in a poorly received sequel to *Once Were Warriors*.

21 ***WHAT IS IT?***
A: Pretentious.

22 ***WHAT'S LOVE GOT TO DO WITH IT***
A: Very little. A better question would be, "Why do you stay with this guy?"

23 ***WHO'S THE MAN?***
A: The hosts of *Yo! MTV Raps*. Remember them?

24 ***WHO'S THAT KNOCKING AT MY DOOR***
A: Catholic guilt.

25 ***WHAT WOULD JESUS BUY?***
A: Nothing.

26 ***WHAT'S THE WORST THAT COULD HAPPEN?***
A: When you try to rob somebody's house, they steal your lucky ring. Then everybody acts like an offensive stereotype.

27 ***WHAT'S EATING GILBERT GRAPE***
A: Small-town life, a handicapped brother, and his fat-ass mama.

28 ***WHAT DO YOU SAY TO A NAKED LADY?***
A: Mostly, you giggle uncomfortably.

29 ***WHAT TIME IS IT THERE?***
A: Time for alienated longing. Also, time to buy a new watch.

30 ***ARE WE DONE YET?***
A: If only.

LET IT DIE

23 SONGS THAT SHOULD NEVER BE COVERED AGAIN

1 **"HOW SOON IS NOW?"**
Perhaps because it's The Smiths' most recognizable song, "How Soon Is Now?" has endured countless ignoble recreations since it debuted more than 20 years ago. It's high time for it to retire with dignity. In spite of what bands may think, the nearly seven-minute epic is hard to cover, and it quickly exposes their shortcomings—few things are worse than someone trying to be Morrissey. Sadly, the song's association with the '80s and The Smiths' cool cred guarantees more ill-advised reprises down the road. See faux-lesbian Russian teen-pop duo t.A.T.u., which made it sound like a number by The Chipmunks.

2 **"REVOLUTION"**
Does any Beatles song need more cover versions? It's tough to resist a great song, but apart from early covers by R&B greats like Stevie Wonder, Aretha Franklin, and Ray Charles (and some digressions from Frank Sinatra and Elvis), does anyone actually shine new light on a Beatles hit? "Revolution" could stand in for the whole catalog, but it deserves special mention, if only for Rascal Flatts' 2007 cover for the *Evan Almighty* soundtrack. When the blandest possible country act is covering a song on the soundtrack to a sequel to a Jim Carrey movie without Jim Carrey, the word "revolution" shouldn't be involved in any way.

3 **"BORN TO BE WILD"**
What says "I'm a rebel who plays by my own rules" less than the Steppenwolf song that's become an "I'm a rebel who plays by my own rules" cliché? Nothing. Nobody told that to Hinder or NASCAR, which teamed up for a cover in 2007. But the real offenders are the thousands of bar bands who've made it into a late-set staple. There's one playing it to drunken yahoos somewhere right now.

4 **"I MELT WITH YOU"**
A staple of myriad "Best Of The '80s" compilations, Modern English's biggest hit has been flogged into oblivion by numerous ad campaigns, bands tapping '80s nostalgia, and Modern English itself. (The band re-recorded it for 1990's *Pillow Lips*.) Since the cult

of the '80s developed in the mid-'90s, countless terrible versions of "I Melt With You"—particularly by shitty emo/punk bands—have assaulted listeners. Check out Bowling For Soup's version from the *Sky High* soundtrack, which changes the lyrics "Making love to you" to "Being friends with you," in order to protect impressionable Disney ears.

5 "ALL ALONG THE WATCHTOWER"

Some estimates say that Bob Dylan has played this song 1,400 times—more than any of his others—but that number pales in comparison to the number of covers out there, by performers including Pat Boone, Dave Matthews Band, Heart, Tiny Tim, and virtually every jam band ever. In one regard, "All Along The Watchtower" is an argument for covers, as Jimi Hendrix's version is virtually definitive. Then again, there's still Heart.

6 "LOVE WILL TEAR US APART"

Cover songs make a statement about the band playing them, and this one says, "We like Joy Division, so we're cool, right?" Yes and no: Released just a month before Joy Division frontman Ian Curtis killed himself, it's become his band's defining song. As such, countless bands have unwittingly pissed on Curtis' grave—which actually features the inscription "love will tear us apart"—by massacring his song. The members of Fall Out Boy must have pretty empty bladders by now.

7 "RESPECT"

Another seeming case in favor of covers, "Respect" was originally released by Otis Redding in 1965, though Aretha Franklin owned it from 1967 on. Bold for its time, the song addresses racial and gender issues with a forceful, no-bullshit refrain. Nearly half a century later, *American Idol* contestants use it to show their "soulfulness" and "spunk." (It figured prominently in the repertoire of inaugural winner Kelly Clarkson.) Reinterpretations by the likes of Dexys Midnight Runners don't fare much better.

8 "COME ON EILEEN"

Speaking of Dexys Midnight Runners, the group's 1982 hit "Come On Eileen" desperately needs to find eternal rest, along with the pointless '80s nostalgia it embodies. And what was it about shitty '90s ska bands and hits from the '80s? Save Ferris was all over this back in 1997. "Eileen" was played out even then, when it was a mere 15 years old.

9 "CRAZY"

No one in country music—or perhaps any kind of music—could convey gut-wrenching vulnerability and loneliness like Patsy Cline. Granted, her entire catalog basically boils down to "Why you treat me so bad?", but no one asked the question better. Her voice makes "Crazy"—written by a young Willie Nelson—especially haunting. Not so haunting is the version by crappy industrial band Kidneythieves, which covered it for the *Bride Of Chucky* soundtrack.

10 "WHAT THE WORLD NEEDS NOW IS LOVE"

How do you definitively know a song should be retired? How about when 10 second-season finalists from *American Idol* join together to release it as a single? You can generally find the CD—one song with all the finalists, another version with just Clay Aiken, Ruben Studdard, and Rickey Smith—for a penny on Amazon.com.

11 "I HEARD IT THROUGH THE GRAPEVINE"

"Grapevine" presents the strongest argument for covers, as Motown songwriters Norman Whitfield and Barrett Strong shopped it to several artists before anyone bit, and three different versions became hits (Gladys Knight & The Pips in 1967, Marvin Gaye in 1968, and, uh, The California Raisins in 1987). Creedence Clearwater Revival also memorably converted it into a 10-minute jam in 1970. Regardless, it basically remains Gaye's, and renditions by groups like The Average White Band, Kaiser Chiefs, Michael McDonald, Psychic TV, and Señor Soul are patently inessential.

12 "TAINTED LOVE"

Another journeyman of a song, "Tainted Love" began life back in 1964 when Ed Cobb wrote it for soul singer Gloria Jones. It reappeared 11 years later with Ruth Swan, but for more than 25 years, it's been mostly associated with Soft Cell, which made it a staple of '80s pop. That version's dark electropop made it a favorite

among industrial and techno bands such as Coil, Deathline Int'l, Atrocity, and that paragon of clichéd rebellion, Marilyn Manson. His "dark, twisted" music video is guilty of a number of crimes, perhaps none worse than the image of his "GOTH THUG" vanity license plate.

13 "REBEL REBEL"

Supposedly David Bowie's most-covered song, "Rebel Rebel" has lived a long, full life since he debuted it on *Diamond Dogs* in 1974—so full, in fact, that Bowie retired it after a 1990 tour, though he inexplicably re-recorded it in 2003. Even if he had let sleeping dogs lie, plenty of other bands have it covered. And really, who wouldn't want to hear Dead Or Alive's take on it? Or let Bryan Adams rework it? Duran Duran, maybe? Def Leppard? (Seu Jorge, you get a pass.)

14 "99 RED BALLOONS"

No song better embodies '80s musical nostalgia than Nena's "99 Red Balloons"—ahem, "99 Luftballons"—and for that reason alone, it deserves retirement. Not enough? How about a slew of terrible covers by the likes of Reel Big Fish and Goldfinger, or a Harry Potter-themed version called "99 Death Eaters" by Draco And The Malfoys, or the raved-up version by Airbag? Maybe that isn't enough: When VH1 Classic auctioned airtime for Hurricane Katrina victims in 2006, one viewer donated $35,000 to have the station play Nena's video continuously for an hour.

15 "ROCK AND ROLL ALL NITE"

If cover songs make statements, this one says, "We just like to fuckin' party, bro. Go to the lake, take the T-top panels off, spark one up, and just get wild! Ooooowwwwwoooooooo!" (It's best if you imagine Matthew McConaughey in *Dazed And Confused* saying that.) Or, to use Paul Stanley's introduction at the 1996 Video Music Awards: "Everywhere around the world, we try to tell people there are no borders, there are no prime ministers, there are no presidents, there's only one nation: That's Kiss nation! There's only one rock 'n' roll national anthem: 'Rock And Roll All Nite,' party every day!" It's tough to argue with that logic, but bands, take note: It's inhumane to subject the world to more Kiss... especially if you're re-casting it as ska (SKAndalous All-Stars) or dance-pop (Daytona).

16 "BLITZKRIEG BOP"

At the corner of Bowery and Second in New York, there should be a panel of pure black granite, à la the Vietnam Veterans Memorial. At the top will be inscribed "Si monumentum requiris circumspice" ("If you seek a memorial, look around"), with the names of the bands who should have never covered "Blitzkrieg Bop": Skid Row, Rob Zombie, The Beautiful South, Hanoi Rocks, and untold anonymous groups appearing at a bar near you. May we never forget.

17 "BROWN EYED GIRL"

Can you kill something that's already been played to death on your local oldies station? According to BMI, Van Morrison's "Brown Eyed Girl" has been played an astounding 8 million times on radio and TV since its debut more than 40 years ago. Please, bands, there's no reason to add to that... Not that it's stopped groups like Rockapella, Jimmy Buffett, Everclear, Boyz Night Out, and something called the Caribbean Magic Steelband, which included it on the album *Island Favorites*. Well, Van Morrison's native Ireland is technically an island...

18 "ONE"

Harry Nilsson wrote it, Three Dog Night made it famous, and dozens of bands beat the crap out of "One" (a.k.a. "One is the loneliest number") for years thereafter. Aimee Mann reclaimed it for the sane populace with her gentle cover (featured in *Magnolia*), which erased years of abuse, including a version by Dokken. It would be best for everyone involved if Mann's version provided a bookend to Nilsson's.

19 "(I CAN'T GET NO) SATISFACTION"

Two covers of The Rolling Stones' staple have brought incredible new life to this clear classic: Devo's jittery new-wave shot, and Cat Power's deliriously slow, wandering version. Hundreds of others have attempted to recreate the power of Keith Richards' massively recognizable lead and Mick Jagger's pouting about the life of a rocking man. There's no shame in leaving this one to the masters, and to karaoke bars.

20 "WONDERWALL"

Every time earnest coffeehouse troubadours strike the simple chords of "Wonderwall" and feel its majesty coursing through their veins, an angel dies. Just because a song is easy to play doesn't mean it's easy to play well. Ryan Adams does a suitable version, adding some soulful smoke, but other singer-songwriters haven't had any luck, and there's even a cottage industry of half-serious covers (Radiohead, Robbie Williams, Mike Flowers Pops). Write your own "Wonderwall," coffeehouse crooner.

21 "IMAGINE"

Imagine a world in which John Lennon's "Imagine" is only covered by people who actually understand and embrace its message about how religion, nationalism, and capitalism are essentially insane. Unitarian churches go nuts with it, and that's fine, but Avril Lavigne, the physical embodiment of crass consumerism? That's just painful. Even A Perfect Circle mangles it, rendering a hopeful, beautiful song into something foreboding and scary. Too bad Lennon wrote such a beautiful melody—it lends itself to empty renditions.

22 "HALLELUJAH"

Leonard Cohen's "Hallelujah" passed into the realm of pop standard long ago. To be fair, two cover versions were arguably better than the original: John Cale's mournful take (only slightly marred by its appearance in *Shrek* and *Scrubs*) and Jeff Buckley's gorgeous rendition. But apparently no one can settle on a "definitive" edition and just let it be, because Bono, Imogen Heap, k.d. lang, Bon Jovi, and too many others have tried, with increasingly sterile results. Even actor Anthony Michael Hall (yes, that Anthony Michael Hall) growled out his own version. Can William Shatner's take be far behind?

23 "WHAT A WONDERFUL WORLD"

Considering that an aged Louis Armstrong sang the original, it's hard to believe this song is a scant 40 years old—it sounds far more old-timey in sentiment and performance. Maybe that's because the world has endured countless renditions over the years by a who's who of the enemies of good taste: Celine Dion, Kenny G, Michael Bolton, Rod Stewart, and John Tesh. Even Joe Pesci felt compelled to share in 1998. But when *America's Got Talent* featured a ventriloquist singing it through a stuffed turtle who was doing an impression of Kermit The Frog covering Louis Armstrong, we as a society should have finally said "Enough!"

Guest List: ZACH GALIFIANAKIS

MY 5 FAVORITE FAX NUMBERS

1. **(314)** [redacted]
   Youth hostel in Missouri
2. **(928)** [redacted]
   Quality Plus Fax Machine Maintenance And Repair
3. **(910)** [redacted]
   James Sprunt Community College Cafeteria, NC
4. **(860)** [redacted]
   Freedom Candle And Switchblades
5. **(803)** [redacted]
   Vitamin Organizer

REDACTED BY LEGAL

Zach Galifianakis is an actor and comedian who has toured with the Comedians Of Comedy and starred in Into The Wild, Visioneers, Out Cold, *and* The Hangover, *among many others.*

SO IT GOES

15 THINGS KURT VONNEGUT SAID BETTER THAN ANYONE ELSE EVER HAS OR WILL

1 **"I urge you to please notice when you are happy, and exclaim or murmur or think at some point, 'If this isn't nice, I don't know what is.'"** The actual advice here is technically a quote from Kurt Vonnegut's "good uncle" Alex, but Vonnegut was nice enough to pass it on at speeches and in *A Man Without A Country*. Though he was sometimes derided as too gloomy and cynical, Vonnegut's most resonant messages have always been hopeful in the face of almost-certain doom. And his best advice seems almost ridiculously simple: Give your own happiness a bit of brain space.

2 **"Peculiar travel suggestions are dancing lessons from God."**
In *Cat's Cradle*, the narrator haplessly stumbles across the cynical, cultish figure Bokonon, who populates his religious writings with moronic, twee aphorisms. The great joke of Bokononism is that it forces meaning on what's essentially chaos, and Bokonon himself admits that his writings are lies. If the protagonist's trip to the island nation of San Lorenzo has any cosmic purpose, it's to catalyze a massive

tragedy, but the experience makes him a devout Bokononist. It's a religion for people who believe religions are absurd, and an ideal one for Vonnegut-style humanists.

3 "Tiger got to hunt, bird got to fly; Man got to sit and wonder, 'Why, why, why?' Tiger got to sleep, bird got to land; Man got to tell himself he understand."
Another koan of sorts from *Cat's Cradle* and the Bokononist religion (which phrases many of its teachings as calypsos, as part of its absurdist bent), this piece of doggerel is simple and catchy, but it unpacks into a resonant, meaningful philosophy that reads as sympathetic to humanity, albeit from a removed, humoring, alien viewpoint. Man's just another animal, it implies, with his own peculiar instincts, and his own way of shutting them down. This is horrifically cynical when considered closely: If people deciding they understand the world is just another instinct, then enlightenment is little more than a pit-stop between insoluble questions, a necessary but ultimately meaningless way of taking a sanity break. At the same time, there's a kindness to Bokonon's belief that this is all inevitable and just part of being a person. Life is frustrating and full of pitfalls and dead ends, but everybody's gotta do it.

4 "There's only one rule that I know of, babies—God damn it, you've got to be kind."
This line from *God Bless You, Mr. Rosewater* comes as part of a baptismal speech the protagonist says he's planning for his neighbors' twins: "Hello, babies. Welcome to Earth. It's hot in the summer and cold in the winter. It's round and wet and crowded. At the outside, babies, you've got about a hundred years here. There's only one rule that I know of, babies—God damn it, you've got to be kind." It's an odd speech to make over a couple of infants, but it's playful, sweet, yet keenly precise in its summation of everything a new addition to the planet should need to know. By narrowing all his advice for the future down to a few simple words, Vonnegut emphasizes what's most important in life. At the same time, he lets his frustration with all the people who obviously don't get it leak through just a little.

5 "She was a fool, and so am I, and so is anyone who thinks he sees what God is doing."
A couple of pages into *Cat's Cradle*, Bokonon recalls being hired to design and build a doghouse for a lady in Newport, Rhode Island, who "claimed to understand God and His Ways of Working perfectly." With such knowledge, "she could not understand why anyone should be puzzled about what had been or about what was going to be." When Bokonon shows her the doghouse's blueprint, she says she can't read it. He suggests taking it to her minister to pass along to God, who, when he finds a minute, will explain it "in a way that even you can understand." She fires him. Bokonon recalls her with a bemused fondness, ending the anecdote with this typical Vonnegut zinger. With it, he perfectly summarizes the inherent flaw of religious fundamentalism: No one really knows God's ways.

6 "Many people need desperately to receive this message: 'I feel and think much as you do, care about many of the things you care about, although most people do not care about them. You are not alone.'"
In this response to his own question—"Why bother?"—in *Timequake*, his last novel, Vonnegut doesn't give a tired response about the urge to create; instead, he offers a pointed answer about how writing (and reading) make a lonesome world a little less so. The idea of connectedness—familial and otherwise—ran through much of his work, and it's nice to see that toward the end of his career, he hadn't lost the feeling that words can have an intimate, powerful impact.

7 "There are plenty of good reasons for fighting, but no good reason ever to hate without reservation, to imagine that God Almighty Himself hates with you, too."
Though this quote comes from the World War II-centered *Mother Night* (published in 1961), its wisdom and ugly truth still ring. Vonnegut (who often said "The only difference between Bush and Hitler is that Hitler was elected") was righteously skeptical about war, having famously survived the only one worth fighting in his lifetime. And it's never been more true: Left or right, Christian or Muslim, those convinced they're doing violence in service of a higher power and against an irretrievably inhuman enemy are the most dangerous creatures of all.

8 "Since Alice had never received any religious instruction, and since she had led a blameless life, she never thought of her awful luck as being

anything but accidents in a very busy place. Good for her."
Vonnegut's excellent-but-underrated *Slapstick* (he himself graded it a "D") was inspired by his sister Alice, who died of cancer just days after her husband was killed in an accident. Vonnegut's assessment of Alice's character—both in this introduction and in her fictional stand-in, Eliza Mellon Swain—is glowing and remarkable, and in this quote from the book's introduction, he manages to swipe at a favorite enemy (organized religion) and quietly, humbly embrace someone he clearly still missed a lot.

9 "That is my principal objection to life, I think: It's too easy, when alive, to make perfectly horrible mistakes."
The narrator delivering this line at the end of the first chapter of *Deadeye Dick* is alluding both to his father's befriending of Hitler and his own accidental murder of his neighbor, but like so many of these quotes, it resonates well beyond its context. The underlying philosophy of Vonnegut's work was always that existence is capricious and senseless, a difficult sentiment that he captured time and again with a bemused shake of the head. Indeed, the idea that life is just a series of small decisions that culminate into some sort of "destiny" is maddening, because you could easily ruin it all simply by making the wrong one. Ordering the fish, stepping onto a balcony, booking the wrong flight, getting married—a single misstep, and you're done for. At least when you're dead, you don't have to make any more damn choices. Wherever Vonnegut is, he's no doubt grateful for that.

10 "Literature should not disappear up its own asshole, so to speak."
Vonnegut touchstones like life on Tralfamadore and the absurd Bokononist religion don't help people escape the world so much as see it with clearer reason, which probably had a lot to do with Vonnegut's education as a chemist and anthropologist. So it's unsurprising that in a "self-interview" for *The Paris Review*, collected in his non-fiction anthology *Palm Sunday*, he said the literary world should really be looking for talent among scientists and doctors. Even when taking part in such a stultifying, masturbatory exercise for a prestigious journal, Vonnegut was perfectly readable, because he never forgot where his true audience was.

11 "All persons, living and dead, are purely coincidental."
In Vonnegut's final novel, 1997's *Timequake*, he interacts freely with Kilgore Trout and other fictional characters after the end of a "timequake," which forces humanity to re-enact an entire decade. (Trout winds up too worn out to exercise free will again.) Vonnegut writes his own fitting epigram for this fatalistic book: "All persons, living and dead, are purely coincidental," which sounds more funny than grim. Vonnegut surrounds his characters—especially Trout—with meaninglessness and hopelessness, and gives them little reason for existing in the first place, but within that, they find liberty and courage.

12 "Why don't you take a flying fuck at a rolling doughnut? Why don't you take a flying fuck at the mooooooooooooon?"
Even when Vonnegut dared to propose a utopian scheme, it was a happily dysfunctional one. In *Slapstick*, Wilbur Swain wins the presidency with a scheme to eliminate loneliness by issuing people complicated middle names (he becomes Wilbur Daffodil-11 Swain) which make them part of new extended families. He advises people to tell new relatives they hate, or members of other families asking for help: "Why don't you take a flying fuck at a rolling doughnut? Why don't you take a flying fuck at the mooooooooooooon?" Of course, this fails to prevent plagues, the breakdown of his government, and civil wars later in the story.

13 "So it goes."
Unlike many of these quotes, the repeated refrain from Vonnegut's classic *Slaughterhouse-Five* isn't notable for its unique wording so much as for how much emotion—and dismissal of emotion—it packs into three simple, world-weary words that simultaneously accept and dismiss everything. There's a reason this quote graced practically every elegy written for Kurt Vonnegut upon his 2007 death: It neatly encompasses a whole way of life. More crudely put: "Shit happens, and it's awful, but it's also okay. We deal with it because we have to."

14 "I have been a soreheaded occupant of a file drawer labeled 'science fiction' ever since, and I would like out, particularly since so many serious critics regularly mistake the drawer for a urinal."
Vonnegut was as trenchant when talking about his life as when talking about life in general, and this quote

from an essay in *Wampeters, Foma & Granfalloons* is particularly apt; as he explains it, he wrote *Player Piano* while working for General Electric, "completely surrounded by machines and ideas for machines," which led him to put some ideas about machines on paper. Then it was published, "and I learned from the reviewers that I was a science-fiction writer." The entire essay is wry, hilarious, and biting, but this line stands out in particular as typifying the kind of snappishness that made Vonnegut's works so memorable.

15 "We must be careful about what we pretend to be."
In *Mother Night*, apolitical expatriate American playwright Howard W. Campbell Jr. refashions himself as a Nazi propagandist in order to pass coded messages on to the U.S. generals and preserve his marriage to a German woman—their "nation of two," as he calls it. But in serving multiple masters, Campbell ends up ruining his life and becoming an unwitting inspiration to bigots. In his 1966 introduction to the paperback edition, Vonnegut underlines *Mother Night's* moral: "We are what we pretend to be, so we must be careful about what we pretend to be." That lesson springs to mind every time a comedian whose shtick relies on hoaxes and audience-baiting—or a political pundit who traffics in shock and hyperbole—gets hauled in front of the court of public opinion for pushing the act too far. Why can't people just say what they mean? It's a question Don Imus and Michael Richards—and maybe someday Ann Coulter—must ask themselves on their many sleepless nights.

NIGHT OF THE KILLER LAMP

22 RIDICULOUS HORROR-MOVIE ADVERSARIES

1 FLOOR LAMP *(AMITYVILLE 4: THE EVIL ESCAPES, 1989)*
So far, *The Amityville Horror* has spawned a whopping eight sequels, remakes, and spin-offs, but surely none of them is as ridiculous as the cheapie *Amityville 4*, in which Satan stops possessing a house and starts possessing bad household décor. After scaring some flinchy priests, an ugly brass lamp full of evil escapes the much-filmed Amityville and winds up in a California house occupied by recent widow Patty Duke, her three kids, and her mom, Jane Wyatt. (In the process, it gives Wyatt's sister tetanus, in a particularly low-key display of Satanic might.) Even though it has the power to flash ominously, cover itself with flies, somehow stuff the family bird into a toaster oven, and activate a chainsaw and a garbage disposal at inopportune moments, the lamp makes a phenomenally inert villain, and the film's constant attempts to make it frightening border on camp—particularly in the scene where it slowly edges across a room, sneaking up on the unsuspecting Duke.

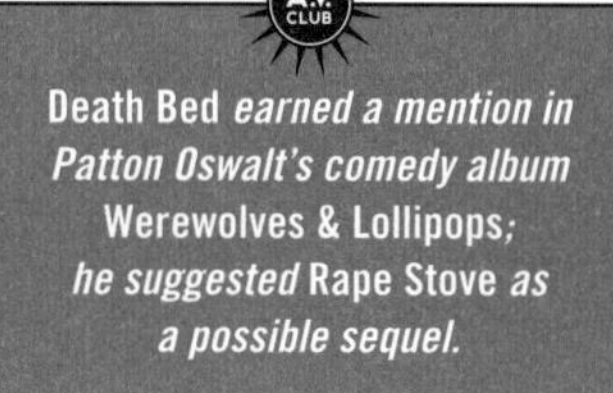
Death Bed *earned a mention in Patton Oswalt's comedy album* Werewolves & Lollipops; *he suggested* Rape Stove *as a possible sequel.*

2 DEMONICALLY POSSESSED BED *(DEATH BED: THE BED THAT EATS, 1977)*
The title says it all, really. Made for $30,000 over a five-year period—and never officially released until it was dug up for DVD in the early '00s—George Berry's inexplicable, surreal camp-horror film features a bed that lures in nappers and love-makers. Here's how the devilish contraption works: Victims are disrobed and sucked into an acid-filled waterbed mattress that dissolves their flesh and bones in a burbling yellow goo, while making the completely inappropriate sound of someone chomping vigorously on an apple. Then the bed makes itself, on the off chance that another orgy

might develop within the next decade or so. The bed also snores, leaving viewers to ponder the metaphysical paradox of a bed sleeping on itself.

3 GIANT TREE
(THE GUARDIAN, 1990)

Dealing with an evil tree? Try staying out of the forest. Like the death bed, the tree in William Friedkin's *The Guardian* can't really go anywhere, so it relies on sexy nanny Jenny Seagrove to bring it infant sacrifices as part of a druidic ritual. (For holding up her end of the bargain, the frequently naked Seagrove gets fondled by twigs.) Still, Friedkin and company come up with increasingly ridiculous reasons for potential victims to flee into the forest, where they're beheaded by branches, impaled by roots, and swallowed up by a trunk that bleeds the blood of the innocent. Too bad this ancient menace lived to see the birth of its unstoppable modern adversary, the chainsaw.

4 LAUNDRY-FOLDING MACHINE *(THE MANGLER, 1995)*

The capitalist machine may be oiled by the blood of the workers, but that metaphor was never meant to play as literally as it does in *The Mangler*, a supremely goofy adaptation of a Stephen King short story. Even when working properly,

Stephen King's idea for "The Mangler" was inspired by his own, presumably less supernatural, stint working in a laundry.

the giant industrial laundry-folding machine at Blue Ribbon Laundry looks like it could rip off a non-union limb or two. But this one is demonically possessed, fueled by virgin's blood and kept in operation by a Mr. Burns/ Dr. Strangelove-like figure (Robert Englund) who convinces safety inspectors to look the other way whenever the body of another sweatshop worker winds up neatly pressed. Like many of the adversaries on this list, the machine is heavy and completely inanimate, but it's surprisingly resourceful. Then again, it needn't be too clever, not when people keep trying to get a closer look by crawling into its hungry maw.

5 WHIPPED CREAM
(THE STUFF, 1985)

The B-movie king of great ideas and so-so execution, writer-director Larry Cohen came up with a doozy of a premise for his satirical horror movie *The Stuff*, but the satire was only half-realized, and he seemed

to forget about the horror part altogether. Found bubbling up from a snow bank like delicious, delicious oil, "The Stuff" is a whipped-cream-like substance that becomes a taste sensation, a low-calorie, ready-to-eat option for families across America. Minor caveat: It eats people from the inside, turning them into dead-eyed zombies. In concept, Cohen has come up with an ingenious dig at capitalism—the consumer being consumed by consumables. But he has a hard time turning tubs of whipped cream into the Stuff of nightmares.

6 KILLER BABOON

(SHAKMA, 1990)

In theory, a killer baboon driven mad by experimental injections—administered by callous professor Roddy McDowall, no less—sounds like a wicked cool beastie. In practice, said baboon most often takes the form of a limp doll that its "victims" jerk about while pretending to be mauled. *Shakma*'s few shots of a live baboon going apeshit look suitably unhinged, though more in a comic way than a scary way.

7 THE FOUKE MONSTER

(THE LEGEND OF BOGGY CREEK, 1972)

Director Charles B. Pierce takes an unusual approach to the horror genre by structuring *Boggy Creek* like a documentary, full of grainy nature footage and "interviews" with people who survived encounters with the legendary woodland ape-man that some know as Sasquatch, some as Bigfoot, and some—the people from Fouke, Arkansas, anyway—know as The Fouke Monster. *The Legend Of Boggy Creek* is sleepily episodic, and about as intense as a bloodless, G-rated monster movie can be, which means that most of the scares consist of people almost seeing The Fouke Monster, then making wide escapes. Whew! That was... not that close, really.

8 GOBLIN ARMY *(TROLL 2, 1990)*

There's a good reason there's a documentary in the works about the making of *Troll 2* titled *Best Worst Movie*. This Italian production—originally called *Goblin*, which more accurately describes its bad guys—follows an American family trying to escape a legion of mythical creatures who turn humans into plants, then eat them. Atrocious acting aside, *Troll 2's* goblins are extra-ridiculous because of their costumes, which resemble potato sacks topped with Halloween masks. Frankly, they're nowhere near as scary as the ghostly grandpa who advises young hero Michael Stephenson to piss all over his family's dinner so they won't undergo "the change."

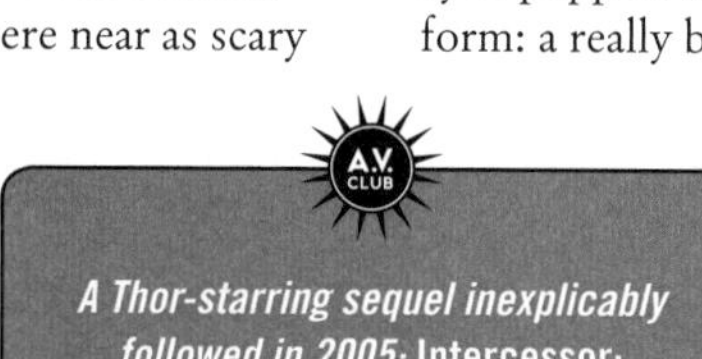

9 KILLERS FROM SPACE

(KILLERS FROM SPACE, 1954)

A trio of space aliens plans to use America's atomic technology to grow giant mutated animals, destroy all humans, and colonize the Earth. And they'd be a lot easier to take seriously if they didn't make this threat while wearing heavy, hooded black tunics and flashing their ping-pong-ball eyes. If you crossbred Marty Feldman with a Muppet, you'd just about equal the level of menace of the killers from space.

Killers From Space ***was directed by Billy Wilder's brother. See if you can spot the telltale Wilder sophistication.***

10 SEMI-MOBILE PUPPETS

(ROCK 'N' ROLL NIGHTMARE, 1987)

Canadian bodybuilder/metal star Jon Mikl Thor scripted and stars in this low-budget, claustrophobic, batshit-insane film about a Canadian metal star who's actually an archangel called The Intercessor. He's itching to fight Satan himself, but for some reason, the Father Of Lies chooses to manifest in the form of disturbingly phallic, one-eyed puppets before showing his true form: a really big, slightly less phallic two-eyed puppet. Or half of one, anyway. The climactic fight scene displays virtually every inch of Thor's body, but only the barely mobile upper half (and feet) of His Satanic Majesty. Hey, even Beelzebub has to make budget.

11 HOMICIDAL VENDING MACHINE

(MAXIMUM OVERDRIVE, 1986)

Under the influence of either a comet tail or alien invaders—writer-director Stephen King never makes it entirely clear—all the machines in *Maximum Overdrive* suddenly turn homicidal. Even a lowly soda machine tries to take out an entire Little League team by launching cans from its dispenser. One can, naturally, nails a guy in the crotch. All that's missing is someone quipping, "I told you soda was bad for you!"

12 VAMPIRE DOGS *(ZOLTAN: HOUND OF DRACULA, 1978)*

Pity poor Zoltan. Once he was a peasant's happy dog. Then, after interrupting Dracula mid-bite, he was forever enslaved to the bloodsucking ways of his new master. After a couple centuries, Zoltan resurfaces in 1970s California, intent on terrorizing the family of Dracula's distant relatives, starting with their dogs. A vampire dog isn't the worst idea for a horror-film foe but there's nothing particularly scary about Zoltan, a perfectly pleasant-looking Doberman outfitted with a pair of unconvincing prosthetic fangs (courtesy of a young Stan Winston). Even less scary: Fight scenes in which the actors appear to be fighting off doggie kisses, and a finale that sets up a sequel involving Zoltan's downright adorable Dracu-pup offspring.

13 FETUS IN A BOTTLE *(THE JAR, 1984)*

Eraserhead was a cult classic, but it understandably didn't prompt a lot of knockoffs. One exception: the 1984 shocker *The Jar*, a bizarre psychodrama about a hirsute, sullen loner (Gary Wallace) tormented by a mysterious, bottled embryo-like creature that gradually tears his life apart and induces ostensibly frightening hallucinations involving crucifixion and the Vietnam War. Wallace shifts the jar's location around, but he can't outrun its extremely silly, abstract evil. The titular fiend ultimately drives Wallace to kill in what can only be described as the apex of storage-unit-based horror.

14 EVIL BRAINS *(THE BRAIN FROM PLANET AROUS, 1957)*

Earth is invaded by an extraterrestrial evil criminal mastermind—a literal mind. The inhabitants of the planet Arous are brains—giant, disembodied brains with glowing eyes, who can take over human bodies and use them for nefarious criminal purposes, including leering at their host bodies' girlfriends. In practice, though, the brains from planet Arous look more like helium balloons with light bulbs for eyes.

15 ROBOT MONSTER *(ROBOT MONSTER, 1953)*

Often mentioned alongside Ed Wood's *Plan 9 From Outer Space* as a science-fiction movie so incompetent it becomes charming, *Robot Monster* was made in four days for $16,000 with mainly amateur actors, and it shows. Director Phil Tucker cast veteran stuntman and actor George Barrows as Ro-Man the robot monster for one simple reason: Barrows already owned his own gorilla suit. Because that's what a robot looks like, right? A diving helmet was added to give Ro-Man at least some semblance of actually being a mechanical creature, but as *Mystery Science Theater 3000's* Joel Hodgson quipped, "I've seen Salvador Dalí paintings that made more sense than this."

16 RUG/SLUG THING *(THE CREEPING TERROR, 1964)*

Unlike Ro-Man, the alien beast in *The Creeping Terror* actually is kind of creepy. And in fact, the same basic concept—an amorphous, amoeba-like creature that eats and eats and eats—was handled well in a similar movie, *The Blob*. What dooms *The Creeping Terror* to laughability is a combination of general filmmaking incompetence and legendary bad luck. The story goes that the filmmakers' original alien costume was either stolen or destroyed only days before filming. The replacement they were forced to build in order to finish the movie is, well, not great. Intended to be a giant slug-like creature, the monster looks like it was sewn together from carpet remnants and tarp. The crewmembers' feet are often clearly visible underneath, and the whole assemblage moves so slowly that the actors playing its victims literally have to stop and wait for it to catch up to them.

The Brain From Planet Arous has enjoyed an unexpected afterlife. Footage from it can be seen in the opening credits of Malcolm In The Middle, *and a screening serves as a destination for the young protagonist of Neil Jordan's* The Butcher Boy.

17 OCTOPUS-MAN *(OCTAMAN, 1971)*

Makeup artist Rick Baker has won six Oscars for his work, which includes highly praised creature designs on *An American Werewolf In London* and *Star Wars*. But everyone's gotta start somewhere, and Baker's first movie was the inauspicious *Octaman*, a cheapie horror-thriller about a deadly man/octopus hybrid mutant terrorizing a Mexican town. It was written and directed by Harry Essex, who basically rehashed the major ideas from his considerably more successful 1954 screenplay, *Creature From The Black Lagoon*. The monster in *Black Lagoon* is an iconic classic; *Octaman* is just a guy in a very unconvincing rubber suit. To fake the appearance of eight limbs, Baker simply suspended two extra arm-tentacles by wires attached to the actor's real arms, and attached two pathetic-looking rubber legs to the back of the real legs.

18 BULLDOZER *(KILLDOZER, 1974)*

Based on a 1944 novella by celebrated science-fiction writer Theodore Sturgeon, the TV movie *Killdozer* has one of the weirdest premises—and most awesome titles—of its era. A group of construction workers on a Pacific Island accidentally strike a meteorite with the blade of a bulldozer, releasing a malevolent blue light that possesses the earthmover, creating a rampaging, driverless mechanical killer with no apparent need for gas, but plenty of bloodlust. Too bad the film is a made-for-TV blandfest, though it does boast an early credit for future TV star Robert Urich.

19 GENERAL PROXIMITY TO NATURE *(FROGS, 1972)*

Frogs just aren't scary. In theory, though, a whole swamp full of poisonous snakes, alligators, spiders, lizards, scorpions, and leeches, with some frogs thrown in as garnish, might be kind of frightening. George McCowan's *Frogs* seems to get this—in spite of the title and the poster depicting a pop-eyed frog with a bloodied human hand in its mouth, the frogs in *Frogs* never actually kill anyone. They just hang around sort of menacingly while cranky billionaire Ray Milland insists his poison-and-pollute anti-nature policies are right and just, no matter how many members of his extended family fall prey to vengeful nature. Unfortunately, their deaths are laughably choreographed, and usually involve shots of victims rolling around screaming in mud or water, interspersed with close-up shots of animals swimming or sitting around peacefully. Moral: Don't get within 50 feet of nature, or some Spanish moss might fall off a tree and bury you to death while tarantulas watch nearby.

Killdozer inspired the name of the influential 1990s-era punk band. That has to count for something.

20 RABBITS *(NIGHT OF THE LEPUS, 1972)*

The trailer for William F. Claxton's *Night Of The Lepus* is all about the mystery: What hideous creature is haunting the night? What's killing all those people? What the heck is the adversary in this film? Answer: bunnies. Giant, carnivorous mutant bunnies. Which look suspiciously like perfectly normal bunnies hopping around in slow motion, with scary roaring and snarling noises superimposed on the soundtrack. Hey, at least they're more ferocious than those frogs.

21 ELEVATOR *(THE LIFT, 1983)*

Elevators conjure up two very real fears: being trapped in a confined space, and falling to your death. But making an entire movie (two movies, actually, since director Dick Maas remade his original Dutch production as 2001's *The Shaft*, with Naomi Watts) revolving around a murderously sentient lift takes a certain amount of chutzpah. There's only so much an elevator can do to kill people, though it does somehow empty itself of oxygen to suffocate its passengers, and it gets the drop on an unwitting victim by descending unexpectedly, cutting his head off. Next time, we'll take the stairs.

22 THE WIND *(THE HAPPENING, 2008)*

Ready for a big ol' spoiler? In M. Night Shyamalan's laughably clumsy horror film *The Happening*, people start committing suicide en masse when plants suddenly start emitting a neurotoxin that reverses humanity's self-preservation impulse. It's silly, but no dumber than many classic horror and science-fiction premises. But how do you personify such an impersonal, diffuse threat? Shyamalan does it by communicating that the toxin is carried on the wind, then having his hapless, overacting protagonists try to stare at the wind in terror, then run away from it. Never has "racing the wind" seemed so unpoetic, and so profoundly dumb.

WASTE OF A GOOD FLIGHT RING

5 CRAZY-ASS MEMBERS OF THE LEGION OF SUPER-HEROES

1 BOUNCING BOY

Back in 1958, *Adventure Comics'* flagship character Superboy met three superpowered teenagers from the future who called themselves the Legion Of Super-Heroes. Their story proved so popular with readers that *Adventure* writers kept bringing the Legion back, adding newer, stranger heroes with each appearance. One of the earliest oddities? Bouncing Boy, a Legionnaire who accidentally drank the formula for a super-plastic, and gained the power to balloon up and bounce like a big rubber ball. He came in handy whenever the Legion needed someone to roll over villains who were already lined up like bowling pins, or to bounce up high enough to scout the area.

2 MATTER-EATER LAD

Shortly after the introduction of Bouncing Boy, *Legion* writer (and Superman co-creator) Jerry Siegel went even weirder by creating Matter-Eater Lad, a hero with the power to, well, eat stuff. Eat *anything*, really. Matter-Eater Lad comes from the planet Bismoll (ha-ha), where food has become inedible, forcing the Bismollians to consume inorganic material. Siegel and the writers who followed had a hard time coming up with things for Matter-Eater Lad to do—he went insane for a while, then became a senator—but once in a blue moon, when a crisis requires something unusual to be eaten, Matter-Eater Lad is on the scene, fork in hand.

3 QUISLET

It isn't that Quislet's superpowers are *dumb*. They're just confusing. Introduced in the mid-'80s, Quislet emerged from an alternate dimension, completely formless except for a miniature flying vehicle that contained his life force. His ethereal spirit leaped from the spaceship to inhabit inanimate objects, bending them to his will for a few minutes before his power disintegrated them. Quislet's major worry while in possessive mode? Steering clear of Matter-Eater Lad.

4 CALAMITY KING

While it might be useful in some situations to have a hero on the team who "causes bad luck," the unpredictability of Calamity King's powers—as well as the weak explanation that he "exploits stress fractures in material objects"—probably explains why he never had a major presence on the team. In fact, in his first *Adventure Comics* appearance, Calamity King was rejected by the Legion, only to appear without explanation as a team member in the '90s, shortly before his whole era of Legion continuity was destroyed and rebooted. Coincidence, or just another Calamity King jinx?

5 INFECTIOUS LASS

Formerly a member of The Legion Of *Substitute* Heroes—an organization that also included the likes of Chlorophyll Kid and Porcupine Pete—Infectious Lass got a brief call-up to the majors during a time of need. Her ability to spread disease is actually a pretty useful way to wipe out enemies, provided that they don't attack during the microbial incubation period. But while beating people up or zapping them with rays has a certain panache, making them sick just feels *wrong*.

Guest List:
"WEIRD AL" YANKOVIC

FRAK BOIMP!: THE 27 ALL-TIME COOLEST DON MARTIN SOUND EFFECTS

1. SNAP PLOOBADOOF
The sound of Wonder Woman unhooking her brassiere. —*Mad* magazine #210, pg. 22

2. DING DING DING DING DING DING DING GLUK
The sound of an alarm clock falling from the sky into a man's mouth. —*Mad* #61, pg. 9

3. THUTHHHH... THOT
The sound of a deflated human head re-inflating back to normal. —*Mad* #93, pg. 33

4. SIZAFITZ
The sound an eyeball makes when poked with a lit cigarette. —*Mad* Special #23, insert sticker

5. FLAT FLOK SWIT GLAP
The sound of a man being folded up as if he were a folding chair. —*Mad* #144, pg. 23

6. SKWEEK SKWEEK
The sound of a giant Q-Tip cleaning out one of Abraham Lincoln's ears on Mount Rushmore. —*Mad* #178, pg. 48

7. FWISK GLURK
The sound of a bottle being forcefully removed from a wino's mouth. —*Mad* #117, pg. 38

8. KLINGDINGGOON
The sound of a man's nose being chopped off by an electric fan. —*Mad* #113, pg. 17

9. ZIT-SREEK SKRAK ZIDIT-POW
The sound of an electric drill malfunctioning after it drills through a ceiling and into a human head. —*Mad* #87, pg. 40

10. KACHUNK SHOOK SHOOK SHOOK SHOOK
The sound of a prince climbing up Rapunzel's armpit hair. —*Mad* #129, pg. 38

11. GLINK
The sound of a toenail landing in a beer can. —*Mad* #162, pg. 39

12. CHK CHK CHA-GONK BRBBRBBRING!
The sound of a man's eyeballs being punched like cash-register keys, whereupon his jaw springs forward as if it were a change drawer. —*Mad* #61, pg. 18

13. BZZOWNT!
The sound produced by a Vend-O-Hair machine when a human head is inserted. —*Mad* #143, pg. 15

14. MAMP SPWAT TOK
The sound of cannibals having a food fight with human body parts. —*Mad* #242, pg. 35

15. KACHUNK GING PSSSSH
The sound of an elderly woman being ironed by a vending machine. —*Mad* #203, pg. 48

16. BPLFLT!
The sound of a man's head being crushed by the enormous posterior of a fellow bus passenger. —*Mad* #64, pg. 27

17. POIT!
The sound of a coat hanger being extracted from a man's mouth, or the sound of an eyeball being retrieved from the end of a vacuum cleaner. —*Mad* #52, pg. 48; *Mad* #89, pg. 48

18. SKNITCH
The sound of a pin being poked into a baby's head as if it were a pin cushion. —*Mad* #91, pg. 26

19. FARRAPPGHT FPFWORPFT FFFPFWRAP
The sound of three news anchors deflating like balloons and flying around the room after pulling out their earpieces. —*Mad* #254, pg. 36

20. SPLOYDOING
The sound of a man's internal organs springing out of his body while he's on the operating table. —*Mad* #110, pg. 11

21. KLOONK KA-DOONK
The sound of a blind man and his seeing-eye dog both walking into a metal pole. —*Mad* #181, pg. 15

22. SHKLURCH
The sound of food being squeezed out of a hippie's beard. —*Mad* #139, pg. 48

23. GA-SPLORTCH... BLUB BLUB BLUB BLUB BLUB... BLORP
The sound of a boy walking onto wet concrete, then disappearing completely into it. —*Mad* #190, pg. 48

24. PADAP PADAP PADAP, KADOONK
The sound of a prison guard dribbling a meatloaf like a basketball, then slam-dunking it into a prisoner's mouth. —*Mad* #249, back cover

25. GISHKLURK
The sound of Moses parting a bowl of soup. —*Mad* #186, pg. 15

26. DOIP! DIT DIT DIT DIT DIT... SKLORK
The sound of an eyeball popping out of its socket, rolling down the street, and getting flattened by a steamroller. —*Mad* #140, pg. 31

27. PITTWEEN SPLATCH THORK BLOOF THLIK GLITCH GLUTCH PITTWOON PLAF PLOOF SPLITCH THUK THAP PLOOP
The sound of a bullet ricocheting off a ceiling, piercing the heads of six people, bouncing off a wall, and then piercing six more heads. —*Mad* #189, pg. 11

"Weird Al" Yankovic is the world's foremost song parodist and the genius behind the cult movie UHF.

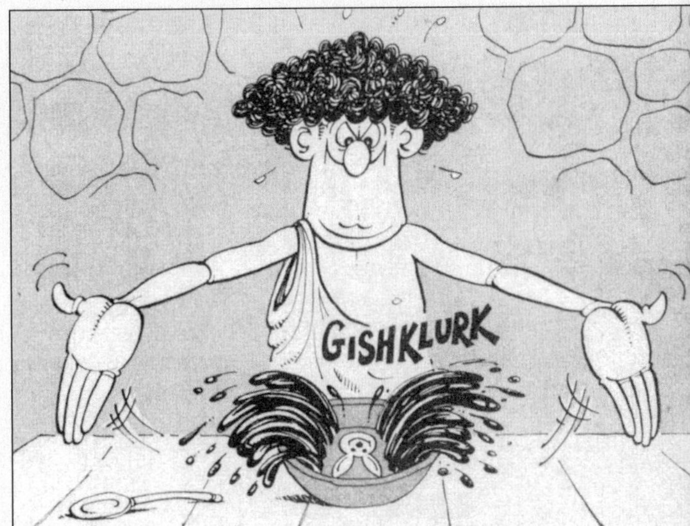

IT WAS ONLY AN OTTER!

9 CLASSIC INSTANCES OF ANIMAL SNUFF FOR KIDS

1 *THE RED PONY* *(JOHN STEINBECK, 1933)*

Where does the tradition of heart-rending children's classics in which a central character spends an entire book caring for and loving a very special animal, only to have it die in the end, usually granting life lessons, hard-won maturity, and heavy-duty pathos come from? Possibly from John Steinbeck's seminal, semi-autobiographical classic *The Red Pony*, in which a boy's beloved and highly symbolic pony loses a gruesome, graphic battle with illness. Like every other title on this list (but one), this depressing classic book later became a depressing classic movie.

2 *OLD YELLER* *(FRED GIPSON, 1956)*

About the only popular-entertainment-related childhood trauma that can compete with the death of Bambi's mom is the death of Old Yeller, a brave farm dog who redeems himself for bad behavior by saving his master's life. As a reward, he gets a bullet to the head from his owner, who manfully saves Yeller from hydrophobia the only way he can. Fortunately, Old Yeller had a sequel—er, a son—to carry on the family tradition.

3 *THE YEARLING* *(MARJORIE KINNAN RAWLINGS, 1938)*

An earlier example of gritty miserabilism in which a young farm boy saves a cherished animal companion from pain by killing it himself, *The Yearling* is a bit unusual in that it's about a domesticated deer rather than a more traditional pet. The hero, Jody, adopts the deer as a fawn after his family slaughters its mother; he raises it to adulthood, whereupon he has to shoot it. It's like *Bambi* all over again, only Bambi and his mom *both* bite it in this version.

4 *RING OF BRIGHT WATER* *(GAVIN MAXWELL, 1960)*

In Gavin Maxwell's real-life-inspired book *Ring Of Bright Water*, a stodgy Brit buys a pet otter, and finds that its fun-loving, insatiably curious nature livens up his life. The 1969 MGM film adaptation is sweet, low-key, almost naturalistic magic, right up to the point where a Scots road-worker offhandedly bludgeons the otter to death, and is then astonished at the horror of the woman who was taking it for a stroll. "It was only an otter!" he protests, not that the millions of shrieking children in the theaters likely heard him.

5 *JULIE OF THE WOLVES* *(JEAN CRAIGHEAD GEORGE, 1972)*

The only one of these books to feature a female protagonist, and—hmm—the only one that hasn't been made into a film, Jean Craighead George's best-loved novel wriggles out of the mold a bit, in that the adored animals here aren't pets; they're wild wolves that adopt the eponymous Julie and enable her to survive after her home life turns spectacularly sour. But their freedom doesn't let them escape the animal-snuff pattern: They die, and Julie winds up accepting the tragic ways of the world, and going home to their killer. Two sequels continued Julie's story for anyone whose heart didn't break with the first installment.

6 *J.T.* *(JANE WAGNER, 1969)*

A poor boy coming of age in the Harlem ghetto comes back from the brink of apathetic criminality and finds self-worth in caring for something outside himself: a battered, one-eyed, scrawny old alley cat. Then he finds out how the world really works when some local kids who hate him make a point of tormenting the cat, and while trying to escape, it gets run over. Fortunately, in the way of uplifting children's stories about dead animals everywhere, J.T. is rewarded with a cute new kitten, and the cycle of life continues.

7 *WHERE THE RED FERN GROWS* (WILSON RAWLS, 1961)

Where The Red Fern Grows yanks extra-hard on the heartstrings, with not one but two loyal, beloved hounds dying at the end—one to save his master, the other out of grief for the first. Like so many of these books, it's a beautiful but anguished paean to love, devotion, and sacrifice, with a lengthy buildup in which the book's boy protagonist works his ass off for two years to buy the dogs—a pair of purebred coon hounds—and spends much of the rest of the book thoroughly enjoying his childhood with them. Then that childhood comes to an end with their deaths, which simultaneously save his life and let his family achieve a long-held dream. Yay?

8 *SOUNDER* (WILLIAM H. ARMSTRONG, 1970)

The dog companion of this classic about poor black Southern sharecroppers isn't as much the central focus as the animals in most of these books, in part because he gets shot early on while trying to protect his family, and he disappears for a good chunk of the story. But he gets the title to himself, and his climactic death, peaceful and weirdly uplifting as it is, pretty much sums up the exhausting miseries his owners live in, and one of the few reliefs they can hope for.

9 *NEVER CRY WOLF* (FARLEY MOWAT, 1963)

Wolves again, hunters again, the frozen arctic again… It's like *Julie Of The Wolves II*, except with an adult white-guy hero instead of a teenaged Eskimo heroine. Oh, and this one came first. The gorgeous film version was directed by Carroll Ballard, who started his career with *The Black Stallion* and went on to helm *Fly Away Home* and *Duma*. In those stories, the people rather than the animals die sorry deaths to impart powerful symbolism, possibly indicating that authors have lightened up a little on the animal snuff in the last couple of decades. Or maybe just that the time is ripe for this decade's great animal-death novel.

POSSIBLE GERMANIES

7 SPECULATIVE FICTIONS ABOUT WORLDS RULED BY NAZIS

1 DC COMICS, EARTH-X

Remember when the Japanese invaded California, distracting the U.S. military to such a degree that the Nazis developed nuclear weapons and won World War II? No? Then you must not live on Earth-X, one of the infinite alternate realities in DC Comics' multiverse. But if you do live on Earth-X, don't worry: The good fight is still being waged by Freedom Fighters, a band of superheroes that includes The Human Bomb, Doll Man, The Ray, Phantom Lady, and Black Condor, all led by the red-white-and-blue-festooned, top-hatted Uncle Sam. They'll get those Ratzis yet! (Or DC will eliminate them from continuity in a multi-title crossover. Whatever.)

2 *THE MAN IN THE HIGH CASTLE*

Thanks to the 1933 assassination of Franklin Roosevelt, the U.S. lacks a strong leader to see it through World War II. Nazi Germany rules the East Coast. Imperial Japan controls the West. The South is a Nazi-sympathizing mess, and nobody cares about what goes on in the middle of it all, where Hawthorne Abendsen lives. He's the author of *The Grasshopper Lies Heavy*, an alternate-history novel in which the Axis powers lose World War II. Head spinning yet? That's just one example of *The Man In The High Castle's* obsession with the distinction between reality and illusion, a theme that author Philip K. Dick approached from seemingly every angle throughout his career. But never again from this one. He planned a sequel but never followed through, in part because his extensive research into Nazi Germany left him shaken.

3 *FATHERLAND*

On the surface, Robert Harris' 1992 bestseller is just a whodunit set in an alternate universe. As Hitler's 75th birthday rolls around in April 1964, protagonist Xavier March is an SS detective not doing a good enough job of hiding his disillusionment with the Nazi state. His investigation of a murdered Nazi elder doesn't help matters, and his troubles deepen as he asks questions, particularly once he starts linking the death to the disappearance of the Jews. The German people have been told that the Jews were simply relocated to the East, and while it's implausible how generally that tale was accepted, that's part of the point. Harris finds a way to reiterate the horror of the Holocaust by summoning up a world in which everyone agrees to pretend it never happened.

4 *1945*

This alternate-history novel got a profile boost from its co-author's ascent to power: Newt Gingrich was the controversial Speaker Of The House when it was published in 1995. In this novel, the U.S. fought only Japan in World War II, letting Germany have its way with Europe. The book ends with Rommel invading Scotland, but the cliffhanger has yet to be resolved, though Gingrich and *1945* partner William Forstchen have subsequently co-authored an alternate-history trilogy in which the Confederacy wins at Gettysburg.

5 *STAR TREK*, "PATTERNS OF FORCE"

Investigating the disappearance of famed historian John Gill, the starship *Enterprise* travels to the planet Ekos, where Gill was observing the local population. Landing, Kirk and Spock find a planet filled with terrifying fascists united by their hate for the nearby planet Zeon, and decked out in undoubtedly-budget-friendly Nazi uniforms. Turns out that Gill, wanting to give the chaotic planet some order in the form of the "most efficient state Earth ever knew," made himself Der Führer. Then his plan, unsurprisingly, went horribly awry. And that's why that whole bit about non-interference is the Prime Directive.

6 *THE PLOT AGAINST AMERICA*

Philip Roth's profoundly chilling novel *The Plot Against America* stakes its plot on a simple question: What if famed aviation hero Charles Lindbergh defeated Franklin Roosevelt in the presidential election of 1940? It could have happened—Lindbergh was a major player in the Republican party at the time, in part because of his isolationist views and his proud conciliation with Hitler's rise to power—and the results would have made for a very different world. At least that's how Roth imagines it in a book that casts fear and paranoia as proxies for actual Nazis on the march. The sound of footsteps is the same either way.

7 *IT HAPPENED HERE*

It Happened Here co-directors Kevin Brownlow and Andrew Mollo (future film and military historians, respectively) started working on this 1966 film when they were both still teenagers. It took them 10 years to make the movie, and while the seams show, their vision of a Britain under fascist control actually benefits from the grit, which lends the movie a documentary plausibility. The sight of officious Brits goose-stepping and dropping lines like, "We don't accept your decisions. We accept ours," reinforces the central conceit: Stay on guard, because once fear and deprivation enter the picture, fascism could happen anywhere.

SHOOT YOUR OWN FEET

15 REALLY GOOD BANDS WITH REALLY BAD NAMES

1. Archers Of Loaf
2. The Dismemberment Plan
3. Blue Öyster Cult
4. Orange Juice
5. Orchestral Manoeuvres In The Dark
6. Broken Social Scene
7. Loose Fur
8. Ned's Atomic Dustbin
9. Flamin' Groovies
10. The Flaming Lips
11. Kitchens Of Distinction
12. Blonde Redhead
13. Prefab Sprout
14. Black Moth Super Rainbow
15. Death Cab For Cutie

THE DISMEMBERMENT PLAN

THE McRIB HAS NO BONES!

13 PARTICULARLY HORRIBLE FAST-FOOD INNOVATIONS

1 McGRIDDLE (McDONALD'S)
In the early '00s, McDonald's tried to satisfy a craving that most Americans didn't even know they had—and thereby kill as many of those Americans as possible—by introducing the Sausage McGriddle, a simple breakfast sandwich consisting of a greasy, salty sausage patty slapped between two miniature pancakes. The original McGriddle ingeniously combined the savory with the sweet, and the chewy with the doughy. Plus, the pancakes had the syrup cooked right in, which made the whole mess relatively un-sticky. It was the kind of stick-to-the-ribs breakfast that a farmer would eat before heading out into the fields, assuming they were located near a turnpike. But not content to leave well enough alone, McDonald's added eggs. And bacon. And cheese. That's right: cheese on a pancake. It's breakfast for those who enjoy heart disease *and* acid reflux.

2 PHILLY CHEESE STEAK BURGER (HARDEE'S)
While other fast-food restaurants upped the meat content of their burgers by piling on a little bacon, Hardee's—also known as Carl's Jr. in some regions—raised the bar with the Philly Cheese Steak Burger, which modified a regular hamburger by adding sliced flank steak, creamy cheese, and grilled onions, recreating the overall peppery, savory flavor of a cheese-steak sandwich. Experience-wise, the Philly Cheese Steak Burger did what it was supposed to, such as inducing that unique sensation of "instant heartburn" familiar to cheese-steak aficionados. But steak and roast beef tend to be iffy sandwich ingredients, because of their varying degrees of chewability. Diners frequently bit into the steak and accidentally pulled it right out of the sandwich, leaving it to dangle greasily against their chins.

3 FRENCH FRIES WITH BUMPS (BURGER KING)
Just as some beer companies emphasize the coldness of their product rather than the taste, Burger King pushes its fries based on the crunchiness. And certainly, BK has the loudest fries the fast-food industry has to offer. But the bumps that cover each fry like an acne breakout cancel out the joys of crunch with an icky, moldy texture. So while they sound great in your mouth, BK fries don't *feel* great, and it all seems like way too much distraction before the actual flavor sets in.

4 OREO PIZZA (DOMINO'S)
"Dessert pizza" just sounds wrong, but crossing the line from savory to sweet is surprisingly easy when the line is completely obscured with generous drizzles of thick, white frosting and heaps of Oreo crumbs. It's also surprisingly easy when it appears that no baking is required at all. In the box, Domino's Oreo Pizza resembles a work by Jackson Pollock via Nabisco: heaps of broken cookies scattered about underneath splatters of white frosting. It's unclear why anyone would pay Domino's for a dessert they could make themselves with a tube of squeeze frosting, a box of Oreos, and a sledgehammer.

5 ORIGINAL KREME FROZEN BLEND (KRISPY KREME)
Ever wanted to drink a Krispy Kreme doughnut? Yes? Then check to see if your jaw is wired shut, because there's no other reason that the words "liquid doughnut" should sound appealing. Some foods—fruit, for instance—naturally lend themselves to liquid or smoothie form. Hot Krispy Kreme glazed doughnuts don't. Still, that didn't stop Krispy Kreme from trying—and failing. The Original Kreme Frozen Blend shake, the frothy

blended beverage the company touted in 2004 as a "drinkable doughnut," didn't taste like a glazed doughnut so much as like syrupy powdered sugar you could slurp through a straw. Close, yet so far.

6 SNACK WRAPS (McDONALD'S)

It's all too easy to deduce the inspiration for the McDonald's Snack Wrap. Some enterprising McEmployee must have looked around the McKitchen one night and noticed that the average day's leftovers included a bunch of fried "Chicken Selects," and that there was plenty of cheese, ranch dressing, and tortillas on hand just waiting to be McSlapped together and sold. Since that beautiful McEureka moment, McDonald's has expanded the Snack Wrap repertoire to include other apparent leftovers, including leftover grilled chicken patties for its Honey Mustard Snack Wrap, and leftover barbecue sauce for its Chipotle BBQ Snack Wrap. The McInnovation never stops!

7 CHEESY GORDITA CRUNCH (TACO BELL)

So over-the-top it inspired a *Saturday Night Live* parody commercial (Taco

Town, where food is wrapped in more food, then dumped in a tote bag and covered with sauce), the Cheesy Gordita Crunch was launched in 2000 with a carpet-bombing ad campaign. Apparently Taco Bell customers were jamming the company switchboards with complaints that their tacos weren't bready enough. So the Bell spread cheese sauce on flatbread and wrapped it around an entire tortilla. We couldn't bring ourselves to try one, for fear that the starchy mess would stick to our upper palates like an insufficiently jellied peanut-butter sandwich, but somebody must have liked this Frankenfood—the company brought it back with great fanfare in 2006.

8 STUFFED CRUST GOLD PIZZA (PIZZA HUT)

"Where else can we cram cheese?" the Pizza Hut engineers mused as they stared at a pie in their gleaming white 2002 test kitchen. "We've put extra mozz on top of the pie. We baked it in a ring inside the outer crust, and had Jessica Simpson eat it backwards on TV. But still they demand more cheese!" And that's when some brilliant, anonymous functionary suggested that they could coat that cheese-stuffed crust with a greasy layer of even more cheese—creating Stuffed Crust Gold. The pizza equivalent of the six-blade disposable razor debuted during the Super Bowl pre-game show in 2003, and weary hearts everywhere gave up even *trying* to pump blood through those stuffed arteries. Excuse us—Stuffed Arteries Gold.

9 INSIDER (PIZZA HUT)

In 2000, millennial anxiety caused Americans to demand cheese-covered bread products, uncontaminated by any liquid that might make the yeasty, dairy goo easier to swallow. Hence Pizza Hut's Insider pizza, which starts with a thin crust covered with cheese, then adds a complete cheese pizza on top. "That's not inside, that's insane!" a prototype advertisement accurately claimed. As for how all this extra cheese might be contributing to the obesity epidemic, Pizza Hut CEO Allan Huston had already exonerated the company five years earlier when he defended its then-new stuffed-crust pizza with a combination blame-the-victim and we're-just-following-orders alibi: "We've found that when people make the decision to have pizza, they've already made the decision to indulge."

10 PIZZAM BREAKFAST PIZZA (DOMINO'S)

Tested in a few Ohio markets in the mid-'80s, the Pizzam was pretty much what you'd expect from a breakfast pizza, assuming you'd expect an unholy union of a pizza and a Denny's platter. Egg, ham, bacon, cheese, and other ingredients rested on a crust not discernibly different from those used for more daylight-oriented meals, and the whole thing arrived with a serving of coffee and a copy of *USA Today*, presumably allowing Pizzam consumers to take their mind off breakfast with the latest stories about Tammy Faye Bakker and the latest in *Miami Vice*-inspired clothing.

11 CHEESECAKE POPPERS (ARBY'S)

Debuting in late 2007, this item modified the classic deep-fried jalapeño-poppers concept for dessert fans, packing a cream-cheese filling inside a graham-cracker shell with a side of tart raspberry dipping sauce. Structurally, the crust held the poppers together better than expected; problem is, cream cheese exposed to fryer temperatures takes on the texture and consistency of warm snot.

12 MAC 'N' CHEESE BITES (SONIC)

Macaroni and cheese is about as low-brow and Middle American as it gets, so leave it to those mad Southern scientists at Sonic Drive-In to transform it into some truly next-level shit by balling it into little clumps and tossing it into the fryer. Introduced in late 2007, the Sonic Mac 'N' Cheese Bites externally resembled any of the chain's other greasy, golden-brown nuggets, but the inside was a gluey mess of limp pasta and rehydrated cheese sauce, flavored with subtle notes of poverty and blissful ignorance. (Although, like everything on the menu, they went down fairly easy when slathered in ranch dressing.)

13 McRIB (McDONALD'S)

It's named after bones. It's shaped like bones. But it has no bones!

LOVE YOU LIVE

6 LIVE ALBUMS THAT DEFINITIVELY SUM UP THE ARTISTS WHO MADE THEM

1 CHEAP TRICK, *AT BUDOKAN* (1979)

Cheap Trick was a critically acclaimed, low-selling American power-pop act in the mid-'70s, but Japan loved the band's music, and when it played Tokyo's Nippon Budokan arena in 1978, more than 10,000 screaming fans turned up. The live document of that show put Cheap Trick's walloping guitar-driven rock in the proper context, and the album became the band's first big hit, driven by steady radio play for the singles "I Want You To Want Me" and "Ain't That A Shame," as well as by the distant roar of the Japanese.

2 BOB SEGER, *LIVE BULLET* (1976)

Like Cheap Trick, Bob Seger was a hardworking Midwesterner who couldn't catch a break on mainstream radio until he found success by recording the live show that was making him a regional favorite. Still a few years away from the clunky mid-tempo roots-rock that would turn him into a millionaire, the Seger of *Live Bullet* is more of an R&B-inflected dynamo, leading his crackerjack band through fiery covers of Tina Turner, Van Morrison, Bo Diddley, and Chuck Berry songs, plus originals like "Heavy Music" and "Ramblin' Gamblin' Man," which stand up to the songs that influenced them.

3 KISS, *ALIVE!* (1975)

Dressing up like kabuki drag queens and spitting fire and blood in the faces of gobsmacked teenagers did wonders for Kiss' concert business in the mid-'70s. But it didn't carry over to big sales for the band's spotty, relatively pedestrian studio albums, which put the focus on music—never Kiss' strong point—rather than spectacle. So a live album was inevitable, and crucial to building the Kiss Army. While numerous overdubs undermine its "live" credibility, *Alive!* is the closest approximation to "being there" for unlucky fans who weren't around at the height of arena rock. While no Kiss studio effort deserves an introduction as arrogantly confident as "You wanted the best, you got it!" *Alive!* is more than loud, dumb, and entertaining enough to justify the claim.

4 JAMES BROWN, *LIVE AT THE APOLLO* (1963)

An artist as important and restlessly creative as James Brown demands more than one entry in any music collection. But if the breadth, energy, innovation, and power of the Godfather Of Soul must be represented by one record, let it be 1963's *Live At The Apollo*, one of the greatest live albums ever made in any genre. While it predates Brown's biggest hits by a couple of years, *Live At The Apollo* is a potent expression of the man's showmanship and musicianship. Commanding his expansive band with the ruthlessness of a Third World dictator, Brown plays his musicians like a single instrument, leading them in a series of soul hollers

and proto-funk vamps that sum up where he came from and point out where he was headed.

5 **PETER FRAMPTON,** ***FRAMPTON COMES ALIVE!*** *(1976)*

As much a triumph of herd mentality as music, *Frampton Comes Alive!* was the album everybody in the late '70s had to have, even people who'd never bought a Frampton record or heard any of his music prior to 1976. The record spawned three radio hits—the wispy ballad "Baby I Love Your Way," the anthemic "Show Me The Way," and the epic, TalkBox-aided show-closer "Do You Feel Like We Do?"—all of which were immeasurably improved by a San Francisco crowd that made seeing a Frampton show sound like a near-religious experience.

6 **THE GRATEFUL DEAD,** ***EUROPE '72*** *(1972)*

The Grateful Dead made studio records, live releases, and live records that were never "legitimately" released. That makes for a lot of entry points into one of America's most popular and important rock bands. What sets the live record *Europe '72* apart in the Dead catalog is that it highlights some of the better examples of the band's "noodling" side—particularly on the standout "Morning Dew." Plus, it includes topflight folk and country numbers first heard on record in these live incarnations, including the gently chugging "He's Gone" and the classic road song "Brown-Eyed Woman." Equally jammy and song-oriented, *Europe '72* covers all the Dead bases in a relatively succinct package.

Guest List: PATTON OSWALT

6 QUIET FILM REVOLUTIONS

Stagecoach, Snow White And The Seven Dwarfs, Breathless, and *Star Wars* caused major changes in the history of film. They sparked entire subgenres of features that we still enjoy (or don't) today. But there are some quiet revolutionary moments in movies, if you look for them. They don't set the world on fire, but sad movie ghouls like me cherish them like a shot of rare old scotch. Maybe it's better that these momentary rebellions only went as far as the films they appeared in. But the fact that they exist—these tiny protests against formulaic deadness—gives me hope.

1. *THE LATE SHOW*: "You're not gonna believe this shit..." Robert Benton wrote this movie, along with many others—for instance, *Bonnie And Clyde*, which altered the cinematic landscape. All his subsequent films have the easygoing confidence of a creator who sees the change he wrought all around him, and no longer needs to raise his voice.

But Benton remains a prankster, rebel, and innovator. He just does it with a wink. From Christopher Reeve's double-take at the phone kiosk in *Superman* to Jeff Bridges and David Huddleston's verbal sparring in the criminally underappreciated *Bad Company*, all Benton's screenplays have at least one "Oh yeah, why don't they do that all the time in movies?" moment.

The Late Show, a loopy, comic-violent 1977 ur-sequel to every Hollywood film noir ever made, contains just such a moment. Robert Altman's *The Long Goodbye* is Philip Marlowe time-shifted to the present with his youth and wits intact. Benton's *The Late Show* is Philip Marlowe with an ulcer, hearing aid, and bus pass, trying to survive in post-hippie Los Angeles.

In a blissful scene about halfway through the movie, an aging gumshoe played to cranky perfection by Art Carney beats the punk and plaster out of the bad guy's sadistic henchman (terrifying and pathetic as portrayed by John Considine). The scene is blissful because Considine wipes the floor with Carney in an earlier scene, just because his character is a bully who likes beating up an old man. So it's particularly satisfying to see Carney's life force well up and take charge. It's even better when he marches Considine—camel-hair coat and all—into the bad guy's pool at gunpoint.

But the sequence is all the more touching and real thanks to the scene afterward. Carney is in a cafeteria with client

Lily Tomlin, telling her how he got one better on Considine. He's enjoying his victory: bragging about it, reveling in it. It's a basic human moment, but we almost never see moments like that in movies.

2. *ANIMAL HOUSE*: Victory through exodus

The fun-loving misfits of the Delta Fraternity at Faber College spend the entirety of 1978's *Animal House* doing battle with—and usually losing to—the narrow-hipped, pretty-boy conformist assholes at Omega House. Then the Deltas get thrown off campus. None of them are going to graduate. They've lost. So they wreck the homecoming parade. The head Delta—pussy-hound supreme Otter—punches the smarmy head Omega. But that's pretty much it, as far as vengeance goes.

And then... The Deltas leave college. As do the Omegas.

The Deltas all, to varying degrees, go on to happiness and fulfillment. The Omegas go on to personal ruin. *But not at the Deltas' hands*. Everyone just continues their lives, and the assholes are left to their fates.

Nowadays, movie misfits overcome their abusers by becoming even more violent abusers. Or if their opponents are mainstream and career-oriented, the misfits win by becoming even more faceless and driven. We've lost the capacity to say "Well, fuck it, let them have their boring-ass goals and victories. I've got my own thing going on, which will make me so much happier."

When did the weirdoes, misfits, and oddballs start craving the lives of uncreative thugs?

3. *ALIEN*: Space is a goddamn job

Ridley Scott's 1979 classic *Alien* is a lot of things—a super-fun haunted-house-in-space movie, a triumph of design, and a parable for the decline of Gary Glitter's career. But it also has a sly, ethereal dig at all the gee-whiz *Star Wars* space-adventure mania that was gripping Hollywood and the nation at the time.

The engineers and troubleshooters on an interstellar mining platform find evidence of alien life on a remote planetoid. And not just life. Maybe... a distress signal! But all anyone thinks about is whether they'll get extra pay for the investigation. Or, in the case of the ship's officers, whether their asses are on the line for not following company regulations.

I can't think of another science-fiction film—apart from the *Alien* sequels—where space travel and alien encounters mostly center on pay scale and vacation time. Except for Han Solo's token griping about credits due once the *Millennium Falcon* reaches the debris of Alderaan, nothing comes to mind. Yes, one day man will sail among the stars. And the paycheck will probably suck.

4. *DIE HARD*: I'll just sit this one out

When *Die Hard* came out in 1988, we were in the ascendancy of Arnold Schwarzenegger, Sly Stallone, and their second-team legions of indestructible supermen. They played the sort of men who could, say, hurl a pipe through a man's body, with enough surplus velocity to pierce the steel hide of a huge steam exchange behind him. Then, as superheated water escaped through the hollow pipe, they'd say something profound to that dying adversary, like "Let off some steam."

But *Die Hard* is a strange case. It did create a viable subgenre, namely, "*Die Hard* in a ________" films. But it contained an element so radical and refreshing that it's no surprise I've never seen its equivalent since.

The hero tries to sit out the action.

Terrorists take over a Los Angeles building. Bruce Willis plays a New York cop trapped inside. *Three* times, he tries to call for help. When the police finally arrive, he happily sits back and has a Twinkie.

Arnold would have punched out the terrorists before they cut a single phone line. He would have done it with his neck.

5. *HENRY: PORTRAIT OF A SERIAL KILLER*: Quipless killing

I saw *Henry* in a theater in

Washington, DC in late summer 1989. By that time, I'd been to countless screenings of the *Nightmare On Elm Street* and *Child's Play* movies, along with dozens of Jean-Claude Van Damme, Steven Seagal, Chuck Norris, Sly, and Arnold shoot-'em-ups.

As noted above, in these movies, the hero (or killer-hero) would slaughter someone, then deliver a pun or quip that made light of the murder method. Now that I think of it, these guys rarely killed anyone instantly—they needed their victims to maintain a flickering consciousness long enough to hear the goodbye joke.

A month before seeing *Henry*, I saw *A Nightmare On Elm Street 3: Dream Warriors*. A skinny, skittish kid sat behind me, in a denim jacket covered with hand-drawn ballpoint sigils of burning skulls, anarchy symbols, various weapons, and band logos.

And all throughout the movie, this quiet, gentle-looking soul, safe in the anonymous darkness, was screaming, "Cut that bitch, Freddy! Yeeeeee-AAAAAAH! Fuck you, wheelchair boy!" When the lights came up, I turned around and looked him in the eyes, and he crumpled. Drooped his head, stood/stooped, and shuffled out.

I am not an intimidating presence. I think this kid—probably not a bad kid, in reality—had no real identity of his own, and any contact with the outside world produced a coat of quills that stuck inside of him, instead of out at the world. Freddy Krueger, a scarred child molester with supernatural powers, was his proxy for interaction. I'm telling this long-winded story so you'll understand how miraculous the *Henry* screening was, months later.

It was midday, and the theater was about two-thirds full of slightly older, more intense versions of that meek *Nightmare* scarecrow. Now they had menial jobs that afforded them skull rings, black leather jackets, and studded belts. They'd come, consciously or not, to anoint a new quip-killer icon.

Half of them left before the movie was over.

Henry: Portrait Of A Serial Killer is the most brutal, realistic horror movie since *The Texas Chain Saw Massacre*. As someone famously said about *TCSM*, "It looks as if the killers themselves got hold of a camera and filmed their killing spree."

Henry goes one step further, with Henry and his accomplice, the subhuman Otis, clumsily videotaping a home invasion/murder. Except neither of them says, "Smile, you're on candid camera!" or "Honey, I'm home!" while dispatching their victims. The movie is a necessary antidote to every giggly, pseudo-witty Chucky *bon mot*.

The crowd of (to quote Jim Goad) "murder pussies" came ready for some reliable call-and-response. What they got was a yawning void that emitted silence, death, and ultimately, nothing.

6. *THE SIXTH SENSE*: It isn't about you

"What do you think the dead people are trying to tell you?" a child psychologist—Bruce Willis again—asks a troubled boy who can see and communicate with dead people in M. Night Shyamalan's perfect *The Sixth Sense*.

Wow! That question, asked of someone who truly has access to the netherworld, was a precious—and, ultimately, ignored—breath of fresh air.

When *The Sixth Sense* came out, the country was tit-deep in stories of angels and otherworldly spirits with messages for us. Actually, not "us"—one special, chosen person. If that person looked like Meg Ryan, even better.

There's something specifically alarming to me about *anyone* who says a deity or one of said deity's agents came looking for *them* to deliver a message or perform a task. That's a scary strain of religion, wherein someone's actions are preemptively justified by the infinite. *The Sixth Sense* tried to gently remind us that maybe the dead, the spirits, and the gods have their own agendas and problems, and that they aren't here to justify us in any way.

As I write this—Labor Day of 2008—we're ending an eight-year period of our history where two sides of an opposing holy war are both represented by individuals who—wouldn't you know it?—say they were chosen *directly* by their respective gods to square off for the fate of the planet. In the world of *The Sixth Sense*, maybe those gods would have reminded everyone to be humble and get along. Or just let the gods be.

Patton Oswalt is a stand-up comedian, writer, and actor who loves pop culture as much as we do. He once wrote an essay on KFC's Famous Bowl for us.

HELEN HUNT THINKS SHE CAN FLY

10 HILARIOUS ONSCREEN DRUG FREAK-OUTS

1 ***REEFER MADNESS: THE MOVIE MUSICAL*** *(2005)*

The original 1936 cult film *Reefer Madness* didn't really gain a following until the '70s, when stoners started watching it to giggle over its histrionic, antiquated anti-drug message. So far as the filmmakers were concerned, marijuana doesn't cause lassitude, enjoyment of dumb comedy, and excessive Twinkie consumption; it causes shrieking, wild thrill-driving, suicide, rape, and manslaughter. The Off-Broadway musical comedy and eventual film adaptation *Reefer Madness: The Movie Musical* parodied this mentality to the hilt: Literally one puff of a "giggle-stick" sends bow-tied, fresh-faced Christian Campbell off into a wild, orgiastic musical number, while a few drags instantly turn his girlfriend, simpering all-American sweetie Kristen Bell, into a kink-crazed, leather-clad dominatrix. Practically every high in the movie is hilarious, from the wacky animated fantasy that emerges from a hash brownie to the eventual horror as a stressed-out habitual pothead smokes up and suddenly mistakes human flesh for food.

2 ***DESPERATE LIVES*** *(1982)*

In this made-for-TV drugs-are-scary flick, wooden actors play students and teachers in a high school filled with drug experimentation. Helen Hunt is a good girl, but under pressure from her studly boyfriend, she snorts some angel dust—then smashes through a second-story window and plummets to the ground, screaming all the way down. But she isn't done! When she hits the ground, she picks up glass shards and starts attacking herself. This scene would be awesome to watch while high.

3 ***SKIDOO*** *(1968)*

Longstanding rumor has it that director Otto Preminger actually indulged in LSD himself in order to get into the heads of the young people he was apparently trying to reach in this disastrously unhip abomination. If that's true, he must have had the squarest freak-out in history, as the end result was a laughably bad mess of a film featuring Carol Channing in hippie drag. Its basement-surrealist low point comes when Jackie Gleason hallucinates the hokiest musical number of the '60s, complete with dancing garbage cans.

4 ***SUPER TROOPERS*** *(2001)*

Nothing strikes fear into a stoner's heart like having to deal with the cops while high, a nightmare scenario that comedy troupe Broken Lizard plays for some of the sharpest laughs in

Super Troopers. In its opening scene, a carload of joint-toking cruisers are pulled over by prank-happy police who are more interested in messing with heads than busting them. That's bad news for the poor guy in the back seat, who's forced to dispose of his friends' evidence by swallowing inhuman amounts of weed and mushrooms. As the officers torture the kids by endlessly repeating the phrase "Littering and...," he loses his already shaky grip on reality and winds up a basket case, licking the bulletproof glass—a punishment far crueler than county jail.

5 FLIRTING WITH DISASTER *(1996)*

Real-life accidental overdoses on hallucinogens? Not funny. But in cinema, they're generally played for hilarity. For instance, in David O. Russell's *Flirting With Disaster*, a complicated road comedy in which Ben Stiller tries to get in touch with his birth parents. For ridiculous reasons, he winds up traveling with his wife, his adoption caseworker, and a pair of gay ATF agents played by Josh Brolin and Richard Jenkins. Once they get to Stiller's parents' house, Brolin makes an unexpected play for Stiller's wife, while Jenkins accidentally winds up eating Stiller's dinner, which Stiller's jealous newfound brother has just spiked with a massive dose of LSD. (The cheery little song he sings to himself while painting roasted quail with acid is almost as much fun as the results.) Before long, Jenkins is complaining that he's seeing colors he doesn't want to see, asking if the dining room has "a musical table," and threatening Stiller's parents (a beautifully goofy Alan Alda and Lily Tomlin) with arrest... on behalf of his agency, "the Bureau Of Tobacco, Tobacco, and Tobacco."

6 DEATH AT A FUNERAL *(2007)*

A similar accident befalls high-strung Alan Tudyk (best-known as Wash from Joss Whedon's *Firefly*) in Frank Oz's similarly crowded, chaotic, dark family comedy *Death At A Funeral*. Determined to make a good impression on his fiancée's father, Tudyk stresses and twitches until his wife-to-be finally pushes him to take some Valium. Instead, he accidentally swallows a powerful designer drug. This leads to him freaking out during the eulogy, dumping the corpse on the rug, then retreating to a bathroom, stripping naked, and climbing around on the roof. And this is just one small part of the wackiness at hand.

7 AROUND THE FIRE *(1999)*

Ah, the prism: the cheap filmmaker's best friend. When Devon Sawa first takes acid in the hilariously misguided anti-pot, anti-LSD coming-of-age movie *Around The Fire*, his world suddenly fills up with all the pretty colors of the rainbow. A simple water fountain becomes an explosion of pure beauty. But Sawa ends up paying a steep price for his vision quest, transforming instantly into a sullen, depressed, angry, verbally abusive drug-dealing monster. The casting of professional party girl and fearless nipple-slip pioneer Tara Reid as a granola enthusiast who teaches Sawa that jam-band music and recreational drug use just don't mix adds an additional layer of irony to this amusingly heavy-handed manifesto.

8 AVENGING DISCO GODFATHER *(1979)*

Since most of their audience had little or no experience with PCP, '70s B-moviemakers took limitless license with angel-dust freak-outs in order to indulge their wildest flights of surrealistic fancy. In the anti-PCP message movie *Avenging Disco Godfather*, angel dust transforms rising hoop star Julius J. Carry III from a disco-dancing innocent to a wild-eyed fiend convinced he's being pursued by a cackling, machete-wielding witch, demonic basketball players with glowing red eyes, and perhaps most horrifying of all, uncle Rudy Ray Moore in a too-revealing baby-blue pantsuit cut below the navel. Carry's freak-out lands him in the overflowing PCP ward of a mental hospital, where Moore subsequently encounters such oddities as a young man who thinks he's an unborn caterpillar and a young woman who mistook her 4-month-old baby for a ham and served it to her horrified family on a silver platter "with all the trimmings." Oh well, at least she didn't neglect the side dishes.

9 DEATH DRUG *(1978)*

In the blaxploitation cheapie *Death*

Drug, rising musician Philip Michael Thomas attacks the wack by giving up his beloved angel dust, only to learn that he can't outrun his PCP-stained past and hopelessly fried synapses. While shopping with his sweetie, a seemingly reformed Thomas experiences the mother of all PCP flashbacks. Hallucinating wildly, he sees snakes, spiders, and rats everywhere, devolves into frothing hysteria, and over-emotes wildly as familiar faces morph into ghoulish monsters in homemade Halloween masks. Only death via truck-assisted accidental suicide can end this hilariously bad, ridiculously cheap, wonderfully over-the-top trip.

10 *TRAINSPOTTING* *(1996)*

For a movie that stakes its credibility on an unflinchingly truthful look at the day-to-day reality of drug addiction, *Trainspotting* comes across as pretty corny a lot of the time. From its blasé attitude to its creaky heist plot, it has a lot of contrivance mixed in with the realness. Nowhere is this more apparent than the horror-show psychedelia scene where heroin addict Ewan McGregor suffers through withdrawal, as what appears to be a Baby Drink 'N' Wet crawls mechanically across his ceiling like toddler Spider-Man. Mixed in with flash-edited condemnations from McGregor's near and dear, the whole sequence comes across less as a nightmarish scene of withdrawal than it does the centerpiece of a really bad student film.

THE HARDEST PART

25 MUSICIANS ANSWER THE QUESTION "WHAT ARE YOU WAITING FOR?"

1. **Damien Jurado:** Her to come home.
2. **Sebadoh:** Their turn to be with you.
3. **Paul McCartney:** Your friends to leave so he doesn't have to hide.
4. **John Mayer:** On the world to change.
5. **White Lion:** Just a moment before our love will die.
6. **The Kinks:** You, though they're so tired of it.
7. **Green Day:** This moment to come, when they're destined for anything.
8. **Ying Yang Twins:** A bitch to accept his love so he can pop her cherry.
9. **The Flaming Lips:** A superman.
10. **Violent Femmes:** The bus.
11. **The Doors:** The sun.
12. **Foreigner:** A girl like you to come into their life.
13. **Pink Floyd:** To follow the worms. (Also, to cut out the deadwood, to clean up the city, to put on a black shirt, etc.)
14. **Matthew Sweet:** You. Because he wants to have you.
15. **Erasure:** The day that you come back.
16. **Rufus Wainwright:** A dream.
17. **Tom Petty:** Tonight.
18. **The Velvet Underground:** His man.
19. **Graham Parker:** The UFOs—we know that they're there.
20. **The Rolling Stones:** A friend, and not a lady.
21. **Depeche Mode:** The night to fall and save us all.
22. **Jimmie Rodgers:** A train.
23. **Bob Dylan:** Only for his boot heels to be wanderin'.
24. **Elvis Costello:** The end of the world.
25. **Mickey Avalon:** To die.

I FOUGHT THE LAW

18 (MOSTLY NEGATIVE) SONGS ABOUT COPS

1 N.W.A., "FUCK THA POLICE"
It's easy to forget those simpler times—on the back cover of *Straight Outta Compton*, this classic of legal-civilian relations is listed as "F___ Tha Police." The track, in which the members of N.W.A. take the witness stand to testify about mistreatment at the hands of the L.A.P.D., inspired an angry letter from the FBI and U.S. Secret Service, which in turn inspired massive sales, cementing *Straight Outta Compton's* place in gangsta-rap history. While that all sounds serious, "Fuck Tha Police" is actually a witty song, if you can get past the killing. Quoth Eazy-E: "Without a gun and a badge, what do ya got? / a sucker in a uniform waitin' to get shot."

2 THE BOTTLE ROCKETS, "RADAR GUN"
The Bottle Rockets' seminal 1995 album *The Brooklyn Side* contains many evocative song-stories, none more potent than this swift, devastatingly funny single about a young cop getting off on a petty abuse of power. The song pegs its subject as a dim-witted local who never made it past junior college, yet did well enough on his police exam to consider it a rite of passage. ("Got me a gun and a badge / I'm a man.") Now with his "shiny new radar gun," he's "makin' money" and "havin' fun" running speed traps, presumably on all the jerks who looked down on him in high school.

3-4 JOHNNY CASH, "HIGHWAY PATROLMAN" AND BRUCE SPRINGSTEEN, "STATE TROOPER"
No one knew better than Johnny Cash that the common man often grows to hate the law. But sometimes the common man is the law. Bruce Springsteen originally recorded "Highway Patrolman" for his *Nebraska* album, and Cash's cover brings a sober view and hard-won sympathy to a state cop named Joe Roberts, who lets his reckless brother Frankie off easy, time and again. Then things get nastier, and he lets Frankie escape into Canada. This isn't a happy ending—in Springsteen's bare, acoustic version especially, it seems Joe's just doing his best to improvise his way out of a hopeless cycle. And in case that sounds too sentimental, *Nebraska* follows the song with the much more paranoid "State Trooper." The Boss and the trooper never actually meet in this spooky classic; it's all about the tension around what might happen if they do. The character, on the edge, knows what evil lurks within, and begs the cop not to pull him over—for the cop's sake. Creepiest line: "Maybe you got a kid / maybe you got a pretty wife / the only thing I got / been botherin' me my whole life."

5 THE STROKES, "NEW YORK CITY COPS"
Pulled from the U.S. release of *Is This It* due to the line, "New York City cops / they ain't too smart"—not exactly a popular sentiment in the wake of 9/11—The Strokes' most infamous song is hardly the incendiary piece of anti-authoritarian polemic it was initially made out to be. Really, it's a fairly standard Strokes track, full of typically vague lyrics about leaving a paranoid girlfriend (or, uh, something). In fact, if there's anything truly offensive about it, it's that the song—widely hailed as one of the band's best—was replaced with the middling B-side "When It Started," denying American audiences the fillerless album that international audiences enjoyed. Thanks, terrorists.

6 HAPPY MONDAYS, "GOD'S COP"
In 1975, Sir James Anderton was appointed Chief Constable of Greater Manchester. Fiercely conservative and devoutly Christian, Anderton marked his controversial career with frequent proclamations against homosexuality (which he declared should be illegal),

such as famously saying that AIDS victims were "swirling about in a human cesspit of their own making." To make matters worse, Anderton claimed to be "an instrument of divine judgment" who spoke directly with the Lord, leading the press to dub him "God's Cop." Anderton was embroiled in scandal when his Deputy Chief was accused of collusion, and while nothing was ever proven, that didn't stop Shaun Ryder from giving him a tongue-in-cheek ribbing in this biting tribute, which claims he "pilfered the bag and AmEx Gold." Of course, being falsely accused of embezzlement probably wouldn't upset the straitlaced Anderton nearly as much as the image of him and the chief getting "slowly stoned."

7 THE DICKS, "HATE THE POLICE"

Austin hardcore pioneers The Dicks—led by crazy "commie cross-dresser" Gary Floyd—burst onto the '80s punk scene with this classic debut single featuring the incendiary refrain, "You can't find justice / it'll find you." Snarling about a cop who "got himself a good job killing niggers and Mexicans" would be a bold move for anyone, let alone an openly gay liberal in the heart of Texas, but even removed from its historical and geographical contexts, "Hate The Police" remains a powerful song. This was later proved by Mudhoney, which included a cover of it on *Superfuzz Bigmuff* with the altered words, "Mudhoney hates policemen, yes it's true."

8 KRS-ONE, "SOUND OF DA POLICE"

KRS-One's solo career-making screed boasts one of the most heavily sampled and recognizable hooks in hip-hop history; the next time you're at a show, try throwing out a "Woop woop!" and you're bound to hear someone echo back, "That's the sound of da police!" Besides clever onomatopoeia, the track offers a side-by-side comparison of today's police officer with a field-slave overseer: "The overseer could stop you what you're doing / the officer will pull you over just when he's pursuing / the overseer had the right to get ill / and if you fought back, the overseer had the right to kill."

9 ALKALINE TRIO, "COP"

Like N.W.A., Alkaline Trio's Matt Skiba reacts to authority with a mixture of braggadocio and anger, sneering—like all young punks—at the kind of person who might choose a life in law enforcement to begin with. ("Maybe as a baby you dropped your rattle.") It's funny and fierce, and one of the best songs on one of pop-punk's semi-lost treasures, the Trio's debut album, *Goddamnit!*

10 LE TIGRE, "BANG! BANG!"

Le Tigre was known mostly for crafting delicious dance-punk anthems spiked with feminist sloganeering, but "Bang! Bang!" isn't an attempt to move hips as well as minds: It's a bluntly brutal protest song. Citing the NYPD's wrongful killings of Amadou Diallo in 1999 and Patrick Dorismond in 2000, leader Kathleen Hanna amps up the rage and bile that once fueled her band Bikini Kill: "Who gave them the fucking right to run around like they own the night?" she screeches, concluding with a call for Giuliani's head. The song's nod to Joe Cuba's warm-fuzzy boogaloo anthem "Bang Bang" doesn't make Hanna's punches any less pulverizing.

11 RICK JAMES, "MR. POLICEMAN"

A fugitive at age 16 after going AWOL from the Navy, Rick James got off on the wrong foot with the long arm of the law. His most infamous crime and incarceration wouldn't come until the '90s, but in 1981, he had already stored up plenty of hatred for cops. "Mr. Policeman"—a track off *Street Songs*, the album that yielded his biggest hit, "Super Freak"—is a loping, reggae-flavored harangue against the 5-0. "It's a shame, it's a disgrace / every time you show your face somebody dies," James cries over some uncharacteristically restrained funk. "Mr. Policeman, I saw you shoot my good friend down / he was just having fun." Of course, James' idea of fun was burning women with crack pipes, so his opinion might be a little suspect.

12-13 DEAD KENNEDYS, "POLICE TRUCK" AND BLACK FLAG, "POLICE STORY"

It seems '80s hardcore is an almost bottomless repository of anti-police songs. Some are acidly hilarious, such as Dead Kennedys' "Police Truck," in which Jello Biafra adopts the persona of an officer of the peace—then rakes cops over the coals for brutality, abuse of power, and rape, via lines like "Tonight's the night that we've got the truck / we're goin' downtown, gonna beat up drunks." But there's nothing funny about Black Flag's "Police Story." Fronting an outfit whose shows were regularly raided by the cops, Henry Rollins—in one of the high points of his checkered tenure with Black Flag—sums up the era's tension savagely and succinctly: "Understand we're fighting a war we can't win / they hate us, we hate them / we can't win."

14 THE CLASH, "POLICE ON MY BACK"

"Police On My Back," from 1980's *Sandinista!*, represents one of music's

Rick James appeared as a plaintiff on a 1999 episode of* Judge Joe Brown. *James loaned his guitar to a friend but never got it back. During the proceedings, James also claimed the defendant groped his buttocks.

rare occurrences: a cover outdoing the original. Originally by Eddy Grant's British reggae/R&B outfit The Equals, "Police On My Back" speaks to the disenfranchisement The Clash continually expressed. Here, police harassment is a daily threat; against a siren guitar, Mick Jones and Joe Strummer sing, "I've been running Monday, Tuesday, Wednesday, Thursday, Friday, Saturday, Sunday / what have I done?"

15 BODY COUNT, "COP KILLER"

A mediocre metal song from a mediocre metal band fronted by Ice-T, "Cop Killer" caught the ears of the then-fledgling alternative nation when Body Count played it at the inaugural Lollapalooza in 1991, the same year Rodney King was beaten by L.A.P.D. cops. By the time it was put to tape and released on the band's debut the following year, the rest of the country had an opinion about it, including George H.W. Bush, Dan Quayle, and Tipper Gore, all of whom joined a chorus of protests that eventually led to the song being removed from the album. The first-person fantasy—featuring a sawed-off shotgun, a "long-assed knife," and an intro that announces, "I'd like to take a pig out here in this parking lot and shoot 'em in their motherfucking face"—is plenty incendiary, but the music isn't nearly as imaginative.

16 OPERATION IVY, "OFFICER"

In 1987, a *Maximum RocknRoll* compilation introduced the first two songs ever recorded by the young Bay Area band Operation Ivy. Op Ivy went on to become a ska-punk legend—as well as a launching pad for the far more successful Rancid—and those early tracks still pack an uppercut. But "Officer" is more than just some punk-rock temper tantrum; besides screaming against the strong-arm excesses and psychological shortcomings of certain members of the law-enforcement community, singer Jesse Michaels ends the song on an up note: "Tough-guy asshole, do what you can / whatever you destroy, we'll create again."

17 KILLDOZER, "THE PIG WAS COOL"

Leave it to the crudely perverse band Killdozer to write a song about a relatively nice cop—even if "The Pig Was Cool" drips with sarcasm and menace. "Jammin' the Foghat on my eight-track / with a case of malt liquor and a bong in back," Michael Gerald growls through a mudslide of rotted distortion. "From out of nowhere came the man in blue / I thought we were busted, but the pig was cool." Turns out Gerald and the merciful officer went to school together—and later in the song, a different simpatico policeman even shares a joint with him. Cue the *Bad Lieutenant* montage.

18 **LEONARD BERNSTEIN AND STEPHEN SONDHEIM, "GEE, OFFICER KRUPKE"**

After being chewed out by Officer Krupke for wanton loitering, *West Side Story* street gang The Jets strikes back by singing an upbeat, scathing retaliation—*after* Krupke leaves. They blame society and their upbringing for turning them into juvenile delinquents, putting themselves on trial and mocking the cops' doltishness and the warped view the adult world must have of them. The Jets can point fingers all they want, but it's a safe bet that fewer of them and their enemies The Sharks would have died in a knife fight had Officer Krupke been around to intervene.

Guest List: PAUL THOMAS ANDERSON

2 MOVIES THAT WITHOUT FAIL OR QUESTION WILL MAKE ME STOP DEAD IN MY TRACKS AND WATCH THEM ALL THE WAY TO THE VERY END, NO MATTER WHAT ELSE IS HAPPENING OR NEEDS TO GET DONE

1. ***THE BIRDCAGE***
2. ***THE SHINING***

Paul Thomas Anderson is the director of five amazing films: Hard Eight, Boogie Nights, Magnolia, Punch-Drunk Love, *and* There Will Be Blood.

EITHER THAT WALLPAPER GOES OR I DO

10 MOVIE SCENES IN WHICH CHARACTERS DESTROY ROOMS

1 *CITIZEN KANE* *(1941)*
After C.F. Kane's wife Susan gathers up the gumption to leave him, the aging lord of Xanadu tries in vain to work the clasp on one of her suitcases, then throws it across the room. What follows is one of the strangest and most uncomfortable rampages on film, as Orson Welles lurches around pulling down draperies, upending furniture, and sweeping books off shelves, until he's brought up short by a snow globe and utters, once again, the cryptic word "Rosebud." The camera hovers near the floor, making Welles' bald head look like it's about to crash into one of the painted beams on the low ceiling. There's no music in the scene—just the stiff-jointed old man blundering about almost mechanically, swinging his arms like Frankenstein alarmed by the peasants' torches. Frankly, it's one of the masterpiece's low points; introduced by a jarring special-effects error (the transparent-eyed cockatoo), the scene never overcomes a feeling of forced significance and artificiality. But it leads into one of the most touching moments in the movie's final act, as Kane slowly walks down a hall past his silent army of servants, reflected endlessly in a series of giant mirrors.

2 *BEFORE THE DEVIL KNOWS YOU'RE DEAD* *(2007)*
In a performance that seems like a calculated homage to Kane, Philip Seymour Hoffman dispassionately destroys the scenery after Marisa Tomei hits the road. The muted carnage even begins the same way, with Hoffman pulling the sheets off the bed before moving on to knock over the bedside lamp, rip the phone out of the wall, shove all the toiletries off the vanity, and toss a potted orchid into the bathroom. Moving into the living room, Hoffman picks up a bowl of decorative rocks and slowly upends it over the glass-topped coffee table, creating a cascade of chipping and rattling that ends the slow, sad scene. As with the parallel scene in *Kane*, Hoffman seems more determined to destroy the evidence of his failure to keep Tomei satisfied than angry at the woman who didn't properly appreciate his attempts.

3 *THE CONVERSATION* *(1974)*
Francis Ford Coppola's slowly disintegrating thriller *The Conversation* is a lot like its protagonist, Harry Caul: melancholy, mysterious, emotionally close to the vest, and in the final scene, quietly unhinged. Caul (brilliantly played by Gene Hackman) spends most of the film wrestling with the moral and ethical quandaries posed by being a surveillance expert paid to spy on a young couple who appear to be in danger because of the information he's collecting. A man who can find a way to bug any conversation, Caul is predictably paranoid about being bugged himself, and after the fate of the young couple is decided, he has reason to believe that his apartment is under surveillance. So Caul methodically rips his place apart, carefully taking out every floorboard, gutting every pillow, and destroying every possession, to no avail. Even with a trashed apartment, Harry can't escape the invisible (and possibly nonexistent) eyes and ears tracking his every move.

4 *PUNCH-DRUNK LOVE* *(2002)*
Adam Sandler's violent *Punch-Drunk Love* character isn't necessarily that different from his usual roles. It's just that in Paul Thomas Anderson's difficult romantic comedy, Sandler's explosive outbursts aren't played for laughs; they're creepy manifestations of a troubled soul. One of the most unsettling scenes comes during his first date with quirky paramour Emily Watson, a co-worker friend of one of

his many sisters. When Watson shares an embarrassing story about Sandler that his sister told her, he excuses himself to the bathroom, which he rapidly dismantles in a blind fury, a reminder that violence is always just under the surface for this man, even as he's falling in love.

5 *PINK FLOYD: THE WALL* (1982)

Given that *The Wall* tracks a rock star through his emotional and mental disintegration, a big hotel-room-wrecking rockstar tantrum seems almost mandatory. Sure enough, it arrives midway through the film. As the song "One Of My Turns" begins, the eponymous fictional rocker, Pink Floyd (played by Bob Geldof) is all but comatose after learning that his wife has moved on to another, presumably less insane man. Pink shows a momentary interest in moving on himself by bringing an American groupie (Jenny Wright) back to his hotel room, but then he loses interest and zones out in front of the TV. When she gently attempts to arouse him, he goes berserk, smashing furniture, slamming breakables into each other, and eventually heaving the TV through a window onto the street below. Did Wright's ministrations stir him far enough back to reality that he could briefly express his anger at his wife? Or is he striking out at Wright, trying to drive her away like he's driven away everyone else who tries to care about him? Either way, he isn't likely to be welcome in that hotel again.

6 *SHORT CUTS* (1993)

There's a similar motive and even possibly a similar passion to Peter Gallagher's behavior in Robert Altman's loose Raymond Carver adaptation *Short Cuts*, but the execution is notably different. Perhaps Gallagher has accepted that his ex-wife isn't coming back; perhaps he's almost ready to move on. But first, he declares his feelings about the dissolution of their marriage by visiting their former home while she's away, and methodically, meaningfully breaking the furniture down to its component parts. It takes a full weekend and a chainsaw, but by the time he's done, even the sofa is just kindling and fluff. Which is a pity for the traveling vacuum-cleaner salesman who shows up to try to demonstrate his wares in the middle of the resultant mess.

7 *THE SEVENTH CONTINENT* (1989)

Few directors exert as much control over their viewers as Michael Haneke, whose tense, methodical dramas often hinge on a single moment when all the air gets sucked out of the room. Haneke fans refer to these moments in shorthand, such as "Majid's death" (*Caché*), "the subway" (*Code Unknown*), or "the remote control" (*Funny Games*). In his chilling feature *The Seventh Continent*, the shorthand is "the fish tank": After resolving to get rid of all earthly possessions and leave this mortal coil, a husband and wife, along with their young daughter, set about destroying their home. Every piece of furniture, every appliance, even all the cash liquidated from their account—nothing is spared. But the moment the father smashes his daughter's fish tank, the piercing horror and violence of their radical actions come rushing to the fore.

8 *FEAR AND LOATHING IN LAS VEGAS* (1998)

"There was evidence in this room of excessive consumption of almost every type of drug known to civilized man since 1544 AD. What kind of addict would need all these coconut husks and crushed honeydew rinds? These puddles of glazed ketchup on the bureau?" After his attorney Dr. Gonzo (Benicio Del Toro) advises him to sample a drug that "makes pure mescaline seem like ginger beer," Johnny Depp's Hunter S. Thompson character wakes to a hotel-room apocalypse: ketchup spattered on the wall like swaths of blood, a crater-sized burning hole in the bed, a smashed mirror, water from an overflowing, filth-filled hot tub at his feet, and Gonzo adding a fresh layer of vomit to the floor. Hunter is so stunned by the wreckage that he fails to notice the lizard tail growing out of his backside.

9 *DODGE CITY* (1939)

The swashbuckling classics that Errol Flynn and director Michael Curtiz made together tend to overshadow their Westerns, but for sheer entertainment, *Dodge City* can hold its own against movies like *Captain Blood* and *The Adventures Of Robin Hood*, even though Flynn wears boots instead of tights. But even without the stunning Technicolor and the sexual tension between Flynn and frequent co-star Olivia de Havilland, it would deserve some fame for the central scene in which a saloon fight starts small, then spirals out of control until there's almost no saloon left to fight in. It's a thrilling moment that Curtiz plays for laughs without overlooking how neatly it captures the thin divide between civilization and chaos on the American frontier.

10 *THE TALL GUY* (1989)
It isn't always hate that drives destruction. In the mostly amusing comedy *The Tall Guy*, Jeff Goldblum plays an American actor struggling to make a name for himself on the London stage. Nothing much goes his way. Even when he falls desperately in love with a nurse (Emma Thompson), her no-nonsense attitude seems to preclude hand-holding, much less sex. But when the two finally hook up, they make love with a frenzy that leaves Thompson's one-room flat a mess and the happy couple covered in stray bits of toast, shattered crockery, and dislodged picture frames.

AGING BADLY

9 STARS WHO FELL VICTIM TO HORRIBLE AGING MAKEUP

1 JAMES DEAN, *GIANT* (1956)
Adapting Edna Ferber's novel of passion and greed in Texas, director George Stevens kept his source's multi-generational scope, so each of its movie-star leads had to age several decades. While Rock Hudson and Elizabeth Taylor make the transition well—they have better makeup, and they tailor their performances to their characters' ages—James Dean's swept-back hair, unconvincing wrinkles, and sleazy mustache don't sit well with acting that's just youthful angst dressed up in middle-aged clothes.

2 WINONA RYDER, *EDWARD SCISSORHANDS* (1990)
Hollywood seemingly operates by a simple template when it comes to aging costumes: glasses + white hair + rubbery fake skin = old. Winona Ryder has all three in *Edward Scissorhands*, and she adds her best shaky old-lady voice for extra "authenticity." Ryder tells the film's story in flashback, but viewers don't see her age-ravaged-but-surprisingly-taut face until the film's final moments. She's got some wrinkles and a bit of a bend in her spine, but she still looks like a young actor playing dress-up.

3 ELIZABETH McGOVERN, *ONCE UPON A TIME IN AMERICA* (1984)
It isn't that Elizabeth McGovern has a bad makeup job in Sergio Leone's otherwise masterful *Once Upon A Time In America*. It's that she has *no* makeup job. As the twentysomething actress supposedly moves through nearly four decades of American gangster history, she doesn't appear to age a day. Co-stars Robert De Niro and James Woods don't age all that convincingly, either, but at least they get some receding hairlines and wrinkles. Leone didn't even run a streak of gray through McGovern's hair. She's every bit as fresh-faced as she was at the beginning, which is bound to confuse viewers who doze during the film's mammoth four-hour running time.

4 JOE PANTOLIANO, *EDDIE AND THE CRUISERS* (1983)
The 1983 cult favorite *Eddie And The Cruisers* skips back and forth in time between the early-'60s heyday of its mysterious rocker protago-

nist and the present-day attempts by foxy lady reporter Ellen Barkin and songwriter Tom Berenger to uncover the mystery beyond his disappearance. Berenger barely seems to age at all over the ensuing decades, but that's okay, since shifty manager Joe Pantoliano ages enough for both of them. His wispy gray hair is fussily arranged into a comb-over, while his wrinkly, distracting old-before-his-time makeup threatens to melt under the hot lights.

5 BILLY CRYSTAL, *MR. SATURDAY NIGHT (1992)*

There's no schmaltzier film in existence than Billy Crystal's self-serving, tear-stained reminiscence about an aging comedian who looks back on his glory days as king of the Borscht Belt zinger. It's told mainly in flashback, but the present-day scenes of Crystal slurping soup with his brother (David Paymer) or trying to revive his career with a new agent (Helen Hunt, squinting sympathetically) are made somehow cornier and heavier by a slathering of old-age makeup. The middle-aged Crystal didn't really need much to make him look older, but with his pallid visage, purple lips, and thin gray comb-over, he looks like he's a few embalming injections away from a funeral viewing.

6 ROBIN WILLIAMS, *BICENTENNIAL MAN (1999)*

What happens when a sentimental robot lives for more than 200 years? He has to say goodbye to his master, his master's wife, his master's children, and his master's children's children. And in *Bicentennial Man*, that means an endless procession of teary deathbed scenes in which various ancient, liver-spotted, latex-y incarnations of Sam Neill and Embeth Davidtz have to bid adieu to their faithful robot friend. (Chapter 20 on the DVD is titled "Yet Another Goodbye," as if in exasperation.) And then Robin Williams' robot, finally converted into a freedom-loving mortal, gets his own dire, rubbery makeup job and delivers a speech about how he'd rather "die a man than live for all eternity as a machine." Because only men could have such mighty jowls!

7 THE ENTIRE CAST, *BACK TO THE FUTURE II (1989)*

The hype over the colorful 2015 depicted in *Back To The Future's* sequel overshadowed the movie itself: Hoverboards! Flying cars! The Michael J. Fox of the future! Obviously, not everything cutting-edge from 1989 held up perfectly years later, but the problem with *Back To The Future II* was that too many gimmicks, tricks, and callbacks spoiled the proverbial stew. The aging makeup used to differentiate the characters in 1955 from 2015, 1985, and the alternative 1985 was rendered ineffective by a silly script and hammy acting, which made the cosmetics more of a novelty than actual effective costuming. Thus, Lea Thompson compromised her 80-year-old-woman makeup with her creeeaky old-lady voice, and Fox's middle-aged face looked merely rubbery, not old. Maybe part of the problem was that it was simply impossible to make Michael J. Fox old: As a middle-aged man, even with health problems, he still looks like an eternal high-schooler. (That may be why he looked most believable when playing his character's daughter, which only required a long red wig.)

8-9 JAVIER BARDEM AND GIOVANNA MEZZOGIORNO, *LOVE IN THE TIME OF CHOLERA (2007)*

In his novel *Love In The Time Of Cholera*, Gabriel García Márquez described seventysomething Fermina, the woman at the novel's center, as a woman "ravaged by age." In Mike Newell's sweeping big-screen adaptation, the elderly Fermina (as played by Giovanna Mezzogiorno) instead resembles someone ravaged by a high-school drama-club costume department. Put simply, Mezzogiorno looks less like a senior citizen awaiting her long-lost love than like a young woman in a gray wig, dressed in Bea Arthur's *Golden Girls* castoffs. Granted, it isn't easy to believably, gradually age young actors 50 years in the space of a two-hour movie, but that doesn't mean the filmmakers couldn't have *tried*. Javier Bardem's glasses-and-white-mustache 75-year-old-man costume at the end looks so artificial that it might as well have come with a rubber cigar.

SOON YOU'LL NEED A MAN

3 OLDIES SONGS FOR PEDOPHILES

1 NEIL DIAMOND, "GIRL, YOU'LL BE A WOMAN SOON"

Grunge-era second-stringer Urge Overkill put a knowing edge on its cover of "Girl, You'll Be A Woman Soon" for the *Pulp Fiction* soundtrack. But Neil Diamond's 1967 original seems to play it with a straight face. The singer-songwriter was 26 when the single climbed the charts, which is a little old to be pining for a girl who clearly hasn't reached the age of consent—or possibly puberty, depending on how you read it. "I'd die for you, girl / and all they can say is, 'He's not your kind,'" Diamond croons; later, he adds "I've been misunderstood for all of my life." A creepy uncle couldn't have said it better.

2 GARY PUCKETT & THE UNION GAP, "YOUNG GIRL"

Unlike Neil Diamond, '60s pop star Gary Puckett at least feels a bit of guilt about his pedophiliac impulses. His band's 1968 hit sparked controversy with its lyrics portraying an underaged girl with potent womanly charms. And the song just gets creepier with lines like "You're just a baby in disguise" and the chorus, where Puckett advises his underage paramour, "My love for you is way out of line / better run, girl." Hey, at least he's giving her a head start. The jury might go easy on him.

3 THE AMES BROTHERS, "THE NAUGHTY LADY OF SHADY LANE"

The Ames Brothers' gee-whiz wholesomeness catapulted them to the Top 10 throughout the '50s—the perfect example of the kind of whitebread vocal group rock 'n' roll sought to topple. But The Ames' first hit, 1950's "Rag Mop," proved they could be demented, and their 1954 song "The Naughty Lady Of Shady Lane" crossed the line into downright unsettling. A goofy, semi-novelty tune, "Naughty Lady" is the story of a young woman who moves to town and gets the entire populace panting with excitement. She's known for her "come-hither glances" and for never turning down "liquid refreshment." The Brothers explain: "Beneath the powder and fancy lace, there beats a heart sweet and pure / she just needs someone to change her, and she'll be nice as can be." Then comes the punchline: As the last line reveals, the naughty lady is "only 9 days old." Ha ha, but also... ewww.

ROLL THAT CLIP!

13 MOVIES WITH KEY SCENES FEATURING CHARACTERS WATCHING OTHER MOVIES

1 BRUCE WILLIS AND MADELEINE STOWE WATCH *VERTIGO* IN *12 MONKEYS* *(1996)*

In a brief respite from their attempts to ward off a grim, plague-filled future, Bruce Willis' half-crazed time traveler and psychiatrist Madeleine Stowe take in a revival of Alfred Hitchcock's *Vertigo*. In one scene, Kim Novak uses a cross-section of a redwood tree to point out the birth and death of someone whom she believes she was reincarnated from. That moment strikes a chord with Willis and Stowe, who are beginning to suspect that fate has them in its pincers, dooming them to repeat what's come before. Directing a rethinking of Chris Marker's "La Jetée," director Terry Gilliam offers a nod to his film's overarching themes and to the fact that sometimes movies repeat other movies in an attempt to get at truths bigger than a screen can contain.

2 HARVEY KEITEL WATCHES *THE SEARCHERS* IN *MEAN STREETS* *(1973)*

After low-level hoods Richard Romanus and David Proval trick a couple of kids from the suburbs into giving them money for illegal fireworks, Harvey Keitel decides they should blow the chump change at the movies. They take in a showing of John Ford's *The Searchers*, though the group is more entertained by the shouting going on between audience members than the film itself. It's a minor scene, but an unquestionably personal touch by director Martin Scorsese. *The Searchers* was an important touchstone for the "film-school generation" of 1970s Hollywood, particularly Scorsese, who referenced the same John Wayne Western in *Who's That Knocking On My Door*. A couple of years later, Scorsese directed Paul Schrader's *Searchers*-inspired screenplay for *Taxi Driver*, a film that captures a different sort of moviegoing experience.

3 ROBERT DE NIRO TAKES CYBILL SHEPHERD TO SEE *KÄRLEKENS SPRÅK* IN *TAXI DRIVER* *(1976)*

There's no reason at all you should ever have heard of *Kärlekens Språk* (*The Language Of Love*). The 1969 Swedish "white-coater," or sexploitation movie released under the guise of being an educational film, likely would have entirely disappeared from the moviegoing consciousness if it weren't the movie Robert De Niro's sociopathic hack Travis Bickle chooses as the venue for his first date with the beautiful Betsy (Cybill Shepherd). His belief that a tawdry piece of pornography is a good way to impress a girl establishes how pitifully clueless and detached Travis is, setting the stage for the deepening alienation that leads inexorably to *Taxi Driver's* bloody conclusion.

4 *NOSFERATU* MAKES AN OMINOUS APPEARANCE IN *KILLING ZOE* *(1994)*

So where does the eye go? To the foreground, where a topless Julie Delpy, playing a Parisian prostitute, goes to work on her American client? Or to the background, where F.W. Murnau's silent classic Nosferatu flickers ominously on the television? The choice is surprisingly difficult: Both are mesmerizing in their own way while suggesting opposite sensations—immediate pleasure and impending doom. It's the first sign that our hero (Eric Stoltz), a professional safecracker about to enter into a robbery scheme with some highly unstable and unprofessional cohorts, may be seduced into a bad situation. But under the spell cast by Delpy—and *Nosferatu*, for that matter—he's helpless to resist.

5-6 *WOODSTOCK* IN *THE OMEGA MAN* (1971) / *SHREK* IN *I AM LEGEND* (2007)

In Richard Matheson's short novel *I Am Legend*, vampires rise up and wipe out humanity, except for one ragged survivor who huddles behind garlic-covered walls by night and roams the streets with wooden stakes by day, slowly going mad in his isolation. Most of the film adaptations have thrown Matheson's details and storyline out the window, but the basic idea of the last man on earth has been tempting enough to keep filmmakers coming back to the book again and again. In *The Omega Man*, survivor Charlton Heston shows just how crazy solitude has made him: By night, he dresses up in velvet and lace to play chess against a bust of Caesar, and by day, he goes to a local movie theater to watch the film that was playing there when society broke down, 1970's *Woodstock*. The way he recites along with the film shows how many times he's seen it, but his giggly joy over the film is far more telling: If a conservative, gun-toting, macho-man nut-job like Heston can so thoroughly enjoy the lengthy documentary about a druggy hippie love-fest, he's clearly beyond desperate for any form of human contact. Similarly, when supposed last-man-on-Manhattan Will Smith meets other people in the later Matheson adaptation *I Am Legend*, he's shell-shocked, confused, and hostile. By way of explanation and apology, he eventually walks into a room where *Shrek* is playing on TV and robotically recites along with it, word for word, to show that he's spent so much time bored and lonely that he voluntarily watched *Shrek* multiple times. It's a clear sign that someone should have gotten him a rubber room before he did something dumb involving vampire-fighting.

7 E.T. WATCHES *THE QUIET MAN* IN *E.T.: THE EXTRA-TERRESTRIAL* (1982)

Like Scorsese, Steven Spielberg was a John Ford devotee, which he makes clear in a loving tribute during one of the most memorable scenes in *E.T.: The Extra-Terrestrial*. When Elliott goes to school and leaves E.T. alone for the first time, the alien—as unsupervised aliens are wont to do—gets drunk on cheap domestic beer while watching TV. Suddenly, Ford's *The Quiet Man* comes on, and E.T. is transfixed. So, it turns out, is Elliott, who through some interspecies psychic connection, can feel everything E.T. is feeling, including a buzz. As drunken Elliott tears apart his science class, freeing the frogs slated for dissection, E.T. watches the scene where John Wayne kisses Maureen O'Hara during a storm. And before he's sent off to the principal's office, Elliott recreates the scene with future *Playboy* Playmate and *Baywatch* cast member Erika Eleniak.

8 GREMLINS TAKE IN A LATE-NIGHT SCREENING OF *SNOW WHITE AND THE SEVEN DWARFS* IN *GREMLINS* (1984)

Set in a picturesque small town where the televisions are always tuned to classic movies—it was produced by Steven Spielberg, after all—the Joe Dante-directed horror-comedy *Gremlins* uses vintage film moments to comment on the action throughout. Clips from *It's A Wonderful Life* and *Invasion Of The Body Snatchers* acknowledge story parallels that none of the characters seem to notice, but the late-film sequence where a horde of evil gremlins files into a theater and fires up *Snow White And The Seven Dwarfs* really brings Dante's vision of childhood fantasies gone wrong full circle. The twisted little monsters seem to sense it, too. They're transfixed by what they see, and it briefly seems like Disney's vision of pint-sized innocence has rubbed off on them. Then the moment passes and the destruction resumes.

9 *PRETTY WOMAN* LAYS DOWN THE GROUND RULES FOR *ROMY AND MICHELE'S HIGH SCHOOL REUNION* (1997)

The opening scene of *Romy And Michele's High School Reunion* sums up the protagonists (Mira Sorvino and Lisa Kudrow) and their relationship simultaneously by observing them at home, watching a movie together. Specifically, *Pretty Woman*, which Kudrow says she never gets tired of mocking, even though they've watched it together, like, 36 times. They proceed to make fun of poor onscreen Julia Roberts as she's thrown out of a high-end boutique for being a skanky ho: "Aw, poor thing. Look, they won't let her shop," Sorvino sneers gleefully. One short pause later, they're both watching with sentimental relief as Roberts is finally permitted to shop. The massive gap between how they see themselves—as clever people looking down on lowbrow entertainment from a refined distance—and the way the audience sees through their pretenses continues through the film: They consistently believe they're sexier, smarter, and more successful than they really are. At the same time, their delusions are so harmless and positive that they're endearing—as endearing as Roberts' hurt, melancholy, shopping-denied expression.

10 *STRANGERS ON A TRAIN* INSPIRES DANNY DEVITO IN *THROW MOMMA FROM THE TRAIN* (1987)

There's no point in complaining that director-star Danny DeVito and screenwriter Stu Silver ripped off Alfred Hitchcock's classic 1951 thriller *Strangers On A Train*, because DeVito and Silver don't hide from it, they embrace it. Early in their 1987 comedy *Throw Momma From The Train*, DeVito's nebbish character goes to see *Strangers On A Train* and gets the bright idea to "swap" murders with his creative-writing instructor, Billy Crystal: DeVito will kill Crystal's shrewish, duplicitous ex-wife if Crystal will kill DeVito's overbearing mother. The story that follows is wildly different from the Hitchcock film (and the Patricia Highsmith novel it's based on), even though the premise is exactly the same. That's one way to silence nitpickers: Head 'em off at the pass.

11 YOUNG INVESTORS WORSHIP AT THE ALTAR OF *WALL STREET* IN *BOILER ROOM* (2000)

The "head 'em off" strategy is slightly different in *Boiler Room*, though it also directly acknowledges its primary influences. Set in the world of young, cocky, not-exactly-legit stock traders, *Boiler Room* owes clear debts to *Wall Street* and *Glengarry Glen Ross*—which is probably why writer-director Ben Younger has his characters quote both movies at every opportunity. At one point, they even sit around a bare luxury apartment and watch *Wall Street* together, reciting the "greed is good" speech with a mixture of irony and awe.

12 *THE SHINING* PLAYS AT A DRIVE-IN THEATER IN *TWISTER* (1996)

Though no one would mistake Jan de Bont's frenetic, weather-carnage-filled *Twister* for a Stanley Kubrick film, that didn't stop it from giving multiple nods to Kubrick. These range from the inconsequential—minor characters named "Stanley" (Ben Weber) and "Kubrick" (Nicolas Sadler)—to the overt: A drive-in theater screens *The Shining* (and, offscreen, *Psycho*) just before a tornado destroys the place. For a couple of seconds, the destructive parallels are literal: Just as a "finger of God" shreds the drive-in screen, a psychotic Jack Nicholson takes his axe to a door. But the film also juxtaposes two kinds of horror: the homicidal/paranormal variety in *The Shining*, and the sudden, inexplicable horror of nature. Still, don't give *Twister* too much credit—the scene owes just as much to good old-fashioned corporate synergy. *The Shining* was a Warner Bros. film, *Psycho* was owned by Universal, and *Twister* was reflecting the fact that it was a joint production between the two studios.

13 *HELLO, DOLLY!* EVOKES A CHARMING LOST PAST IN *WALL-E* (2008)

The quaint 1969 Barbra Streisand movie-musical *Hello, Dolly!* comes up several times in *Wall-E*: A battered old videotape copy is the titular robot's favorite possession, and he moons over certain scenes on a regular basis, observing this quaint human thing called "love." (Or at least this quaint human thing called "Dressing up in frilly clothes and dancing like lunatics.") Eventually he shows it to the robo-girl of his dreams, hoping she'll get the hint. Of course, taking a date back to your place to watch a notorious box-office flop on video is about as big a risk as *Wall-E* co-writer/director Andrew Stanton heavily centering the love story in his $180 million movie around that same notorious box-office flop.

I CAN THINK OF AT LEAST TWO THINGS WRONG WITH THAT TITLE

18 MOVIES WITH INAPPROPRIATE NAMES (BESIDES NAKED LUNCH*)

1 *Funny Ha Ha*
2 *Scary Movie*
3 *Last Action Hero*
4 *Reservoir Dogs*
5 *Everything You Always Wanted To Know About Sex But Were Afraid To Ask*
6 *Funny Games*
7 *The House Of Mirth*
8 *Happy Together*
9 *Isn't She Great*
10 *Men Don't Leave*
11 *Reindeer Games*
12 *True Romance*
13 *Happiness*
14 *Last Tango In Paris*
15 *The Truth About Cats & Dogs*
16 *Chopping Mall*
17 *Alice, Sweet Alice*
18 *The NeverEnding Story*

Chopping Mall *actually contains 0 percent chopping, and 100 percent laser-blasting robots. Though it does feature a mall.*

* WHY NO *NAKED LUNCH? THE SIMPSONS'* NELSON MUNTZ ALREADY POINTED OUT ITS INAPPROPRIATE TITLE IN THE EPISODE "BART ON THE ROAD."

Guest List: DANIEL HANDLER

10 SONG TITLES WITH ALTERED MEANINGS DUE TO PARENTHETICALS

1. **"I Wasn't Meant To Live My Life Alone (with Vince Gill)"**
2. **"Where Were You When They Crucified Our Lord (with the Carter Family)"**
3. **"As You Turn To Go (with Momus)"**
4. **"When I'm Out Of Town (with Chris Knox)"**
5. **"Pillow Fight (with Mitch Easter)"**
6. **"Under Pressure (with Queen)"**
7. **"Pleasure Of The Dance (with Ruts DC)"**
8. **"Waltzing Me All The Way Home (with Odetta)"**
9. **"I Like It (featuring Nate Dogg)"**
10. **"U Can't Touch This (Instrumental)"**

Daniel Handler is best known to the literary world as Lemony Snicket, author of the book series A Series Of Unfortunate Events. *He's also published books for grown-ups,* Adverbs *and* The Basic Eight, *under his own name and played accordion with The Magnetic Fields.*

STILL ROCK AND ROLL TO WHOM?

8 UNROCKING SONGS ABOUT ROCK MUSIC

1 STARSHIP, "WE BUILT THIS CITY"

In its former incarnation as Jefferson Airplane—or, to be generous, its interim identity as Jefferson Starship—Starship might have properly claimed that it built a city on rock 'n' roll: Jefferson Airplane was a significant part of San Francisco's mid-'60s redefinition of rock. But by the mid-'80s, after lineup shifts and name changes, the group's slick, commercial sound was as corporate as it comes. Released in 1985, the ubiquitous No. 1 hit "We Built This City" found the band leaning on some of the era's most ubiquitous songsmiths for hire, including Peter Wolf and Elton John lyricist Bernie Taupin. Taupin is probably to blame for lines like "Marconi plays the mamba, listen to the radio," but ultimately the band is responsible for the dissonance between its pro-rock message and its lifeless if-this-is-rock-let-it-die sound.

2 PETER, PAUL AND MARY, "I DIG ROCK 'N' ROLL MUSIC"

Peter, Paul And Mary gained fame by sucking the bile and irony out of Bob Dylan songs and turning them into pretty AM pop hits. As folkies, they were lightweights of questionable credibility. As rockers, they registered somewhere between The Turtles and Garry Lewis And The Playboys. So while a song as smug and condescending as "I Dig Rock 'N' Roll Music" would be annoying coming from anybody, it's even more grating coming from a group whose sense of superiority is completely unearned. "The message may not move me / or mean a great deal to me / but hey, it feels so groovy to say," the trio warbles. Somehow, they manage to harmonize even while holding their noses over this "rock" tune.

3 ELVIS PRESLEY, "RAISED ON ROCK"

By the '70s, kids who grew up on rock 'n' roll were getting nostalgic for the early days, as their hairlines receded and waists expanded to rock-prohibiting dimensions. None other than The King himself tapped into the trend with this 1973 single. Guitarist James Burton provides a truly rocking contribution, but Elvis sounds dispiritingly lifeless. Listen to it enough, and you can almost hear the genre disappearing into its own navel.

4 SHAUN CASSIDY, "THAT'S ROCK 'N' ROLL"

Is it, Shaun Cassidy? Is it *really*? Because while this power-pop anthem from The Raspberries' Eric Carmen has all the gilding of rock 'n' roll (a stomping backbeat, a riff nicked from Chuck Berry, a swingin' horn section), there's also the small matter of *you*. The fake-Elvis sneer that can't hide those pearly whites, the hair so feathered that it's like an ass-pillow for angels, the watertight satin pants—you're the dictionary definition of "prefabricated '70s teen idol." You're not fooling anyone when you claim "I played at parties, played at bars / I spent my money buyin' new guitars." More accurately, you had a famous older brother, you landed a record contract when *Partridge Family* fever started to wane, and Warner Bros. spent its money on a stable of songwriting ringers specializing in middling retro-'50s pastiche. If that's rock 'n' roll, sir, you can have it.

5 BAD COMPANY, "ROCK 'N' ROLL FANTASY"

"Here come the jesters, one two three / it's all part of my fantasy." And with those words, Bad Company sets up a "Rock 'N' Roll Fantasy"—an unrestrained vision of the ultimate rock-dream scenario. And the best it could come up with is three jesters? The band makes no mention of women, drugs, eight-necked guitars being played by some sort of mythical octopus rock-god—nothing. Which makes you wonder if it was the lamest band of all time, or just had no idea what a fantasy is. This "rock utopia" sounds like it came from a set decorator at Medieval Times. Oh, and the music sucks, too.

6 ASIA, "ROCK AND ROLL DREAM"

When it formed in 1981, the anthem-slinging outfit Asia actually had bona fide rock credentials in the form of Yes guitarist Steve Howe and ELP drummer Carl Palmer. But any goodwill earned by Asia's 1982 hit "Heat Of The Moment" was squandered by pretty much everything else the band ever did. A great example of its snowballing crappiness is "Rock And Roll Dream," from 1985's *Astra*. With Howe, Asia's coolest member, already gone, the soggy-synthed "Dream" sounds like a seven-minute tutorial in exactly how *not* to rock, which doesn't restrain singer-bassist John Wetton from unleashing a melodramatic, mythologized account of what it's like to ride in limousines and take the stage of stadiums. It comes complete with samples of roaring fans trying to drown out the guitar solo—or maybe that's just wishful thinking.

ULTIMATELY THE BAND IS RESPONSIBLE FOR THE DISSONANCE BETWEEN ITS PRO-ROCK MESSAGE AND ITS LIFELESS IF-THIS-IS-ROCK-LET-IT-DIE SOUND.

7 DAVID ESSEX (AND, LATER, MICHAEL DAMIAN), "ROCK ON"

One sad, lonely day in 1973, a marginally talented British actor/singer best known for his role in *Godspell* thought, "I wonder what would happen if I crammed together a bunch of lame clichés and overused pseudo-references into something called a song?" What happened was it became a monster hit, and millions of innocent people were forced to suffer through the horror that was "Rock On." Sixteen years later, an even less talented American actor/singer, best known for his role in *Joseph And The Amazing Technicolor Dreamcoat*, thought "I wonder what would happen if I took the exact same song, wrung every last bit of actual rock out of it, and dropped it, steaming and unashamed, at the doorstep of the American public?" A second generation of suffering innocents answered his question.

8 THE RIGHTEOUS BROTHERS, "ROCK AND ROLL HEAVEN"

By 1974, The Righteous Brothers hadn't had a serious hit since the 1966 single "(You're My) Soul And Inspiration." Their gorgeous blue-eyed-soul harmonies had been driven out of style by changes in the musical landscape. But they still had one trick up their sleeves: exploitative nostalgia. Songwriters J. Stevenson and Alan O'Day, who had a hit a few years later with the equally execrable "Undercover Angel," handed Bill Medley and Bobby Hatfield a song about dead rock stars. The chorus lays out a simple premise: "If there's a rock and roll heaven, you know they've got a hell of a band." The verses elaborate on that notion with a cheesy roll call of dead stars, asserting that "Jimi gave us rainbows" and "Janis took a piece of our hearts." Et cetera, ad nauseam. Not content to let the dead rest in peace, the Brothers' 1991 *Reunion* album added lines about Elvis ("...loved us tender"), John Lennon ("...cried 'give peace a chance'"), and others. There's a great place for this song, but rock 'n' roll heaven isn't it. Think somewhere warmer.

WHO WAS THAT MASKED BAND?

8 MUSICAL ACTS THAT KEEP THEIR FACES HIDDEN

1 THE RESIDENTS

The Residents have kept their identities secret for a remarkably long time, forming The Cryptic Corporation as a front for their songwriting, and more importantly, never appearing without masks. The band has employed a variety of disguises, but by far the most iconic are the giant eyeball-heads, often accompanied by natty tuxedos. Stranger still, such weirdness pales in comparison with the music the 40-year-old band produces.

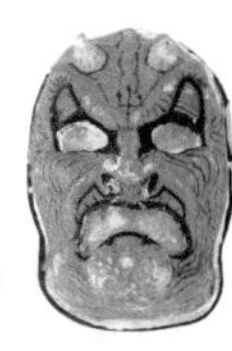

2 BUCKETHEAD

Avant-metal guitarist Buckethead has collaborated with everyone from Guns N' Roses to Viggo Mortensen to the composers of *Mighty Morphin' Power Rangers: The Movie*. His motives for never performing without wearing a mask and a KFC-bucket hat have to do with an elaborate character he's built, a man raised by chickens, and determined to alert the world to the "chicken apocalypse" taking place in fast-food joints. It might also have to do with the fact that the man behind the mask, Brian Carroll, is reportedly painfully shy.

3 BLOWFLY

Clarence Reid initially wore a mask for practical reasons—to protect his identity as a legit songwriter while performing insanely sexual parodies. As Blowfly, he writes new lyrics to popular songs, giving each a stupidly graphic edge. Over the years, he's rewritten everything from "What A Difference A Day Makes" ("What A Difference A Lay Makes") to "Should I Stay Or Should I Go?" ("Should I Fuck This Big Fat Ho?").

4 DAFT PUNK

Robot helmets are so hard-wired into Daft Punk mythology that it's surprising they don't just grow directly from the French dance-music duo's brains. The robot look suits an electronic sound given to hard mechanical grooves, and it never hurts to have an extra reflective agent in visual presentations that owe their luster to lasers and lights.

5 CLINIC

Clinic singer Ade Blackburn has said that his band's look—everyone wears surgical masks—is an homage to The Residents and a way to keep the focus away from any individual member. Over the years, the band has kept the masks but changed up the rest of the outfits, from Masonic garb to Hawaiian shirts. Meanwhile, the music—droning, sometimes terrific garage-inspired weirdness—has remained remarkably consistent from album to album.

6 MF DOOM

When Daniel Dumille, a.k.a. Zev Luv X of cult hip-hop group KMD (and creator of the "Gas Face"), was looking to radically reinvent himself in the late '90s, he looked no further than his outsized collection of *Fantastic Four* comic books, and recreated himself in homage to the supervillain Dr. Doom. (The identity is also a twist on his birth name, Dumille.) MF Doom doesn't often rap about villainous topics, but he's otherwise unusually committed to the character. He's never seen in public without his mask (a gothic number cribbed from Ridley Scott's *Gladiator*), he litters his albums with comic-book sound bites, and he sometimes records under the name Viktor Vaughan, a reference to Dr. Doom's birth name, Victor Von Doom. Doom is the rare rapper who appeals equally to hip-hop heads and comic-book super-nerds.

7 LOS STRAITJACKETS

What does blazing surf and rockabilly-inspired instrumental music have to do with Mexican wrestling masks? Nothing, really, but that doesn't stop the combination from working for Los Straitjackets, a bunch of Nashville aces who started bringing an elaborate, mask-heavy stage show to eager fans in the early '90s. Need a little holiday spirit? They also do a nice Christmas act, masks and all.

8 SLIPKNOT

A nine-member band whose members are named after the numbers zero through eight, perform in jumpsuits, and call their fans "maggots" (affectionately, of course) probably doesn't need any more gimmicks. Apparently the Des Moines nü-metal act Slipknot felt otherwise. Hence a parade of homemade masks that recast the band as pigs, clowns, and, um, a burlap sack sprouting dreadlocks. If only the music were half as creative.

HOMELAND INSECURITIES

8 HORROR FILMS THAT RESPONDED TO 9/11

1 *28 WEEKS LATER* (2007)

With George Romero leading the charge, zombie movies have always been the most pliant horror subgenre for smuggling political metaphor, because zombies—once human, now empty husks of mindless need—are only one stop removed from ourselves. In the ingenious sequel to *28 Days Later*, the "turbo zombies" from the original film represent a terrorist threat, but they're only half the problem. Just as dangerous are the government's attempts to thwart the zombie uprising through the sort of heavy-handed military operation that mucked things up in Iraq. After clearing a section of London, the authorities create a heavily fortified Green Zone. But once that space is infiltrated, out come the bombs and artillery fire, and there's no room for distinctions to be made between zombies and the innocents. Everyone dies.

2 *THE DEVIL'S REJECTS* (2005)

Rob Zombie's startling follow-up to *House Of 1000 Corpses* might seem like another grisly *Texas Chain Saw Massacre* knock-off, but the subtext lies close to the surface. Early on, the film introduces a vengeful cop (William Forsythe) who wants to take down the gleefully malicious "Rejects," a group of outlaws responsible for killing members of his family. But Zombie questions the proper response to those murders, and asks at what point the avenger loses his moral bearings. By the time the cop has the Rejects tied to chairs and is torturing them, the film's sympathies have shifted, and the cop's all-consuming desire for revenge has morphed from righteous to hideously, sadistically compromised.

3 *GEORGE ROMERO'S LAND OF THE DEAD* (2005)

"We don't negotiate with terrorists," Dennis Hopper says in the fourth of Romero's zombie movies, each of which attempted to capture the tenor of its time with pointed social commentary. A sweeping metaphor for the Iraq war, *Land Of The Dead* pitches the battle between the humans cloistered in a heavily guarded luxury high-rise and the teeming zombies at the gate as a war between the haves and the have-nots, and it extends its sympathies to the latter camp. As Hopper's elitist mogul sits in his high tower, chaos reigns on the streets below; Romero asserts that the War On Terror is, as much as anything else, about keeping the world safe for the wealthy at any cost. And with abundant visual references to current events like Abu Ghraib—right down to the point where humiliating pictures are taken of chained zombies—Romero hammers the point home.

4 *HOSTEL* (2005)

Since the Bush administration quickly drained the vast reserves of worldwide sympathy in the wake of 9/11, ordinary Americans have been greeted with a less-hospitable reception in other countries, particularly in Europe. Add to that the tradition of "Ugly Americans" overseas, and it's become a toxic situation: tourists puffed up with entitlement, hosts teeming with resentment. Like a horror riff on the comedy *EuroTrip*—which was originally titled *The Ugly Americans*—Eli Roth's *Hostel* follows a trio of debauched frat-guy types who travel to deepest Slovakia in search of good times and loose women. What they find is payback: an organization that lets people buy American tourists to torture and kill for sport.

5 *WAR OF THE WORLDS* (2005)

In reconceiving an H.G. Wells story that was previously staged as an Orson Welles broadcast and a 1953 science-fiction staple, director Steven Spielberg looked to 9/11 as an example of people responding en masse to a surprise attack on their home turf. Spielberg's images should be eerily familiar to viewers who watched on TV as the horrors of 9/11 unfolded: the dust-covered masses emerging from the scene, searching for a way home; the dozens of handmade "Missing" notices plastered to billboards and buildings; the spontaneous bonding of strangers who were personally affected by the attack. Given that Welles' version was in part a response to Hitler's rise to power, and the '53 version was fueled by Cold War hysteria, Spielberg had appropriate reasons to dust off an old classic.

6 *FUNNY GAMES* (2008)

The inevitable question greeting Michael Haneke's shot-for-shot English-language remake of his Austrian home-invasion thriller *Funny Games* is "Why?" Why shoot the same movie in the same way twice? Part of the reason is that Haneke always intended his scolding treatise on film violence to reach an American audience, because Hollywood is the main purveyor of the thoughtlessly violent entertainments that prompted his objections. The other, more pertinent reason is that the *Funny Games* reboot, by extension, becomes a movie about Americans complicit in torture. Haneke breaks the fourth wall by having the two young sadists who terrorize a middle-class family speak directly to the camera, suggesting that their "funny games" are being played out for our edification.

7 *THE HOST* (2006)

Bong Joon-ho's thrilling Korean horror-comedy is to the post-9/11 world what *Godzilla* was to the Atomic Age—a manifestation of America's toxic intervention overseas. In the opening scene, a U.S. officer running a lab forces an assistant to dispose of vast quantities of unwanted chemicals by pouring them down a convenient drain, even knowing that it pipes directly into Seoul's Han River. The environmental catastrophe that follows starts with a mutated tadpole that develops into a massive monster that stalks the river and surrounding area. When the Americans intervene a second time, the solution is nearly as bad as the problem: Their Agent Orange-like gas, "Agent Yellow," threatens to wipe out far more than a single amphibious adversary.

8 *CLOVERFIELD* (2008)

Lots of early 9/11 footage came from home video, as amateur videographers lucked into shots of the planes hitting the buildings, then captured on-the-ground reactions from all over the city. In the YouTube age, there are cameras everywhere, so it's fitting that if a monster swooped down on New York City and started knocking over buildings, the attack would be recorded from the shaky vantage point of palm-corders and cell-phone cameras. With props due to *The Blair Witch Project*, the smartly conceived *Cloverfield* adopts a pea-sized perspective on a large-scale catastrophe, underlining the terror of individuals in the face of something much larger than themselves.

THIS PREMISE GOES TO 11

9 MUSICAL ARTISTS WITH ELABORATE MYTHOLOGIES

1 DEVO

Devo has been through so many incarnations over the decades that it's easy to forget that Gerald Casale and Mark Mothersbaugh conceived it as a multimedia art project that included film, music, art, and performance. Partially inspired by the notorious shootings at Kent State, where they were both students at the time, Casale, Mothersbaugh, and their early bandmates developed the theory of "devolution," which stated that thanks to selfishness, dysfunction, and subservience to authority, humanity was actually moving back down the evolutionary ladder. Many of the characters who illustrated the devolutionary concept would appear in their later work: Jocko Homo, the stereotype of evolutionary regression; the mutated, simian Booji Boy and his father, the government operative General Boy; and the sinister Communist infiltrator known as the Chinaman. Many of the ideas were also incorporated in the Church Of The Sub-Genius, with which Mothersbaugh was involved for decades.

2-3 SUN RA AND GEORGE CLINTON

In addition to being two of modern music's biggest talents and farthest-out characters, Sun Ra and George Clinton are often linked as avatars of Afro-Futurism, a philosophy that explores the African-American tradition through space-age themes and science-fiction narratives. Sun Ra was born Herman Blount in Birmingham, Alabama, though he later declared he came from Saturn. His concerts, his early adoption of electronic synthesizers, and even his record label all expounded a network of beliefs that he referred to as "equations." On hundreds of major and minor releases, Ra led his Arkestra from hard swing to atonal synth-driven improv while wearing the funkiest Egypt-inspired space costumes this side of his follower, funk genius George Clinton. According to Clinton's cosmology, which he explored with key bands Parliament and Funkadelic, the funk has been trapped in the pyramids for 5,000 years. It's up to Dr. Funkenstein to awaken it and save the Earth—the "Unfunky UFO"—from the regressive ideology of Sir Nose, D'Void of Funk. Ra and Clinton didn't miss the struggle for civil rights during their head-trips to Egypt; their positivity reacted to the full gamut of the black experience in America. As Ra once put it: "The Impossible attracts me, because everything possible has been done and the world didn't change."

4 MAGMA

With the rise of the long-playing album came the long-playing concept album, a format made infamous by a series of successful UK progressive-rock bands that told outlandish stories over the course of one, two, or four album sides: Emerson Lake & Palmer's mechanized armadillo, Yes' riffs on Shastric scriptures, and Pink Floyd's giant-balloon-inspiring *The Wall*. The concept album became synonymous with indulgence and overreaching. Yet other artists have taken mythologies and premises to heights so impressive that they leave pretension behind. Take France's Magma. Its first albums tell the story of a small band of humans who leave a decaying Earth to start an enlightened, technologically progressive society on the far-off world of Kobaia. Trouble starts when another band of human refugees finds them and lures them back to Earth, starting a conflict that's told across a series of albums—and that's sung entirely in the made-up language of Kobaian. Magma is steeped in the work of composers like Carl Orff, while its spiritual reach pays debt to John Coltrane. The results eschew flash and indulgent solos for focused intensity, and it pursues an enlightenment that goes beyond a 30-foot inflatable pig.

5 GONG

Though born out of England's Canterbury scene—where founder Daevid Allen helped start the legendary Soft Machine—Gong made its seminal records from a commune in the woods of France. And while its work is full of humorous names and whimsical fantasy—from the Pot Head Pixies and the Octave Doctors to Allen's own reedy, gnomish voice—it includes a sustained philosophy. The Radio Gnome Trilogy was told over the course of three albums, from 1973's *Flying Teapot* to 1974's *You*, and revisited in some later works. Born from a vision Allen had on an Easter full moon in 1966, it tells the story of Zero The Hero, who starts picking up radio transmissions from the planet Gong. He's called on to bring about a new era of enlightenment by organizing a feast on the Isle of Everywhere, at which the Switch Doctor will open mankind's third eyes. Zero pulls off the festival, but at the key moment, he's distracted by "earthly pleasures"—

specifically, a fruitcake—and he misses his shot at enlightenment. In its way, the story is a tragedy, with Zero its sacrificial fool. After all, what's the point of tuning in and dropping out if you never get to turn on?

6 SUBTLE

In the early '00s, avant-rapper Doseone (a.k.a. Adam Drucker) started bringing characters and symbols into his work like images slipping into a dream. With the formation of his mid-'00s ensemble Subtle, he wove them into the story of a middle-class rapper who struggles with commercial pressure, society's apathy, and fears and anxieties embodied by such nightmarish characters as Dr. MoonOrGun and the Long Vein Of The Law. The protagonist, Hour Hero Yes, loosely follows Doseone's life and artistic ambitions. Dose has always been conflicted about his career plan: He's ambitious enough to sign a major-label contract, but stubborn enough not to compromise his dense, highly personal poetry, which has drawn a devoted cult audience but doesn't lend itself to quick hits. Can a true artist hide behind a simple pop face to make accessible music? And more importantly, if an artist creates such a remarkable, personal, engrossing body of work, how could the whole world not want to tune in?

7 COHEED AND CAMBRIA

Heavy metal, among all the rock genres, has always seemed particularly vulnerable to infection by crazy cosmologies. Even so, New York prog-metal superstars Coheed And Cambria take the idea to particularly ridiculous extremes. Each of Coheed And Cambria's four studio albums furthers the "Amory Wars" saga, an impenetrable science-fiction epic told through Claudio Sanchez's lyrics. Based around the adventures of a space messiah named Claudio (ahem), the son of two royals named Coheed and Cambria, the saga is also told in at least one side project, a series of monthly comics. Now that's sticking to a theme.

8 THE RESIDENTS

Starting in 1981, the masked electronic noisemakers known as The Residents launched their most elaborate project to date: a proposed trilogy, beginning with *Mark Of The Mole*, telling the deeply mythological story of a conflict between the subterranean Mole People, a group of savage Calvinists, and the above-ground Chubs, distant cousins of the Moles who grew fat and decadent off their own junk culture. The follow-up was the terrific *The Tunes Of Two Cities*, which contrasted the harsh, atonal work-songs of the Moles with the vapid, burbling lounge music of the Chubs. After that, it gets a bit puzzling: Following the provocative "Mole Show" live tour, a rift developed within the band about whether to continue the trilogy, and there was never a third installment. There was, however, a fourth: *The Big Bubble*, released in 1985, was meant to be followed by a fifth and sixth part that never materialized. Confusing? Sure. But no more so than anything else about one of the most mysterious bands in rock history.

9 THE MOUNTAIN GOATS

Even sensitive, emotionally honest poet-philosopher types like Mountain Goats' John Darnielle aren't entirely immune to the appeal of a good sprawling mythology. First appearing on the 1995 *Zopilote Machine* album, the "Alpha Series" tells the story of an alcoholic Florida couple (never named) who were once very much in love, but now seem to stay together only in the hopes that one of them will see the other die. Unlike most such concepts, the Alpha series wasn't initially concentrated on one record; it was spread out over nearly two dozen songs (almost all of which contain the word "Alpha" in the title) until 2002's *Tallahassee*. The pinnacle and culmination of the bittersweet story of the Alpha couple, *Tallahassee* features songs portraying them at their most loving, their most bitter, and memorably—on the darkly hilarious "No Children"—both. It ends fittingly, with the Alpha male asking his wife to sing along with him as they contemplate dying together in their burning house.

MOVIES FOR EARS

11 SOUNDTRACK ALBUMS BETTER THAN THE FILMS

1 ***PURPLE RAIN** (1984)*
The year was 1984, and we hadn't yet realized exactly how bad Prince was at making movies. (We'd know two years later, thanks to *Under The Cherry Moon*.) But *Purple Rain* gave us plenty of hints: Director Albert Magnoli did nothing to make the semi-autobiographical story of one of the most electrifying performers of the last 40 years worth watching, and Prince himself is as bad at acting as he is good at singing and playing guitar. Only professional flash in the pan Apollonia saves him from being the worst actor in the movie. But oh, the music! *Purple Rain* the album is a masterpiece, every bit as great as its reputation, and the breathtaking performances are almost enough to convince viewers that they're watching a good movie. Prince absolutely kills on tracks like "Let's Go Crazy," "When Doves Cry," and "Take Me With U." Amazingly, he isn't even the film's best performer. That title belongs to The Time's astounding Morris Day, who steals the show whenever he's onscreen.

2 ***JUDGMENT NIGHT** (1993)*
In 1993, "rap-rock" hadn't yet become the played-out province of the Limp Bizkits of the world, and a "mash-up" was something old people and babies ate. In spite of proven hits like Aerosmith/Run-DMC's "Walk This Way" and Anthrax/Public Enemy's "Bring The Noise," collaborations between hip-hop acts and alternative-rock or metal groups were still a novelty until *Judgment Night's* ambitious soundtrack kicked open the door. Granted, pairings that seemed inspired on paper didn't always pan out in the studio, and some collaborations (Teenage Fanclub and De La Soul's trippy run through "Fallin'"; Sonic Youth and Cypress Hill's hazed-out "I Love You Mary Jane") fared far better than others (Biohazard and Onyx's barking title track; Helmet and House Of Pain's embarrassingly overwrought "Just Another Victim"). And the world should band together to make sure certain unholy alliances (Slayer and Ice-T; Mudhoney and Sir Mix-A-Lot; Cypress Hill and Pearl Jam) never happen again. Yet even when *Judgment Night's* soundtrack fails, it fails spectacularly, making for a wildly entertaining ride. Unfortunately, the same can't be said for the film, a formulaic guns-and-gangs actioner that doesn't

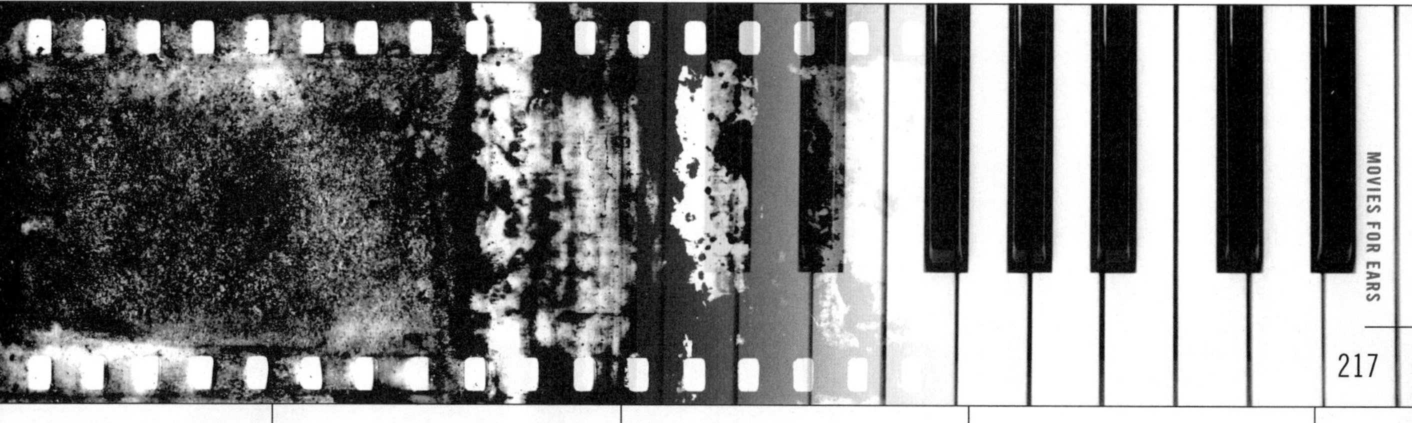

even try to match its soundtrack's innovation.

3 *XANADU* *(1980)*

How good is Electric Light Orchestra? So good that its music almost single-handedly rescued *Xanadu* from being a forgettable flop, and landed it in the cult canon of terrible movies that are fun to watch. The ridiculous plot follows a roller-skating Greek goddess who comes to life to help Gene Kelly and a struggling artist start a roller disco, and even the dance numbers are outlandishly corny, but at least the choreographers had ample ammunition: The shimmering sounds and hustling beats of "Xanadu" or "All Over the World" deserve better than the painfully dumb film that accompanies them. Audiences seemed to recognize this; the movie barely broke even at the box office, but the soundtrack went double-platinum and scored six Top 20 singles, including tunes by Olivia Newton-John and Cliff Richard. As a side note, *Xanadu* enjoyed a rare happy transition to Broadway, as the producers kept the great songs and transformed the hacky plot into something knowingly campy and winking.

4 *ONE FROM THE HEART* *(1982)*

It was supposed to be the other way around. Francis Ford Coppola sank everything he had into his innovative American Zoetrope studio, and tried to invent an entirely new method of filmmaking, combining the traditional stagecraft of a giant Las Vegas set with the high-tech wizardry of sophisticated electronics, remote cameras, and untested editing equipment. Unfortunately, Coppola put all this gadgetry and innovation at the service of a bland, un-involving romance between Frederic Forrest and Teri Garr. Audiences didn't know about the backstage wizardry and didn't care about the onscreen characters, and the movie took such a bath that Coppola spent the better part of 15 years making commercial movies just to make good on the massive debts he'd incurred. The upside is that he hired just the right people to do the film's sad, beautiful soundtrack: Postmodern cabaret singer Tom Waits and underrated country singer Crystal Gale crafted a fantastic album full of songs that deliver on the sometimes sour, sometimes transcendent romance that the movie promised.

5-6 *UNTIL THE END OF THE WORLD* *(1991)* AND ***THE END OF VIOLENCE*** *(1997)*

German director Wim Wenders made some striking movies in the '70s and '80s. Then he just kept making movies. Fortunately, by then he'd cultivated a lot of friends in the music world, so at least his soundtracks found an audience. Set in the far-off year of 1999, *Until The End Of The World* involves a device that allows viewers to watch their own dreams, and… beyond that, we're really not sure. Wenders insists that his longer director's cut is much better than the two and a half hours that saw release; if his version ever sees the light of day, we'll check it out. Meanwhile, we'll stick with the soundtrack that features a (briefly) reunited Talking Heads, Lou Reed, Elvis Costello doing The Kinks, and one of Nick Cave's best songs. Wenders' 1997 film *The End Of Violence* had a marginally more comprehensible plot and an almost-as-good soundtrack featuring U2, Tom Waits, Whiskeytown, Eels, and score excerpts from Ry Cooder. Why bother with all those pesky images?

7 *NICK & NORAH'S INFINITE PLAYLIST* *(2008)*

An alternate title for this Peter Sollett film could be *Indie Rock: The Movie*, as it's wall-to-wall hip bands, with a predictable love story underneath the buzzworthy songs. In the film, stars Michael Cera and Kat Dennings spend a night in New York going from one live-music venue to the next, listening to music, talking about music, and even getting it on in the legendary Electric Lady Studios. The *Nick & Norah* soundtrack follows suit, with appearances by Devendra Banhart, Vampire Weekend, Bishop Allen, Takka Takka, We Are Scientists, Band Of Horses, Shout Out Louds, and others. Even "Nick & Norah's Theme," the final track, is by a ringer: Mark Mothersbaugh of Devo.

8 *THE CROW* *(1994)*

As a film, *The Crow* was a decent-enough comic-book adaptation that benefited critically and financially from a real-life tragedy: The on-set death of actor Brandon Lee added a certain cachet and demanded some reverence, so only a few brave souls dared nitpick its superficial plot and one-dimensional characters. Regardless, the film's gothic, nihilistic pall endeared it to a whole generation of angsty teens, in part thanks to a soundtrack that served as a primer on mid-'90s alternative music. Like the film's victim-turned-vigilante, it volleys in mood from self-pity to anger to crying-in-the-rain wistfulness, with contributions from seemingly disparate groups like Helmet, Medicine, Rage Against The Machine, For Love Not Lisa, Pantera, and Violent Femmes. And yet somehow, it hangs together, thanks to its common dark thread. Of the originals, The Cure's wailing "Burn" (the last gasp of the band's *Wish*-era heyday), The Jesus And Mary Chain's thundering "Snakedriver," and Stone Temple Pilots' soon-to-be-signature hit "Big Empty" are all indispensable, but even the covers of stark post-punk songs of yore succeed (Nine Inch Nails' reverential take on Joy Division's "Dead Souls"; Rollins Band's meathead version of Suicide's "Ghost Rider"). Even better, they offer suggested further reading for fans looking to expand their "miserable music" repertoire.

9 ***SIESTA*** *(1987)*

Mary Lambert's *Siesta* is, frankly, a mess. Crammed full of Eurotrashy surrealism, its incomprehensible plot alternately shambles around and dashes past viewers at top speed, in hopes that they'll miss how many bits of it are falling off. Lambert was one of the first directors to nail a feature-film gig on the strength of her work in music videos, and it does that career arc no credit that *Siesta* wastes a terrific cast (including Gabriel Byrne, Julian Sands, Isabella Rossellini, and Jodie Foster) on this flashy but totally pointless disaster. It has something to do with Ellen Barkin, an heiress/stuntwoman, passing out in Spain. And, uh, maybe she killed someone, and she's being stalked by a midget and a scary cab driver, and... Well, leave it at this: The movie is so bad that not even Foster and Barkin making out can save it. What does make it worthwhile is Miles Davis' stunning soundtrack. One of the jazz master's finest late-period works, it features his successful collaboration with producer Marcus Miller on warm, loose, inviting songs suggestive of Davis' legendary *Sketches Of Spain* album.

10 ***TOYS*** *(1992)*

The forced-mirth fantasy *Toys* is a sloppy embarrassment even for a director as inconsistent and oft-hacky as Barry Levinson; it veers around tonally and struggles to cram childish whimsy into grown-up packages, with Robin Williams (the king of forced, grown-up childish whimsy) leading the charge. The soundtrack collects songs that are similarly all over the place, with Enya's dreamy "Ebudae" bumping up against Frankie Goes To Hollywood's rattling instrumental mix of "Welcome To The Pleasuredome." But where the actors and the script are trying too hard, and the eye-popping (and Oscar-nominated) art direction and costumes tend to overwhelm the film's too-artificial stabs at humanity and humor, the soundtrack adds up to an interesting, sweet, sparky package on its own merits. It even has a purer, less cramped sense of wonder than the film (expressed via Grace Jones' stately ballad "Let Joy & Innocence Prevail" and the sweet theme song "The Closing Of The Year"), and a better sense of humor, typified by Thomas Dolby's "The Mirror Song" and Tori Amos' pointedly perky "The Happy Worker."

11 ***THE WACKNESS*** *(2008)*

Jonathan Levine's 1994 period piece *The Wackness* starts off breezy and funny, with a dopey, mildly depressed NYC high-school senior (Josh Peck) getting advice from his eccentric shrink (Ben Kingsley) in exchange for weed. Soon, Peck is riding the subway, thinking aloud about the mysteries of life (read: girls), and the train is taken over by dancing Fly Girls, all part of an *In Living Color* fantasy that was probably far too common among male teens in 1994. From there, however, the movie shifts from original coming-of-age story to maudlin, trite coming-of-age story. Levine ramrods in a lot of awkward '90s slang as Peck's dopiness devolves into an irritating slowness, as if he's acting inside a vat of quick-dry cement. But the soundtrack never suffers such a sharp turn. With tracks from Notorious B.I.G., KRS-One, Nas, Craig Mack, and R. Kelly, plus "Summertime," the last Will Smith song that doesn't make listeners instinctively cringe, the music is far more evocative of the early '90s than the movie itself. To put it in Levine's clumsy '90s slang, the soundtrack is the dopeness, while *The Wackness* as a whole lives up to its title.

THE PARTY'S OVER, GO HOME

15 PIECES OF MUSIC SURE TO CLEAR A ROOM

1 STEVE REICH, "COME OUT"
Just because a piece of music is groundbreaking and important doesn't keep it from emptying a room faster than a fire alarm. Case in point: "Come Out," an early piece of "process music" by avant-garde composer Steve Reich. The whirling, disorienting effect caused by its piling on of one out-of-phase sample after another can be hypnotic—even beautiful, if you're in the right mood. But at 2 a.m., people full of Keystone Light rarely have the patience for 13 minutes of someone saying "come out to show them" over and over. And over and over. And over and over.

2 KEIJI HAINO, *EXECRATION THAT ACCEPT TO ACKNOWLEDGE*
Japanese experimental guitarist Keiji Haino has made a career out of finding that tiny corner where free jazz, noise-rock, and doom metal meet, then throwing firecrackers into it. It's hard to find, but this 40-minute-plus, single-track live album is a sure bet to alienate listeners as Haino, his amps turned up to 100 or so, throttles the neck of his custom Stratocaster with the strings as he bellows and moans like someone shot him in the stomach on the way to the studio.

3 MERZBOW, *TAUROMACHINE*
What is it about the Japanese? As with electronics, vending machines, and kitten-related merchandise, their aptitude with brutal, punishing noise music puts America's to shame. Merzbow (the *nom de bruit* of Masami Akita) records the kind of horrible, unlistenable aural assaults that make Lou Reed's *Metal Machine Music* sound like the work of a petulant teenager trying to annoy his parents. If some of the choicer tracks on this 1998 album, like "Soft Water Rhinoceros" or the painful "Minotaurus," don't clear the dance floor, nothing short of a SWAT team will.

4 RHODA WITH THE SPECIAL A.K.A., "THE BOILER"
Released by the 2 Tone label as part of the late-'70s/early-'80s ska revival, this single finds the lead singer of The Bodysnatchers teaming up with members of The Specials for a harrowing/jaunty tale of date rape. Rhoda plays the part of a woman usually "left on the shelf" who's thrilled to catch an attractive guy's attention. The good mood sours as the encounter turns violent and the song ends with Rhoda in tears and screaming as she recalls the rape. Remarkably, this was released as a single, complete with a cartoon sleeve that did nothing to suggest the contents.

5 ORTHRELM, *OV*
Aside from Mick Barr and Josh Blair's inhuman prowess, nothing about their extreme technical-death-metal outfit Orthrelm makes them especially more heinous than similar bands. What makes the *OV* album special is its formal structure. It's a single song, more than 45 minutes long, with no bass or vocals, and a crushingly repetitive riff that doesn't break for more than 20 minutes. Not entirely unlike Philip Glass if his métier was speed metal, *OV* will try the patience of even the most dedicated metal fanatic; it's really something to survive, not something to listen to.

6 JANDEK, *PUT MY DREAM ON THIS PLANET*
It's easy to argue that any release by the cryptic, seldom-seen singer-songwriter from Corwood is a party-ender. But for some reason, starting in 2000, Jandek decided to dispense with music entirely, and put out a handful of albums featuring nothing but him

muttering his creepy, incomprehensible lyrics to anyone who will listen. (As with most other Jandek releases, the microphone is either 10 feet away or right next to his face.) *Put My Dream On This Planet* is the next-best thing to a live appearance by a raving, homeless derelict.

7 HAPPY FLOWERS, "MOM, I GAVE THE CAT SOME ACID"

Happy Flowers' output has been so consistent that choosing just one song for this list is difficult. So why not go to the beginning? A duo consisting of a vocalist named "Mr. Hideously Charred Infant" and a guitarist named "Mr. Anus," the Flowers burst onto the Virginia punk scene in the '80s with this shouty song in which a child apologizes for giving the cat some acid. Repeatedly. And loudly. Other violent tales of childhood—"They Cleaned Out My Cut With A Wire Brush," "If This Were A Real Gun (I Could Shoot You And Sleep In The Big Bed With Mom)," "If It Was Broken, You'd Be Screaming"—followed. All of them are equally good at room-clearing.

8 ABRUPTUM, *EVIL GENIUS*

Black-metal founding father Euronymous called Abruptum "the audial essence of pure black evil." Who can argue with that? Featuring dark, almost ambient blasts and hums, occasionally shattered by searing guitar noise and the horrible wounded shrieking (in Latin!) of lead singer It, *Evil Genius* sounds like a recording of a blind, badly injured man

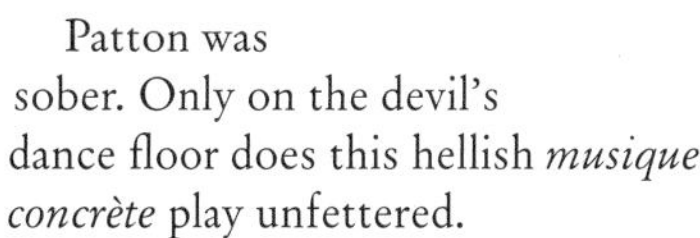

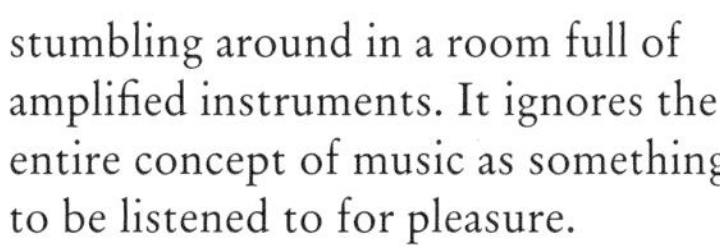

stumbling around in a room full of amplified instruments. It ignores the entire concept of music as something to be listened to for pleasure.

9 MIKE PATTON, "PORNO HOLOCAUST"

While the rest of Faith No More was out sampling the wares and women of various nations on the band's '95 world tour, front-freak Mike Patton stayed in, sampling his own elastic voice for hours on end. The result was an album of intricately edited pileups of guttural disturbance that crest in "Porno Holocaust" with what sounds like Popeye gagging on his own fist. If Prefuse 73's Scott Herren completely lost his shit on mescaline and woke up wearing nothing but a TASCAM 4-Track duct-taped to his chest, he might whip up something half as raw and brainsick as this. Of course, Patton was sober. Only on the devil's dance floor does this hellish *musique concrète* play unfettered.

10 BROTHA LYNCH HUNG, "SICC MADE"

Even horrorcore has its heroes, and Brotha Lynch Hung, "that cannibalistic nigga with the 9-millimeter," is a legend in his field. Never has a self-made rapper-producer matched a bit of the old ultra-violence to surging, beat-damaged soundscapes with such ability and aplomb, which makes this song a floor-clearer in a class of its own. Thick, vintage G-funk lulls listeners into 40-swinging gangsta jamdom, but when a pitch-shifted voice comes in to define "the siccness" (hint: it involves an Oedipal threesome with an infant!), any revelry should instantly turn into retching. If that doesn't do it, the line about eating "pussy meat" prepared in a pan "full of nuts and guts and intestines and shit" should be a clincher.

11 NEGATIVLAND, "QUIET PLEASE"

Generally speaking, there are two types of folks in this world: the ones who find culture-jamming collage artists Negativland amusing, and the ones who hate those people. When it comes to raising the ire of the latter group, it's tough to beat the band's 1987 SST debut, *Escape From Noise*, which announces its intentions to annoy (but in a clever, self-aware way!) with this track resembling a sped-up Jan Hammer theme—all shuffling disco beats and blaring synth-horns—overlaid with endless samples of pratfalls and spills culled from Hanna-Barbera cartoons. Acting as a snarky surrogate for the audience, a voice exclaims, "I can't hear a thing! Quiet please!" while another answers archly, "Is there any escape from noise?" Not for the next two minutes and 15 seconds.

12 TERRY RILEY, "YOU'RE NO GOOD"

When a Philadelphia club owner commissioned avant-garde composer Terry Riley to create a theme for his disco, Riley obliged with this 20-minute opus using "You're No Good," a soulful dis track by obscure R&B artist Harvey Averne. Opening with several minutes of droning Moog that slowly rises to a teeth-grinding fever pitch, Riley first lulls the audience into a sense of relief by letting the catchy, funky song spin through once unsullied before he starts toying with it, looping lines here and there, toggling the channels, and feeding bits and pieces through delays. At first, it's as hypnotically fascinating as any of his more "traditional" minimalist works, but as those various echoed bits start to unravel, Riley introduces more and more signal noise until the song finally disintegrates into a gibbering mess. It's as close as anybody's come to the sound of losing one's mind.

13 REDNEX, "COTTON EYE JOE"

How could the traditional folk song "Cotton-Eyed Joe"—that insidiously catchy staple of barnburners and hoedowns—possibly become more annoying? Swedish novelty act Rednex found out by layering it with cheesy synths and oontz-oontz beats, as part of an evil plan to fuse banjo-pluckin', fiddle-sawin' country with Eurodance, thereby creating the world's most instantly regrettable form of music. By grafting the song's already gratingly repetitive square-dance patter onto thumping rave rhythms, and turning the verses over to a girl whose larynx is located somewhere in her nostrils, the group created a surprise hit with the power to bring nations together… in agreement that it sucks.

14 CHUCK BERRY, "MY DING-A-LING"

Which is the worst thing about Chuck Berry's cutesy novelty hit? The way the agonizingly simple, lurching tune sticks in the brain? The herky-jerky shout-along choruses and pandering Berry performance on the best-known recorded version, the 1972 live cut recorded at the Lanchester Arts Festival? The smirking innuendo of the verses, which invite listeners to picture Berry clinging to and playing with his "ding-a-ling"? The fact that it was Berry's only American No. 1 single, effectively eclipsing his many better songs? How about all the above? Maybe the worst part is the risk that it'll send half of any given group of unwanted party guests screaming into the night, but get the other half enthusiastically singing along.

15 YOKO ONO, "DON'T WORRY, KYOKO (MUMMY'S ONLY LOOKING FOR HER HAND IN THE SNOW)"

Before popping up on her 1971 solo album, *Fly*, Yoko Ono's "Don't Worry Kyoko" was released as the B-side of The Plastic Ono Band's 1969 single "Cold Turkey"—infamously recorded in the aftermath of Ono's and John Lennon's heroin withdrawals. Accordingly, the song is a narcotic nightmare: From Ono's opening notes, which sound like either a constipated goat or a throat-singer being strangled, "Don't Worry" has the opposite of its intended effect. While a nauseating guitar riff churns beneath her, Ono tries to calm the listener—presumably Kyoko Cox, her daughter from her tumultuous first marriage, who was 6 at the time of the song's release—with a series of nerve-scraping squawks that occasionally coalesce into the phrase "Don't worry." The song won't just clear a room, it'll clear your sinuses.

OH, I GET IT NOW

6 MOVIES THAT MAKE A LOT MORE SENSE IF YOU'VE READ THE BOOK

1 *THE MAN WHO FELL TO EARTH* (1976)

Nicolas Roeg's *The Man Who Fell To Earth* and Walter Tevis' 1963 novel of the same name reach a common destination by different routes. Tevis crafted the story of an alien who arrives on Earth with a plan to save his drought-stricken planet by using advanced technology to insinuate himself into a position of power. Then he gets sidetracked by Earthly distractions. Though filled with science-fiction details, it ultimately reveals itself as a parable about the burdens of genius, the way time erodes youthful promise (shades of Tevis' *The Hustler*), and the trap of alcoholism. Roeg's film, on the other hand, explains just enough of what's going on to let viewers piece the story together. It would be elliptical to a fault, but Roeg's striking imagery and David Bowie's wasted appearance as the eponymous alien tell the same story almost subliminally, opening with otherworldly wonder and futuristic promise, and closing in some nowhere bar where lost souls try to forget that yesterday happened and tomorrow is on its way.

2 *TRISTRAM SHANDY: A COCK AND BULL STORY* (2006)

Anyone who hasn't read Laurence Sterne's brilliant *The Life And Opinions Of Tristram Shandy, Gentleman* is likely to get really confused really quickly when confronted with Michael Winterbottom's loose quasi-adaptation. It features a nearly impenetrable interweaving of story and meta-story, film and meta-film-within-a-film, actor-as-actor, and actor-as-character. Steve Coogan plays Steve Coogan and Tristram Shandy, and both of their stories seem needlessly complicated; the film itself never seems to get going. Anyone who's read the book knows that's the entire point, though. *Tristram Shandy*

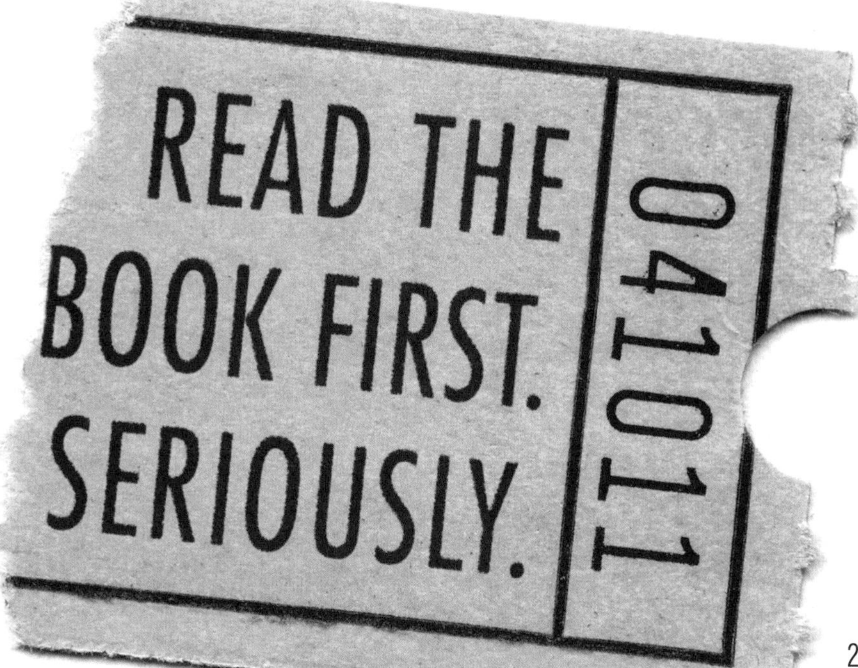

was a postmodern masterpiece before there was even modernism; it's all about distractions, complications, and confusions. Reading the book, and discovering that much of its abundant humor comes from its deliberate inability to get anywhere, makes the movie's shaggy-dog format much more effective.

3 *DUNE* (1984)

David Lynch doesn't normally do anything conventionally, but his adaptation of Frank Herbert's science-fiction classic *Dune* came close, by unfortunately incorporating all the conventional problems of a book-to-film adaptation. Herbert's *Dune* is a dense yet sprawling book, packed with warring factions and interests, each with their own history, methodology, and cause-driven scions. Lynch attempted to get across some of that complexity with extensive opening narration that laid out the key planets and players, but he still misses out on much of the depth, and his convoluted, weird, culty film wound up full of characters with unclear motivations, using unexplained powers to confusing ends, and trying to explain it all with stilted internal monologues. Reading the book fills in the extensive backstory, makes all of the political maneuvering much clearer, and turns several blustering ciphers into nuanced characters. But it also tends to engender a lot of frustration with Lynch's radical departures from the story, particularly in the film's goofy ending.

READING THE BOOK FILLS IN THE EXTENSIVE BACKSTORY... AND TURNS SEVERAL BLUSTERING CIPHERS INTO NUANCED CHARACTERS.

4 *LOLITA* (1962 & 1997)

Neither film adaptation of Vladimir Nabokov's classic tragicomedy *Lolita* got things exactly right, even though Nabokov himself scripted the 1962 version, directed by Stanley Kubrick. Though this takes a lot longer than it's probably worth, the best approach may be to read the book first, then view both films in succession. The 1962 version is improved by the knowledge that Clare Quilty (played by a delightfully hammy Peter Sellers) isn't the book's main character; the 1997 Adrian Lyne adaptation is better served by the realization that *Lolita* is really supposed to be funny. And both films take on a whole different tone with the knowledge that the title character is supposed to be 12 years old, which isn't apparent when she's played by Dominique Swain in the 1997 version, or even more so, by Sue Lyon in 1962.

5 *THE FOUNTAINHEAD* (1949)

It's actually a bit of a stretch to say that *The Fountainhead* makes sense even for those who've read the book. Ayn Rand penned both the novel and the screenplay, and making sense isn't one of her strong suits. However, the book communicates a far better sense of Objectivism, the grandiose political philosophy that informed all of Rand's books; in particular, those who love Gary Cooper's overblown, self-impressed courtroom speech at the movie's conclusion will love it even more in the book, where it seems to go on for 300 pages. The book also makes it clear how Cooper was miscast; his simple, jus'-folks delivery was entirely inappropriate to the character of Howard Roark, a windy gasbag who would have been much better played by Charlton Heston.

6 *2001: A SPACE ODYSSEY* (1968)

Stanley Kubrick's *2001: A Space Odyssey* is a movie with enigmas at its core. Where did humanity come from? Where is it going? The film opens with a group of hominids being gifted with intelligence by way of a monolithic black slab, and it ends with a glowing baby that means... well, opinions vary. Arthur C. Clarke's novel, prepared in conjunction with the film, but different from it in some key details, is better about spelling out what's happening and why. But is that a good thing? Clarke was a science-fiction master, but the clarification doesn't improve *2001* so much as brings it back down to earth. Sometimes it's best to let the mystery be.

WILD THINGS

16 FILMS FEATURING MANIC PIXIE DREAM GIRLS

1 *ELIZABETHTOWN* *(KIRSTEN DUNST)*

Ah, the Manic Pixie Dream Girl, the sentient ray of sunshine sent from heaven to warm the heart and readjust the attitude of even the sulkiest, most uptight male protagonist. In a 2007 column on *Elizabethtown*, *A.V. Club* head writer Nathan Rabin coined the phrase to describe that bubbly, shallow cinematic creature that "exists solely in the fevered imaginations of sensitive writer-directors to teach suicidally soulful young men to embrace life and its infinite mysteries and adventures." In *Elizabethtown*, Kirsten Dunst plays the archetypal Manic Pixie Dream Girl, a flirty, flighty chatterbox stewardess who razzles and dazzles brooding sensitive guy Orlando Bloom. Coked up, or merely high on life? You be the judge. Though Dunst in *Elizabethtown* and Natalie Portman in *Garden State* epitomize the contemporary Manic Pixie Dream Girl, the strangely resilient archetype has its roots in the nutty dames of screwball comedy. For every era, there's a Manic Pixie Dream Girl perfectly suited to the times.

2 *I LOVE YOU, ALICE B. TOKLAS* *(LEIGH TAYLOR-YOUNG)*

Like the Magical Negro, the Manic Pixie Dream Girl archetype is largely defined by secondary status and lack of an inner life. She's on hand to lift a gloomy male protagonist out of the doldrums, not to pursue her own happiness. In the late '60s and early '70s, MPDGs often took the comely form of spacey hippie chicks burdened with getting grim establishment types to kick back and smell the flowers. In that respect, they mirrored mainstream culture's simultaneous suspicion and fascination with the open sexuality of the emergent counterculture. With the help of pot-laced brownies, *I Love You, Alice B. Toklas'* groovy free spirit Leigh Taylor-Young helps transform uptight Jew Peter Sellers from a stone-cold square to a swinging proponent of free love and sense-derangement. But what does Taylor-Young ultimately want? As is usual with Manic Pixie Dream Girls, the filmmakers don't seem to have given the matter much thought.

> A.V. CLUB
>
> *Critic Christopher John Farley laid out the annoying film stereotype of what he called "Magical African-American Friends" in a bitter 2000* Time *article. Spike Lee later started calling the type the "super-duper magical negro." The term describes a black character who has magical powers instead of a personality, and who exists largely to teach or enlighten a white protagonist.*

3 *GARDEN STATE* *(NATALIE PORTMAN)*

Pharmaceutical companies have made billions peddling antidepressants to twentysomething white people who are, like, totally stressin' over people not appreciating them enough. Zach Braff did similarly well peddling two unusual but no less popular antidepressants in *Garden State*: The Shins and Natalie Portman. Braff's character is completely transformed when the latter introduces him to the former in a doctor's waiting room, with the plucky, annoying promise, "It'll change your life, I swear." Of course, anything sounds profound coming from such a dreamy woman. Oh, Natalie, your unconventional ways are so inspiring, and your beauty is surprisingly nonthreatening! In *Garden State*, she's a loveably eccentric little angel in the body of a smokin'-hot goddess, spreading good cheer and tuneful indie rock to depressed boys everywhere.

4 *BUTTERFLIES ARE FREE* (GOLDIE HAWN)

Hawn began her acting career playing the ditz on TV comedies like *Good Morning World* and *Laugh-In*, but by the end of the '60s, her bubble-headed persona became less a figure of fun and more a love-generation ideal. She was the uncomplicated free spirit, unduly hassled by the establishment. Hawn won an Oscar for bringing that character to film in 1969's *Cactus Flower*, and then in 1972's *Butterflies Are Free*, she played a happy hippie who helps blind lawyer Edward Albert learn to live on his own and stand up to his fretful, frightful mother. Hawn's boyfriend doesn't care for her friendship with Albert, but what can he do? Hawn is a butterfly, man.

5 *ALMOST FAMOUS* (KATE HUDSON)

In Cameron Crowe's gilded memories of being a teenage rock critic on assignment for *Rolling Stone*, his protagonist's muse is an idealistic groupie named Penny Lane. With blinkered idealism, the boy-critic gets all starry-eyed at her visions of the power of music, the freedom of life on the road, and the fantasy of staying young and beautiful forever. Even though Penny's incandescent charisma gets tarnished by that sex she claims she isn't having, not to mention an overdose that might not have been accidental, Crowe's stand-in has been transformed enough to defend her version of rock 'n' roll against the cynicism, infighting, and weariness of the band who won't return her devotion.

6 *JOE VERSUS THE VOLCANO* (MEG RYAN)

Ryan plays three roles in 1990's *Joe Versus The Volcano*, only one of whom is a self-described "flibbertigibbet" (a sort of antiquated version of the MPDG). But since all Ryan's characters are aspects of the same dream woman, they all sport a little flibber. Their collective goal? To get mopey, nebbishy Tom Hanks to overcome his fears—including his concern that he's about to die from a fatal "brain cloud"—and enjoy life for a change. But if Hanks doesn't make it out of the film alive, no worries. The chipper, ever-life-altering Ryan is waiting for him in *Sleepless In Seattle* and *You've Got Mail*, too.

7 *THE APARTMENT* (SHIRLEY MACLAINE)

All Jack Lemmon wants to do is ascend the corporate ladder, even if that means loaning his bosses his terrific bachelor pad for their illicit trysts. Then one day he comes home to find that the peppy elevator operator he likes is lying comatose on his sofa, feeling suicidal after an affair gone wrong. He nurses her back to health and she turns his life upside down, talking a blue streak until she convinces him to adjust his values. This kind of troubled, worldly, yet surprisingly ebullient character became Shirley MacLaine's stock in trade throughout the late '50s and early '60s, in films like *Some Came Running* and *Two For The Seesaw*. Three years after 1960's *The Apartment*, she reunited with Lemmon and director Billy Wilder for *Irma La Douce*, in which she played the ultimate MPDG: a prostitute who corrupts the policeman trying to save her from the streets.

8 *BRINGING UP BABY* (KATHARINE HEPBURN)

For the bulk of her career, Katharine Hepburn played strong-willed patrician types who defied convention, but still maintained a baseline gravity. But in Howard Hawks' 1938 screwball comedy *Bringing Up Baby*, Hepburn let gravity go, playing a giggly, scatterbrained heiress who torments stuffy scientist Cary Grant with her crazy demands and pet leopard. By the end of the film, Hepburn has turned Grant as nutty as she is, and as they hang from a crumbling dinosaur skeleton, he confesses that following her manic whims has led to the best day of his life.

9 *WHAT'S UP, DOC?* (BARBRA STREISAND)

In Peter Bogdanovich's 1972 homage to *Bringing Up Baby* and *Looney Tunes* cartoons, Streisand plays a pesky chatterbox who endeavors to help dreary musicologist Ryan O'Neal get the grant he's after, but instead succeeds in driving a wedge between O'Neal and his fiancée, and getting him embroiled in espionage and jewel thievery. Streisand's character never really has any plausible motivation: She's just an anarchic change agent, pitched halfway between a screwball heroine and a cartoon character. Yet after spending a weekend with her, O'Neal is in a better place financially, romantically, and career-wise. Funny how things work out.

10 *ANNIE HALL* (DIANE KEATON)

The grand champion of the MPDG fighting league, '70s division, just might be Diane Keaton as the title character in Woody Allen's most good-natured film. The fact that she pulled this off in a world that let Goldie Hawn run around loose is just a further testament to how completely Keaton filled out the role of what otherwise could have been a shallow wish-fulfillment fantasy. Her character certainly does have wish-fulfillment elements. But while it's hard to believe such a woman could exist, it's very easy to believe that if she did, she'd be a perfect match for Allen's prototypically nebbishy character, Alvy Singer. If ever there was a comedian who needed to lighten up, it was him, and if there was ever a woman who could make him do it with just a "la-di-dah," it was her.

11 *BREAKFAST AT TIFFANY'S*
(AUDREY HEPBURN)

In Truman Capote's short novel *Breakfast At Tiffany's*, Holly Golightly is a sexually adventurous woman who jumps from man to man, living off the gifts she extorts from them, and changing casually with the seasons. In the film version, Audrey Hepburn plays Holly as a chaste party girl who shares her opinions easily, but keeps her affections to herself (and her cat). Nevertheless, Hepburn-Holly charms writer George Peppard to such an extent that he's able to give up the rich older woman who helps subsidize his work, and instead offer his devotion to his erratic dream woman—who improbably, in contradiction to Capote's book, accepts.

12 *SOMETHING WILD*
(MELANIE GRIFFITH)

Straitlaced corporate drone Jeff Daniels desperately needs some screws loosened: His life sucks, and his family is suffocating him. But in the movies, there's always a MPDG around to show the buttoned-up bores how to live. In this case, it's crazy Lulu—later transformed into demure Audrey—who kidnaps him and pushes him into a road trip, complete with assumed identities and murderous mobsters. For a generation of young urban professionals, the indelible image of Griffith ripping her tank top apart while straddling a mortified but excited Daniels forever defined what kind of mania they wanted to see in their pixie dream girls, even if Jonathan Demme's film took some left turns that undermined the fantasy a bit.

13 *SWEET NOVEMBER*
(CHARLIZE THERON)

Terminally ill Earth mother Charlize Theron makes things easy for uptight business-dude Keanu Reeves in 2001's *Sweet November*, an appropriately maudlin remake of the 1968 tearjerker. She enters Reeves' life, imbues it with meaning, then leaves, saving her new beau from the agony of watching her perish. Theron promises to change Reeves' life in a single month, and through highs, lows, and rampant quirkiness, she does just that. By the time she exits, he's regained his joie de vivre and has been blessed with a haunted, vulnerable look that will be catnip to future MPDGs looking for a man to inspire.

14 *AUTUMN IN NEW YORK*
(WINONA RYDER)

See above. Joan Chen's directorial debut, *Autumn In New York*, is a strange cross between *Sweet November* and the culture-clash square-dude-meets-hippie-chick romantic subgenre of the Woodstock era. In 2000's *Autumn In New York*, the square dude in question is uptight businessman Richard Gere, and the charming minx who breathes life into his sorry existence and reawakens his libido is delightful pixie/crazy free spirit Winona Ryder, who, like Theron, nurses the tragic secret that she's terminally ill. They live, they love, and then that whole tragic-early-death thing enters the equation. Bummer city.

15 *THE LAST KISS*
(RACHEL BILSON)

In this remake of the stylishly annoying 2001 Italian film *L'Ultimo Bacio*, MPDG magnet Zach Braff goes to a wedding soaked through with thirty-something ennui, and with the oppressive weights of adulthood, responsibility, and attractive, utterly devoted girlfriend Jacinda Barrett hanging around his neck. Clearly, he needs an escape from his prison of a life. Trailed by a cloud of flowing brunette hair, in walks Rachel Bilson, a chatty, smiley, flirty college student so diminutive that she's technically a regulation-sized pixie. They laugh, they chat, they exchange meaningful glances, and Braff discovers that she's everything his girlfriend isn't: short, 22 years old, and carefree. Unfortunately, Bilson is also manic, and her mania doesn't surface until after they have sex in her dorm room, once Braff's regret is in full, watery-eyed bloom.

16 *MY SASSY GIRL*
(ELISHA CUTHBERT)

If there's an assembly line for Manic Pixie Dream Girls, Elisha Cuthbert went straight from the manufacturing facility and onto a subway railing to be saved by Jesse Bradford in *My Sassy Girl*, a remake of a 2001 Korean hit. The endearing way she slaps him without provocation, the adorable ways she sabotages his job interviews, the absolutely cute anger she displays when he won't jump into a freezing river… Cuthbert puts the "charming" in "charmingly mentally impaired." She's just the dash of acute manic depression (spiked with what appears to be severe alcoholism) that a staid, sensible-sweater-wearing business major like Bradford needs. But Cuthbert's aggressive, allegedly charming lunacy might not be organic: By the end of the movie, she reveals that her fiancé committed suicide only a few weeks before she met Bradford, so she dove headfirst into a kind of manic downward spiral. "Grief can make us crazy," she reminds Bradford between their lengthy break-up and their predestined reconciliation. She doesn't mention why her fiancé killed himself in the first place, but considering her personality, she doesn't really have to. As Bradford's token chubby best friend reminds him, "She's a nut-job!" Bradford's response: "But I love her." Those lines fully sum up the plot of any movie featuring a MPDG.

THE AMAZING DR. WHAT?

26 REAL TITLES FROM OLD MOVIES, SHORTS, AND CARTOONS THAT WOULDN'T FLY TODAY

1. *The Amazing Dr. Clitterhouse* (1938)
2. "Billion Dollar Boner" (1960)
3. "Don't Get Gay With Your Manicure!" (1903)
4. *The Bank Dick* (1940)
5. "Pussy Willie" (1929)
6. "The Boob Detective" (1914)
7. *Three Nuts For Cinderella* (1973)
8. "On The Knocker" (1963)
9. *Dandy Dick* (1935)
10. "Oh, What A Boob!" (1913)
11. "Burlesque Cock Fight" (1903)
12. "The Gay Shoe Clerk" (1903)
13. "Bush Doctor" (1954)
14. "Beaver Trouble" (1951)
15. "A Boob For Luck" (1915)
16. *The Gay Divorcee* (1934)
17. "The Boob's Nemesis" (a.k.a. "Nuts Nuts") (1914)
18. "The Hairy Ainus" (1913)
19. "Dick Wakes Up" (1954)
20. "Three Arabian Nuts" (1951)
21. "Boobs In The Woods" (1925)
22. "Jim Post, The Great Facial Comedian, And His Troubles" (1903)
23. "Two Nuts In A Rut" (1948)
24. "The Coming Of Sophie's 'Mama'" (1914)
25. "Pimple Gets The Hump" (1915)
26. *Death Race 2000* (1975)

TALK THE TALK

9 DVD COMMENTATORS ALWAYS WORTH A LISTEN

1 PAUL VERHOEVEN

Cinematic provocateur Paul Verhoeven is as high-spirited in his commentary tracks as in his filmmaking, which means he turns discussions of the likes of *RoboCop* and *Total Recall* into freewheeling lectures on American cinema, theology, fascism, human sexuality... whatever pops into his head, really. Perhaps his best-known commentary track is the one for his cult classic *Starship Troopers*, in which he reads excerpts from the movie's negative reviews and explains point-blank why he thinks the critics are idiots. But even Verhoeven's commentary on his lesser-known films can be a treat. His track for the medieval war film *Flesh+Blood* includes an eloquent history of early Christian thought, along with hilarious anecdotes about coming to work in Hollywood for the first time. And throughout, Verhoeven's rapid-fire speech, loud tone, and thick Dutch accent make him sound like a character out of one of his movies: brilliant, larger-than-life, and more than a little unhinged.

2 STEVEN SODERBERGH

It isn't just that Steven Soderbergh is an affable, analytical guy willing to talk about movies in ways that are informative and unpretentious. He's also developed playfully fresh approaches to the commentary concept. On the *Schizopolis* track, he interviews himself, satirizing the fatuousness of arthouse filmmakers. On the track for *The Limey*, his conversation with screenwriter Lem Dobbs is cut up and rearranged, reflecting the film's jumbled editing style. Soderbergh has also been helpful to director pals like Lodge Kerrigan and Mike Nichols, assisting them on their commentary tracks by engaging in collegial conversation. Soderbergh is like everyone's high-school über-nerd—the one who made nerddom look cool.

3 PAUL THOMAS ANDERSON

Paul Thomas Anderson confesses early in the commentary track for *Boogie Nights* that he learned a lot about filmmaking from listening to other commentary tracks. Anderson's own commentary tracks are similarly enlightening for film fans curious about his specific creative process, and what goes into making a movie in general. For *Hard Eight* (which he stubbornly refers to by its original title, *Sydney*) Anderson offers this sage advice to blocked writers: "Put your characters in a coffee shop, and get them talking. Eventually you'll find your direction." For *Boogie Nights*, Anderson shows off a professorial-style knowledge of '70s porn films, and talks about how porn gag reels gave him insight into how the films were made. Anderson is always engaging, funny, and passionate (sometimes defiantly so), and he isn't above dishing a little behind-the-scenes dirt. (His intense dislike for *Hard Eight* producer Robert Jones is barely concealed.) So far, Anderson has recorded commentary tracks for only his first two films, but hopefully his contagious enthusiasm will carry over to his other projects.

4-5 KURT RUSSELL AND JOHN CARPENTER

Sometimes a commentary track shared by two or more people gets lost in the confusion of crosstalk, nonsensical in-jokes, and other meaningless jibber-jabber that's a lot less fun for listeners than it was for the jibber-jabberers. But with long-time collaborators Kurt Russell and John Carpenter, who teamed up for commentaries on *The Thing* and *Big Trouble In Little China*, the meaningless jibber-jabber couldn't be more entertaining. While the duo has plenty to say about the films in question—mostly about how sadly misunderstood these career watermarks were upon their original release—Russell and Carpenter spend a lot of time just bantering like old buddies catching up over a couple of beers. On the *Big Trouble* commentary, Carpenter ribs Russell good-naturedly over *Captain Ron*, and Russell laughs about toughing out injuries during the making of *Soldier* to keep his fat paycheck. Russell and Carpenter make such an affable pair, chatting about their kids and getting older, that they should record commentary tracks for every DVD, regardless of whether they were involved in the film.

6 JOSS WHEDON

It wouldn't be right to say that Joss Whedon is a fan of his own work, exactly, but he knows better than almost anyone how to give the obsessives what they want. Whedon's commentary tracks on select episodes of his TV shows *Buffy The Vampire Slayer* and *Firefly* (as well as his *Firefly* movie *Serenity*) have the effect of going deep into the shows' universe without spoiling their mysteries. His commentaries may or may not be planned out in advance, but they sound like they've been as carefully crafted to entertain as the material he's commenting on. Whedon's brilliant idea to do a singing commentary track for the DVD edition of his web musical *Dr. Horrible's Sing-Along Blog* speaks to his commitment to entertaining his fans at a time when most special features are numbingly superfluous.

7 DAVID X. COHEN

In a way, David X. Cohen is lucky: as a writer and producer for *The Simpsons* and the co-creator of *Futurama*, any DVD commentary on which he appears will find him surrounded by smart, funny people. But Cohen's distinct, reedy voice usually takes the lead: He combines a fanboy's encyclopedic knowledge of the material with an insider's perspective and a storyteller's flair for dishing the inside scoop. His sense of humor is as dry when he speaks as it is absurd when he writes, and his scientific background—a quality he shares with a surprisingly large number of great contemporary TV writers—lets him gamely explain the innumerable nerdy jokes he and his crew drop into every episode. He never seems to be having less than a good time, and it's usually his jokes that bring down the house, no matter how many other funny people are in the recording studio. No matter which show's commentary he appears on, he comes across like the world's most awesome math teacher.

8 DAVID MILCH

When David Milch began working on *Deadwood*, the show that brought him his greatest acclaim as a television writer and producer, his choice to have the denizens of the Old West town speak in an amalgam of florid Victorianisms and vulgar street argot was highly informed by H.L. Mencken's *The American Language*. On commentary tracks, Milch comes across as Mencken-esque: cynical, irascible, confident, and low-key. On the very first *Deadwood* commentary, he watches a white stallion gallop through the opening credits, dryly noting that it seems very symbolic, but if anyone could actually explain to him what it means, he would be deeply in their debt. Elsewhere, he comes off like a *Deadwood* character himself, alternating between highfalutin talk about dramatic structure, and introducing a recurring character by saying, "Look at this ugly motherfucker." His follow-up series, *John From Cincinnati*, wasn't very good, but his DVD commentaries are still entirely entertaining: At one point, he relates how he tried to get himself in the right frame of mind to tell a mystical story by dropping acid every day for three months. "That," he notes flatly, "helped my brain power a *lot*."

9 UWE BOLL

The Teutonic cult videogame-movie hackteur behind *Alone In The Dark*, *Bloodrayne*, and *Postal* might just be the most predictably unpredictable audio commenter around. He's certainly the least diplomatic: His perversely essential DVD ramblings spew vitriol and invective in every direction. In his wonderfully paranoid, conspiracy-minded commentaries, he lashes out semi-coherently at critics, Internet haters who've made him a walking punchline, spineless studio executives, his competitors, and actors who had the audacity to refuse to appear in his films. He's also been known to crack racist about Asian drivers, bemoan actresses' unwillingness to indulge in gratuitous nudity, and make tasteless jokes about Owen Wilson's suicide attempt. Boll's uncensored, unhinged audio commentaries are just one of the reasons he's a filmmaker that cinephiles and casual moviegoers love to hate.

WHITTLING A SPOON FROM A BIGGER SPOON

50 LIST IDEAS WE REJECTED FOR THIS BOOK

1 **Mallory's dumb and Alex is an asshole—but both so endearingly so!:** The 170 best episodes of *Family Ties*

2 **Heady entertainments:** 11 memorable beheadings in non-horror movies

3 **Bugs!** (This never went any further.)

4 **"Don't turn your back on me, sucka!":** 68 great quotes from Mr. T

5 **You got to lick it before we kick it:** 9 people famous mainly, if not exclusively, for their oral-sex prowess

6 **Going Postal:** 5 great Uwe Boll films

7 **All decked out like a cowgirl's dream:** 21 classic country songs that objectify men

8 **I got riddims:** 14 rock bands that had no business playing reggae

9 **Batman is a racist!:** 125 compelling arguments from imdb.com

10 **Tell Coppola to go fuck himself:** 12 movies made under the influence of cocaine

11 **Hola, Señor Heston:** 3 films about Mexicans starring people who clearly aren't Mexican

12 **The Bennifer effect:** 8 films ruined by offscreen couples

13 **Starting with Jim:** 14 fat comedians who aren't John Belushi

14 **Born into this:** 6 films in which Larry The Cable Guy doesn't play a cable guy

15 **"You can't handle the truth!":** 14 Aaron Sorkin dialogues that changed the world

16 **Disputing Lil Wayne:** 31 rappers who claim to be the best alive

17 **If Shakespeare were alive, Macbeth would guzzle Red Bull:** 18 triumphant moments in product placement

18 **Paging Fredric Wertham:** 12 great eye-injury scenes

19 **James Hurley sings:** 6 of the worst moments of *Twin Peaks'* second season

20 **Mahir ate my balls:** 211 embarrassingly dated Internet memes

21 **A slice of Humble Pie:** 19 edible band names

22 **Hey, it's Harvey Keitel's penis!:** 5 films with uncomfortable nude scenes

23 **Sorry, Stephen:** 3 notable Baldwins

24 **Artfully Naked Gun:** 12 dramas starring Leslie Nielsen

25 **"KHAAAAAAAAAAAN!":** 76 great moments where hammy actors yell things at the sky

26 ***CHiPs*, the complete series? Seriously?:** 5 TV shows needlessly available on DVD

27 **Honky-tonk badonka-what?:** 11 badly executed appropriations of hip-hop culture by country singers

28 **Hey now, you're an all-star:** 29 movies, TV shows, and commercials featuring that annoying Smash Mouth song

29 **You had me at "menu screen":** 13 DVD menus worthy of their own commentaries

30 **To the moon, Alice!:** 12 hilarious depictions of domestic violence

31 **I Was An Amnesiac Call Girl:** 20 Lifetime movies to solve every woman's problems

32 **Blah blah blah *The Wire*:** 15 something something *The Wire*

33 **You had to have been there:** 26 things Keith said during book-planning meetings that made no sense

34 **From Seals & Crofts to Zager & Evans:** 29 horrible rock duos

35 **A way a lone a last a loved a long:** 24 books a lot of people pretend they've read

36 **Whipped cream and roses:** 15 cinematic replacements for the brassiere

37 **We must find another brain:** 14 horror movies that couldn't have happened without World War I

38 **Sugar Sugar Sugar:** 2 songs about candy that aren't actually about sex

39 **The morning sun when it's in your face really shows your age:** 10 oldies songs for gerontophiles

40 **"Evidently his death was a somewhat unpleasant experience for him":** 23 things Bob Greene said better than anyone else ever has or will

41 **Where have you gone, dancing Itos?:** 5 almost-amusing Jay Leno routines

42 **No shirt, no shoes, no justice:** 100 great *COPS* arrests

43 **Bread, for example:** 18 things that taste better toasted

44 **The rose goes in the front, big guy:** 8 funny scenes involving dudes in lingerie

45 **The bell tolls for...:** 6 bands with "thee" in their names that don't play garage-rock

46 **"Grandma Got Run Over By A Reindeer" got run over by a reindeer:** 31 ways to destroy all copies of Xmas' most annoying song

47 **Major movie star:** 8 inessential Jessicas in pop culture

48 **You remember that one time when...?:** 46 flashback episodes worth remembering

49 **Delicious redundancy:** 48 list books from the past three years

50 **Okay, what about, like, every song with the word "love" in the title?:** 1,111 suggestions so bad they didn't even make THIS list

ACKNOWLEDGMENTS

Acknowledging everyone who helped inspire and create *Inventory* would require a list the size of another book. But here are a few without whom it never could have happened: Sean Mills, Daniel Greenberg, Steve Hannah, Brant Rumble, the staffs of *The Onion* and Decider, Stephen Thompson, Brian Carmody, Scott Gordon, Michaelangelo Matos, our special guest contributors, and of course, *The A.V. Club*'s devoted readers. Without you, we're nothing but a bunch of opinionated, fact-filled nerds.

IMAGE CREDITS

P. iii: Photo: istockphoto.com
P. v: Photo: istockphoto.com
P. 1: Illustration: Danny Hellman
P. 5: Photo of Keanu Reeves by Retna Ltd., copyright Retna Ltd.
P. 7: Photo of *Wonder Showzen* puppets by John Tanzer
P. 10: *Reno 911!* photo of Ben Garant by Daniel Longmire, used with permission by Comedy Central ©2009. All Rights Reserved.
P. 11: Illustration: Danny Hellman
P. 19: Photo: istockphoto.com
P. 21: Photo of Johnny Cash by Michael Putland, copyright Retna Ltd.
P. 27: Photos: istockphoto.com, Hemera Photo-Objects Collection
P. 28: Graphic: Jon Resh
P. 30: Photo: istockphoto.com
P. 33: Photo of John Hodgman by Jan Cobb
P. 35: Photo of Ringo Starr by Gary Gershoff, copyright Retna Ltd.
P. 41: Illustration: Danny Hellman
P. 46: Photo of Robert Altman by Sara Deboer, copyright Retna Ltd.
P. 47: Photo: Hemera Photo-Objects Collection
P. 50: Photos: istockphoto.com, Hemera Photo-Objects Collection
P. 61: Photo: istockphoto.com
P. 67: Photo of Andrew W.K. by Victoria Stevens
P. 69: Photo: Hemera Photo-Objects Collection
P. 73: Illustration: Danny Hellman
P. 79: Photo: Hemera Photo-Objects Collection
P. 89: Photo: Hemera Photo-Objects Collection
P. 91: Illustration: Jon Resh
P. 94: Photo of Amy Sedaris by Michael Ingulli
P. 96: Image courtesy of the Criterion Collection
P. 102: Illustration: Danny Hellman
P. 103: Image courtesy of the Criterion Collection
P. 107: Photo: Hemera Photo-Objects Collection
P. 110: Photo of Tom Lennon by Seth Olenick
P. 113: Illustration: Danny Hellman
P. 114: Photo of David Cross and Bob Odenkirk by Marina Chavez
P. 118: Photo: istockphoto.com
P. 122: Photo: istockphoto.com; graphic: Jon Resh
P. 125: Illustration: Danny Hellman
P. 126: Photo of Tim Heidecker and Eric Wareheim by Pamela Littky
P. 127: Image courtesy of the Criterion Collection
P. 129: Photo: istockphoto.com
P. 142: Photo: Hemera Photo-Objects Collection
P. 144: Photo: Hemera Photo-Objects Collection
P. 146: Graphic: Jon Resh
P. 153: Photo: Hemera Photo-Objects Collection
P. 161: Image courtesy of the United States Department of Energy
P. 165: Photo: Justin Fluck
P. 170: Photo of Zach Galifianakis by Ryan Russell
P. 171: Illustration: Danny Hellman
P. 175: Illustration: Danny Hellman
P. 180: Illustration: Don Martin image from MAD #162 copyright 1973 E.C. Publications, Inc. All rights reserved. Used with permission.
P. 181: Photo of Al Yankovic by Mark Seliger
P. 181: Illustration: Don Martin image from MAD #186 copyright 1976 E.C. Publications, Inc. All rights reserved. Used with permission.
P. 183: Photo: istockphoto.com
P. 185: Photo of The Dismemberment Plan by Dave Holloway
P. 187: Illustration: Danny Hellman
P. 189: Photo: stock.xchng
P. 191: Photo of Patton Oswalt by Mike Carano
P. 193: Photo: Hemera Photo-Objects Collection; graphic: Jon Resh
P. 197: Photo: stock.xchng
P. 199: Photo of Daniel Day-Lewis and Paul Thomas Anderson by Melinda Sue Gordon
P. 204: Photos: stock.xchng, Hemera Photo-Objects Collection
P. 208: Photo of Daniel Handler by Meredith Heuer
P. 209: Photo: Hemera Photo-Objects Collection
P. 210: Photo: Hemera Photo-Objects Collection
P. 211: Photos: Hemera Photo-Objects Collection
P. 215: Illustration: Danny Hellman
P. 217: Photo: istockphoto.com
P. 221: Photos: Hemera Photo-Objects Collection
P. 223: Graphic: Jon Resh
P. 231: Photo: Hemera Photo-Objects Collection

INDEX

A.V.
CLUB